Volume Two: Since 1865

A HISTORY OF THE AMERICAN PEOPLE

Volume Two: Since 1865

A HISTORY OF THE AMERICAN PEOPLE

STEPHAN THERNSTROM
Harvard University

HARCOURT BRACE JOVANOVICH, PUBLISHERS

San Diego   New York   Chicago   Washington, D.C.   Atlanta
London   Sydney   Toronto

Illustration Credits

Cover: © Frank Siteman MCMLXXX/Jeroboam

Maps and graphs: Evanell Towne

Pictures: 380, Caterpillar Tractor Company; 383, 431, 457, 479, Library of Congress; 407, Museum of the City of New York; 421, From David Ward, *Cities and Immigrants: A Geography of Change in Nineteenth Century America* (Oxford University Press, Inc., © 1971); 426, From Harold M. Mayer and Richard C. Wade, *Chicago: Growth of a Metropolis* (University of Chicago Press, © 1969), 177; 510, Lewis Hine from International Museum of Photography at George Eastman House; 513, Jacob A. Riis Collection, Museum of the City of New York; 541, Brown Brothers; 565, Ford Motor Company; 593, Wide World Photos; 613, The Bettman Archive; 630, NASA; 633, Dorothea Lange, FSA, Library of Congress; 663, Robert Jakobsen, © Los Angeles Times; 695, © 1984, Harvey Stein; 719, © Bernie Boston from Washington Evening Star; 745, © 1984, Melanie Kastner/Zepher Photo.

ISBN: 0-15-536531-2
Library of Congress Catalog Number: 83-081524
Printed in the United States of America

To Melanie and Sam

Preface

After taking an examination in American colonial history as a graduate student at Johns Hopkins University in 1884, Woodrow Wilson wrote in disgust that he went into it "crammed with one or two hundred dates and one or two thousand minute particulars of the quarrels of nobody knows who with an obscure governor for nobody knows what. Just think of all that energy wasted! The only comfort is that this mass of information won't long burden me. I shall forget it with great ease." History presented as an endless string of names and dates, battles and treaties, can be excruciatingly boring, and it is natural to wonder about the point of studying it.

In writing this book, I have been mindful of Wilson's complaint. Inevitably this book includes a good many names, dates, and descriptions of key historical actors and events—but only those details I consider truly important to the beginning student. An American history without George Washington, Abraham Lincoln, or Woodrow Wilson would be like a *Hamlet* without the Prince of Denmark. Chester A. Arthur, though, can safely be left out of the main story, although he occupied the White House from 1881 to 1885. So too can chief executives whose administrations were uneventful, obscure bills, treaties, battles, and scandals that authors of textbooks customarily feel obliged to cover because all the other texts include them.

Too many details overwhelm the reader. A textbook can also be boring not just from an excess of facts but from a lack of a strong connective tissue of *ideas* to give those facts meaning. History is not "one damned thing after another"—X happened, then Y happened, then Z happened. History examines the relationship between X, Y, and Z, and explores how one led to the next. A description of five acts passed by Congress in 1863 will not interest anyone unless he or she is prodded to think about why the measures passed when they did and what their consequences were. The historian must be analytical, asking not only what happened but how and why it happened in that sequence and what difference it made. The descriptive passages in this volume serve a purpose too. They provide the necessary raw material to make the "how" and "why" questions comprehensible. Asking why things turned out as they did and not some other way is always central to this book's purpose.

Like most historians today, I believe that history is more than past politics. Therefore, the central focus of this book is not on political life, although major political developments are indeed treated. I think the central question to ask about American history is: Who are the American people and how did they come to be that way in the nearly four centuries that have elapsed since the first British settlement at Jamestown in 1607? Scholarly inquiry in such new fields as urban, ethnic, family, and women's history has shed much new light on that overarching issue in recent years. Studies of life at the "grassroots" now tell us far more about the millions of anonymous Americans in the past than we knew before. I have drawn upon this recent literature, as well as upon still valuable older studies, to fashion a fresh overview of the contours of American history.

I hope then that readers will take from this book something more meaningful than what Woodrow Wilson claimed from his study of colonial history. If I have succeeded in my aim, readers will gain a greater measure of self-understanding and a stronger sense of connection with their ancestors, a new feeling for what Abraham Lincoln called "the mystic chords of memory" that tie successive generations of Americans together. Another of our greatest presidents, Franklin D. Roosevelt, spoke of why our history matters:

> A nation must believe in three things. It must believe in the past. It must believe in the future. It must, above all, believe in the capacity of its people so to learn from the past that they can gain in judgment for the creation of the future.

I am grateful to the following historians who reviewed portions of the manuscript in its various drafts: Barton J. Berstein, Stanford University; John Morton Blum, Yale University; A.M. Burns, University of Florida; Maurice A. Crouse, Memphis State University; Jack Diggins, University of California at Irvine; Michael Frisch, State University of New York at Buffalo; Sheldon Hackney, Princeton University; Donald W. Hensel, California Polytechnic State University; Stanley N. Katz, Princeton University; Dr. Myron A. Marty, formerly at Florissant Valley Community College, now with the National Endowment for the Humanities; John M. Murrin, Princeton University; Nell Irvin Painter, University of North Carolina, Chapel Hill; James T. Patterson, Brown University; Raymond Robinson, Northeastern University; Laurence Veysey, University of California at Santa Cruz; and Daniel J. Walkowitz, New York University.

Contents

Part Three _____

From Farm to Factory:
Technology Takes Command

Part Four _____
Regulation and Reform:
The Consequences of Progressivism

Part Five —————————————————————
Modern Times: From Depression to Detente

Volume Two: Since 1865
A HISTORY OF THE
AMERICAN PEOPLE

Chapter Sixteen

Reunion and Reconstruction

The Civil War was a revolution that destroyed the Old South and struck the chains from four million black people. Once the military struggle was over, however, the victors treated the vanquished with a mildness rare in the history of revolutions. Mass executions for political crimes and confiscation of vast lands and other wealth accompanied great social revolutions in France, Russia, and China. The dozen years of "reconstruction" following the American Civil War, by contrast, saw remarkably little vengeance. Although Union troops had marched into battle singing, "We'll hang Jeff Davis on a sour apple tree," the chief political leader of the rebellion merely went to prison for two years. Robert E. Lee was never even arrested. Of the hundreds of thousands of rebels who took up arms against the federal government, none was forced into exile. Only one was tried and executed, and that not for treason but for war crimes—his administration of the ghastly prison at Andersonville, Georgia, where thousands of Union captives died. The only significant bloodshed after Appomattox was caused not by the winners but by the losers—southern whites who banded together in the Ku Klux Klan and similar organizations to topple the recently established Republican regimes through systematic terrorist raids.

The planters, it is true, lost $2.5 billion worth of human property. But they generally managed to hang onto their land, and a new system of sharecropping allowed them to continue to exploit black labor. New modes of political and social control were devised to put the freedmen back "in their place."

The impressive resilience of the southern social order was testimony not only to the fierceness of the resistance displayed by its defenders but to the weakness of

"The First Vote" of freed Negroes is depicted in this drawing by A.R. Waud for an 1870 issue of **Harper's Weekly.**

the radical impulse in the triumphant North. There were moments when truly fundamental changes seemed possible, changes that would radically and permanently alter not only southern society but the place of black people in American life. But beneath the turbulent surface was a bedrock consensus that was missing in convulsive social upheavals in other countries. Some visionaries, like Senator Charles Sumner of Massachusetts and Representative Thaddeus Stevens of Pennsylvania, challenged it, but in the end white Americans agreed on the sanctity of private property, the limited right of the central government to intervene in state affairs, and the inferiority of the black race. A dozen years after Appomattox, the reconstruction effort had faltered, and proponents of white supremacy were back in power in all the ex-Confederate states. The Union was restored, but the South was not drastically reconstructed.

PRESIDENT JOHNSON'S RECONSTRUCTION PROGRAM

Three major questions faced the nation in 1865. On what terms would the defeated rebel states be brought back into the Union as normally functioning states? Could the ruling Republican party retain its national ascendancy once that happened? What would be the place of the millions of "freedmen" in southern society? These contentious and intricately interwoven issues provoked a prolonged political struggle that almost resulted in the removal of a President from office for "high crimes and misdemeanours."

Slavery was, of course, dead. The Emancipation Proclamation had not done the job completely, because it only applied to areas not under Union control in January of 1863. Congress had completed the task by approving the Thirteenth Amendment. It was ratified by the necessary three-fourths of the states and became the law of the land in 1865. Once blacks were no longer slaves, however, what were they? Were freedmen full citizens with all the rights enjoyed by white Americans? Could they vote, hold political office, serve on juries, testify in court, own property, move freely from place to place, attend school, enter any occupation? In 1865 southern whites obviously were not prepared to grant their former servants equality in all these spheres. What is less obvious, and crucial to an understanding of the period, is that many northern whites were not either. Only 7 percent of northern blacks lived in states that allowed them to vote. Most states forbade blacks to join the militia, to serve on juries, and to testify against whites in court. Housing was segregated. So were public transportation, hotels, restaurants, theaters, schools, hospitals, prisons, and cemeteries. Only a year before the Emancipation Proclamation, Lincoln's own state of Illinois approved a referendum forbidding blacks from entering the state by a two-to-one margin.

Such racist policies did not go unchallenged in the Reconstruction years. Radical Republicans committed to egalitarian ideals led courageous campaigns to extend the franchise to blacks and to protect them from discriminatory treatment throughout the North. But a lot of courage was required, for the issue was politically dangerous. Between 1865 and 1869, Republicans sponsored eleven referenda on black voting rights in northern states; nine were defeated.

Democratic politicians found white supremacy their best issue, practically their only issue. In the 1867 Democratic campaign in Ohio, a parade of young girls, in white dresses, carried banners reading, "Fathers, Save Us from Negro Equality." The Democrats roundly defeated the Republican equal suffrage proposal that year and captured both houses of the Ohio legislature as well. In 1868, the Democratic literature for the presidential contest included a pamphlet called "White Men Must Rule America." A Democratic victory, it pledged, would "maintain the supremacy of the white race at all hazards, and restore negroes to that condition where they can exist in accordance with the laws of their being and where they will become in the future as they were in the past, the happiest and most valuable race of subordinates on earth." The widespread racial prejudice to which the Democrats appealed was felt by a good many Republicans as well. It was a powerful constraint on the policies that Republicans could devise for the South. The 1868 Republican platform avoided entirely the issue of black suffrage in northern states.

The Freedmen's Bureau

After passing the Thirteenth Amendment in early 1865, Congress took another significant action. Most of its members regarded the centralization of power in Washington that had taken place during the war years as a temporary aberration, the product of an emergency that was now over. The Constitution delegated only certain powers to the central government and left such matters as education, control of crime, and preservation of law and order to states and local communities. The enormous disruptions caused by the war and the freeing of the slaves, however, seemed beyond the capacity of the individual states to manage. Consequently, Congress reluctantly created a temporary agency to provide assistance to the war-torn South, and to ease the transition of black Americans from slavery to freedom—the Freedmen's Bureau. The Bureau was to administer relief for the needy, and in its five years of existence it supplied more than 20 million free meals, a quarter of them to impoverished southern whites. It established schools and hospitals for freedmen.

The central aim of the Freedmen's Bureau was to assist blacks to find employment. General O.O. Howard, its head, told a group of former slaves that he would "promise them nothing but freedom, and freedom means work." Bureau officials wanted freedmen to have the same rights as northern workingmen—to bargain for wages and freely choose their employers. However, the major source of work was obviously in the cotton fields, and planters pleaded that they lacked the capital to pay regular cash wages. As a transitional measure, the Bureau printed contracts committing plantation owners to provide food and shelter to ex-slaves in exchange for labor from all able-bodied members of the family, who were put to work in gangs as they had as slaves. Blacks were pressured to sign these agreements by the threat that no more rations would be forthcoming from the Bureau. There were provisions for what the contracts referred to as "wages," but they were not truly wages, a fixed sum for a given unit of time. Freedmen would receive income only if the plantation returned a profit at the end of the season, which was of course quite beyond their control.

The legislation authorizing the Freedmen's Bureau also pointed to another more promising solution to the problem of black employment. The bill empowered the Bureau to "set apart for the freedmen" abandoned lands in plots of 40 acres at nominal rents, with the option to purchase later. Two similar efforts to create a class of independent black yeoman farmers had already begun under military auspices during the war. After the fall of Vicksburg, General Grant had resettled some 2,000 blacks on former plantation land at Davis Bend, Mississippi, and allowed them to farm the land cooperatively. Likewise, General Sherman had set aside a portion of the South Carolina and Georgia coasts for 40,000 ex-slaves, and had given them temporary titles to farms. When a Carolina planter returned to claim his estate, his former slaves greeted him with "overflowing affection," but told him, "We own this land now. Put it out of your head that it will ever be yours again." Congress now seemed prepared to move further in this direction. Although the Freedmen's Bureau had only enough abandoned plantation land for 20,000 out of almost one million families, the principle was vitally important; the federal government was beginning to assume responsibility for satisfying the freedmen's ardent desire for "forty acres and a mule."

Johnson Takes Command

Congress adjourned in March of 1865, not to reconvene until the end of the year. When southern military resistance collapsed in April, the task of reconstructing the governments of the rebel states fell to the President, who would have a free hand for eight months. Andrew Johnson, a life-long Democrat from Tennessee, had been made Vice President in 1864 in a gesture of wartime bipartisanship. That responsibility fell to him, thanks to Lincoln's assassination. The situation was doubly ironic. The victorious North now had a southern chief executive, and a former slaveholder at that. The Republican Party which had directed the war effort had to contend with a Democratic President. Although Johnson claimed that his reconstruction policies would adhere strictly to the guidelines established earlier by Lincoln, he had none of Lincoln's flexibility and gift for compromise. He was the most rigid and obstinate man ever to occupy the White House. Congress had already made plain its determination to play a powerful role in the formation of Reconstruction policy. Johnson rashly ignored this. He assumed that if he could establish new regimes in the rebel states before Congress returned in December, the legislators would have to accept them as a *fait accompli*.

Before the year was out, governments acceptable to Johnson had been created in all but one of the former Confederate states. But the character of these new governments shocked and infuriated many northerners. They were led, almost without exception, by the same planters who had steered the South down the road to secession. The men southern voters elected to the new Congress included four Confederate generals, five colonels, six Confederate cabinet officers, fifty-eight

A BLACK CODE

All freedmen, free Negroes and mulattoes in this State, over the age of eighteen years, found on the second Monday in January, 1866, or thereafter, with no lawful employment or business, or found unlawfully assembling themselves together, either in the day or night time, and all white persons so assembling with freedmen, free Negroes or mulattoes, on terms of equality, or living in adultery or fornication with a freedwoman, free Negro, or mulatto, shall be deemed vagrants, and on conviction thereof shall be fined in the sum of not exceeding, in the case of a freedman, free Negro or mulatto, fifty dollars, and a white man two hundred dollars, and imprisoned at the discretion of the court, the free Negro not exceeding ten days, and the white man not exceeding six months. . . .

And in case any freedman, free Negro or mulatto shall fail for five days after the imposition of any fine or forfeiture upon him or her for violation of any of the provisions of this act to pay the same, that it shall be . . . the duty of the sheriff of the proper county to hire out said freedman, free Negro or mulatto, to any person who will, for the shortest period of service, pay said fine and forfeiture and all costs. . . .

—*Laws of Mississippi, 1865*

Confederate Congressmen, and the Vice President of the Confederate States of America! Almost all were Democrats, with predictably negative stances on the tariff, federal aid for railroads, river and harbor improvements, and other developmental expenditures. Some of the conventions at which these new regimes were formed were so unrepentant that they refused to fly the Stars and Stripes. Republicans who hoped that the South could generate a more moderate, loyal, progressive leadership group were appalled at the return of the old guard.

The actions the Johnson-sponsored governments were taking toward the freedmen were equally troubling. Although the President had made ratification of the Thirteenth Amendment a condition for readmission to the Union, some states did so with great reluctance and much defiant rhetoric. And if they grudgingly conceded the end of slavery, they seemed determined to recreate it in everything but name by passing restrictive Black Codes. It was not terribly disturbing to most northern Republicans in 1865 that every one of the secessionist states denied blacks the right to vote. The average Republican favored, at best, only a qualified suffrage for a black minority—those who were literate, owned property, or had served in the Union Army.

The Black Codes, however, denied far more than black suffrage. They were often lifted from the old slave codes, with the word "negro" for "slave." In

Mississippi, Negroes were denied the right to purchase or even rent land. In South Carolina, they needed a special license to hold any job except that of field hand. Almost all the state codes contained restrictions protecting white labor from black competition. Most denied blacks the right to purchase or carry firearms, and even the right to assemble after sunset. Most brutal were the typical vagrancy provisions. Any black discovered by the authorities "wandering or strolling about in idleness" could be arrested and put to work on a state chain gang, or auctioned off to a planter and forced to work without pay for as long as a year. Freedmen were therefore forced to remain with their employers, normally their former masters, because they could not travel in search of better opportunities.

The Black Codes, a Louisiana newspaper explained, created "a new labor system prescribed and enforced by the state." General Howard had advised freedmen to "begin at the bottom of the ladder and climb up," but powerful whites were determined to keep them on a quite separate ladder with only one rung. They believed, as one said candidly, "The general interest both of the white man and the negro requires that he be kept as near to the condition of slavery as possible, and as far from the condition of the white man as is practicable." As a northern traveler said, the codes were "a striking embodiment of the idea that although the former owner has lost his individual right of property in the former slave, the blacks at large belong to the whites at large." President Johnson, nonetheless, defended them as measures "to confer upon freedmen the privileges which are essential to their comfort, protection, and security."

Congressional Reactions

When Congress convened in December of 1865, Johnson declared that the task of reconstruction had been completed, and requested that the duly elected representatives of the ex-Confederate states be allowed to take their seats. Not surprisingly, outraged Republicans refused. Instead, they created a special joint Senate and House Committee, the Committee of Fifteen, to develop an alternative program. After hearing testimony on what was happening in the South, they proposed two measures. One bill enlarged the power and extended the life of the Freedmen's Bureau. Another, the Civil Rights Act of 1866, was the Republican answer to the Dred Scott Decision and the Black Codes. It extended citizenship to blacks and guaranteed them equal protection of the laws.

The angry President vetoed both measures and denounced the Congress in intemperate terms. They were unconstitutional federal intrusions into matters best left to the states, he said, the work of fanatics who aimed to "destroy our institutions and change the character of our Government." Although he was undoubtedly sincere in his constitutional scruples, he was also influenced by the fear that the bills threatened white supremacy. In his view, blacks had "shown less capacity for self-government than any other people. Whenever they have been left to their own devices they have shown an instant tendency to lapse into barbarism." After a meeting with Frederick Douglass and other black leaders, he told his private secretary: "I know that damned Douglass; he's just like any nigger, and he would sooner cut a white man's throat than not."

Because representatives from the former Confederate states had been denied their places, the Republicans had the votes to override the vetoes by the required two-thirds majority. But the measures were threatened from a different quarter as well—the Supreme Court had the power to strike them down as unconstitutional. To guard against that, Congress sought to write the necessary safeguards for equal rights into the Constitution itself via the Fourteenth Amendment. Republicans pushed it through Congress, and required that rebel states ratify it *before* they were readmitted to the Union. The Fourteenth Amendment extended citizenship to blacks, and forbade any state to "abridge the privileges and immunities" of citizens, to deprive citizens of "life, liberty, or property, without due process of law," or to "deny any person within its jurisdiction the equal protection of the laws." This seemed to rule out the most obnoxious features of the Black Codes, although the Supreme Court was later to ignore the clear meaning of this language, and also to find in it other quite unanticipated meanings.

Another important provision of the Fourteenth Amendment barred from federal or state office anyone who had taken a federal oath of office and then participated in the rebellion. This was a blow at the South's traditional leadership, of course. It specified, however, that such persons might be pardoned by a two-thirds vote of Congress.

The Fourteenth Amendment also protected the black man's right to vote, albeit in a rather sneaky way. Some Republican radicals had argued for equal political rights for the freedmen all along. By the summer of 1866, when the amendment was framed by Congress, others had come to favor it out of fear for the future of their party. The Democrats were experiencing a resurgence in the North. They would obviously grow even stronger when the South reentered the Union, if only whites were allowed to vote. The South had been solidly Democratic since the 1850s. The Republicans had long complained of the disproportionate political clout the three-fifths clause of the Constitution gave the South. The end of slavery, ironically, only increased it more. Because the entire black population—not just three-fifths—would count in apportioning seats in Congress and the Electoral College, the South would gain 24 additional Representatives and electoral votes. The only hope of making the Republican party a contender for those seats would be to open the polls to the freedmen, who would surely favor the party that gave them their freedom. It was an issue, said a Republican official, in "which the highest requirements of abstract justice coincide with the lowest requirements of political prudence."

Given the racist climate in the North, the "lowest requirements of political prudence" ruled out a straightforward provision barring racially discriminatory voting laws anywhere in the land. Idealistic proposals to do that were rejected in Congress, as were the pleas of Susan B. Anthony to delete the word "male" from the voting provision. A devious compromise measure was adopted instead. The states would control the franchise, as was traditional, excluding blacks from the polls if they wished. However, they would lose congressional seats in proportion to the number of persons so excluded. With its large black population, the South could expect its congressional delegation to shrink by at least a third, whereas no northern states had enough black residents to lose any seats at all as a result of racially restrictive policies. Northern Republicans could thereby weaken southern Democrats without incurring the wrath of their constituents who shuddered at the thought of blacks voting in Philadelphia or Chicago. Either the rebel states would be forced to extend the vote to blacks, who would probably vote overwhelmingly Republican, or there would be a good many fewer southern Congressmen in Washington.

The Failure of Compromise

The congressional Reconstruction program of 1866 was less generous with the South than President Johnson would have wished, but its terms—readmission to the Union in exchange for acceptance of the Fourteenth Amendment—were far from harsh. Most members of the pre-Civil War southern political elite—perhaps 25,000 people—were barred from political office. These people could still vote, however, and were eligible for future pardon. (All but 500 were pardoned by 1872.) The elementary human rights denied former slaves by the Black Codes would have to be granted, but the vote could be withheld, although at the cost of losing congressional representation.

Most reassuring of all to southern leaders, there would be no serious attempt to redistribute rebel property to the freedmen. This was partly because the President had quickly crippled the experiments of Grant, Sherman, and the Freedmen's Bureau in settling ex-slaves on the plantations. Within a few months of the war's end, Johnson offered amnesty to the owners of most of these estates and allowed them to reclaim their property. Officials of the Bureau were forced to evict the unbelieving freedmen from the land.

It was Johnson who ordered the Freedman's Bureau to put an end to the land redistribution effort. But the President, of course, had no monopoly of political power. Congress found much of his Reconstruction program wanting when it came back into session. It could have passed legislation mandating a continuation, or even a drastic expansion, of the land distribution experiments, and it did not. The betrayed freedmen petitioned Congress in protest, but only a few isolated legislators on the radical fringe supported them. Thaddeus Stevens, the most dedicated egalitarian in the House, argued the case at every opportunity. Although he favored the granting of full political rights to blacks as well, he had no doubt about what the priorities should be. "In my judgment we shall not approach a measure of justice until we have given every adult freedman a homestead on the land where he was born and toiled and suffered. Forty acres of land and a hut would be more valuable to him than the immediate right to vote." To obtain the necessary land, Stevens proposed to confiscate 400 million acres of land belonging to 70,000 Confederate planters with estates of more than 200 acres. This program would have brought a true social revolution to the South, but such an assault on private property was unthinkable to most Americans of the day.

The Reconstruction effort would probably have ended with the Fourteenth Amendment had the new Johnson-sponsored state governments been wise enough to bend with the wind and accept the bargain as the best they could expect. Encouraged by President Johnson, however, all but Tennessee rejected the amendment. Northern opinion was further outraged by a mounting wave of southern violence against blacks and white sympathizers. In April of 1866, a white mob in Memphis attacked black neighborhoods, killing 47 men, women, and children and burning down four churches and twelve schools. In July, white New Orleans police fired on a convention of black suffrage advocates, killing 48 and wounding 200. Convinced that the organizers of the meeting were part of a radical Republican conspiracy to stir up the "passions and prejudices of the colored population" and stage a *coup d'etat*, Johnson refused to condemn the perpetrators of the New Orleans massacre. The "cause and origin of the blood that was shed," he said, was the actions of "the radical Congress."

CONGRESSIONAL RECONSTRUCTION

The campaign preceding the congressional elections in the fall of 1866 was as vicious as any in American history. Johnson went on an extended speaking tour, denouncing his opponents as "a common gang of cormorants and blood-suckers," and comparing himself to a persecuted Christ. Thaddeus Stevens responded with a quite different biblical metaphor, saying:

> You all remember that in Egypt He sent frogs, locusts, lice, and finally demanded the first-born of every one of the oppressors. Almost all of these have been taken from us. We have been oppressed with taxes and debts, and He has sent us worse than lice, and has afflicted us with an Andrew Johnson.

The election was a referendum on the conflicting reconstruction policies of the President and congressional Republicans, and the verdict was clear cut. A Republican landslide gave them 42 of 53 Senate seats, and a House of Representatives with 143 Republicans to 49 Democrats. With margins of command like that, the President's veto power was an empty threat and the Republicans were free to do what they wished with the South.

That smashing victory marked the beginning of what is usually termed Radical Reconstruction. Radical it was in certain ways—in its assertion of congressional supremacy over the executive, in its determination to transform the political complexion of the rebel states, in its assumption of the superiority of Yankee ways. The "spirit of the North," declared the most influential religious journal of the day, must become "the spirit of the whole country." A popular poem summed it up:

> Make 'em Amerikan, and they'll begin
> To love their country as they loved their sin;
> Let 'em stay Southun, an' you've kep' a sore
> Ready to fester ez it done afore.

But Radical Reconstruction was not very radical in the dictionary sense of the term—"going to the roots or origins"—if one accepts Thaddeus Stevens' view that the root problem was the continued economic dependence of the freedmen on the master class that held the land. The abolition of serfdom by the Russian Czar in 1861 did not give the freed serfs political rights, but it did provide them with some of the land they had worked. The reverse was true in America. At the height of "radical" Reconstruction, equal political rights were granted and enforced by Union soldiers. But after Johnson torpedoed the first land redistribution experiments, nothing further was done to assure the preservation of those political rights once the troops were withdrawn. The dominant view was that all men would be rewarded fairly in the marketplace, and that interference on behalf of particular disadvantaged elements of the population was unnecessary. One of the most powerful Senate Republicans declared that giving land to freedmen was "more than we do for white men," and was unmoved by Charles Sumner's response, "white men have never been in slavery." Once they were granted equal political rights, declared the leading liberal journal, *The Nation*, blacks were "on the dusty and rugged highway of competition," and henceforth "the removal of white prejudice against the Negro would depend almost entirely upon the Negro himself." Any "attempt to justify the confiscation of southern land under the pretence of doing justice to the freedmen," said the *New York Times*, "strikes at the root of all property rights in both sections. It concerns Massachusetts quite as much as Mississippi."

Congress had been able to block Johnson's plan for restoring the Union on easy terms, by failing to seat the representatives the old guard regimes had sent to Washington. But those white supremacist governments were still operating as the supreme authority in their respective states. Had they read the 1866 election returns correctly and promptly ratified the Fourteenth Amendment, they might well have won readmission to the Union without further conditions. But only Tennessee did so. The intransigence of the other ten forced sterner measures—Military Reconstruction. In February of 1867, *The Nation* summarized the political dynamics that caused it:

> Six years ago, the North would have rejoiced to accept any mild restrictions upon the spread of slavery as a final settlement. Four years ago, it would have accepted peace upon the basis of gradual emancipation. Two years ago, it would have been content with emancipation and equal civil rights for the colored people without the extension of suffrage. One year ago, a slight extension of the suffrage would have satisfied it.

The Reconstruction Act of 1867 declared that "no legal State governments or adequate protection for life or property now exists in the rebel States." It divided the South into five military districts, and empowered Union Army officers to supervise the actions of state and local governments, conduct military trials, and remove officeholders for misconduct. Military Reconstruction was not as draconian as is sometimes alleged. There were less than 20,000 federal troops available to supervise a population of more than ten million, and no one proposed expanding the army. But to the intransigent southern whites it was an astonishing and appalling extension of federal power.

The act provided that military rule would end after the states held conventions to prepare new constitutions. Delegates were to be elected by universal suffrage, without racial bars. Former rebels denied political office by the terms of the Fourteenth Amendment could not serve in them, although the amendment itself had not yet been ratified by enough states to make it part of the Constitution. The conventions were to be followed by elections for new state governments. Once their legislatures had approved the Fourteenth Amendment, their representatives would be accepted in Congress.

Johnson raged at Military Reconstruction. It was "an act of military despotism," a "tyranny as this continent has never witnessed." Equal suffrage would give power to a race of men "corrupt in principle and enemies of free institutions." "Of all the dangers which the nation" had yet encountered, "none are equal to those which must result from the success of the effort now making to Africanize the half of our country." Because the military commanders responsible for enforcement were subject to his authority as Commander-in-Chief, he did his best to obstruct the implementation, removing the four of the five he found too vigorous in defending the rights of the freedmen. He could not, however, prevent the holding of conventions and the creation of new governments chosen by universal suffrage, and that soon happened throughout the South.

Impeachment

Johnson's resolute efforts to frustrate congressional Reconstruction made his supporters a dwindling minority on Capitol Hill, and brought him within a hairsbreadth of losing his office through impeachment. The storm that almost drove him from the White House began with his February, 1868 decision to fire Secretary of War Edwin Stanton, the last surviving member of Lincoln's cabinet and a favorite with congressional radicals. This was arguably a violation of the Tenure of Office Act passed by Congress the year before to prevent Johnson from purging the government of Republican civil servants. The act was loosely worded and of questionable constitutionality, and it was unclear that it even applied to Stanton, who had not been appointed by Johnson. But Republican rage at the President had reached such a peak that they were ready to use the pretext that he had violated the law to throw him out. In three days, the House approved an impeachment resolution by a vote of almost three to one.

Johnson's six-week trial before the Senate focused on the issue that resurfaced again more than a century later in the Watergate era—whether the "high crimes and misdemeanours" that the Constitution refers to were to be defined in narrow legal or broad political terms. Can a President be unseated only for a serious criminal offense, or is it sufficient to establish that his actions had been "subversive of some fundamental or essential principle of government or highly prejudicial to the public interest?"

The result of the trial was seemingly a victory for Johnson and the office of the Presidency. In May of 1868, he was acquitted, although the prosecution failed to obtain the two-thirds majority needed for conviction by only one vote. The claim that that single vote "marks the narrow margin by which the Presidential element in our system escaped destruction" seems exaggerated, but a conviction of Johnson would doubtless have diminished the independence of subsequent chief executives.

In an important sense, however, congressional Republicans achieved much of what they had sought. If in the end they had to live with Johnson for the remaining months of his term, they had tamed him. The President had persuaded a group of conservative Republican senators to vote for acquittal by promising that he would refrain from further interference with congressional Reconstruction and would enforce the Reconstruction Acts properly, and he lived up to that promise. Many Americans would later take the decision as a precedent that no President could be impeached unless caught holding "a smoking gun," but the immediate political lesson suggested otherwise. A chief executive who failed to faithfully execute laws approved by a strong majority in both houses of Congress could suffer a punishing political defeat. Johnson hoped to win a second term in the 1868 elections, and angled for the Democratic nomination, but he won only a handful of southern votes at the convention and had to return reluctantly to Tennessee.

The Fifteenth Amendment

In the November, 1868 elections the Republicans retained their lopsided majorities in both houses of Congress, and elected their presidential candidate, General Ulysses S. Grant. With that hurdle cleared, Congress proceeded to pass the last major constitutional change of the period—the Fifteenth Amendment, which provided that the right to vote could not be denied any citizen "on account of race, color, or previous condition of servitude."

This amendment fell considerably short of what the most devoted egalitarians wanted. It did not forbid racial barriers to the holding of political office, only to voting. It did not provide national control of the suffrage and federal protection of voting rights, but only specified something states could not do. Most important, it did not bar a variety of techniques that could be employed to restrict the access of black people to the polls—property requirements, poll taxes, literacy tests and a host of others that were in fact soon to be used successfully for that purpose. Despite these limitations, however, the Fifteenth Amendment was a great step forward: it struck a blow for equality in the North as well as in the South. At the time it was passed, all but seven northern states denied blacks the franchise, and it was courageous of the Republicans to make it a matter of national policy. After strenuous organizational efforts by Republican state machines, the necessary number of states approved the Fifteenth Amendment.

STRUGGLE IN THE SOUTH

Between 1868 and 1870, all of the former rebel states held constitutional conventions and carried out free elections, open for the first time to freedmen. Some 700,000 new black voters were added to the electoral rolls, and 150,000 southern whites were disenfranchised for having held federal or state office before 1861 and having violated their oath to uphold the Constitution of the United States. Everywhere but in Virginia, the new governments were under Republican control. These were the so-called "carpetbagger" regimes of "Black Reconstruction." Both labels are misleading.

"Carpetbagger" was the invidious term applied by southern white conservatives to northerners who migrated south following the war in search of wealth and power, allegedly men with only enough possessions to fit in a carpetbag. In fact, those who came were from no single social group, and many brought with them funds the war-torn southern economy badly needed. The number of Yankee newcomers was vastly exaggerated by political opponents who argued that no southern white could possibly cooperate politically with blacks. The 1870 Census found a total of less than 50,000 northern-born persons living in the ex-Confederate states—a mere .6 percent of the population. And many of them had undoubtedly come before the war. In 1850, almost 85,000 northerners lived in the South, and it is highly unlikely that all of them had died or moved away by 1870. Fewer than 50,000 true carpetbaggers, probably many fewer, resided among the more than eight million people of the region. It is true that newly arrived Yankees assumed posts of political leadership far out of proportion to their numbers. They constituted approximately 60 percent of the Congressmen sent to Washington from the reconstructed states. But the political success of this infinitesimal fraction of the population depended on their ability to persuade others to vote for them.

Many who did, of course, were blacks, who joyfully seized the opportunity to participate in politics despite white efforts to intimidate and coerce them into staying away from the polls. The extent of black political dominance in these years has often been exaggerated. Whites were a majority of the voters in five of the ten elections to select delegates for constitutional conventions in the reconstructed states, and were nowhere outnumbered by much. A majority of delegates elected were white in eight out of the ten contests, and in a ninth—Louisiana—an equal number came from each race. The willingness of blacks to transcend racial loyalties and give their votes to whites they felt they could trust was even more evident in subsequent elections of state and local officials. During the entire era, blacks were in a majority in the legislature of only one state, and then in the lower house alone. No black governors were chosen, and only two senators.

This is not to suggest that able black politicians did not develop. The number and quality of the black leaders who emerged during Reconstruction was impressive, given the lives the vast majority of them had lived as slaves and the prohibitions that the small free black community of the South had to endure. Not surprisingly, few former field hands became politically prominent at the state level. Most of those who rose to prominence were literate, and had been free before the war or had been skilled craftsmen as slaves. At the grassroots level, however—which has been little studied—there is evidence that some ordinary agricultural laborers were quite active in mobilizing their neighborhoods on election day.

Scalawags

Blacks formed only about a third of the southern population, and the number of northern whites who came south during Reconstruction, we have seen, was much too small to make a majority capable of governing. The new Republican governments, it follows, must have had the backing of at least a significant minority of southern whites. The whites who supported the Republicans, at least for a time, were denounced by their opponents as "scalawags," traitors to the cause of white supremacy. They were the critical swing vote, whose eventual disaffection allowed opponents of Reconstruction—the "Redeemers"—to carry the day.

Some of the scalawags were oldtime planters of Whig persuasion, who had been lukewarm about secession and believed that with paternalistic skill they might be able to manipulate the black vote for their own ends. Some were rising businessmen from outside the planter class, who found the business-oriented economic policies of the Republican party attractive. The most important source of scalawag support, however, were the poor whites from marginal farming areas.

Many small farmers living on relatively infertile soil outside the large plantation areas of the Black Belt had long been resentful of planter domination. Although potential class conflict had generally remained submerged in the antebellum South, it had surfaced on the eve of the war, in the crucial elections on the question of secession. Almost three-fourths of the plantation areas voted in favor of withdrawal. In counties with few or no slaves, however, the pattern was reversed: Almost two-thirds of them opposed provoking a war to defend an institution in which they had no stake. Such places—in mountain areas from West Virginia into northern Georgia, Alabama, and Mississippi, in particular—were centers of Unionist disaffection from the Confederacy during the war and of Republican strength after it. Few of the poor whites there relished association with blacks—most had strong prejudices—but significant numbers were willing for a time to join an electoral coalition that included the freedmen, a coalition of the poor against the master class. The scalawags, said one opponent, were "the party paying no taxes, riding poor horses, wearing dirty shirts, and having no use for soap." It was a biased but broadly accurate generalization about the social base of the movement.

Accomplishments of Reconstruction Governments

The reconstructed governments were relatively short-lived. The most enduring, in Florida, Louisiana, and South Carolina, fell in less than a decade. Most survived hardly half that time before being overturned by white "Redeemers." In that brief time, the governments accomplished a good deal. The new constitutions they drew up were considerably more democratic than the ones they replaced. They reduced the number of crimes punishable by death, enlarged the rights of women, and established fairer apportionments of seats in the legislature.

Opponents of reconstruction regimes denounced them for profligate spending and rampant corruption. Corruption there was, although not notably more than in other states or after "Redemption." State debts increased sharply, but largely to finance the physical redevelopment of a war-torn region and to develop what the South had always lacked—a public school system. In the old South, slaves received no schooling and ordinary white children precious little. The reconstructed governments, assisted by a flood of volunteer Yankee school mistresses who came south to enlist in the crusade, made valiant efforts to develop a comprehensive common school system. (It was racially segregated everywhere but in New Or-

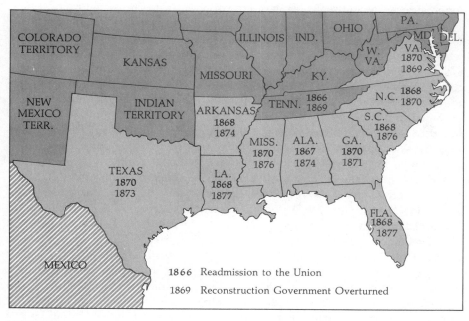

MAP 16-1
The Reconstruction Governments

leans.) In South Carolina in 1868 only 12 percent of school-age white children and 8 percent of the blacks were enrolled. By 1875 the figures had risen to 50 percent for whites and 41 percent for blacks. In Florida the number of pupils in public schools tripled between 1869 and 1873. At the close of Reconstruction, the southern educational system still lagged far behind that of the rest of the nation, but a giant stride forward had been taken.

In a variety of other ways the Republican governments acted to protect the interests of those who were less well-to-do, white as well as black. They put an end to debt imprisonment, and repealed laws favoring landlords over tenants. They reduced high poll taxes and increased levies on landed property. They provided salaries for public officials, so that someone other than a wealthy planter could afford to serve.

Collapse

The radical phase of Reconstruction lasted only an average of four and a half years; by November of 1876, only three southern states were still under Republican rule, and those fell within the next few months as the last federal troops were withdrawn. The Redeemers employed two strategies to topple them. They whipped up racial fears to win back the scalawag vote, persuading many that having a government in all white hands was more important than having a government responsive to the needs of the masses of common people. At the same time, they discouraged blacks from turning out to vote, by measures ranging from economic coercion and social ostracism to whipping, torture, and murder.

Throughout the South, the Ku Klux Klan, militia organizations with names like the White League and the Red Shirts, and local "rifle clubs" murdered blacks on the road on election day. On the eve of the elections that redeemed Mississippi in 1875, the Democratic press adopted the forthright slogan: "Carry the election peaceably if we can, forcibly if we must." Accurate statistics are not available, but the number of blacks murdered in that campaign in one state almost certainly numbered in the hundreds. Six heavily black Mississippi counties that produced more than 14,000 Republican votes in 1873 returned a mere 723 in 1876. The lesson of the "Mississippi Plan" was not lost on white conservatives in other unredeemed states; similar savagery produced equally devastating results.

The first instances of large-scale antiblack violence brought forceful federal action. Congress passed a series of measures that provided machinery to enforce the Fourteenth and Fifteenth Amendments. In October of 1871, President Grant proclaimed that nine South Carolina counties in the grip of KKK violence were in a state of rebellion again, and put them under martial law. After that, however, the North's determination to uphold the civil liberties of Republican voters in the South flagged. In 1872, Congress declared a general amnesty for ex-Confederates, allowing them to re-enter public life. The federal courts that were supposed to bring terrorists to justice were pathetically understaffed, and Congress refused to appropriate funds to expand them. A Democrat committed to ending all federal intervention in the South nearly won the Presidency in 1872, and in 1874 the House of Representatives fell to the Democrats. "The whole public," said President Grant, "is tired of these outbreaks in the South." Radical leaders like Stevens and Sumner died or retired from politics, to be replaced by younger men more concerned with issues of economic policy than with events south of the Mason–Dixon line. The final surrender came after the 1876 elections, the outcome of which hinged on the returns from the last three unredeemed states—Louisiana, Florida, and South Carolina. A congressional commission awarded the electoral votes of those states to the Republican Rutherford B. Hayes, in exchange for his pledge that he would withdraw all federal troops from the South, appoint a southern white to his cabinet, and support the construction of a southern transcontinental railroad.

The Rise of Sharecropping

While blacks were being forced out of politics, they were also falling into a new form of economic dependency—the sharecropping system. The failure to give land to the freedmen meant that they would be forced to work for those who did own it—by and large, the old planter group. The common impression that the Civil War meant the death of the planter class is quite false. Although they lost the ownership of their slaves, they usually held onto their land, and not infrequently expanded their holdings. The richest 10 percent of landowners in one Alabama cotton county in 1860 owned 55 percent of the landed wealth; by 1870 the figure was up to 63 percent. Without the capital to establish farms of their own, former slaves had to turn to the master class for employment.

They were, however, able to resist the planters' efforts to recreate the plantation system. Despite the spur of the Black Codes (until those were repealed by the reconstructed governments) and pressure from Freedmen's Bureau officials, most freedmen flatly refused to work in the fields in gangs under the supervision of an overseer. Even though some planters offered high wages for gang labor, they found few takers—it was too reminiscent of slavery. Blacks would work only if granted a degree of independence and autonomy. The sharecropping system that developed was, as an Alabama paper put it, "an unwilling concession" to the freedman's desire to be a proprietor. The essence of the concession was to decentralize the plantation, dividing it into many separate small plots farmed by individual black families. A striking symbol of their hunger to be free of supervision was the way that freedmen sometimes hitched a team of mules to their old slave cabins and dragged them off to the acres assigned them. They would live out of sight of "the big house," and would refuse to let their wives and young children toil in the fields.

Although these were great gains from the freedmen's point of view, their independence was sorely limited in one critical respect: They were not ordinary renters who could grow whatever crop they pleased and had a prospect of substantial profits if the harvest was good and crop prices high. Slavery had left them no capital, and they needed credit—funds for tools, seed, farm animals, and food until harvest time. Under the sharecropping system, these were supplied by the landlord (or sometimes a country merchant) who determined what was to be grown, and took half of the crop at harvest time as his share in return for having

A TYPICAL SHARECROPPING AGREEMENT, 1886

This contract made and entered into between A.T. Mial of one part and Fenner Powell of the other part both of the County of Wake and State of North Carolina—

Witnesseth—That the Said Fenner Powell hath barganed and agreed with the Said Mial to work as a cropper for the year 1886 on Said Mial's land on the land now occupied by Said Powell on the west Side of Poplar Creek and a point on the east Side of Said Creek and both South and North of the Mial road, leading to Raleigh, That the Said Fenner Powell agrees to work faithfully and dilligently without any unnecessary loss of time, to do all manner of work on said farm as may be directed by Said Mial, And to be respectful in manners and deportment to Said Mial. And the Said Mial agrees on his part to furnish mule and feed for the same and all plantation tools and Seed to plant the crop free of charge, and to give the Said Powell One half of all crops raised and housed by Said Powell on Said land except the cotton seed. The Said Mial agrees to advance as provisions to Said Powell fifty pound of bacon and two sacks of meal pr month and occationally Some flour to be paid out of his the Said Powell's part of the crop or from any other advance that may be made to Said Powell by Said Mial. As witness our hands and seals this the 16th day of January A.D. 1886.

Witness
W.S. Mial (*signed*)

A.T. Mial (*signed*) (Seal)
Fenner (*his mark*) Powell (Seal)

supplied the land, a cabin, tools, and seed. In fact, he often took the other half of the crop as well for having provided the food and clothing needed by the cropper's family. The tenant had to accept a "crop lien" agreement that gave landlords and merchants first claim on the crop. Once the Redeemers came to power, they repealed Republican legislation that protected debtors, and passed new laws slanted to favor creditors. Towering interest rates, higher prices for goods bought on credit (the "two-price system"), and sometimes outright cheating that could not be detected by an illiterate customer usually produced debts that matched or exceeded the income from the sale of the tenant's share of the crop. Moving away to escape the unpaid debt was fruitless, for other landlords would not enter into a sharecropping arrangement with a new tenant without checking with the previous landlord.

Only an extraordinarily diligent minority of blacks could save enough under this system to purchase land of their own. In Georgia in 1880, for example, the black half of the population owned less then 2 percent of the taxed land. The

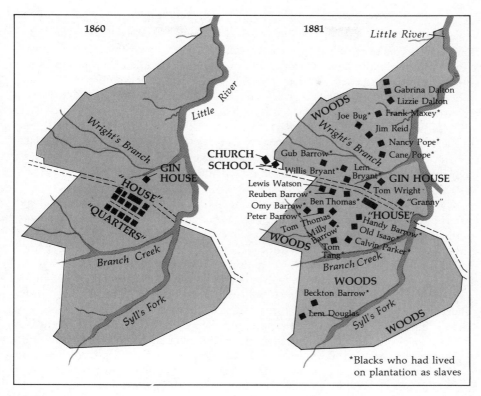

MAP 16–2
A Georgia Plantation, 1860 and 1881

overwhelming majority of blacks were chained in poverty. Some economic historians argue that 15 years after the war the average sharecropper had a *lower* standard of living than the average slave in the 1850s. A more sanguine analysis estimates that freedom gave blacks 29 percent more income, for considerably less arduous labor. Even in the most optimistic appraisal, the economic results of emancipation in the United States were deeply flawed. It left blacks the most impoverished element of the population in by far the most impoverished region of the country.

The Effects of Reconstruction

Reconstruction left its mark upon America. The Thirteenth, Fourteenth, and Fifteenth Amendments, which were in effect the final terms of peace between North and South, were the only major alterations in the U.S. Constitution during the entire century. The thrust toward equal rights they represented was soon blunted by judicial interpretation in an altered political climate, but they remained on the books and in the following century would become powerful levers for social change. The freedmen, although finally stripped of many of the rights they enjoyed temporarily and reduced to a condition of semiservitude in communities devoted to white supremacy, had tasted freedom and had gained confidence in their ability to govern themselves if given the chance. The schools established by the reconstruction regimes survived, although expenditures—particularly for black schools—were sharply cut by the Redeemers when they seized power. In 1879, one southern state spent $1.60 per pupil on white schools and only $.52 per black student. The tide of change, however, was not reversed entirely. At the time of emancipation, hardly 1 black in 20 could read and write; by 1890 it was 9 in 20, by 1910 almost 14 in 20.

The Reconstruction experiment might have effected still more far-reaching and enduring changes in American life. Three fundamental circumstances, however, set the limits beyond which experimentation could not go. First, too few Americans understood the sociology of freedom well enough to grasp that regimes whose continued existence depended so heavily on the votes of a propertyless black proletariat could not long survive without external support. Americans' faith in the fairness of the race along the "dusty and rugged highway of competition," and a general blindness to the realities of economic coercion led them to reject any scheme that would alter existing property relations on behalf of the freedmen. The effort to make dramatic changes of a purely political character was bound to fail.

Second, the dominant American suspicion of strong central government and attachment to the federal system made it necessary to conceive of Reconstruction as a temporary emergency effort. To engineer a deeper change in southern society would have required strong external pressure for decades rather than years. A few radicals called for a long-term occupation of the South on those grounds, but to most that seemed vindictive and unconstitutional.

Finally, the depth of racial prejudice in the North limited the moral energy that might have gone into the struggle for black rights, and gave southern whites reason to denounce northern hypocrisy. To appease fears that fleeing slaves would flock into the North during the war, the Union army had carried out a "containment policy" to keep them in the South. The same determination to discourage large-scale northward migration of southern blacks manifested itself at many points during Reconstruction. After one Congressman suggested placing freedmen in jobs in northern industrial areas, even Charles Sumner of Massachusetts, the most liberal state in the Union on racial matters, denounced the scheme as "utterly untenable." When another key northern senator assured his nervous constituents that the objective of Reconstruction was to give freedmen "liberty and rights" in the South so that "they will stay there and never come into a cold climate to die," solicitude for the health of potential black migrants was not his primary motive. It would be cynical but not altogether inaccurate to say that Reconstruction was the North's attempt to keep southern blacks where they were by pressuring southern whites to treat them more decently than the relatively few blacks of the North were treated. The racism that underlay the thinking of most northerners surfaced more and more as the reconstructed regimes began to founder. Instead of blaming their collapse on the violence of the Redeemer crusade, the feebleness of preventive federal intervention, or the inability of landless blacks to resist economic coercion, northerners advanced a quite different explanation, that conveniently exempted the nation from further responsibility. A New York Republican newspaper, once in the vanguard of the struggle, announced in 1877 that blacks "had been given ample opportunity to develop their own latent capacities," and had succeeded only in proving that "as a race they are idle, ignorant and vicious." This was the self-serving lesson the masses of white Americans, North and South, seemed to have learned from the Reconstruction experiment.

SUGGESTED READINGS

For compact overviews, see John Hope Franklin, *Reconstruction After the Civil War* (1961), Kenneth M. Stampp, *The Era of Reconstruction* (1965), and Rembert Patrick, *The Reconstruction of the Nation* (1967). On the political struggles within the North over Reconstruction policies, LaWanda and John Cox, *Politics, Principles, and Prejudice, 1865–1866* (1963), W.R. Brock, *An American Crisis: Congress and Reconstruction, 1865–1867* (1963), Eric L. McKitrick, *Andrew Johnson and Reconstruction* (1960), David Donald, *The Politics of Reconstruction* (1965); Michael Les Benedict, *A Compromise of Principle: Congressional Republicans and Reconstruction, 1863–1869* (1974), and Martin Mantell, *Johnson, Grant and the Politics of Reconstruction* (1973) present contrasting views. Michael Benedict, *The Impeachment and Trial of Andrew Johnson* (1973) and Hans L. Trefousse, *The Impeachment of a President* (1975) are stimulating recent treatments. Constitutional issues are skillfully dissected in Stanley Kutler, *Judicial Power and Reconstruction Politics* (1968) and Harold Hyman, *A More Perfect Union* (1973). Michael Perman, *Revolution without Compromise: The South and Reconstruction, 1865–68* focuses on Southern white resistance to change.

The fullest and richest account of the economic situation of blacks in the South is Roger L. Ransom and Richard Sutch, *One Kind of Freedom: The Economic Consequences of Emancipation* (1978). A more optimistic economic analysis is offered in Robert Higgs, *Competition and Coercion: Blacks in the American Economy, 1865–1914* (1977). Further insight into the social and economic adjustment of blacks may be gained from Willie Lee Rose, *Rehearsal for Reconstruction* (1964), William S. McFeely, *Yankee Stepfather: General D.O. Howard and the Freedmen* (1968), Peter Kolchin, *First Freedom* (1972), Louis S. Gerteis, *From Contraband to Freedman* (1973), and Edward Magdol, *A Right to the Land* (1977). Jonathan M. Weiner, *Social Origins of the New South: Alabama, 1860–1885* (1978) reveals the staying power of the planter class. Thomas Holt, *Black Over White* (1978) is an excellent study of South Carolina. Albion W. Tourgee, *A Fool's Errand* (1879) is an illuminating novel by a carpet-bagger who served as a judge in the Reconstruction government in North Carolina.

The campaign of violence that helped to bring the Reconstruction governments down is analyzed in Allen W. Trelease, *White Terror* (1971). The political bargaining that led to final withdrawal of federal troops is exposed in C. Vann Woodward, *Reunion and Reaction* (1956).

Thirty-four mules pulled this early threshing machine across wheatfields of the Northwest in the early 1900s.

Part Three

*From Farm to Factory:
Technology Takes Command*

Chapter Seventeen

Industrialization, 1860–1900

The electric light, the bicycle, the sewing machine, the subway, the sky-scraper, the phonograph, the camera, the telephone, the typewriter, the elevator, petroleum, repeating firearms, and dynamite. All of these essentials—or at least inevitables—of contemporary life either did not exist or were at the very earliest stages of development when the Civil War began, and were commonplace by the close of the nineteenth century. No wonder the author of an 1889 volume called *Recent Economic Changes* could exclaim that his generation had lived through "an almost total revolution in every branch of the industrial and commercial system," an amazing advance in man's "control over the forces of Nature." To say "what the world did not have half a century ago," he declared, "is almost equivalent to enumerating all those things which the world now regards as constituting the dividing lines between civilization and barbarism."

That writer's easy equation of "civilization" with material progress and of "barbarism" with the lack of it displays a simple faith, more common in his age than in ours, in technology as a perfecter of humanity. But surely he can be forgiven for marveling so at the extraordinary economic changes that had recently occurred. Allowing him just a bit of poetic license, examining "the economic experiences and industrial conditions" that had prevailed in America only a generation before was like making an excursion into ancient history.

Dramatic technological innovations like the electric light only hinted at the extent of economic transformation in the United States between 1860 and the close of the nineteenth century. An agrarian society became an industrial society; an economy of small-scale producers became an economy dominated by giant na-

In this late nineteenth century engraving, the human figures seem appropriately dwarfed by the machinery in a Bessemer process steel plant.

tional corporations. These developments made America the world's richest nation and greatest industrial power by 1900. Whether they improved the quality of American life, however, was a question that many who lived through these dizzying changes found deeply troubling.

GROWTH AND STRUCTURAL CHANGE

The Civil War, which took tens of thousands of men from their jobs and wrought widespread devastation, interrupted the surge of economic growth that had begun earlier in the century. Growth quickly resumed after the war ended, and at an accelerated rate. Between 1870 and 1900 the gross national product of the United States increased more than fourfold.

One reason, to be sure, was simply that the population grew substantially in those years, from 40 million to 76 million. All other things being equal, an expanding labor force naturally produces an increasing volume of goods and services. But in late nineteenth century America the growth of production far outpaced the growth in the number of producers. The gross national product *per person* rose two and a quarter times, from roughly $225 in 1870 to almost $500 in 1900. In the two decades before the war, national income per capita had increased at a healthy rate of 1.45 percent per year. In the three decades from 1870 to the end of the century, per capita annual growth averaged 2.1 percent, a good 45 percent higher. The standard of living of the average American was improving rapidly.

The productive advances that allowed this rise in the standard of living came partly in the agricultural sector of the economy. In the boom period following the Homestead Act of 1862, more than three million new farms were started. The total amount of land under cultivation in the United States doubled between the Civil War and the end of the century. The farm labor force grew from less than six million to nearly ten million workers, and the productivity of the average farmer increased by almost 50 percent. The resulting flood of grain and meat, dairy

TABLE 17-1
Gross National Product, 1869–1901*

	Total (billions)	Per Person
1869–73	$ 9.11	$223
1877–81	16.1	327
1887–91	24.0	388
1897–1901	37.1	496

*Measured in constant 1929 dollars to eliminate the distorting effect of changes in the price level.

CUTTING THE COST OF FLOUR PRODUCTION

... In respect to no other one article has change in the conditions or production and distribution been productive of such momentous consequences as in the case of wheat. On the great wheat-fields of the State of Dakota, where machinery is applied to agriculture to such an extent that the requirement for manual labor has been reduced to a minimum, the annual product of one man's labor, working to the best advantage, is understood to be now equivalent to the production of 5,500 bushels of wheat. In the great mills of Minnesota, the labor of another one man for a year, under similar conditions as regards machinery, is in like manner equivalent to the conversion of this unit of 5,500 bushels of wheat into a thousand barrels of flour, leaving 500 bushels for seed-purposes; and...it is reasonably certain that the year's labor of one and a half men more—or at the most, two men—employed in railroad transportation, is equivalent to putting this thousand barrels of flour on a dock in New York ready for exportation, where the addition of a fraction of a cent a pound to the price will further transport and deliver it at almost any port of Europe.

Here, then, we have the labor of three men for one year, working with machinery, resulting in their producing all the flour that a thousand other men ordinarily eat in a year, allowing a barrel of flour for the average consumption of each adult. Before such a result the question of wages paid in the different branches of flour production and transportation becomes an insignificant factor in determining a market; and, accordingly, American flour grown in Dakota, and ground in Minneapolis, from a thousand to fifteen hundred miles from the nearest seaboard, and under the auspices of men paid from a dollar and a half to two dollars and a half per day for their labor, is sold in European markets at rates which are determinative of the prices which Russian peasants, Egyptian "fellahs," and Indian "ryots," can obtain in the same markets for similar grain grown by them on equally good soil, and with from fifteen to twenty cents per day wages for their labor.

—David A. Wells, *Recent Economic Changes*, 1889

products, cotton, and tobacco more than satisfied the needs of the burgeoning urban population, and provided a growing surplus for export.

The chief arena of economic dynamism, however, was the industrial sector. Indeed, it was new mechanical reapers and harvesters, improved steel plows, barbed wire fencing, and a host of other manufactured products that stimulated the growing efficiency of the farmer. Agriculture continued to play a crucial role in the economy well into the twentieth century, but the economy had taken a decisive turn toward industrialism well before 1900.

TABLE 17-2
Percentage of the Labor Force in Agriculture, 1860–1900

1860	53%
1870	52
1880	51
1890	43
1900	40

The Shift from Agriculture to Industry

At the time of the Civil War, the American economy still had a strongly agrarian stamp. For every dollar invested in manufacturing establishments, seven were tied up in farmland, livestock, tools and equipment. Over half of the labor force worked at farming, and farm products represented over half of the value of the country's commodity output. Furthermore, the relatively small industrial sector concentrated on the simple processing of the resources of the land. Flour milling, cotton goods, and lumber were the top three American industries by value of product.

By the end of the century, the shape of the economy had changed. Although the absolute number of people working on farms continued to grow until 1916, other occupations were expanding far more rapidly. Between 1880 and 1890 farmers became a minority for the first time in American history, a minority destined to shrink further with each decade. By 1900, six out of every ten Americans made their living outside agriculture.

The overshadowing of the farm sector appears earlier and more abruptly if we measure the change in terms of contribution to the wealth of the nation. In 1860, of every dollar's worth of commodities produced in the United States, 56 cents' worth were farm products; by 1900, the figure had fallen to only 33 cents. The share of

TABLE 17-3
Sector Shares of Commodity Production, 1860–1900

	Agriculture	Manufacturing and Mining	Construction
1860	56	33	11
1870	53	35	12
1880	49	40	11
1890	37	52	11
1900	33	58	9

TABLE 17-4
Value Added per Worker, 1870-1900 (in 1879 Dollars)

	Agriculture	Manufacturing and Mining
1870	$256	$521
1900	358	984
Rate of increase	43%	76%

manufacturing, only 33 cents per dollar in 1860, rose to 58 cents by 1900. That the share of commodity production coming from the agricultural sector declined much more sharply than did the proportion of the labor force engaged in farming suggests that farm productivity must have been lagging behind manufacturing productivity, which was indeed the case. Value added per farm worker rose an impressive 43 percent between 1870 and 1900, but the increase for employees in manufacturing was a striking 76 percent, almost twice as much. In the four decades after 1860, the number of Americans employed in manufacturing increased five times, while the value of what they produced rose ten times.

The Makeup of American Industry

As agriculture gave way to industry, the character of American industry itself was undergoing a transformation. Resource processing and light manufacturing continued to expand, but heavy industry—in which technological innovation proceeded most rapidly—made especially dramatic gains. Steel is the classic case. Until the 1860s, iron was the primary metal used in American industry. Although iron rails, for example, were so brittle that heavy locomotives soon pounded them to pieces, manufacturers had neither the know-how nor the capital to begin the more challenging task of producing strong, flexible steel. The little steel available came from Britain, still the world's industrial leader, and was expensive and of poor quality. In 1864, the Bessemer process for converting iron ore to steel was introduced into the United States, and shortly after, the Siemens–Martin or open hearth process, which was better suited to the type of ore which came from the immense deposits in the Lake Superior region. Steel output soared from a mere 19,000 tons in 1865 to an amazing 10 million tons by the century's end. In 1900, one giant American firm—the Carnegie Steel Company—outproduced the entire steel industry of Great Britain!

A part of the economy that had been little developed before the war was the "capital goods" or "producer's goods" sector. These industries—tool and diemaking, for example—produced machinery and equipment not for the immediate use of consumers but for the use of other producers. Rapid expansion in this sphere

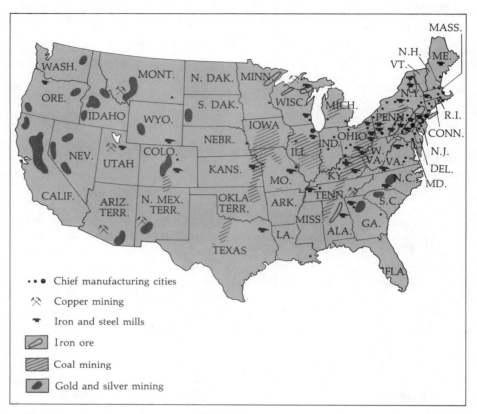

MAP 17-1
Industrial Development in the Late Nineteenth Century

was responsible for much of the dynamism in the American economy as a whole during the period; it facilitated mechanization in other industries, not only in the manufacture of consumer goods but in transportation, communications, and agriculture. By 1900, the machinery industry was the nation's largest by "value added" (that is, the value of the product minus the cost of the raw materials used to make it).

Increasingly sophisticated mechanized production made it possible to substitute energy derived from inanimate sources for human muscle, which is always in short supply. Although there had been progress in tapping natural sources of power during the early nineteenth century industrial transformation, on the eve of the Civil War the total amount of such energy generated annually was only five million horsepower. In the next four decades, the figure multiplied ninefold.

There was an important shift too in the *kind* of power available, a shift that allowed industry to develop in places that had been inappropriate in earlier times. The main source of inanimate energy in the prewar years was waterpower. As late

ANDREW CARNEGIE
ON COST ACCOUNTING

As I became acquainted with the manufacture of iron I was greatly surprised to find that the cost of each of the various processes was unknown. Inquiries made of the leading manufacturers of Pittsburgh proved this. It was a lump business, and until stock was taken and the books balanced at the end of the year, the manufacturers were in total ignorance of results. I heard of men who thought their business at the end of the year would show a loss and had found a profit, and *vice-versa*. I felt as if we were moles burrowing in the dark, and this to me was intolerable. I insisted upon such a system of weighing and accounting being introduced throughout our works as would enable us to know what our cost was for each process and especially what each man was doing, who saved material, who wasted it, and who produced the best results.

To arrive at this was a much more difficult task than one would imagine. Every manager in the mills was naturally against the new system. Years were required before an accurate system was obtained, but eventually, by the aid of many clerks and the introduction of weighing scales at various points in the mill, we began to know not only what every department was doing, but what each one of the many men working at the furnaces was doing, and thus to compare one with another. One of the chief sources of success in manufacturing is the introduction and strict maintenance of a perfect system of accounting so that responsibility for money or materials can be brought home to every man. Owners who, in the office, would not trust a clerk with five dollars without having a check upon him, were supplying tons of material daily to men in the mills without exacting an account of their stewardship by weighing what each returned in the finished form.

—Andrew Carnegie, *Autobiography*, 1920

as 1869, almost half (48 percent) of the power employed in manufacturing came from water, which forced industrial concentration along rivers whose energies could be harnessed, most of them in rather isolated rural areas. After that, coal-burning steam engines were introduced on a large scale; by 1890 they accounted for about four-fifths (78 percent) of the energy supply. Manufacturers thereby gained much greater freedom in selecting plant sites, and gravitated toward the cities, which could supply workers as well as the transportation connections to obtain the necessary fuel and raw materials. (The implications this shift had for urban development are more fully discussed in the next chapter.)

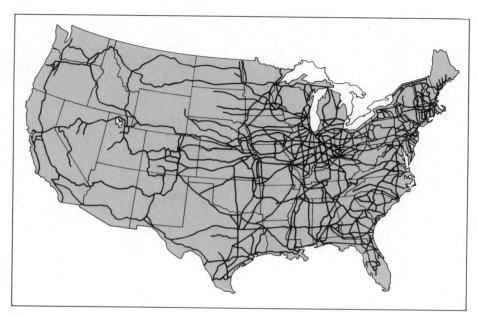

MAP 17-2
The Rail Network in 1890

Transportation and Communication

Changes in the structure of the American economy and the increased productivity of the average worker depended to a significant degree on improvements in transportation and communication. What might be called the Second Transportation Revolution occurred after the Civil War. In the railroad boom of the prewar decades, an impressive 30,000 miles of track had been laid. The railroads had become the country's first billion dollar industry. The system was largely confined to the states east of the Mississippi, however, and even in the East there were a great many gaps. Because of the number of small railroad companies, most routes were short-line, and passengers on long journeys had to change trains several times. The absence of long-distance routes was compounded by the lack of agreement on a standard gauge (width) for the track. No less than eleven different gauges were used by competing companies, so that one road's cars could not ordinarily pass over another's route. Freight between locations not served by the same road had to be laboriously reloaded into different cars. The primitive locomotives had a top speed of 30 miles per hour. Even at that speed, travel was dangerous because there was no standard signal system and brakes were poor.

In the last third of the century, the rail system was expanded enormously and these limitations were overcome. The Union Pacific Railroad reached the Pacific Coast in 1869, to be followed by other transcontinental roads. Small companies were merged into regional systems. By 1900 track mileage had been increased almost ninefold and the gauge had been standardized at the Union Pacific's 4'8''. Steel tracks had replaced iron, and were able to bear loads 20 times heavier. More powerful locomotives made rail travel much faster, and the introduction of standard signals and air brakes made it far safer. In scope and efficiency, the American railroad system had reached its peak of development, and the cost of shipping goods long distances had fallen to new lows. In 1865 it cost $3.45 to move a barrel of flour from Chicago to New York by rail; in 1895 it was a mere 68 cents.

A modern communications network was laid down in these years as well. In 1860 it took three weeks for news from San Francisco to reach New York. Although the first telegraph lines had been built in 1845, none extended across the continent, and there was little cooperation between the competing companies that operated them. Shortly after the war they merged to form the Western Union, which proceeded to extend its lines from coast to coast. Almost instantaneous communication between cities thousands of miles apart became possible. The development of the telephone system after Alexander Graham Bell's successful 1876 experiments was no less revolutionary. Within a quarter of a century there were 1.3 million phones in service and long-distance calls were routine. To avoid the confusion that would have been created by rapid communication between communities operating on dozens of different local times, as well as to facilitate railroad scheduling, standard time zones were established in 1883. The volume of communication via the printed word increased enormously as well. The circulation of daily newspapers, for example, increased sevenfold between 1870 and 1900. The ever more rapid and economical flow of information across the land lubricated the wheels of commerce and industry and enlarged the national market.

Investment in Physical and Human Capital

The great productive advances of the late nineteenth century all required capital investment on a massive scale. The building of the railroads, for example, took a capital expenditure valued at more than $13 billion in 1900, at a time when the country's gross national product for an entire year was less than $20 billion. And there were other great capital needs. Farmers needed better tools and machines. New plants had to be built and equipped with technological devices of unprecedented cost. The urban population needed houses, roads, bridges, sewers, warehouses, schools and hospitals.

Although part of the increment to the national income produced by economic growth was devoted to personal consumption, a large and growing share was not. In the late nineteenth century the physical basis of the modern American economy was firmly established. This was a time of what is termed "capital deepening"—a rise in the share of the national income withheld from consumption and invested in further production. Even before the Civil War, the proportion of the national income going to capital formation was a solid 15 percent; by the 1870s, however, it had leaped to 25 percent—and it rose another 4 percent in the 1880s. As a result, the total material capital stock of the nation soared from $27 billion (in constant 1929 dollars) in 1870 to four times that by the century's end. On a per capita basis, the

TABLE 17-5
U.S. Material Capital Stock
(net of capital consumption), 1870–1900 (in 1929 Dollars)

	Total (billions)	Per Worker
1870	$ 27	$2,110
1880	42	2,490
1890	68	3,060
1900	108	3,790

capital stock per worker rose from $2,110 in 1870 to $3,790 in 1900, a gain of 80 percent.

The capital embodied in a new factory building, a massive Bessemer converter, or a steam locomotive is the most obvious, but not the only important kind of capital. If we consider capital "any form of wealth employed or capable of being employed in the production of further wealth," then any spending that improves people's capacities to work effectively is a capital investment. Schooling may not be quite the same thing as *learning*, but the best measure we have of investments in "human capital" is educational expenditures. Already the most educationally advanced country in the world at the time of the Civil War, the United States devoted a growing share of its wealth to education in the decades that followed. Total school expenditures per year rose from $60 million to more than $500 million, a much sharper increase than the rise either in children of school age or in the GNP. Expenditures per child quadrupled, and the percentage of the national income going to education jumped from 1.4 to almost 3 percent.

As a result, the quality of the labor force improved substantially. The number of workers unable to read and write fell considerably, from one in five in 1870 to one in nine in 1900. Illiteracy among blacks declined dramatically, thanks to the efforts of the Reconstruction governments, but the percentage decline in illiteracy

TABLE 17-6
Resources Invested in Education, 1860–1900

	Costs of Resources Devoted to Education (millions of current dollars)	Costs per Child Aged 5 to 19	Cost as Percentage of GNP
1860	$ 60	$ 5.33	1.4
1900	503	20.53	2.9

TABLE 17-7
Some Measures of Educational Progress, 1870–1900

	Illiteracy (percentage of the population 10 or older)			High School Graduates (percentage of 17-year-olds)	College Enrollments (Percentage of 18–21-year-olds)
	Total	White	Black		
1870	20	11	80	2.0	1.7
1900	11	6	45	6.4	4.0

among whites throughout the nation was actually just as great. Primary schooling was becoming all but universal, and more students were undertaking more advanced training.

THE RISE OF BIG BUSINESS

Between 1860 and 1900, American business organization underwent a transformation as momentous as the change from an agricultural to an industrial economy. On the eve of the Civil War, railroad companies were virtually the only large corporations in America. Within the next four decades, giant corporate enterprises sprang up in virtually every branch of the economy, firms of unprecedented size, complexity, geographic scope, and power. Many did more business than all of their competitors put together. By the end of the century, the American Tobacco Company produced 75 percent of the country's cigarettes, Standard Oil over 80 percent of its petroleum, the National Biscuit Company 90 percent of its biscuits and crackers. Pabst beer, Ivory soap, Singer sewing machines, Kodak cameras, Campbell's soup, Quaker oats, Heinz pickles, Borden's milk, Pillsbury flour—these are but a few of the staples of today's consumer society that were first developed in the closing decades of the nineteenth century by new firms that grew to be giants. The rise of big business had immense and enduring effects on the life of the nation.

Chartered business corporations have a long history in America, but as late as 1860 much the most common form of business enterprise was the one-man firm. The individual proprietorship must normally be small and short-lived. Its resources are limited to the wealth of the owner, and its life span to his life span. They can be expanded by allowing one or more partners to buy in, but there is a serious deterrent to this kind of expansion: The partners become liable for the full debts of the firm. In the event of failure, they risk losing not only their original investment but any other assets they might have. So long as it was confined to individual proprietorships and partnerships, American business would necessarily remain small-scale.

The limited liability corporation is a device that maximizes the size and longevity of the firm while minimizing the risk to investors. It is free to generate capital by selling as much stock as the public will buy. The investor cannot lose more than his investment, because the corporation's liability is limited to its corporate assets. The firm's life span will not be endangered by the death of the owner, because there is no single owner. Investors or their heirs are not entitled to demand company repayment for their share of the business. To retrieve their funds, they must sell to another investor, which leaves intact the corporation's invested capital.

The extraordinary flexibility and expansive capacity of the corporate device had not become apparent to American manufacturers before the Civil War. The manufacturing corporations that did exist were small and primitive by later standards. The largest New England textile mill employed only 800 hands, the average mill some 200 to 300. The peak capitalization for these establishments was $1 million. They typically confined themselves to the manufacturing stage, leaving both the procurement of raw materials and the sale of the final product to independent commission agents. Although some part of their output went to distant markets in other parts of the country, none of these companies had branch offices or factories across several states, or a complex managerial hierarchy.

The only giant corporate enterprises on the scene were the railroads, the pioneers in the most dramatic change in business organization the world had seen in centuries. The largest railroads employed at least five times as many men as the largest textile mills, and were capitalized at levels as high as $20 million. Their workers were dispersed over the length of the road, often hundreds of miles, and there was need for the most precise coordination of their activities to avoid calamitous wrecks. The number of financial transactions railroads engaged in each year, collecting freight charges from tens of thousands of shippers and fares from hundreds of thousands of passengers, presented a staggering accounting task. Generating profits from so complex an operation required accurate statistics on operating costs and revenues. America's railroads consequently carried out a managerial revolution, developing a complex coordinating and controlling bureaucratic structure that would spread into other spheres of the economy in the late nineteenth century.

Changes in state laws in the third quarter of the century made incorporation even more convenient by simplifying procedures and eliminating the necessity of obtaining charters from the legislature. The increasing availability of cheap and rapid transportation and communications—the completion of the rail network, and the laying of first telegraph and then telephone lines across the country—dramatically enlarged the potential market. The successful example of the railroads prompted emulation, and it was no accident that the first man to introduce railroad management techniques into manufacturing was steelmaker Andrew Carnegie. He had learned them from the inside during his climb from telegraph boy to Division Superintendent of the Pennsylvania Railroad.

Why some firms became as gigantic and powerful as they did, however, is a more difficult problem. One possible answer is that they became giants through superior efficiency in production, by delivering the goods at a price their competitors could not match. Their ascendancy, in this view, represented the survival of the fittest. At the other extreme is the argument that the growth of companies like Standard Oil stemmed from their efficiency not at producing but at destroying their competitors through ruthless and underhanded methods. Were the business leaders of this era great "industrial statesmen" who deserve credit for revolutionizing the system of production? Or were they "robber barons," who beat their business rivals into submission and then plundered the consumer, whose only choices were to pay monopoly prices or do without? Americans who lived through this era were divided on the issue, as historians have been ever since. The most important aspects of the issue follow.

Reasons for Business Concentration

In many industries, there were clearly large "economics of scale." The higher the total output, in other words, the lower the average cost of each item produced. The gains in productivity that accompanied the enormously expensive technology employed in such advanced industries as steel, petroleum, electrical equipment and chemicals made it impossible for even a small enterprise to approach the levels of efficiency the giants could attain. When Carnegie entered the steel business in 1874, it cost more than $100 to make a ton of steel. The phenomenal expansion of Carnegie Steel thereafter was attributable in considerable measure to his remarkable success in driving down costs as output increased, to $50 a ton within two years, to $20 before a dozen had elapsed, to $12 by the late 1890s. Similarly, the price of lamp oil was 18 cents per gallon in 1873. It plummeted after John D. Rockefeller established Standard Oil as the dominant oil refining firm, and remained at 8.5 cents or below for the rest of the century. That was indeed delivering the goods.

Such economies of scale were most often achieved by firms that expanded by means of what is called "vertical integration." Vertical integration means adding other operations to the company's original function at earlier or later stages in the production process. For example, Standard Oil made the barrels to contain its oil, owned the warehouses in which it was stored, and bought a fleet of tankers and a system of pipelines to carry it to market. Similarly an official of Federal Steel remarked that his company "takes the ore from the ground, transports it, manufactures it into pig iron, manufactures pig iron into steel, and steel into finished products, and delivers those products." Such integration lowered costs of production because it allowed administrative coordination of the many differing operating units brought under common management.

Vertical integration may proceed "forward" or "backward." A manufacturing firm integrates "forward"—closer to the final consumer—by entering directly into distribution and sales instead of relying on independent commission agents, wholesalers and retailers. "Backward" integration—farther away from the consumer—is securing the needed raw materials without depending on other suppliers.

A classic example of successful vertical integration in both directions came in the meatpacking industry in the 1870s and 1880s. The swelling populations of the eastern cities were demending more and more fresh meat. The limited supply of

JOHN D. ROCKEFELLER ON THE VIRTUES OF ECONOMIC CONCENTRATION

It is too late to argue about advantages of industrial combinations. They are a necessity. And if Americans are to have the privilege of extending their business in all the states of the Union, and into foreign countries as well, they are a necessity on a large scale, and require the agency of more than one corporation. Their chief advantages are:

(1) Command of necessary capital.
(2) Extension of limits of business.
(3) Increase of number of persons interested in business.
(4) Economy in the business.
(5) Improvements and economies which are derived from knowledge of many interested persons of wide experience.
(6) Power to give the public improved products at less prices and still make a profit for stockholders.
(7) Permanent work and good wages for laborers.

—Report of the United States Industrial Commission, 1899

eastern land available for pasture kept the price of livestock high. It would obviously be cheaper to grow the beef cattle in Texas, if western beef could be brought to the tables of New York or Boston. A group of meatpacking companies in Chicago known as the "Big Five" capitalized on that opportunity. Improvements in transportation played a key role in their success. The penetration of the rail network into the Far West cut the time and expense of bringing cattle to market, and the perfection of the refrigerated railroad car in the 1870s made it possible to slaughter the animals far from the city where they were consumed and thereby pay freight charges only on the edible portions.

But the crucial innovation, made first by Gustavus Swift, was forward integration into distribution and marketing. Local butchers and wholesale meat distributors lacked refrigerated storage facilities, and they—like many customers at first—tended to doubt the quality of meat slaughtered far away many weeks earlier. Swift bypassed the existing distribution channels by setting up his own national network of warehouses and launched a major advertising campaign stressing the superiority of his prime western beef. His business boomed, and the slaughtering part of the operation was soon operating on a vast scale. An assembly-line method of processing animals allowed new savings, as did the use of parts that had been previously discarded as waste. Fat was made into soap and lard, heads and feet into glue, hog bristles into cushion stuffing, cattle horns into combs and buttons, bones into fertilizer, entrails into violin strings. Swift, it was said, used every part of a pig except the squeal. The result was better meat at lower prices.

American industry, of course, might have developed as rapidly as it did without the direction of capitalists like Carnegie, who earned a comfortable lifetime profit of $50 million for his efforts. Mass production and the resulting economies of scale cannot be equated with production by large capitalist firms; there are socialist alternatives. But questions of that kind occurred to only a small fraction of Americans in these years. The main cleavage was between those who thought economic concentration inevitable and desirable and those who believed it unnatural and dangerous. And in many branches of industry, giant production units clearly were necessary for maximal efficiency.

The growth of big business in the late nineteenth century, however, cannot be explained solely on the basis of the superior efficiency of the emerging giants. Although in some industries—generally those less technologically advanced ones—there were few economies of scale, some companies nonetheless achieved a position of dominance. Even in the industries with significant economies of scale, other factors also promoted concentration. Cutting costs of production is only one way of maximizing profits. The level of profit is a function not only of costs but of revenues, which are determined by price. Control over prices is crucial. The giant firms that grew up in this era did so partly because they succeeded in controlling prices by eliminating or limiting competition.

One common tactic was to exert pressures on other businesses for preferential treatment not given to one's competitors. The rise of Standard Oil, for example, and the demise of hundreds of smaller oil firms was facilitated by John D. Rockefeller's successful demand that the railroads transporting oil from his Cleveland refineries to eastern markets charge less than the announced rates. Under the table "rebates" were given Standard on each barrel of its oil shipped. This, of course, allowed Rockefeller to sell more cheaply than his competitors. Rebates were eventually outlawed, but not before Rockefeller won an even nicer concession—rebates to Standard on the shipping charges paid by his *competitors*, which made it all the easier to undersell them! This is but one example of a more general pattern: Firms large enough to be important customers of suppliers, transporters, or sellers used their power to exact concessions unavailable to their smaller rivals. They could, like Standard Oil, obtain cost reductions enabling them to wage successful price wars and drive their rivals out of business, after which they could raise the price. Or they might directly limit the market, as when leading firms forbade their distributors to sell competing products as well, and developed a network of spies to report instances of "disloyalty."

The drive to develop consumer loyalty to national brand names was another way of checking competition. In the breakfast food industry, for example, economies of scale in production were negligible. Cornflakes could be produced as cheaply by small companies as by large ones, and tasted much the same. But if the American public could be convinced that there was something very special about *Kellogg's* Cornflakes, the corporation that made them would dominate the market. That conviction could be created only by advertising, and the late nineteenth century saw an extraordinary rise in advertising expenditures, from $50 million at the end of the war to $542 million by 1900, when the proportion of the national income going to advertising was actually higher than today. The appearance of giant firms in the technologically less advanced industries was partly attributable to that.

The effort to control prices was especially urgent for producers with a heavy burden of fixed costs—costs that remained large even if the volume of business was shrinking. It costs almost as much, for example, to run a train with 100 passengers from Pittsburgh to Cleveland as it does to run one with 1,000 passengers. Shutting down a huge blast furnace or oil refinery saves something in labor and material costs, but the larger expense of paying for the plant and equipment continues even if it stands idle. Consequently, producers with heavy fixed costs have a powerful incentive to cut prices below actual costs of production in hopes of capturing a larger share of the market, a tactic that makes short-run sense from the viewpoint of the individual firm, but can lead to widespread bankruptcy if many pursue it.

To deal with this problem, corporations sought to collaborate with their rivals to fix prices at a reasonably high level, or to merge with them into larger units. This is the strategy of horizontal, rather than vertical integration, the combination of separate units performing at the same stage of the production process—refining oil, distilling whiskey, milling flour, or whatever. Early attempts at a loose form of horizontal integration occurred in many industries in the 1870s, when competing firms agreed to fix prices and divide the market into agreed shares. Such "pools" or "cartels," however, proved ineffective, because they had no legal standing and they broke down whenever any member company felt it could capture a larger share of the market by violating the agreement and reducing prices. More binding forms of combination were soon devised. One was the "trust," a particular legal device for centralizing control over separate firms without violating laws against one corporation's owning the stock of another. Rockefeller's Standard Oil Trust, created in 1882, was the pioneer here. A slightly different means to the same end was the "holding company." Both devices began to be used on a large scale in the early 1890s. Some 51 major corporate mergers took place between 1890 and 1893. The trend was reversed temporarily during the depression of the mid-'90s and then resumed with greater force. 1,207 American firms disappeared through merger in the year 1899 alone.

Some of the giant enterprises that occupied the commanding heights of the economy by the century's end clearly became giants by producing more efficiently than their rivals. Others grew by eliminating or controlling competition and charging monopoly prices. Both factors appear, with varying degrees of frequency, in the history of most big firms, making it very hard to assess the overall importance of each. However, leading economic historian, Douglass C. North, has recently calculated that total corporate profits in 1900 were roughly $400 million higher than they would have been under fully competitive conditions. He points out that this is $5 per person in the country, or a mere 2 percent of average annual income.[1] From another vantage point, however, we can say that the profits reaped by big business were 40 percent higher than they would have been under free competition, hardly a trivial figure.

---

[1] See Douglass C. North, *Growth and Welfare in the American Past*, 3rd ed., (Englewood Cliffs, N.J.: Prentice Hall, 1983), p. 140.

The costs and benefits of the new corporate industrial order cannot be measured by any single economic standard. The profound changes that occurred in the organization of the American economy during the late nineteenth century produced a complex public response—a mixture of enthusiasm, bewilderment, and fear.

GROWING PAINS

Americans thrilled at the signs of economic progress they saw all around them. In this era, faith in economic growth was expressed more unreservedly than ever before in American history. The great Philadelphia Centennial Exhibition of 1876, was eloquent testimony to the fact. Although the occasion naturally invited some commemoration of the past, the exhibits resolutely ignored history and celebrated the technological marvels of the present. All would be well in the future, presumably, if it held more of the same. Walt Whitman composed a poem for the affair. He wrote that the American people were engaged in a task of construction "mightier than Egypt's tombs...fairer than Roma's temples." Furthermore, he said, "Business shall be, nay is, the word of the modern hero."

Strong as this faith in technology and industry was, aspects of the great economic changes of the late nineteenth century seemed profoundly disturbing to many. One was the instability, the increasingly violent economic fluctuations, that accompanied growth. Although periods of unusual prosperity and years of depression were not unknown in pre-industrial America, after industrial transformation the cycle of boom and bust was dizzying. The Centennial celebrations at Philadelphia did not boast about the fact that the unemployment rate that year was higher than ever before in American history. Some two million people, one out of every eight workers, were without jobs.[2]

In both its length and severity, the depression that began in 1873 was much worse than any of the pre-Civil War depressions. But two decades later there was an even more acute collapse from 1893 to 1897. In the worst year, 1894, more than 4.5 million persons were unemployed, almost a fifth of the labor force. Three years later, the jobless still numbered almost 4 million.

The men and women who lost their source of livelihood and had to resort to the bread lines and soup kitchens were the most obvious, but far from the only victims of these recurrent depressions. Another telling fact that went uncelebrated in 1876 was that more than 90,000 American businesses, one out of every seven, were forced to close down that year, leaving debts of almost $2 billion. In 1893 more than 150,000 firms collapsed, with liabilities exceeding $3.5 billion. Farmers, too, increasingly dependent on the sale of cash crops to pay for the new machines they

---

[2]The unemployment rate was 13 percent which means in fact that at least a third and possibly as much as half the labor force was probably without work for some months. If the average length of unemployment was six months, a 13 percent rate would mean that 26 percent of workers were out of work for approximately half a year each. If the average term of unemployment was from three to four months, which was generally the case in the late nineteenth century, a 13 percent rate means unemployment for from 39 to 52 percent of the labor force.

TABLE 17-8
Unemployment Rates in Peak Depression Years of the Nineteenth Century

	Percentage
1819	4
1838	7
1858	7
1876	13
1894	18

needed, were hard hit. Declining crop prices created acute hardship; mortgages were foreclosed by banks, and previously independent men found themselves working for others as tenants or laborers. People wealthy enough to ride through the crisis times complacently called these alternate periods of activity and depression only minor "ebbs and flows in the great rising tide of material progress, ending in an adjustment to ever new and better conditions of life." But for ordinary citizens, the harsh fact was that the growth in national wealth had yielded not more but less economic security.

Corporate Morality

A second source of unease about the new order stemmed from the conflict between new business practices and traditional American moral precepts. Books like Henry Demarest Lloyd's exposé of Standard Oil, *Wealth Against Commonwealth* (1894), were disturbing to those who believed in playing hard but playing fair. "Business is not a philanthropy," Henry O. Havemeyer, the head of the Sugar Trust, told a government investigating committee frankly. "I do not care two cents for your ethics. As a business proposition it is right to get out of a business all that you possibly can."

There was suspicion, too, that the wild swings of the business cycle were the result of manipulation by speculators who reaped immense rewards without producing useful things—combining and recombining businesses in ways that increased profits but not productivity. John W. Gates, founder of the Barbed Wire Trust, was nicknamed "Bet-a-Million" Gates for having staked a million dollars on the turn of a card (he lost). There were grounds for fearing that men like Gates were conducting their business lives on the same principles, and that their gambles were affecting the welfare of millions of people.

The practice of "watering" corporate stock well illustrates the clash between the old and new morality. The term "watered stock" derived originally from an inventive business method employed in the cattle trade by a sly scoundrel named Daniel Drew. Drew accumulated a fortune by letting his herds eat salt and then drink as much water as they pleased just before they arrived at the market to be weighed for sale, which inflated the weight of each animal by about 50 pounds. (That Drew's later endowment of a theological seminary assured his soul of eternal heavenly rest may be doubted.) Applied to corporate business, watering of the stock takes place when two companies merge their assets into a new corporation, and issue new stock certificates in amounts exceeding the assets of the two. The excess is called water, for it is not backed by real physical assets.

The analogy with the cattle trade breaks down here, however, for the 50 pounds of water purchased by Drew's unwary customers quickly vanished. It was utterly worthless. But the purchaser of watered stock might or might not lose on the investment. The value of corporate stock is determined not by the size of the company's assets but by the demand for its shares on the stock market. There has to be some relation between the two—a corporation with a million dollars in plant, equipment, inventory, and good will cannot sell a billion dollars worth of stock—but the relation can vary within fairly broad limits. Two companies with combined assets of a million dollars might well successfully market twice that much stock, and buyers might still find it a good investment and be able to sell it in the future at a profit. But to many Americans in the bewildering new world of late nineteenth century corporate capitalism, this seemed sheer alchemy, a means of gulling the public.

Concentrated Power

Perhaps the deepest and most fundamental fear was that the emergence of giant corporations had put an unprecedented concentration of power into the hands of a few people, thereby threatening to freeze the social structure into "a new feudalism." Part of that fear was that the economic power of big business would lead to direct business dominance over the political system. In 1888 the president of Harvard University warned that one Boston railroad employed 18,000 persons and took in $40 million a year, while the government of Massachusetts employed only 6,000 and operated on some $7 million annually. The United States Steel Corporation, created in 1901, merged more than 200 separate firms into a super corporation. It was capitalized at $1.4 billion, three times the annual budget of the federal government. The great corporations often did make their weight felt on the political scales, through lobbying, campaign contributions, and sometimes outright bribery. Standard Oil, Henry Demarest Lloyd quipped, did everything to the Pennsylvania legislature except refine it. In the vivid imagination of one reformer, the growing political influence of giant firms was nothing less than "treason, a conspiracy to usurp and pervert the government, to overthrow free institutions and to establish a despotism and a favored and dominant class."

A broader concern was that a nation of independent producers had been transformed into a nation of dependent employees, and that traditional opportunities to rise in the world by venturing into business for oneself had been blocked. The middle rungs of the social ladder had been broken out, and the society was becoming polarized into "haves" and "have nots." It came as a shock to many when the 1890 census disclosed that less than half (48 percent) of American

WILLIAM JENNINGS BRYAN ON THE DANGERS OF INDUSTRIAL CONCENTRATION

I may be in error, but, in my judgment, a government of the people, by the people, and for the people, will be impossible when a few men control all the sources of production and dole out daily bread to all the rest on such terms as the few may prescribe. I believe that this nation is the hope of the world. I believe that the Declaration of Independence was the grandest document ever penned by human hands. The truths of that declaration are condensed into four great propositions: That all men are created equal; that they are endowed with inalienable rights; that governments are instituted among men to preserve those rights, and that governments derive their just powers from the consent of the governed. Such a government is impossible under an industrial aristocracy. Place the food and clothing, all that we eat and wear and use, in the hands of a few people, and instead of it being a government of the people, it will be a government of the syndicates, by the syndicates, and for the syndicates. Establish such a government, and the people will soon be powerless to secure a legislative remedy for any abuse. Establish such a system, and on the night before election the employees will be notified not to come back on the day after election unless the trusts' candidate is successful.

—Chicago Conference on Trusts, 1900

families owned their own homes, and that the richest 9 percent held 71 percent of all the wealth.

Some of these fears were ill-founded. From the limited evidence available, it appears that the gulf between "haves" and "have nots" did not widen appreciably during the industrial surge of the late nineteenth century. The extent of wealth concentration revealed by the 1890 census was not really greater than it had been by the middle of the nineteenth century. Neither the percentage of Americans without property nor the share of the prosperous elite—whether defined as the top tenth, fifth, or quarter—seems to have risen. It was not that the late nineteenth century pattern was so egalitarian, but rather that sharp stratification had already occurred well before the Civil War.

What was new in the closing decades of the century, and was mistakenly viewed as evidence of a more general trend toward inequality, was the appearance of a new class of super-rich multimillionaires, men dozens and dozens of times richer than any American before the Civil War. The fortunes accumulated by Carnegie, Rockefeller, and their counterparts in other industries—Swift and Armour in meat, Duke in tobacco, Guggenheim in mining, Vanderbilt, Harriman and

Stanford in railroads—were indeed staggering by these standards of an earlier America. Many of these families are still among the wealthiest in the nation. The very wealthy were more visible than ever before, particularly those who indulged in obscene adventures in conspicuous consumption. And, for reasons detailed in the next chapter, the sufferings of the poor in the cities were also becoming more visible. A growing number of Americans felt themselves caught in the middle between these two extremes, and were forced to wonder if further economic progress would divide society into ever more sharply antagonistic classes.

The widespread fear that "traditional" opportunities to rise in the world were declining in an economy increasingly dominated by giant firms was also based on an oversimplified impression of what was happening. Both the level of opportunities that had been "traditional" in the past and the barriers to advancement in the new corporate world were exaggerated by those who looked back in nostalgia. In many areas of the economy, it was still possible to venture into business and eventually prosper without much initial capital. But there was a substantial change in the locus of opportunity for the ordinary person. For increasing numbers, moving up was achieved not by striking out on one's own but by climbing up the corporate ladder. The financial rewards that accompanied such mobility tended to be greater than those from self-employment. The corporations rewarded the ambitious and energetic exceedingly well, and the chances of failure were less than they were for the self-employed. An employee, nonetheless, was not his own man, but a cog in the wheel of an organization.

These growing pains accompanying late nineteenth century industrialization account for much of the confusion and ambivalence that will be seen again and again in the next four chapters treating other aspects of the era. The material benefits that came with the new order eventually proved sufficiently compelling to undermine movements aimed at shaping the economic system in a fundamentally different pattern. But the accommodation of the American people to the forces of industrialization was neither quick, smooth, nor uniform.

SUGGESTED READINGS

J.B. Jackson, *American Space: The Centennial Years, 1865-1876* (1972) is a brilliant description of the American landscape in the early phases of industrialization. Stuart Bruchey, *Growth of the Modern American Economy* (1975) and Robert L. Heilbroner, *The Economic Transformation of America* (1977) are brief and lucid introductions to economic change in the period. E.C. Kirkland, *Industry Comes of Age : Business, Labor, and Public Policy, 1860-1897* (1961) is an outstanding detailed account. The relevant chapters of W. Elliot Brownlee, *Dynamics of Ascent: A History of the American Economy* (1974) and Robert C. Higgs, *The Transformation of the American Economy, 1865-1914* (1971) offer more technical economic analysis. Phillip S. Bagwell and G.F. Mingay, *Britain and America: A Study of Economic Change, 1850-1939* (1970) draws useful comparisons and contrasts, as does H.J. Habakkuk, *American and British Technology in the 19th Century* (1962). On technology, also see E.E. Morison, *From Knowhow to Nowhere* (1974).

Glenn Porter, *The Rise of Big Business, 1860-1910* (1973) is a compact survey. Alfred D. Chandler, Jr., *The Visible Hand: The Managerial Revolution in American Business* (1977) is superb. See also Glenn Porter and H.C. Livesay, *Merchants and Manufacturers: Studies in the Changing Structure of 19th Century Marketing* (1971). Harold C. Livesay, *Andrew Carnegie and the Rise of Big Business* (1975) is a short and illuminating biography. The thought, aspirations, and strategies of business leaders are examined in T.C. Cochran, *Railroad Leaders, 1845-1890* (1953) and Edward C. Kirkland, *Dream and Thought in the American Business Community, 1860-1900* (1960). Public perceptions of the group are analyzed in Louis Galambos, *The Public Image of Big Business in America, 1880-1940: A Quantitative Study of Social Change* (1975) and Sigmund Diamond, *The Reputation of the American Businessman* (1955). For changes in four crucial industries, see George R. Taylor and Irene Neu, *The American Railroad Network, 1861-1890* (1964), Peter Temin, *Iron and Steel in the 19th Century: An Economic Inquiry* (1964), H.F. Williamson, *The American Petroleum Industry, 1859-1959*, 2 vols. (1959-63), and H.C. Passer, *The Electrical Manufacturers, 1875-1900* (1953). James H. Young, *The Toadstool Millionaires: A Social History of Patent Medicines before Federal Regulation* (1962) sheds entertaining light on advertising. Walter K. Nugent, *Money and American Society, 1865-1880* (1968) and Irwin Unger, *The Greenback Era* (1964) explore issues of monetary policy.

T.C. Cochran and William Miller, *The Age of Enterprise: A Social History of Industrial America* (1942), Maury Klein and Harvey A. Kantor, *Prisoners of Progress* (1976), Samuel P. Hays, *The Response to Industrialism, 1885-1914* (1957), Alan Trachtenberg, *The Incorporation of America: Culture and Society in the Gilded Age* (1982), and Robert H. Wiebe, *The Search for Order, 1877-1920* (1968) examine the social repercussions of industrialization. Sigmund Diamond, ed., *The Nation Transformed* (1963), Alan Trachtenberg, ed., *Democratic Vistas, 1860-1880* (1970), and Neil Harris, ed. *Land of Contrasts, 1880-1901* (1970) are fine collections of documents from the period.

Chapter Eighteen

A Nation of Cities

I n 1889 the heroine of Theodore Dreiser's novel *Sister Carrie* (1900) turned her back on her small midwestern hometown and boarded the train for Chicago. Chicago was then the fastest growing city in America, indeed in the world. Dreiser successfully captured the vitality and brute power of this "giant magnet," an instant metropolis with more than half a million residents and an insatiable appetite for more. The city fathers were so confident of the future that they laid new streetcar lines far out into the open cornfields, and "miles of streets and sewers through regions where, perhaps, one solitary house stood out alone—a pioneer of the populous ways to be. There were regions open to the sweeping winds and rain, which were yet lighted throughout the night with long, blinking lines of gas-lamps, fluttering in the wind. Narrow board walks extended out, passing here a house, and there a store, at far intervals, eventually ending on the open prairie."

Millions of Americans followed in Carrie's footsteps in the latter half of the nineteenth century, pulled from the farms and small towns by urban magnets like Chicago. "We are now a nation of cities," remarked one observer in 1895, and it was true. By the end of the century, as many people lived in America's cities as had inhabited the entire country only 40 years earlier (see Table 18–1 and Map 18–1). How and why that transformation took place, and what it meant for the lives of city dwellers, are the subjects of this chapter.

New York's Hester Street was both thoroughfare and marketplace for newly arrived, mostly Jewish, immigrants, as revealed in this 1899 photograph.

TABLE 18-1
Urban Growth, 1860–1900

Population of cities, by size (in thousands)	1860	1900	Percent Increase
2,500–9,999	1,571	6,103	288
10,000–99,999	2,007	9,848	391
100,000–499,999	1,260	6,133	387
500,000 or more	1,379	8,074	485
Total	6,217	30,160	385
Number of cities, by size			
2,500–9,999	299	1,297	
10,000–99,999	84	402	
100,000–499,999	7	32	
500,000 or more	2	6	
Percent of total population in cities			
2,500–9,999	5	8	
10,000–99,999	6	13	
100,000–499,999	4	8	
500,000 or more	4	11	
Total	20	40	
Total excluding the South	27	51	

RISE OF THE INDUSTRIAL CITY

Before the Civil War, most American cities—and all of the largest ones—had a commercial base. A few industrial cities like Lowell, Massachusetts had appeared, but they were small. The factories of that era needed water power, and the fast-moving rivers that could turn water wheels were located far from the major cities. The big cities were primarily centers of commerce and finance for the "hinterland" around them. The top five—New York, Philadelphia, Baltimore, Boston, and New Orleans—were all long-established seaports, each at the apex of a hierarchy of smaller cities and towns in the surrounding area. The farmers of western Massachusetts did not drive their horses 100 miles to Boston to sell their crops and buy the manufactured items they needed. They went to Springfield or Northhampton or Great Barrington, whose merchants in turn dealt with purchasing agents and wholesalers in Boston.

Commerce remained a vital urban function after the Civil War as well. As farmers poured on to the unsettled Great Plains to homestead, hundreds of new cities sprang up to provide the commercial services they needed—storage and marketing facilities for their crops, food, clothing, lumber, fuel, blacksmiths, banks. Until the end of the century, these had to be available every dozen miles or

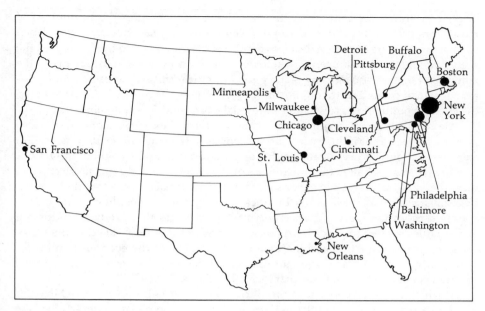

MAP 18–1
Metropolitan Centers with over a Quarter Million Population, 1900

so, so that farmers could reach them by horse and buggy and return the same day. Thereafter, many of these communities declined, as the automobile multiplied the distance that could be covered in a shopping trip, and improved postal services and mail-order catalogs from Sears, Roebuck & Company or Montgomery Ward brought the big city department store into every rural home.

The growth of such traditional commercial centers in farming areas, however, accounted for only a small part of the tremendous urban growth that occurred during the period. The crucial new stimulus to urban development was the shift of industry into the cities, and particularly the largest cities. By 1890, although the ten largest urban centers had only 8 percent of the U.S. population, they produced almost 40 percent of the country's manufactured goods. Industrial expansion had become the key to urban growth.

Why did industry gravitate into the cities in the post-Civil War era? One reason was that the growing availability of steampower and, towards the end of the century, electricity, eliminated the advantage of river sites. At the same time, the greatly improved national rail network made proximity to raw materials used in manufacturing less necessary.

Steam, electricity, and better rail connections eliminated barriers that had earlier deterred manufacturers from locating in the major cities. Changes in the character of manufacturing positively invited urban concentration. The technological advances then occurring introduced new economics of scale in many industries. Costs fell as output rose to very high levels, creating the need for much larger concentrations of workers. In the cities, especially after the beginnings of mass immigration toward mid-century (more about that shortly), the needed workers were to be found. Instead of recruiting labor to come to the factory, as the early manufacturers had been forced to do, industry now brought the factory to the laborers. The creation of new factory jobs in cities, in turn, attracted more migrants, which created further opportunities for large-scale industry. Consequently, the cycle of population growth and industrial expansion was self-reinforcing.

Another important factor—what economists call "external economies"—also promoted the shift of industry into urban centers in the late nineteenth century. An external economy is any advantage that accrues to a firm as the result of the actions of other parties—usually other businesses or the government. Buying more efficient machinery, or obtaining a cheaper source of raw materials is an internal economy. The construction of new roads or track, a telegraph or telephone line, docks, warehouses, or the mere presence nearby of companies that produce equipment and supplies needed for one's own business—any of these external economies may lower costs of production and increase profit margins. In the economic and technological circumstances of the late nineteenth century, large cities offered vital external economies to the firms that located in them.

Much of the urban concentration spurred by industrialization occurred in cities that had already established themselves as leading commercial centers before the war—New York, Philadelphia, and Boston, for example. They, of course, had excellent transportation connections; they were major ports and the rail network had first been laid down to link them more closely to their hinterlands. And they had an ample pool of cheap labor suitable for factory work.

The stimulus industrialization gave to urban growth was most evident, though, in the case of cities that were not among the nation's largest before the Civil War, and that then surged forward largely because of their success in attracting industry. Pittsburgh, for example, was transformed from a trading center with less than 50,000 inhabitants to an industrial metropolis more than ten times larger chiefly because of the remarkable expansion of the iron and steel, coal, and oil industries. By the 1880s, a reporter calculated that Pittsburgh had "thirty-five miles of factories belching forth smoke, glowing with fire, swarming with workmen, all echoing with the clank of machinery." Thriving industry was likewise the prime source of the spectacular growth of Cleveland, Detroit, and Milwaukee, and many smaller industrial cities. By the end of the century a great manufacturing belt extended across the Northeast to St. Louis on its western edge. It is no coincidence that all and from Minneapolis to St. Louis on its western edge. It is no coincidence that all but one of the country's 15 largest cities lay within it; eighth-ranked San Francisco was the sole exception. Here was the urban industrial heartland of the nation.

HOW CITIES GROW IN POPULATION

In 1860 only 6 million Americans lived in cities. In four decades, the urban population had increased by approximately 24 million. Where did these additional 24 million people come from?

A VIEW OF PITTSBURGH, 1868

There is one evening scene in Pittsburg which no visitor should miss. Owing to the abruptness of the hill behind the town, there is a street along the edge of a bluff, from which you can look directly down upon all that part of the city which lies low, near the level of the rivers. On the evening of this dark day, we were conducted to the edge of the abyss, and looked over the iron railing upon the most striking spectacle we ever beheld. The entire space lying between the hills was filled with blackest smoke, from out of which the hidden chimneys sent forth tongues of flame, while from the depths of the abyss came up the noise of hundreds of steam-hammers. There would be moments when no flames were visible; but soon the wind would force the smoky curtains aside, and the whole black expanse would be dimly lighted with dull wreaths of fire. It is an unprofitable business, view-hunting; but if any one would enjoy a spectacle as striking as Niagara, he may do so by simply walking up a long hill to Cliff Street in Pittsburg, and looking over into—hell with the lid taken off.

—James Parton, "Pittsburgh," *Atlantic Monthly,* Jan. 1868

There are only two ways by which the population of a city can grow. Either it must have more births than deaths—what is termed "natural increase"—or it must succeed in attracting outsiders and hence grow through migration.[1] Both of these processes contributed to the urban population explosion in late nineteenth century America, but by no means equally.

More people were being born than were dying in American cities in these years. But the rate of natural increase was not very high for two reasons. First, the birth rate was falling in the entire country, especially in the cities. The decline in fertility that had begun before the Civil War continued without interruption for the rest of the century. The fertility rate—the number of children produced by the average woman during her child-bearing years—dropped from over 7 in 1800 to 5.2 in 1860 to 3.6 in 1900. And the city family was smaller than the rural family on the average.

Second, urban death rates remained high until almost the end of the century,

---

[1]Strictly speaking, there is a third way in which a city can gain population—by extending its boundaries and annexing other communities whose residents then are credited to it in subsequent censuses. Most growing cities in this period did increase their populations through annexation, as we will see later in this chapter. But this would not produce any increase in the percentage of Americans who were recorded as "urban" by the census definition—that is, living in places of 2,500 or more—except in those cases where annexation brought communities of under 2,500 within the boundaries of a larger urban center. Since the question at hand now is how the total number of Americans living in urban areas grew so much, annexation may be safely neglected. Few annexations, in fact, embraced communities of less than 2,500.

TABLE 18-2
Deaths per 100,000 Population in New York, Boston,
Philadelphia and New Orleans (annual averages)

Cause	1864–1888	1899–1913
Tuberculosis	365	223
Stomach and intestinal disorders	299	196
Diphtheria	123	58
Typhoid and typhus	66	19
Smallpox	53	25

when new understanding of the bacterial sources of infectious disease and a newly organized public health movement led to major improvements. Until then, living in the crowded city was dangerous, just as being crowded into Civil War army camps had been dangerous. In 1882, half of the children born in Chicago could not expect to live to the age of five! An 1890 study revealed that almost a quarter (24 percent) of the infants born in cities died in their first year. The infant mortality rate in cities was twice as high as in rural areas, ten times higher than the contemporary American rates, substantially worse even than that of India today.

If the growth of cities in late nineteenth century America had depended on the natural increase of their populations, they would have expanded much less rapidly. The cities of Massachusetts, for example, grew an average of 38 percent between 1885 and 1895, but their rate of natural increase for the decade was only 7 percent. More than four-fifths of their growth, in other words, came from another source: migration. It was chiefly the arrival of wave after wave of newcomers that multiplied the urban population dramatically in these years. Who were these newcomers, and why did they come?

Internal Migrants

When we think of nineteenth century cities, we tend to think first of immigrants from abroad, crowded into Little Italies, Chinatowns, and other ethnic ghettos. Many foreigners did indeed make their way to America's cities then, but an equally large migration stream carried native-born Americans—internal migrants rather than immigrants—from rural areas to urban communities. Dreiser's Sister Carrie, who fled the boredom of small-town life for Chicago, was a representative figure. Historians since Frederick Jackson Turner (1861–1932) have been fascinated with the last great wave of agricultural expansion before the closing of the frontier at the end of the century. They have neglected a population shift that affected even more people—migration of farmers and their children into cities. Evidence on which to base a precise estimate is unavailable. We do know, however, that the number of "old stock" Americans—that is, native-born persons whose parents were native-born as well—who were living in cities more than tripled in the last 30 years of the century, an increase of more than ten million. Some fraction of this gain, of course, was due not to migration from rural to urban areas, but to the natural increase of the old stock population already urbanized in 1870. Even allowing for that, however, something like eight or nine million Americans must have left the country for the city in the late nineteenth century.

Individuals, of course, move from one place to another for many reasons, including pure whim. But massive migratory waves like this one normally have a definite structure, and stem from common circumstances. Such movements can be viewed as the result of one set of forces that "push" people away from their place of origin and another set that "pull" them to their destinations.

The most important factor pushing people away from the countryside in this period was that farm families were still having large numbers of children while the mechanization of agriculture was reducing the number of hands needed to produce a given crop. Another "push" effect of mechanization was the rising cost of farm machinery, which made it harder for farm children coming of age to make a start in farming themselves. The amount of capital invested in equipment and machinery on the average farm rose 56 percent between 1870 and 1900. Because wages for farm laborers did not go up correspondingly during those years—in fact they declined slightly—the number of years of labor it took to accumulate enough savings to buy a farm increased sharply. There were other "push" factors of a social kind—the isolation and drudgery of life on the farm, for example—that must be reserved for discussion in the more detailed treatment of late nineteenth century farming in the next chapter. But the economic and demographic processes that were producing a growing surplus of young men and women in the countryside were the main forces impelling country people to consider moving.

That they did move in such large numbers to cities, however, was the result of "pull" as well as "push" factors. The city was a magnetic force principally because of the economic opportunities it offered. Few country lads and lasses found the fame and fortune they dreamed of in the city, but there were jobs in the city, and exceedingly well paid ones, by rural standards. In 1890 the average farm laborer earned $244, whereas wage earners in manufacturing averaged twice as much ($439). Clerical workers earned almost four times as much ($848), and such white collar occupations were far more accessible to native migrants than to immigrants. In Cleveland in 1890, for example, 23 percent of the native white males of native parentage held clerical or sales jobs, as compared with less than 5 percent of the foreign-born. There were other attractions to the city, to be sure: the freedom, variety, and vitality of urban life. But solid economic advantages like these were the prime impetus to migration.

These rural newcomers were almost all whites; the great migration of black people to the city did not begin until World War I. There was some black urban migration within the South—by the end of the century more than four of ten residents of the larger southern cities were black. But as late as 1900, 90 percent of America's blacks still lived in the South, and the South remained by far the least urbanized section of the country. Although two-thirds of the black people outside

REASONS FOR IMMIGRATING

O James, my well beloved child, what have I done to you that you thus abhor me? Leave me and your sister here and in shame and confusion, not as much as rags of clothes either on one or other of us. Oh, James my darling boy, it is a most pitiful sight your father without a shew on his foot or a coat or shirt on his back and every man and woman saying why don't you write to your children and it can't be but they will take you out of this.

—An Irish Father to His Son in the U.S.

I want to get to America, but I have no means at all because I am poor and have nothing but the ten fingers of my hands, a wife and 9 children. I have no work at all, although I am strong and healthy and only 45 years old. I cannot earn for my family. I have been already in Dombrowa, Sosnowiec, Zawiercie and Lodz, wherever I could go, and nowhere could I earn well. And here they (the children) call for food and clothing and more or less education. I wish to work, not easily only but even hard, but what can I do? I will not go to steal and I have no work.

So I beg the Protective Association to accept me for this journey and not only me, but I should like to take with me two of my children, a boy 16 and a girl 18 years old.

—A Polish Peasant Seeking Assistance to Immigrate
W.I. Thomas and F. Znaniecki, *The Polish Peasant in Europe and America*,
Vol. V., 1920

the South lived in cities, that group was very small. In 1900 blacks formed less than 2 percent of the populations of New York, Chicago, Detroit, and Cleveland, the centers that were to draw them in such great numbers from World War I on. They found themselves confined to segregated ghettos, and to only the most menial unskilled jobs. White collar jobs, the skilled trades, even steady factory work were available to only a fortunate few, and fewer still had access to professions like law and medicine. Until these circumstances began to change, there was little to draw blacks from the southern countryside to the northern city.

Immigrants

When native whites migrating from rural areas reached cities, they encountered other newcomers from more distant places, chiefly from Europe. Mass immigration to the United States began well before the Civil War, of course; some five million immigrants arrived between 1820 and 1860. That large number, however, was dwarfed by the figure for the next four decades—almost 14 million. Some European villages lost half or even more of their residents to "America fever." An American visiting a town in southern Italy was told by the mayor: "I greet you in the name of the 5,000 inhabitants of my village, 4,000 of whom are now in your country."

The push factors that impelled immigration in this period were much the same as those behind the earlier waves—economic and demographic pressures. The populations of the countries from which most immigrants came were growing, at the same time that the mechanization of agricultural production was reducing the need for labor. Not only peasants but village shopkeepers and artisans who depended on them as customers were compelled to seek alternatives.

These expulsive pressures first built up to critical levels in Britain, Ireland, and Germany in the first half of the nineteenth century; seven out of every eight immigrants to the United States in the 1850s were British, Irish, or German. As these pressures subsided in northern and western Europe, they mounted in eastern and southern Europe. By the 1890s, less than a quarter of those arriving were from Britain, Ireland, or Germany. Italy and the multiethnic Russian and Austro-Hungarian empires had become the prime suppliers of immigrants. These changes in the American immigration figures are a sensitive register of changing conditions in the European countryside.

Immigration to the United States should be viewed in the larger context of the movement of European peoples. Not all uprooted Europeans came to America. Movement across the ocean to the United States was only one of many options. Several great migration waves rolled over nineteenth-century Europe. One took people from the countryside to the city within the land of their birth. A second shifted them across national boundaries within the continent of Europe. And for those who did leave the Old World, there were destinations other than the United States: Canada, Mexico, South America, Australia. In the closing decades of the century, only 70 percent of the migrants who left Europe came to America; almost a third went elsewhere.

Whether those who departed from Europe came to the United States or not was largely determined by two factors: the means of transportation available and the state of the American business cycle. From 1800 to 1850 half a million people per decade left Europe. From 1850 to 1900 it was five million per decade. This sharp rise stemmed not only from growing pressures to relocate, but from changes in transportation that made intercontinental movement much easeir. Early in the century, immigrants had to travel from their homes to distant port cities on foot or in carts. The spread of the rail network thereafter permitted quick travel to points of departure. Improved sailing ships, and then the introduction of steam-powered iron vessels made the journey much quicker and safer. Before that, transatlantic voyages of 40 days were not unusual, and they could stretch out two and even three months. Ten to twenty percent of those who started out perished aboard ship before they landed. By the late nineteenth century, the trip could be made in ten days, and a steerage ticket from Naples to New York could be had for $15. America's leading role in the export of bulky raw materials to Europe—timber, cotton, tobacco, and grain—was a principal reason for the cheap fares. The fine

TABLE 18-3
Changes in European Immigration to the United States

Arrivals from	1854	1882	1900
Great Britain	58,647	102,991	12,509
Ireland	101,606	76,432	35,730
Scandinavia	4,222	105,326	31,151
Other Northwest Europe	23,070	27,796	5,822
Germany	215,009	250,630	18,507
Central Europe	208	33,822	114,847
Russia	2	16,918	90,787
Other East Europe	7	134	6,852
Italy	1,263	32,159	100,135
Other Southern Europe	1,508	1,978	8,360

linens, china, and wines brought back on the return voyage left ample space for passengers willing to endure the discomfort of steerage class travel. Many immigrants came to the United States not because of its special attractions but because that was where the ships happened to be going.

The other determinant of the flow of immigrants into the United States, however, did operate through the deliberate choice of individuals. A chart of the number of newcomers entering the country year by year in the latter half of the nineteenth century shows a great deal of fluctuation—a series of major peaks and valleys, and a good many smaller ups and downs. Some of this fluctuation is attributable to events in Europe that accentuated or diminished pressures to leave. But it also has a good deal to do with the changing health of the American economy. The periods of most rapid economic expansion were also the periods of maximum immigration. During hard times, like those of the late 1850s, the mid-1870s and the mid-1890s, the flow of newcomers fell off to half or less of previous levels. As American wages dropped and unemployment rose, the word spread quickly, and Europeans who would otherwise have journeyed here either remained at home or went somewhere else. News of returning prosperity spread just as quickly, and there followed an upswing in immigration.

The most important source of information about American conditions was letters from other kinsmen or friends who were already living in the United States. Few immigrants moved as isolated individuals; most settled in particular cities where they were taken in by relatives or friends from the same village who could help them find a job. More than half of the Italians living in Cleveland around 1900 came from one of ten villages that were the source of major "chain movements" to the city; less than a fifth were from communities that sent less than five other immigrants to Cleveland.

Many—perhaps most—immigrants did not originally intend to make the United States their permanent home. Instead, they came to earn enough money to improve the family fortunes when they returned home. Many found America to their liking

CHAIN MIGRATION TO PITTSBURGH

The workers on the hills of Galicia, in the vineyards of Italy, and the factories of Kiev, earn from 25 to 50 cents in a day. When the American immigrant writes home that he earns from $1.50 to $2.00, the ablebodied wage-earner in the fatherland who hears this will not be satisfied until he also stands where the higher wages govern. It is these homegoing letters more than all else which recruit the labor force. They are efficient promoters of immigration. Said Big Sam to me, in his broken English, "There are no ablebodied men between the ages of sixteen and fifty years left in my native town in Servia; they have all come to America."

When prosperity is at flood, the men in charge of furnaces, foundries, forges, and mills in the Pittsburgh District cannot get the help they need. The cry everywhere is: "Give us men." A foreman, therefore, will assure Pietro and Melukas that if brothers or cousins or friends are sent for, they will get work as soon as they arrive. More than that, the Slav and Italian are no longer dependent upon the English boss in the matter of finding work for their countrymen. The inflow from southeastern Europe has assumed such proportions in the industries of the cities that superintendents have, in some instances, appointed Italian and Polish and Lithuanian foremen; and with these, as with German and Irish, blood is thicker than water. They employ their fellow-countrymen. They know the condition of the labor market and can by suggestion stimulate or retard immigration.

—Peter Roberts, *Wage-Earning Pittsburgh*, 1911

and stayed, of course, using their savings instead to buy tickets for other kin. But a good many were "birds of passage" who stayed only for a time. The federal government did not begin to tabulate return migration until 1908, but after that about a third of all immigrants—and as much as 80 percent in some groups—eventually went back to the "old country." The rate of return migration was highest in years of economic downturn and lowest in boom years, another indication that immigrants weighed alternatives carefully and responded intelligently to changing economic circumstances.

Although it is risky to generalize about 14 million people from so many different cultures, the newcomers shared a number of characteristics. First, the extremes of both wealth and poverty were underrepresented in the immigration stream. The upper classes, of course, had no need to leave. The poorest had the need, but lacked the means, the information, and perhaps the courage and confidence to journey so far into the unknown. There were many exceptions, to be sure, but in general it was not so much those already mired in desperate poverty as those fearful of falling into it who seized the opportunity. And it is probable—though unprovable—that those who took the risk were more ambitious, aggressive, and cunning, and hungrier for material success, than those who remained behind.

The distinctive demographic characteristics of the immigrants magnified their role in the American economy. From 60 to 70 percent of those entering each year in the late nineteenth century were males. Furthermore, the minority who were female were more likely to seek jobs than native American women of the day. Most important, relatively few of either sex were either too young or too old to work. Approximately 75 percent of them were in the prime productive years of 15 to 40, as compared to only 40 percent of the entire population of the United States. As a result, the foreign-born, although only about a seventh of the American population in this period, made up a fifth of the labor force. Through immigration, the American economy was able to profit from the labors of people who had been supported in their early dependent years by the resources of other societies.

Although most immigrants had previously worked on the land, opportunities for those without capital were chiefly to be found in the cities, especially the largest cities of the northeastern and midwestern manufacturing belt. In 1890, the Northeast and Midwest together had some 63 percent of the total population of the country but six out of seven of America's immigrants were living there. Over 40 percent of the residents of New York and Chicago, and over 35 percent of the people in Boston, Detroit, and Cleveland were foreign-born. Virtually every individual immigrant group clustered in urban centers. National groups varied, to be sure, as Table 18-4 reveals. Mexicans in this period were almost all farm laborers. Only 8 percent were located in cities of 25,000 or more in 1890, as opposed to 18 percent of the native American population. Mexicans therefore were less than half as urbanized as native-born Americans. Italians, at the other extreme, were more than three times as urban as native Americans; 59 percent of them lived in good-sized cities. But what stands out most is that of the 20 immigrant groups for which data are available, only the Mexicans—at this point one of the smallest groups—were less strongly clustered in cities than natives. Twelve of the other 19, including most of the largest, were at least twice as urbanized as native Americans. At least 86 percent of the country's foreign-born in 1890 were from those 12 groups that were concentrated in cities two to three times as heavily as the native population.

The immigrant presence was even more visible in the cities than these figures suggest because of another immigrant trait—they tended to have large families. Native-born children of foreign parentage, "second generation" Americans, were therefore a rapidly expanding group. The birthrate of foreign-born women in Boston in 1890, for example, was 40 percent higher than that of native women. Figures such as these led some old stock Americans to worry that they were being swamped by alien elements. Francis A. Walker, President of MIT, warned that Yankees were committing "race suicide," restricting their families out of fear of bringing children into the world to compete with newcomers incapable of understanding "the refinements of life and thought." One nativist writer calculated that after 200 years 1,000 Harvard men would have only 50 descendants, whereas 1,000 Rumanian immigrants would have produced no less than 100,000! The race suicide theorists overlooked the fact that the shrinking of the average native family could hardly have resulted from immigrant competition, since the fertility decline began

TABLE 18-4
The Concentration of Immigrant
Groups in Cities, 1890

	Number (in thousands)	Percent in Cities of 25,000 or More
Native-born Americans	52,468	18
Mexicans	78	8
Norwegians	323	21
Danes	133	23
Welsh	100	26
Swiss	104	31
Canadians	981	31
Swedes	478	32
Dutch	82	34
Chinese	107	40
English	909	41
Scotch	242	41
Hungarians	62	45
French	113	46
Germans	2,785	48
Czechs	118	48
Austrians	123	48
Irish	1,872	56
Poles*	147	57
Russians*	183	58
Italians	183	59

*The U.S. Census did not distinguish immigrants by religion, but the bulk of those identified as Russians and a good many of the Poles were East European Jews.

decades *before* significant immigration took place. Nor did they foresee what proved to be the case—that as ethnic groups assimilated to American ways in other respects they would emulate American fertility patterns as well and limit their families in the same way. This fallacious argument was nonetheless an important weapon in the arsenal of supporters of the movement to restrict immigration that triumphed after World War I.

THE CHANGING FACE OF THE CITY

As city populations multiplied through natural increase and migration, the structure of the urban community was profoundly altered. If you stepped out of a time machine into the streets of Philadelphia or Boston in 1860, you would find the layout of the city quite unlike anything in your experience. If, however, you took a shorter backward journey and visited one of those cities in 1895, you would feel a good deal more at home. The basic shape and social geography of most of our major cities today still shows the strong imprint of developments that occurred between the Civil War and 1900. Slums, suburbs, and skyscrapers are among the legacies of the late nineteenth century urban revolution.

Walking Cities

The urban communities of the pre-Civil War era have been called "walking cities." In the absence of low-cost public transportation, most people had to travel between home and work on foot. There were fairly strict limits on how far a normal person would walk, especially when the ordinary work day was twelve hours long. Consequently, the densely settled portions of even the largest cities rarely extended outside of a circle about four miles across. The walking city was physically very compact.

The city of those days was not divided into distinct specialized areas: a financial district, a warehouse district, a retail shopping district, an industrial district, a tenement district. It did, of course, have a center, with government buildings and perhaps a central market for farm products. If it was a seaport, near the docks would be clusters of merchants, warehouses, and the maritime trades. Perhaps it might have an elegant residential neighborhood such as Boston's Beacon Hill. But in a way which we would find bewildering today, different kinds of people and different kinds of activities were jumbled together within the crowded quarters of the walking city. Most manufacturers and traders lived at or near their places of business, and their apprentices and other employees often lived with them. The cheapest and meanest hovels in town were often located next door to or in the alley behind the homes of the well-to-do. A family's address then was not a strong clue as to its ethnic background or social class.

In the walking city there was little variation in the scale of buildings, and no high-rise structures. The nature of construction techniques and materials and the absence of passenger elevators limited the height of buildings to four or five stories.

Spatial Expansion

Improvements in urban transportation soon allowed cities to break out of their confined boundaries, and transformed their social geography. Streetcars drawn by horses were first introduced in the 1850s, and horsecar lines from the city center extended ever farther into outlying areas in the 1860s and '70s, making it possible to commute downtown to work each day from outlying "streetcar suburbs." A second great wave of urban expansion followed when cable cars and then electrified streetcars ("trolley cars"), elevated trains, and subways replaced the plodding horse. By 1900 the walking city had been transformed into a suburbanized metropolis with a radius four to five times larger.[2]

---

[2]And an area 16 to 25 times larger, of course, since the area of a circle is found by multiplying the *square* of the radius by pi.

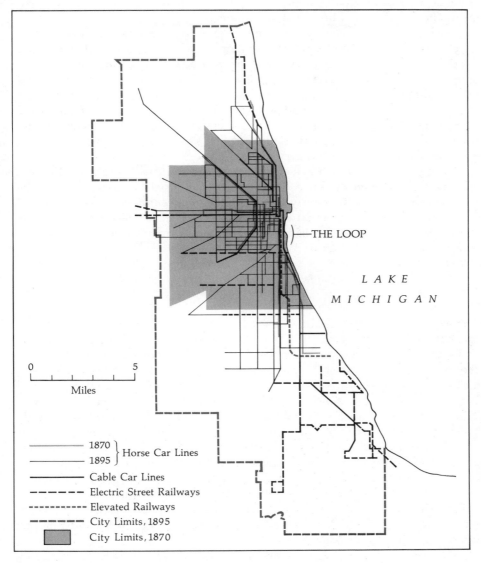

MAP 18–2
The Expansion of Chicago's Transportation Network, 1870–93

More important than the increased scale of urban life was the new segregation of people and activities, the new order that replaced the jumble of the walking city. At the center of the city, the modern central business district took form. There was an area given over to retail shops, including the first department stores—Macy's in New York, Marshall Field's in Chicago, Filene's in Boston. Nearby was an area dominated by banks and insurance companies, corporate headquarters, government offices, and the law firms that served them.

The most sharply bounded central business district grew up in Chicago, where the elevated tracks of the electric railroad formed the "Loop" around it, but similar districts appeared everywhere. Chicago took the lead too in creating vivid symbols of the wealth and power concentrated at its center. Beginning in the late 1880s, land values within the Loop soared. The development of electric elevators, tough structural steel and improved window glass stimulated Louis Sullivan, Frank Lloyd Wright and other great Chicago architects to design the first skyscrapers. The city expanded upward as it expanded outward, the steel and glass towers thrusting above it tangible evidence of the energy it radiated.

Ringing the areas of high-rise construction, and still relatively close to the center, were the growing wholesale, warehouse, and industrial districts in which the manual labor jobs in the city were increasingly concentrated. Now trucks and improved highways have freed such businesses from the need to be near the downtown area, but in the era of rail and water transportation economic activity of this sort was strongly centralized.

Slums and Suburbs

The expansion of urban industry near city centers in the late nineteenth century made these locations increasingly less attractive places to live. The pall of smoke and soot from the blast furnace, the stench of the oil refinery or the slaughterhouse, the pounding of heavy machinery were difficult to tolerate. Soon those families with a choice in the matter—those with a high and steady enough income to buy or rent homes in cleaner and quieter neighborhoods farther out—escaped with relief. Those left behind were soon joined by other working-class families—mainly European immigrants in the largest cities of the industrial heartland, chiefly native rural migrants elsewhere. These were the people who could least afford commuting costs, especially because their incomes were so low that more than one member of their family usually worked, which multiplied transportation expenses unless they could walk to their jobs. Another pressure locking them into inner-city neighborhoods was the menace of unemployment. The greater the number of alternative jobs at their skill level nearby, the more chance they had of finding other work if they were laid off.

The homes left vacant as the more well-to-do moved out along the spreading horsecar and trolley lines had been relatively spacious and attractive when built. But the working-class families entering these neighborhoods could not afford such accommodations, and there were a great many more of the poor arriving than of the prosperous departing. As a result, the structures were converted to higher density uses; four, five, or more families were packed into the space previously occupied by one, with little regard for ventilation and sanitary facilities. If the conversion of existing structures did not meet the demand for housing in the neighborhood, new tenements were erected in back or side yards, obliterating grass and trees and blocking the sunlight previously available to the original

THE SLUMS OF NEW YORK, 1883

In Baxter street in one room there are eight families, composed alto-gether of forty-two people, and three-quarters of them are so destitute of clothing that they cannot go into the street even to beg...

Q. Where is this room; is it above ground or under ground?— A. Well, it is a basement, a half-cellar, and, when the tide comes in the water is eight inches deep on the floor; they have to put scantlings and slabs across to put their clothes on. One small stove is all that can be found in that enormous room to warm a whole crowd of people in the cold weather...

Q. Do you say that there are eight families in one room?— A. Yes, sir.

Q. What is the size of the room?— A. It is a large room—a whole basement. It is, perhaps, longer but not as wide as this room—it extends back...

Q. Do you know how the people who live there employ them-selves?— A. I think they are rag pickers, mainly. I say that the houses for the poor in this city are too dark, too damp, too much crowded, too poorly ventilated, and have altogether insufficient water, and hence are too vile to live in. I refer to the tenements for the masses. Who it is who owns these houses I do not know. I have been told that some of these tene-ments—places of the lowest order—are owned by people like the Astors. How they can ride in their carriages, and dress in silk and velvets, or sleep peacefully at night while they permit their tenants to have such dwellings, I cannot understand.

*—Report of the Committee of the Senate on the
Relations between Labor and Capital, 1885*

building. On the Lower East Side of New York, in 1890, people were squeezed into tenements at the incredible density of 334,000 per square mile. To appreciate that level of density, imagine all of the approximately 225 million people who live in the United States today confined to an area of about 675 square miles, or a circle with a radius of 15 miles!

The Lower East Side was the most extreme case of crowding, but slum neigh-borhoods appeared everywhere. They were overcrowded, deteriorating, pervasive-ly poor. And they were breeding grounds of disease, crime, and vice. The appalling conditions that existed in the worst neighborhoods began to attract some public attention after the publication of Jacob Riis' disturbing *How the Other Half Lives* (1890) and other books like it. But most prosperous city dwellers were comfortably insulated from inner-city problems. And even if the public had been aroused to action, writers like Riis were better at denouncing than at diagnosing and prescribing remedies. Lacking any real understanding of the economic pressures that created the slums and impelled people to live in them, they believed that living in bad housing caused poverty rather than the other way around. Therefore they recommended policies that either did nothing or that were positively counterproductive. Their pleas to the wealthy to invest in model tenements which would somehow offer better quarters for low rents and still yield a profit--"philanthropy plus 6 percent"—were ignored. They did succeed in getting laws passed that specified certain minimum standards of health and safety for tenements, but enforcing these standards caused rent increases. Landlords passed along the cost of upgrading to their tenants; those who couldn't afford the rent hike were forced into even worse slums. Reformers focused more attention on the physical condition of slum neighborhoods than on the condition of the human beings who lived in them. The demolition of a decaying tenement to make way for a new warehouse was applauded because it removed an eyesore. But if that improved the neighborhood, it did not improve the lot of the displaced tenants, who had to crowd in somewhere else nearby. The slums endured, although their locations sometimes shifted in response to changing commercial and industrial needs.

Beyond the slums were the better residential neighborhoods; the farther out, the better they were. There were exceptions to that law, of course. Chicago's Gold Coast, Boston's Beacon Hill and Back Bay, San Francisco's Nob Hill were wealthy areas on the fringes of the central business district. But the general pattern was clear. Within the limits of comfortable commuting, the richest tended to be farthest out. They lived in spacious single-family dwellings on large lots. Two or three miles closer to the city center, lots would be smaller, and apartment buildings or houses for more than one family would begin to appear. Still closer to the center, the proportion of single-family homes, the amount of greenery, and the income of the average resident would all be lower. Where you ranked on the socio-economic scale could now be gauged from where you lived.

As one's address became a badge of status, it became increasingly common for city dwellers to change houses with each change in their status. Although many of the residents of the metropolis at any one time were desperately poor and lived in fearful slums, they were not trapped for life. Few rose from rags to riches, but a great many advanced modestly from rags to respectability by obtaining middle-income jobs. This allowed them to move farther away from the center, following the "tenement trail" to more affluent neighborhoods. In the typical city of this era, about a third of all families moved from one dwelling to another in an average year. A study of Omaha, Nebraska in the closing decades of the century revealed that less than a quarter of the city's families lived at the same place over a five-year period; only 3 percent remained at one address as long as twenty years! Some of this movement, of course, was simply restless shifting about within the neighborhood, between dwellings at about the same rent level. But the overall tendency was for outward residential mobility and upward social mobility to go hand in hand. The youngest, poorest, and most recently arrived city dwellers clustered in the inner city. As their careers unfolded, they tended to move up and out, up the economic ladder and out of the inner city.

The Ghetto

Although city residential patterns were set mostly by economic forces, segregation followed ethnic lines as well. Immigrants from Italy, Poland, Sweden, and dozens of other countries preferred to live together with others with whom they shared a language and culture. Consequently, neighborhoods developed a distinctive ethnic flavor; languages other than English were heard on the streets; there were shops and restaurants offering Old World specialties, and religious, social, and cultural institutions catering to particular groups. These ethnic concentrations have often been called "ghettos," a term first used to describe the section of the medieval city in which Jews were legally compelled to live. The immigrant ghettos, however, differed fundamentally from both the medieval Jewish ghettos and the black ghettos of our cities today. They arose from group preference, not from laws or discriminatory practices enforced by the larger society. They were not as closed and ethnically homogenous. No Italian ghetto was as uniformly Italian as Harlem and Watts are black today. Their inhabitants were free to leave them for other neighborhoods when they chose to and had the funds with which to move. And they characteristically did so as their incomes rose and they became more acculturated to American patterns.

When they did move out, however, they tended to follow trails blazed by earlier members of their group, so that some ethnic clustering continued. The neighborhoods they selected were usually less heavily Italian, Polish, or Swedish than the area of initial settlement, but they were not utterly mixed melting pot areas with no discernible ethnic stamp. The map of the city continued to have ethnic shadings, even after the passing of the immigrant generation.

City versus Suburb

By 1900, the process that sorted out city dwellers by class and ethnic group had produced a social cleavage that remains central in urban life today—between the city and the suburb. For a time it appeared that the emerging big cities of the nation would be able to govern all those who lived within the metropolitan region and were part of its economy. As more and more of the residents of surrounding areas began commuting to work in the central city, pressures to annex these communities to the metropolis grew. This would enlarge the city's tax base and would offer the formerly independent towns in return the superior services the city could offer—fire and police protection, water, improved streets. Within a decade after the close of the Civil War, for instance, the 75,000 people who lived in Roxbury, West Roxbury, Dorchester, Charlestown and Brighton voted to give up their legal independence and become part of the city of Boston.

But as the process of sorting out continued, differences sharpened between the class and ethnic composition of the inner city and the outlying streetcar suburbs. The annexation movement ground to a halt. The middle class, largely Yankee, commuter communities feared becoming submerged in metropolitan centers with

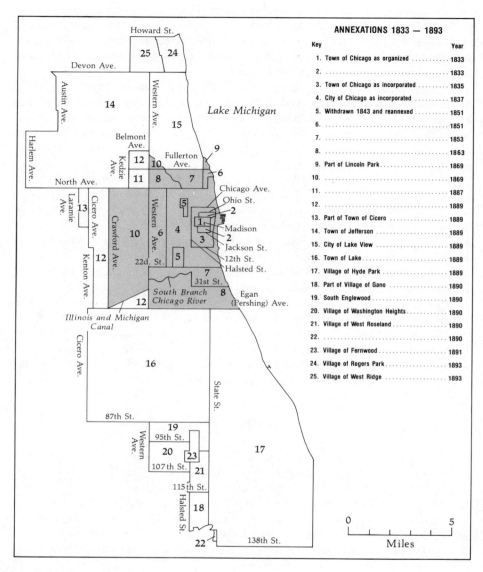

Map 18–3
Annexations to the City of Chicago, 1833–93

massive working-class immigrant populations. Although most suburbanites were economically dependent on the metropolis, there was no way of forcing them to pay their way.[3] The voters of Brookline defeated an annexation proposal in 1879,

---

[3]There might have been if the American city had enjoyed the powerful independent legal status of the typical European city. But in the United States the cities were creatures of the state governments, and

the turning point in Boston. The timing varied from city to city, but the ultimate result was generally the same. The wealthiest communities on the outer reaches of the metropolitan areas retained their independence and became "suburbs," parasitic creatures that profited from the existence of the metropolis without being subject to its taxation or political control.

The major cities were still of sufficient size and diversity to have the potential for sharp internal political conflict. In addition to the division between city and suburb there was a cleft within the city itself, between the inner core and the periphery. The classic big city political machines drew their support primarily from the working class, often immigrant people clustered in the inner city, whereas the reformers who battled the machine and crusaded for a purified politics found their primary constituency in the outer rings, which tended to be middle-class, native, and Protestant. The conflict between bosses and reformers did not reach a climax until the opening decade of the twentieth century, in the Progressive era, and fuller analysis of it can be deferred to Chapter 22. For now, it is sufficient to understand that it grew directly out of the profound changes in the social geography of the city that we have just examined.

By 1900 the United States was indeed "a nation of cities"—and a nation of factories, giant corporations, and immigrants as well. The vast impersonal forces of industrialization and urbanization that caused these remarkable changes have been analyzed in this and the preceding chapter. In the next two chapters, we will narrow our focus to look more concretely at how these developments affected two major elements of the population—first the farmers, then the laboring class. Both farmers and workers felt the shock of rapid change; both struggled in various ways to resist, accommodate themselves to, or change the new industrial order.

SUGGESTED READINGS

Sam B. Warner, Jr., *The Urban Wilderness* (1972), Zane Miller, *The Urbanization of America* (1973), and Howard Chudacoff, *The Evolution of American Urban Society* (1975) are illuminating introductions. Adna F. Weber, *The Growth of Cities in the Nineteenth Century* (1899) compares urbanization in America and elsewhere in the world. Beverly Duncan and Stanley Lieberson, *Metropolis and Region in Transition* (1970) relates urban growth to industrial change.

On the changing shape of the city and the role of immigration in urban growth, see David Ward, *Cities and Immigrants: A Geography of Change in 19th Century America* (1971) and Sam B. Warner, Jr., *Streetcar Suburbs: The Process of Growth in Boston, 1870–1900* (1962). Rowland T. Berthoff, *British Immigrants in Industrial America* (1953) and Charlotte Erickson, *American Industry and the European Immigrant* (1957) help to explain why so many immigrants came and why they settled where they did. The varying experiences of arriving groups may be traced in Stephan Thernstrom, ed., *The Harvard Encyclopedia of American Ethnic Groups* (1980). Patterns of

---

were kept on tight reins by the state legislatures. Because rural, old stock Americans tended to dominate the legislatures, there was little chance of their using their influence on the side of the big cities.

mobility and assimilation are treated in Stephan Thernstrom, *Poverty and Progress: Social Mobility in a 19th Century City* (1964) and *The Other Bostonians: Poverty and Progress in the American Metropolis, 1880–1970* (1973), Josef J. Barton, *Peasants and Strangers: Italians, Rumanians, and Slovaks in an American City, 1890–1950* (1975), Thomas Kessner, *The Golden Door: Italian and Jewish Immigrant Mobility in New York City, 1880–1915* (1977), and Clyde and Sally Griffen, *Natives and Newcomers: The Ordering of Opportunity in Mid-Nineteenth Century Poughkeepsie* (1978). Abraham Cahan, *The Rise of David Levinsky* (1917) is a classic novel about the immigrant quest for success. Alan M. Kraut, *The Huddled Masses: The Immigrant in American Society, 1880–1921* (1982) is a useful synthesis. Barbara Rosenkrantz, *Public Health and the State: Changing Views in Massachusetts, 1842–1936* (1972) illuminates living conditions. Roger Lane, *Violent Death in the City: Suicide, Accident, and Murder in 19th Century Philadelphia* (1979) is a fascinating monograph with broad implications. David P. Handlin, *The American Home: Architecture and Society, 1845–1915* (1979) explores the shaping of the urban landscape. Changing perceptions of city dwellers are analyzed in Thomas Bender, *Toward an Urban Vision: Ideas and Urbanization in Nineteenth Century America* (1975), Paul Boyer, *Urban Masses and Moral Order in America, 1820–1920* (1978), and Gunther Barth, *City People: The Rise of Modern City Culture in Nineteenth-Century America* (1980). Peter J. Schmitt, *Back to Nature: The Arcadian Myth in Urban America* (1969) is delightful. Jacob Riis, *How the Other Half Lives* (1890) is still very much worth reading. Robert H. Bremner, *From the Depths: The Discovery of Poverty in America* (1956) considers other exposés of urban conditions. Ann Cook, *et. al, City Life, 1865–1900* (1973) is an intriguing collection of contemporary documents and pictures.

Chapter Nineteen

Farmers in the Industrial Age

I n the early 1870s one family arrived in western Kansas with "a team of oxen, nine children and eleven cents," to claim the 160 free acres available under the Homestead Act. Between the Civil War and 1900 more new farms were started, and more virgin soil brought under cultivation, than in all preceding American history. The western half of the United States, beyond the frontier in 1860, was wrested from the Indians to become farms and ranches. Despite the relentless push of urbanization and industrialization, the agrarian ideal—the dream of attaining independence and security on the family farm—remained very much alive.

For many of the three million families that launched new farms in this period, the dream became a nightmare. In Kit Carson County, Colorado in the 1890s one family lived for six weeks on nothing but squash. They had no money for fuel or clothing, and wrapped themselves in rags. The result of such suffering was a great surge of agrarian protest, culminating in the Populist Revolt. The political struggle will be examined in detail in Chapter 21. Here we look at the changes in farming life that were fundamental to agrarian protest.

VICTIMS OF EXPANSION: INDIANS AND MEXICANS

By the 1890s millions of angry American farmers were convinced that they had been victimized and exploited. But there were two groups of people who had even stronger grounds for complaint—the Indians and Mexicans who were engulfed by the waves of new settlers and who lost most of their land to them.

The windows, wagons, and windmill indicate the relative prosperity of this family of sheep ranchers posing in front of their sod house near Coburg, Nebraska in this 1887 photo by S.D. Butcher.

The "Empty" West

In 1860 the West was virtually uninhabited by white Americans, except for the westernmost fringe along the Pacific. Although over 60 percent of the land area of the continental United States lay west of the western borders of Minnesota, Iowa, Missouri, Arkansas, and Louisiana, it was populated by little more than a million whites—4 percent of the national total. Average population density in the West was less than one person per square mile. The Census Bureau used a density of two persons per mile to define where the area of "continuous settlement" gave way to frontier, but on the eve of the Civil War only Texas and California were settled by that standard—barely settled at that, with densities of 2.3 and 2.4 people per square mile respectively.

It was revealing, however, that the census takers made no effort to enumerate one group of people quite visibly living beyond the frontier—the Indians. Precise figures for the Indian population of the region are therefore unavailable, but an estimated 250,000 of the approximately 300,000 Indians then living in the United States resided there. The number may seem small for so vast an area. But most of the Indian tribes depended on hunting for their livelihood, and hunting peoples must range over large tracts of wilderness to find enough game to feed themselves. From their point of view, the West was already settled quite enough—at densities appropriate to a hunting economy. The arrival of the eastern tribes forcibly removed to the West in the Jacksonian era had put uncomfortable pressure on the western tribes, but the conflicts provoked by that had subsided. If the United States continued to honor the treaties in which it pledged western lands to the Indians "as long as the grass should grow and water flow," all would be well. "There," Andrew Jackson had said, "your white brothers will not trouble you; they will have no claim to the land. It will be yours forever."

Those solemn pledges, however, were made at a time when Americans saw little reason not to leave the West, except for the Pacific Coast fringe, to the Indians. Almost until the Civil War it was generally believed that the Great Plains and the mountain territory beyond them could not sustain "civilized" existence. The maps of the day identified the area between the Missouri River and the Rockies as the "Great American Desert." It was thought to be as forbidding and as worthless as the Sahara Desert—flat, treeless, arid. Without trees, how could one build a cabin in which to live, and fences to protect crops? With so little rainfall, how could anything grow? Nor did it seem that the great mountain ranges beyond this desert could support settlement. No wonder the migrants who flocked into Oregon in the 1840s jumped some 2,000 miles beyond the Missouri frontier to reach familiar looking wet and wooded farming land. The Oregon Trail began at the Missouri River. Between there and the forests of the Pacific Coast there seemed nothing worth stopping for.

New Incentives to Settle

That unduly pessimistic belief, so fortunate for the western tribes, was soon replaced by an excessively optimistic view of the region's potentials. First came the discovery that the mountains of the West were rich in gold, silver, copper, and lead.

The great rush of gold seekers to California in 1849 was followed by other rushes—to Nevada and Colorado in the late 1850s, Idaho and Montana in the 1860s, the Black Hills of South Dakota in the 1870s. From its initial center in California, the mining frontier thrust inexorably eastward through Indian territory. Similar pressures came from the opposite direction as well, as white ranchers and farmers pushed west across the Great Plains in the 1860s and 1870s. The first arrivals were cattlemen, who found the endless grassy plain superb for grazing. But they soon were followed by much larger numbers of farmers.

What brought the farmers into the Great American Desert? The completion of the transcontinental railroad shortly after the war was a crucial stimulus, because it made it possible to deliver crops grown in Nebraska and the Dakotas to eastern markets at a reasonable cost. An important invention of the 1870s—barbed wire—eliminated the need to employ costly imported lumber for fencing. It was still expensive to build a wooden cabin, but settlers discovered that they could exist in huts made of prairie sod.

The limited rainfall remained a serious problem. One solution was to dig a well and draw up water for irrigation with a windmill. Nature, furthermore, played a trick that fostered positive thinking, for the years of early settlement happened to be unusually wet ones in the Great Plains. This gave rise to the comforting theory that the climate could be manipulated. Observing that trees were abundant in areas with substantial rainfall and rare in arid climates, pioneers mistook the causal relationship and concluded that planting trees would bring down more rain from the heavens. "Rain," it was said, "follows the plough." The disastrous long-term consequences of this misconception for the farmers of the Great Plains will be discussed later. The first casualties, however, were the Indians. The new belief that the Great American Desert could be transformed into a Garden of Eden meant that the Indians were caught between two millstones—the westward-moving farming frontier and the eastward-moving mining frontier.

COSTS OF BUILDING A SOD HUT, CIRCA 1880

1 window	$1.25
18 ft. of lumber (for a door)	.54
1 latch and pair of hinges	.50
1 stovepipe joint (to go through the roof)	.30
3 lbs. nails	.19
	$2.78

The Last Indian Wars

The details of the process by which the Indians of the West were ground into submission vary from tribe to tribe but the broad outlines are easily sketched. White prospectors or land-hungry farmers would pile up along the boundaries of land reserved by treaty to the Indians, and would begin to filter into it. It was difficult for the federal government to prevent such violations, and few officials felt any inclination to try. More often the encroachers were encouraged. In 1874, for example, an army expedition party led by General George Custer explored the Black Hills of South Dakota in the heart of Sioux territory. The ostensible purpose of Custer's mission was to identify possible sites for an army post. This was consistent with the terms of the U.S. treaty with the Sioux. But his party was accompanied by prospectors, and Custer's glowing report of the gold to be found there triggered a rush of miners to the area. In repeated instances like this, American officials showed they shared the belief bluntly expressed by the Commissioner of Indian Affairs in 1872: "The westward course of population is neither to be denied not delayed for the sake of all the Indians that ever called this country their home." Most American whites did not doubt that, as Theodore Roosevelt put it even more bluntly somewhat later, "This great continent could not have been kept as nothing but a game reserve for squalid savages."

As the demand for Indian land mounted, the government pressured tribal leaders to renegotiate the original treaties and to confine themselves to ever more restricted reservation areas. Although this meant that the tribes would become less and less able to support themselves by hunting, they were promised that in exchange the federal government would provide them with the supplies they needed until they could make the transition to becoming self-supporting farmers. Here was a solution, said the Indian Commissioner, which happily allowed "the freest extension of settlement and industry, while affording space and time for humane endeavors to rescue the Indian tribes from a position altogether barbarous and incompatible with civilization and social progress."

The tribes that chose not to be "rescued" by such "humane endeavors," and refused to surrender their lands to the representatives of "civilization and social progress," had no recourse but violent resistance. The army would not expel whites who trespassed on Indian lands, and when the Indians themselves did so, they found the military power of the federal government turned against them. Consequently, a series of Indian wars erupted in the West.

The Sioux, Cheyenne, and Arapaho were formidable warriors, and they won a few striking victories. Provoked by the building of the Bozeman Trail squarely through Sioux hunting grounds to the Montana mining camps, Red Cloud's Sioux warriors defeated small detachments of the U.S. Army in 1864–65 and forced a closing of the trail. In 1876, the most famous Indian triumph occurred when General Custer led a unit of the Seventh Cavalry against Sioux and Cheyenne on Indian land west of the Black Hills; all 264 of his men were wiped out by braves under the leadership of Sitting Bull, Crazy Horse, Two Moon, and Gall.

But that was the last desperate gasp, the end of almost three centuries in which fear of Indian retaliation restrained the actions of white Americans. Further Indian resistance was impossible, and the last remaining hostile tribes were forced to surrender. The Seventh Cavalry got its revenge against the Sioux. At the reservation at Wounded Knee, South Dakota in 1890, the troops had surrounded a band who had left the area against the orders of the Indian agent in charge. As the Indians were surrendering their weapons, a shot was fired, provoking the cavalrymen to an orgy of killing. When it was over, 300 Sioux were dead, including approximately 100 women and children, some of them chased down and murdered as far as three miles from the spot where the shooting began.

Three new developments finally tilted the military balance decisively against the Indian. First, the coming of the railroad to the West gave the U.S. Army superior mobility; troops and supplies could be rapidly transferred to any trouble spot. Repeating firearms, standard issue by the 1870s, provided an awesome increase to the Army's firepower. Finally, the buffalo—the principal source of food for many tribes—was wiped out by white hunters who took the hides and tongues and left the prairie strewn with putrefying corpses. (The skins, ironically, were used as belts to drive machines.) An estimated 10 million bison roamed the United States in 1865; hardly 1,000 remained in 1890—one of the great ecological crimes in history. It was a crime against the Indians as well, for starvation forced them into submission.

The Reservation System

By 1872 the Indian Commissioner could confidently predict that within a few years "the most powerful and hostile bands of today" would be "thrown in entire helplessness on the mercy of the government," and "reduced to the condition of suppliants for charity." He was right. By 1880 all of the tribes had been confined to reservations, controlled by white authorities charged with the duty of "civilizing" them. "If they cannot bear civilization," a popular journal declared complacently, "it will at least kill them decently."

It almost did. The premise of the reservations policy was that the Indians there would be temporary, not permanent, recipients of federal assistance. In the best of circumstances, the transition to self-supporting farming has been difficult for nomadic hunting peoples. And the reservations tended to be located on land that no whites wanted because it was impossible to grow anything on it. The Indians' continued need for aid, however, was taken as evidence not of the deficiencies of the soil but of the supposed shiftlessness and inefficiency of Indian labor.

The white agents in charge of the reservations saw their mission as a complete transformation of the Indian way of life. Most of them lacked any understanding or appreciation of traditional native culture, and were determined to stamp it out as quickly as possible. Many of the agents were chosen from lists of nominees submitted by churches. Not surprisingly, they regarded tribal religious beliefs and practices as mere superstition, and sought to convert the Indians to Christianity. White teachers in the reservation schools, with some honorable exceptions, were equally disdainful of Indian customs. They sought to alienate children from their "backward and superstitious" parents, and penalized families that kept their chil-

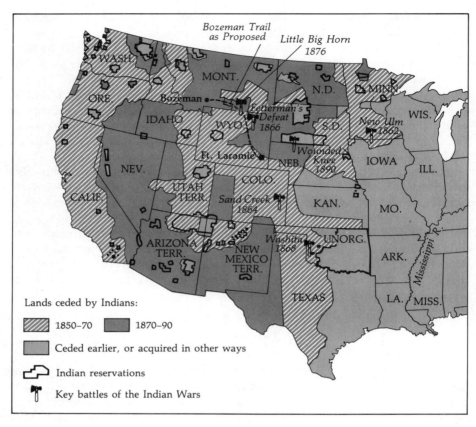

MAP 19-1
The Final Indian Land Cession, 1850–90

dren home by withholding their weekly rations. When schools on the reservation failed to achieve that aim, a new system of Indian boarding schools was created. The rationale, according to the Commissioner of Indian Affairs, was that "the barbarian child of the barbarian parent spends possibly 6 of the 24 hours of the day in a school room. He returns, at the close of his day school, to eat and play and sleep after the savage fashion of his race." The boarding school cut off the child from contact with his parents and other members of the tribe. English was the only language permitted there, and assignment policies deliberately mixed students from different tribes to prevent them from reverting to their native tongues when free of supervision.

There were many other indications of white American intolerance of cultural differences and determination to root them out. Washington mandated that Indian males must cut their hair; on at least one reservation the tribesmen had to be put in shackles before that order could be carried out. Many Indians believed long hair essential for proper conduct of religious ceremonies, and thought disaster would

THE NEAR EXTINCTION OF THE BUFFALO

I saw on plains a great stack of whitening bones. There were perhaps fifty or a hundred tons of skulls and leg bones in the heap, which had been gathered by some of the northern Cree Indians. This is all that is left of the buffalo now out of which the Indian can find profit. Once he obtained food, clothing, building material for his tepees, bones from which he could fashion weapons, and hides which he could sell or use in the making of canoes, and for many other purposes. Now the Eastern sugar-refineries purchase the bones found scattered all over the plains, to be used in clarifying sugar. The Indian picks them up, and he gets for them whatever the teamsters, commission men, brokers, railroad companies, and the other middle-men who stand between the starving savage on the plains and Claus Spreckels' representative choose to give him.

I said to the inspector who rode with me, "Do the Indians make a living gathering these bones?"

"Yes, in a way," was his reply; "but it is a mercy that they can't eat bones. We were never able to control the savages until their supply of meat was cut off. We have had no trouble worth speaking of since 1883, however."

—Hamlin Russell,
"The Story of the Buffalo," *Harper's Monthly,* April 1893

strike a man whose cut hair fell into the hands of an enemy. No matter, thought the agents, that belief was barbaric nonsense. To repress it could only benefit the Indian by prodding him farther down the path toward civilization. Likewise, when some tribes turned loose the cattle the government provided them with and attempted to hunt them down in the manner of the traditional buffalo hunt, the agents intervened. The cattle, they insisted, had to be slaughtered in the proper and sanitary fashion prescribed by American whites.

The Dawes Act

The climax of the effort to force the Indian into the white American mold was a major legislative reform, the Dawes Severalty Act of 1887. Before then, reservation lands were held in common by the tribe, and could not be sold by individual members. In fact, individual ownership of land was alien to Indian tradition. But for late nineteenth century Americans, civilization rested on the sanctity of individual property rights. A group of well-intentioned reformers like Helen Hunt Jackson, whose documentary *A Century of Dishonor* (1881) and novel *Ramona* (1884) amounted to an *Uncle Tom's Cabin* of the Indian cause, argued persuasively that reservation Indians were making little progress. The root problem, they urged, was the practice of communal land ownership, which stifled the incentive for individual self-improvement, and the continued strength of tribal political structures which sustained traditional customs and beliefs. The Dawes Act aimed to remedy that by giving 160 acres of land to each Indian family, and dissolving the tribal governments. As they "adopted the habits of civilized life" Indians were to be granted U.S. citizenship. The land was to be held in trust by the government for 25 years, and could not be sold, but thereafter it could be marketed as freely as any other land.

Some supporters of the Dawes measure were not as well-intentioned as Mrs. Jackson. Though the reservations were far smaller than the original treaty lands guaranteed to the tribes, the 160 acres allowed for each Indian family worked out to a total of even less land. Instead of either increasing the allotment per family to use up the remainder or leaving the balance under tribal ownership, the act provided that it could be sold to whites. A number of the complex provisions of the measure invited exploitation of the Indians by white lumbermen, real estate agents, and farmers, and this happened all too often.

For all of its massive abuses, however, the Dawes Act failed as much because of well-meaning ignorance as because of greed. The legislation rested on a false assumption—that the Indian wished to become an American-style businessman farmer, and would do so if only given a fair chance. The chance given was less than fair, to be sure, but the attempt to impose individualistic, competitive behavior on a people with such strong tribal loyalties and customs of mutual assistance was probably doomed to failure from the beginning.

Whatever the mix of causes at work, the effects of the Dawes Act are clear. Most Indians did not flourish on their homesteads. Half a century later, almost two-thirds (63 percent) of the 138 million acres allotted to them had slipped from their grasp into white hands; many of the 52 million acres remaining were barren desert. Most Indians were sunk in worse poverty than that of southern black sharecroppers. Some tribes managed to resist allotment to some extent, retaining part of their communal holdings and preserving their political structures—providing a basis for a revival of tribal life when the federal government abandoned the allotment program half a century later, in the New Deal Years. Some Indians—an unknown number—were successfully assimilated into white America. But most were caught between two cultural worlds, without the benefits of either. America's "humane endeavors to rescue the Indian tribes from a position altogether barbarous" had yielded them only poverty, disease, alcoholism, and hopeless apathy.

The Annexed Mexicans

Mexicans first became a significant ethnic minority in the United States in the middle of the nineteenth century. They did so not by choosing to immigrate there like the hundreds of thousands of Irish and Germans then arriving, but because the American government seized the land on which they happened to be living, the

LIVING CONDITIONS IN NEW MEXICO, 1895

In the case of the poorer class of Mexicans, one family, often large, usually occupies but a single room of less than 20 by 30 feet. This room has but a single door, and one or possibly two openings in the wall to admit light. These "windows" have no glass, and are guarded by wooden slats set into the wall a few inches apart. The floors of the houses are simply the bare ground, and the roofs are made of poles covered with brush, or some similar material, on top of which is spread a liberal coating of adobe mud. This constitutes the only protection against rain, which, however, seldom falls.

Mexicans of the poorer class raise the greater part of their food, which is almost entirely of vegetable origin. Flour and corn are used, the relative amounts depending upon the amount of money available. If it is necessary to reduce the cost of living to the minimum, as is often the case, more corn and less flour is used.

Southwest from Texas to California. The consequences of the contacts that followed were not as unrelievedly dismal as they were for the Indians, but there is one basic similarity. Like the Indians, the Mexicans lost most of their land and became impoverished and dependent.

Some of the Spanish colonists living in the Southwest at the time of the annexation of Texas, the Mexican War, and the Gadsden Purchase were unwilling to live under the American flag and fled south to Mexico. The great majority, however, chose to remain—an estimated 85,000 of them.[1] The Treaty of Guadalupe Hidalgo that concluded the war gave them the right of American citizenship, including "the free enjoyment of their liberty and property." (Few noted at the time that it did *not* guarantee the validity of the land titles previously granted by the Mexican government—soon to become a source of major conflict.) Most of these "Mexicans" had no particular identification with Mexico, since they had settled in the area long before Mexican independence (1821) and regarded themselves as Spanish. And many must have assumed that absorption into the dynamic American economy would put an end to the poverty that was the lot of most of them in this isolated, arid region.

---

[1] One might expect to find a precise number in the U.S. Census of 1850, which enumerated the foreign-born by country of birth. But the census takers, astonishingly, classified the annexed Mexicans as native-born. Apparently they were so convinced that it was the "manifest destiny" of the Southwest to become part of the United States that they regarded people born in Texas, New Mexico, and California many years before the annexation as Americans all along. This is a bit reminiscent of a famous Texas gunman's reply to the question of how many notches he had on his gun: "Thirty-seven, not counting Mexicans."

It did for some—generally the largest landholders who forged ties with powerful whites and who had the resources and connections to hire competent lawyers to defend their land titles from legal attack. But the influx of American settlers into the Southwest resulted in economic displacement for most. The legal status of the land they held was questionable because of the confused and inconsistent practices of prior Mexican governments, and small farmers and ranchers could not afford prolonged litigation to defend their property. Fundamental changes in the southwestern economy in the latter half of the nineteenth century worked to the same end. The growth of giant, American-owned mechanized farms and ranches relentlessly squeezed out small operators. The timing of this transformation varied considerably, occurring first in Texas and northern California and last in Arizona and New Mexico. But by the end of the century, the Hispanic people of the Southwest were mostly unskilled and ill-paid wage laborers in farming, ranching, railroad construction, or mining. Their living standards were probably no worse than in the days before annexation, but the loss of their land was a source of enduring bitterness.

BOOM AND BUST IN THE COUNTRYSIDE

The nineteenth century ended in catastrophe for millions of American farmers. The crisis, however, was not a general agrarian crisis; it affected some farmers disastrously, but left others untouched. To understand it requires a grasp of the different types of farming practiced in different parts of the country.

The Northeast and Old Northwest

Throughout the period a good many of the nation's farmers continued to live in the midwestern states that were settled before the Civil War (the Old Northwest), or in the agricultural counties that still existed in such highly urbanized northeastern states as Pennsylvania and New York. In both of these developed areas, farmland had become quite expensive. For people without much capital, the prospects of obtaining farms of their own were much poorer than in earlier days. The passage of the Homestead Act (1862), which offered 160 acres of land free to citizens and to aliens who declared their intent to become citizens, did not open up opportunities to start farms in New York or Illinois. By then virtually all of the land east of the Mississippi had already been taken up.

But for those who were already established in farming in these areas, the post-Civil War period was generally prosperous. During the depression of the mid-1870s, many midwestern farmers were drawn to the Granger movement, which demanded a ceiling on the rates charged by the railroads and operators of grain elevators. There was also some support for the Greenback Party, which urged the continued printing of paper money like the Civil War "greenbacks" as a stimulus to recovery. Such grievances never ran very deep or lasted very long, however, largely because most farmers of the Northeast and the Midwest successfully adjusted to the new economic circumstances that confronted them. Once the wheat and corn fields of the Great Plains came into production, farmers in older areas realized the folly of continuing to produce grains, and shifted to products that were increasingly in demand because of the rapid growth of cities. Consequently, the farmers of Illinois and Iowa abandoned wheat and shifted over to hogs and cattle, which they fattened up for slaughter with cheap western grain. The declining grain prices that dismayed their brethren on the Great Plains were not a grievance but a blessing for them. Other farmers in the urban industrial heartland found similar new opportunities, and turned to the production of milk, poultry, eggs, and perishable fruits and vegetables sought by nearby city dwellers. Some benefited from urban growth in yet another way, selling off acres for residential or industrial development at prices far above what they had initially paid for them.

This is not to say that farmers like these regarded the new order with unabashed enthusiasm. Like other American farmers of the era, many of them had deep misgivings about the rise of the city and the new corporate order. Cities seemed alien, unnatural, immoral places, centers of vice and corruption, and the fact that their sons and daughters felt the lure of the city lights filled them with dismay. Sons of the soil and guardians of the Jeffersonian tradition, they felt overshadowed as industrialization took command. Balancing those grievances and apprehensions, however, was the fact that they received a goodly share of the fruits of the tremendous economic growth of those years. The same relatively smooth adjustment to changing economic circumstances was not made by the farmers of the other two principal American farming regions—the Great Plains and the South. In these areas, the lot of the farmer in the late nineteenth century was far grimmer.

The Great Plains

The crushing of Indian resistance and the extension of the rail network across the western half of the country opened up the last farming frontier. Here, it seemed, the common man could make a fresh start in life, carving out a family farm from the wilderness with the help of the Homestead Act. The rich soil offered wondrous bounty; books like *Marvels of the New West* (1887) reported such sights as Kansas corn "eighteen feet high, with ears long and heavy enough for a policeman's club," and stalks so thick that it required an ax to flatten them. Between 1865 and 1890, when the Census Bureau reported that the frontier had ceased to exist, millions of settlers pushed across the Great Plains to the foothills of the Rocky Mountains. Eight new states were added to the Union as a result: Colorado in 1876, North and South Dakota, Washington, and Montana in 1889; Idaho and Wyoming in 1890; Utah in 1896. By the century's end, only Oklahoma, Arizona, and New Mexico remained as territories with too few inhabitants for statehood.

Obtaining land suitable for farming did not prove as simple as enthusiastic western boosters claimed. The amount of land open to homesteading was limited, and much of it was in the least desirable locations. The choicest plots were grabbed up by those first on the scene, often aggressive businessmen who had no intention of farming themselves but, instead, of selling at a high price in the future. The

HOW THE HOMESTEAD ACT OPERATED IN PRACTICE

A young merchant, lawyer, or speculator, rides into the interior, to the unoccupied public lands, pays some settler five dollars to show him the vacant 'claims,' and selects one upon which he places four little poles around a hollow square upon the ground. Then he files a notice in the land-office that he has laid the foundation of a house upon this claim and begun a settlement for actual residence. He does not see the land again until ready to 'prove up,' which he may do after thirty days. Then he revisits his claim, possibly erects a house of rough slabs, costing from ten to twenty dollars, eats one meal and sleeps for a single night under its roof. More frequently, however, his improvements consist solely of a foundation of four logs. He goes to the land-office with a witness, and certifies under oath his desire to preempt the northwest quarter of section twenty-four, township ten, range thirteen, (or whatever the tract may be,) for his 'own exclusive use and benefit.' The witness also swears that the preemptor settled upon the land at the time stated, and erected 'a habitable dwelling,' in which he still resides. In three cases out of four, after 'proving up,' the preemptor never visits his land again unless for the purpose of selling it. Says the Spanish proverb, "Oaths are words, and words are wind." Thus this unequivocal perjury is regarded upon the frontier. The general feeling is that it wrongs no one, and that the settlers have a right to the land.

—Albert D. Richardson, *Beyond the Mississippi*, 1867

Homestead Act required that claimants erect dwellings and live on their claims, but fraud was widespread. Lacking a corps of inspectors, government officials had to depend on the testimony of witnesses who frequently perjured themselves for a consideration. And there were ingenious tactics to avoid outright perjury. Houses were supposed to be a minimum of 12 feet square; some witnesses testified to have seen a 12-by-14 house, when in fact it had been whittled with a penknife, 12 *inches* by 14. In Nebraska one cabin of the necessary size was built on wheels, and shuttled from claim to claim for a rental of $5 a day!

Much of the land that was not snapped up by local speculators was not open to homesteading, but was in the hands of the railroads. To induce the railroad companies to build through areas in which so little traffic could be expected for years to come, the federal and state governments offered them enormous tracts of land as a subsidy—tracts that together amounted to an area five times the size of the state of Ohio! Great strips of land ten to forty miles wide on each side of the railroad line were set aside. Half of the land within them—alternating mile-square sections in a checkerboard pattern—was assigned to the railroad companies, who

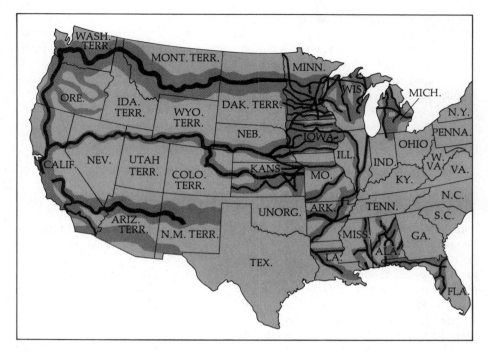

MAP 19–2
Federal Land Grants to Subsidize Rail Construction

sold as much of it as they could. Most of the land that could be obtained free by homesteading was too far from a rail terminal to be farmed properly. The railroad land at $320 or more for a 160-acre plot was therefore a better bargain to those who could afford it.

For these reasons, six of every seven new farms established west of the Mississippi in the late nineteenth century were on acres obtained by purchase from the railroads or private speculators. The Homestead Act undoubtedly gave a boost to some families who were too poor to make a start in farming without it, but its impact was drastically curtailed by the manipulations of speculators and the lavishness with which western land was dispensed to the railroads. Of course the region could not have supported the settlement that it did without railroads. But a society more genuinely committed to the ideal that the Homestead Act was generally thought to embody would have found a means of constructing the transportation network it required without surrendering so much of the public domain to corporate interests, and would have devised and enforced a system of land distribution that was egalitarian in practice as well as in theory.

Finding land they could afford was only one of several problems confronted by the farmers of the Great Plains. There was the physical environment—remarkably bleak, harsh, and forbidding. Winters were long and bitter, summers blazing. Frequent severe droughts devastated crops and soon shattered the myth that "rain follows the plough." The tough prairie grasses the pioneers ploughed under could survive in these conditions, but not tender corn or wheat. Plagues of grasshoppers sometimes descended to destroy every green thing for miles in every direction. L. Frank Baum opened his 1900 children's fantasy *The Wizard of Oz* with an accurate account of the view from a typical farmhouse on the great gray Kansas prairie:

> *Not a tree or a house broke the broad sweep of flat country that reached the edge of the sky in all directions. The sun had baked the plowed land into a gray mass, with little cracks running through it. Even the grass was not green, for the sun had burned the tops of the long blades until they were the same gray color to be seen everywhere.*

The same overwhelming sense of isolation in a hostile physical environment comes through powerfully in the stories of Hamlin Garland, another product of the Great Plains in this era, and in O. E. Rolvaag's classic novel, *Giants in the Earth* (1927). There were no automobiles, no telephones, and few neighbors nearby. Families homesteading on 160 acres lived a minimum of half a mile from each other. Average distances were even greater than that because there were vacant tracts and a good many farms of more than 160 acres. To people accustomed to the village life of rural Europe, or even the more densely settled farming areas back east, the solitude of the Great Plains frontier must have been hard to bear.

It would have been easier if the land had yielded secure prosperity. But for most it did not. Farm families found that their incomes fluctuated sharply from year to year, and in bad times they faced a mountain of debt. Substantial numbers lost their farms to creditors, and were reduced to tenancy or forced to return eastward in wagons with signs that announced "In God We Trusted. In Kansas We Busted." The population of western Kansas dropped 50 percent between 1888 and 1892. Someone must be to blame, they reasoned. They were being victimized and exploited by the railroads that shipped their products, the "middlemen" who handled the sales, the financiers who lent them money, and the great corporations that manufactured necessities.

One cannot fail to sympathize with the plight of the Kansas farmer whose testimony follows:

> *At the age of 52, after a long life of toil, economy, and self-denial, I find myself and family virtually paupers. With hundreds of hogs, scores of good horses and a farm that rewarded the toil of our hands with 16,000 bushels of good corn, we are poorer by many hundreds of dollars than we were years ago. What once seemed a neat little fortune and a house of refuge for our declining years by a few turns of the monopolistic crank has been rendered valueless.*

And he, of course, was better off than those who went bankrupt. It is estimated that two out of three farms established under the provisions of the Homestead Act failed before the end of the century. But understanding as well as sympathy is required. Who or what was to blame for the frustration and suffering of plains farm families? Was it truly the work of the sinister conspirators who were turning "the monopolistic crank?"

Part of the problem was unjustified optimism and simple ignorance of the risks of farming in such a region. Urged on by the glowing prophecies of real estate boosters, railroad land agents, and government officials, some settlers took up lands too barren for cultivation without extensive irrigation or a sophisticated understanding of dry farming techniques only developed in this century.[2]

Excessive optimism of another kind was also involved—speculative overexpansion. Farmers purchased more land than they could use immediately, confident that its value would continue to rise as the population increased and intending to sell for a good profit later. Many crushing mortgage debts were initially contracted not to finance the launching of a modest farm, but for such speculative purchases. In this respect, the actual homesteaders were not very different from hustling businessmen who staked claims with no intention of farming them. The real attachment of the American farmer, the great social critic Thorstein Veblen (1857–1929) observed, "was not to the land but to land values." For evidence of this, one need only look at the behavior of conservative Germans and Scandinavian immigrants in the Great Plains. They tended to be more cautious about borrowing than natives, were content with smaller acreages, and were more successful at weathering the hard times.

Wheat was the principal Great Plains crop. In years of good weather and good wheat prices, the occupants of even the poorest lands could survive adequately, and those on better soil did well enough to extend themselves even further by enlarging their holdings. But prices fluctuated sharply, and tended strongly downward over the period as a whole.

A combination of domestic and foreign circumstances accounted for the extreme instability and the general downward trend of wheat prices in these years (see Table 19-1). The root problem was that for a number of reasons wheat output rose more rapidly than its demand, forcing the price per bushel to fall. Why did supply outstrip demand? One reason was that the introduction of new farm machinery multiplied the productivity of the average farm worker. In 1830 it took three hours of labor to produce a bushel of wheat; in 1896 it took ten minutes.

This rise in productivity need not in itself have resulted in soaring total output; it might have been accompanied by a decline in the number of farmers growing wheat. But that did not happen. To the contrary, for all the imperfections of the Homestead Act, it was relatively easy to enter farming in this period in areas best suited to wheat production, and too many people did so for the economic welfare of wheat farmers as a group. They had no control over how much wheat would be

---

[2]Indeed, there is still a question as to whether even modern scientific agriculture is suited to much of the Great Plains environment. In the 1930s, when almost all of the prairie grasses had been ploughed under to make way for wheat, a series of droughts turned much of the area into a "Dust Bowl" denuded of topsoil. The return of wet weather later in the decade and ample financial and scientific assistance by the federal government brought recovery and reconstruction. But one recent authority argues eloquently that it could happen again; see Donald Worster, *Dust Bowl: The Southern Great Plains in the 1930's* (New York; Oxford, 1979).

TABLE 19-1
Wheat Production and Prices, 1866–1900

	Bushels Produced (millions)	Price per Bushel (dollars)
1866	170	2.06
1867	211	2.01
1868	246	1.46
1869	290	.92
1870	254	1.04
1871	272	1.25
1872	272	1.24
1873	322	1.17
1874	356	.95
1875	314	1.01
1876	309	1.04
1877	396	1.09
1878	449	.77
1879	459	1.11
1880	502	.95
1881	406	1.20
1882	552	.89
1883	439	.91
1884	571	.65
1885	400	.77
1886	513	.69
1887	491	.68
1888	424	.93
1889	504	.70
1890	449	.84
1891	678	.83
1892	612	.62
1893	506	.53
1894	542	.49
1895	542	.51
1896	523	.72
1897	606	.81
1898	768	.58
1899	655	.59
1900	599	.62

produced in the country, and hence no control over the price at which their crop would sell. All the individual farmer could do was try to harvest more and more each year, and hope that the increase in his output would compensate for any fall in the price per bushel. Although for each individual farmer it made sense to produce as much as possible, for all farmers to follow that strategy resulted in such a large output that prices plummeted.

There was, of course, some increase in demand for wheat in these years. The American population increased some two and a half times between 1860 and 1900, so there were more than 40 million new mouths to be fed. But the demand for wheat did not grow as much as we might expect. In these years of industrialization, income levels were rising, and this caused a shift in the national diet that is common in developing societies. As Americans became richer they ate less bread and more meat.

The result, from the point of view of farmers who naturally hoped for high prices, was a problem of overproduction. (To urban consumers, of course, such "overproduction" was not a problem but a blessing.) The difficulty was compounded by a basic change in the world economy in the post-Civil War years. Improvements in international transportation and in agricultural technology transformed the agriculture of long-settled areas and permitted the cultivation of vast new tracts not only in the American West but in such places as Argentina, Australia, Canada, and Russia. The development of this new international market for grain gave American farmers new outlets for their crops. When harvests elsewhere were poor, as much as 40 percent of American wheat was sold abroad at good prices. But it also exposed them to worldwide competition, and made their livelihood even more dependent on forces beyond their control. Before, in poor American harvest years, prices were at least pushed up, making it somewhat easier for the man who had lost half his crop to drought or grasshoppers to scrape by. That compensating mechanism no longer operated. A year of poor crops in South Dakota became disastrous if it happened to be a time of bumper crops in Argentina or the Ukraine.

It happened, furthermore, for reasons too complex to go into here, that the condition of the international agricultural market of the late nineteenth century was generally depressed. American producers of staples who traded internationally had no way of insulating themselves from the world economy, and suffered the consequences.

These factors—speculative overextension, overproduction relative to demand, the sluggish state of the international market—were the root causes of the economic difficulties of western farmers in the late nineteenth century. The grievances the farmers themselves articulated most bitterly in the Grange Movement of the 1870s and the Populist Party in the 1890s were, in comparison, far less important.

The complaint, for example, that railroad monopolies commonly charged farmers exorbitant rates to carry their crops to market was an exaggeration. Certainly there were abuses, but the principal feature of the pattern of railroad freight rates in this era is their overall decline. The prices farmers were receiving for their wheat were also dropping for much of the period, but no more so than railroad charges. A chart displaying the movement of wheat prices and railroad rates over the period shows no long-term change in the relationship between the two between 1867 and 1897. There were periods in which the share of a man's crop that went to pay the freight charges was increasing, but there were as many periods when it was dropping, and no overall trend in either direction. It was not true that an increas-

MAP 19-3
Farming Regions in the Late Nineteenth Century

ingly larger share of the farmers' income was being denied them by predatory railroad interests.

There was more substance to the farmers' complaint that they were being milked by eastern money-lenders who charged excessively high interest rates on western farm mortgages. Rates were indeed higher in the West. In 1890 they averaged 5½ percent in the Northeast and 8 percent in the Great Plains states. Some of that differential was probably justified, because the troubled economic circumstances of the West made farmland there a much riskier investment than, say, in Pennsylvania. But the size of the differential suggests that in the mortgage market some discrimination against the West kept credit tight and the cost of obtaining it higher than it should have been. Had that gap been eliminated, however, and easier credit been provided to the western farmer, still more people might have been induced to start farms, accentuating the root problem of overproduction and falling prices.

Many farmers also blamed eastern moneyed interests for depressing crop prices through manipulation of the money supply. The late nineteenth century was a time of severe deflation; the price level fell by more than half between the close of the Civil War and the 1890s. This was because productivity was rising rapidly, but the money supply was not. As the supply of goods available grew relative to the supply of money with which to buy them, prices had to fall. The supply of money remained more or less fixed due to a series of decisions by the federal government—decisions to remove from circulation the paper money printed during the Civil War, to limit severely the amount of silver coins that could be minted in any year, and to put the economy on the gold standard.

Some farmers saw these decisions as the work of corrupt politicians in the pay of Wall Street. They argued that the resulting deflation hurt agriculture in two ways. For one thing, it unfairly penalized farmers burdened with mortgages. If, for example, prices dropped by 50 percent between 1865 and 1890, a farmer who borrowed $1,000 on a 25-year mortgage in 1865 would be paying it off in 1890 in dollars worth twice as much as when he borrowed them. Second, they charged, deflation depressed farm prices.

The first complaint had a measure of truth. Debtors do suffer from deflation and creditors benefit, in general, and the tight money policy of the government did reflect the greater political influence of creditor interests. Of course, not all farmers were debtors, nor were all debtors farmers. Business loans and corporate bonds, for example, also became increasingly burdensome in deflationary periods. It is not surprising that the farmers in debt, as so many of the Great Plains were, complained of deflation. But the farmer who repaid $1,000 worth of loans with $2,000 in purchasing power in 1890 would have been hard to find in real life. In fact, the typical farm loan lasted nothing like 25 years. The average in Kansas and Nebraska in 1890, for example, was less than four years. Farm property was exchanged or refinanced so frequently, each time at the current price level, that the tax imposed on borrowers by deflation was very little.

The second argument—that the monetary policies producing deflation hurt farmers because they depressed the prices at which their crops could be sold—was fallacious. The general deflation affected all prices, not just farm prices, and did not in itself cut the real incomes of farmers at all. It brought them less cash for their crops, but also meant that they required correspondingly less money to buy commodities they needed. If the price of wheat fell more sharply than the price of manufactured goods—as it did during much of the period—that was the result not of the monetary decisions that depressed the overall price level but of the particular circumstances that governed the supply of wheat and the level of demand for it.

The political program advanced by furious western farmers who rose up in the 1890s therefore failed to strike at the root of their difficulties. The Populist upheaval provoked the sharpest political polarization the country had seen since the 1850s. The politics of the farmer's revolt will be discussed in Chapter 21. Here we need only note that even if the outcome of that struggle had been different—if the key demands of the farmers had been enacted into law—it is doubtful that farmers would have been helped very much. The anguish and frustration of the Populists was real enough, but their analysis of the sources of their problems was too superficial to yield effective remedies.

The South

Southern farmers in the late nineteenth century faced many of the same problems as those on the Great Plains, along with some others peculiar to their region. Despite a generation of publicists calling for a "New South," a South of factories

TABLE 19–2
Regional Differences in Urbanization and Per Capita Income, 1860–1900

| | *Percent Living in Cities of 2,500 or More* | | |
	1860	*1880*	*1900*
Northeast	36	51	66
Midwest	14	24	39
West	16	31	41
South	7	9	15

| | *Per Capita Income as a Percentage of U.S. National Average* | | |
Northeast	139	141	137
Midwest	68	98	103
West	NA	190*	163*
South	72	51	51

*These impressively high western figures are somewhat misleading. They reflect the high levels of income generated by mining, but much of that income was returned to the East in the form of profits to mine owners. Also, the population of a mining region contains mostly adult males with few dependents. Income per capita therefore appears to be higher than it truly is, because a worker's income is not divided among a number of dependents.

and prosperous cities, the area remained stubbornly resistant to change. The South produced a smaller proportion of American manufactures in 1900 than in 1860. About one in seven southerners lived in cities, far below the proportion in any other region. Only 30 percent of the country's population resided in the South, but fully half of all of its farmers did.

The South was still overwhelmingly agricultural, and its people were, on the average, strikingly poor compared to other Americans. Before the Civil War, the region was relatively affluent, with per capita income levels a bit higher than in the free farming states of the Midwest. Subsequently the two regions developed in quite different directions. Improved agricultural productivity and the beginnings of urban-industrial transformation raised midwestern incomes almost up to the national average by 1880, and slightly above it by 1900. The southern economy, by contrast, stagnated. In 1880, per capita income in the South stood at barely half the American average, and it failed to improve for the rest of the century.

The poverty in which so many southerners lived was even greater than these per capita figures suggest, because they do not account for how income was distributed. Definitive studies of southern income distribution in the late nineteenth century have yet to be made, but it appears there was a good deal more inequality—substantially more concentration at the top—than was the case in midwestern agricultural communities. One indication of this is the high percentage of southern farms that were operated by tenants, who had to give up a sizeable share

TABLE 19-3
The Growth of Farm Tenancy, 1880–1900

	Percentage of Farms Operated by Tenants		
Year	United States	South	Non-South
1880	26	36	19
1890	28	38	21
1900	35	47	26

of their crop to the owner of the land. Throughout the country, rising land values, increased capital needs stemming from mechanization, and falling crop prices were forcing an increasing proportion of the nation's farm families into tenancy in these years. Between 1880 and 1900, the percentage of tenant-operated farms grew from 26 to 35 percent. But tenancy was far more common in the South than elsewhere. In 1880, less than a fifth of all farms outside the South, but over a third of the southern farms, were occupied by tenants. By 1900 the tenancy rate outside the South had risen to a quarter, but in the South it had reached almost half.

These tenants were "farmers," but the independence and the opportunities for advancement celebrated in the agrarian myth were unknown to them. The most important single source of profits for the American farmer—rising land values—was closed to them, because they had been unable to accumulate the capital needed for purchase. Even the decision as to what crops they should grow was made by their landlords. And the crop, almost invariably, was cotton, the price of which declined even more precipitously than that of wheat in the late nineteenth century. The tenant's wages—a share of the crop—fell steadily. The failure to provide land to former slaves during Reconstruction left southern blacks with few options other than tenant farming. At the century's end, when the first comprehensive figures were gathered, three-fourths of the black farmers of the South were sharecroppers, as compared to 36 percent of the whites. But tenancy was far from an exclusively black institution. In fact, a majority (55 percent) of all southern tenant farmers were white.[3] The tenancy system was a modified, decentralized form of the old plantation system, with the master class of large landowners still making the basic production decisions and reaping most of the profits, but its tentacles extended over a large minority of southern white farmers as well.

The high concentration of landed wealth, and the great numbers of farmers who were consequently forced to labor on land owned by others was one distinc-

---

[3]These two points—that a much higher proportion of blacks than whites were tenants, and that a majority of all tenants were white—may seem contradictory. They are not. Because there were more than twice as many white as black farmers, it was possible for the *proportion* of whites who were tenants to be lower than the proportion of blacks and yet for the *number* of white tenants to exceed the number of black ones.

tive feature of southern agriculture in the late nineteenth century. Another was the scarcity of credit and the overconcentration on cotton production that suppliers of credit demanded. The small farmers who were fortunate enough to own sufficient land to cultivate still needed credit to obtain necessary supplies and equipment. Civil War banking legislation had been shaped to meet the needs of northern financial interests; few charters for the new national banks it created went to southern institutions. Southern farmers found mortgage money extremely difficult to obtain. Credit was available from local supply merchants, but in a form that had serious drawbacks. Merchants refused to make loans secured by farmland, because land could be difficult to sell in case of default. Instead, they demanded a farmer's forthcoming crop, and that crop had to be what the merchant preferred. Like the tenant, then, the farmer in need of funds was denied the opportunity to experiment with producing other things that might have been more profitable. These loans—"crop liens"—also carried a high interest rate, and were made even more expensive by the requirement that a farmer deal exclusively with the merchant who advanced him the credit, thereby allowing the merchant to charge credit customers prices well above the regular cash price. Debts mounted very rapidly under this system. When their crops were finally harvested and sold, many farmers found that they were still not "paid out," and had to pledge their next crop to the same merchant.

The prevalence of tenancy and crop liens kept a large part of the southern rural population, white and black, in poverty, and heavily influenced the overall stagnation of the southern economy in this period. Too often the economic backwardness of the late nineteenth century South has been uncritically attributed to the terrible devastation wrought by the Civil War. In a material sense, the war cost the South much more than the North. Much more of the fighting took place there, and the Union Army did what it could to shatter the economic basis of the Confederacy. Half of the agricultural machinery in the region was destroyed, for example, and a third of the horses and mules. The destruction of so much physical capital inevitably depressed levels of production. But how long can we reasonably expect the blighting effects of a war to last? The extraordinary economic recovery of Japan, Germany, and other European countries after World War II suggests that it is possible to catch up very rapidly after a disaster. The analogy may not be close, but it seems reasonable to wonder why the South showed no signs of catching up with the rest of the nation economically until well after the turn of the century. The answer may well lie in the hierarchy and rigidity of the region's economic and social structure.

The decentralized plantation system that emerged after emancipation left the land concentrated in the hands of the planters, and allowed them to retain the profits it brought. But the features of the plantation labor system that resulted in high slave productivity—well-coordinated, closely supervised gang labor—were lost. Each sharecropping family worked alone on its small plot. If the land and the profits of their labor had been theirs, they would have had an incentive to work as hard or harder than they had as slaves. But that was not the case, and output per worker fell as a result. Similar demoralization and apathy spread through the ranks

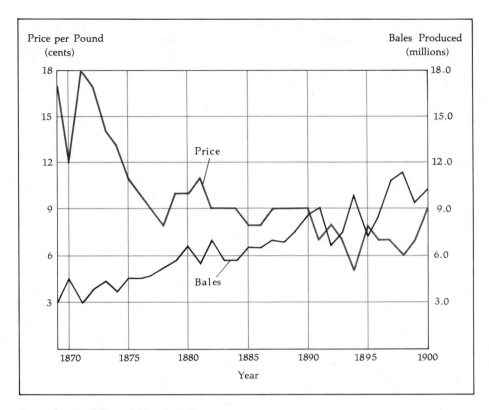

Price per Pound
(cents)

Bales Produced
(millions)

Cotton Production and Prices, 1869–1900

of white farmers as well, as they either resigned themselves to tenancy or watched their futures becoming hopelessly mortgaged to the supply merchant.

The rigidity of the system was damaging, too; it led to overproduction of one crop and prevented diversification. The landlords and merchant-creditors who dictated which crops would be produced remained convinced that cotton was the best paying in spite of a period of abrupt and almost uninterrupted declines in its price. A record harvest in 1894 produced almost ten million bales of cotton. Yet that harvest brought less money into the South than the four million bales turned out 20 years before, because the price had fallen from 13 cents per pound to only 5 cents. As with wheat, the explanation lay in worldwide economic conditions—increased output in other parts of the world and depression in the cotton textile industry that kept demand from expanding as rapidly as supply.

These circumstances made the late nineteenth century South, like the Great Plains, ripe for agrarian revolt. The situation of southern farmers was, if anything, even more desperate than that of those in the West. In addition to the acute problem common to both regions—disastrous price declines stemming from oversupply in the world market—there were the burdens of widespread tenancy and scarce credit. When revolt did finally come, however, these fundamental difficulties were not sharply focused, and a program that might have resolved them was not formulated. When the southern and western farmers joined forces in the Populist movement of the 1890s, they offered an analysis that was relatively superficial. At the climax of their efforts, the presidential campaign of 1896, they let the issue turn on their claim that a single measure—the expansion of the money supply through the unlimited coinage of silver ("free silver")—would be a cure for every ill that beset them. It is hard to resist the conclusion that most protesting farmers had little understanding of the true sources of their misery, and wasted their energies crusading for a panacea that could not have significantly helped.

SUGGESTED READINGS

Henry Nash Smith, *Virgin Land: The American West as Symbol and Myth* (1950) is a brilliant account of shifting popular conceptions of the region. J.B. Jackson, *American Space: The Centennial Years, 1865–1876* (1972) is superb on the changing landscape. Frederick Merk, *History of the Westward Movement* (1978), John A. Hawgood, *America's Western Frontier: The Exploration and Settlement of the Trans-Mississippi West* (1967), and Ray A. Billington, *Westward Expansion: A History of the American Frontier* (1967) describe the course of settlement from different vantage points. The evolution of land policy may be followed in Paul W. Gates, *History of Public Land Development* (1968) and Vernon Carstensen, ed., *The Public Lands: Studies in the History of the Public Land* (1962). Walter Prescott Webb, *The Great Plains: A Study in Institutions and Environment* (1931) is a classic. Howard R. Lamar, *The Far Southwest, 1846–1912* (1966) is a history of the territories. On mining, see R.W. Paul, *Mining Frontiers of the Far West, 1848–1880* (1963) and Mark Twain's delightful *Roughing It* (1871).

William T. Hagan, *American Indians* (rev. ed., 1979), Wilcomb E. Washburn, *The Indian in America* (1975), and Robert Berkhofer, Jr., *The White Man's Indian: Images of the American Indian from Columbus to the Present* (1978) are good general accounts. R.W. Mardock, *Reformers and the Indian* (1971)and Francis P. Prucha, *American Indian Policy in Crisis: Christian Reformers and the Indians* (1976) analyze shifting policies. Robert Utley, *Last Days of the Sioux Nation* (1963) is moving. The plight of former Mexican nationals in the annexed Southwest is described in Edward H. Spicer, *Cycles of Conquest* (1967), D.W. Meinig, *Southwest* (1971), and M.S. Meir and Feliciano Rivera, *The Chicanos: A History of Mexican-Americans* (1972).

Gilbert C. Fite, *The Farmer's Frontier, 1865–1900* (1966) is a good overview. Eric Lampard, *The Rise of the Dairy Industry in Wisconsin, 1860–1920* (1963) and Alan G. Bogue, *Money at Interest: The Farm Mortgage on the Middle Border* (1955) are outstanding monographs. Sharply contrasting views of southern agricultural conditions are presented in R.L. Ransom and Richard Sutch, *One Kind of Freedom: The Economic Consequences of Emancipation* (1977) and Robert L. Higgs, *Competition and*

Coercion: Blacks in the American Economy, 1865–1914 (1977). Robert Dykstra, *The Cattle Towns* (1968) and Julie Roy Jeffrey, *Frontier Women: The Trans-Mississippi West, 1840–1880* (1979) are illuminating. Willa Cather, *My Antonia* (1918) and O.E. Rølvaag, *Giants in the Earth* (1927) are novels that vividly capture farm life on the Great Plains.

Chapter Twenty

Industrialism and the Wage-Earner

In July of 1877, workers on the Baltimore and Ohio Railroad in Martinsburg, West Virginia threw down their tools, seized the local depot, and refused to let the trains move. Like other railroad employees across the country, they had endured sharp pay cuts over the three preceding depression years, and now management had announced another 10 percent reduction. The strike spread quickly to other rail centers, from Baltimore, Philadelphia, and Pittsburgh to as far west as Kansas City and Omaha, interrupting service on about two-thirds of the whole system. When the police, state militia, and federal troops appeared on the scene to restore order, they had to fight pitched battles with angry mobs. In the wake of the first great nationwide strike in American history, more than a hundred people lay dead and $10 million in railroad property had been put to the torch. Some terrified observers warned that the working class had acquired a "Samson-like strength," and might soon pull down the pillars supporting the temple of American civilization. The terrible memory of the Civil War was still fresh, and a character in a popular novel of the day asked whether "the labor question" might not prove to be "the irrepressible conflict" of his generation.

These fears proved unfounded. The American worker was no Samson; the "labor question" did not trigger a second Civil War. But in the closing decades of the nineteenth century, the clash between capital and labor did become an issue of acute public concern. In 1881 the government started keeping statistics on strikes—that in itself was a revealing index of change. From then on, labor disturbances multiplied. During the early 1880s nearly 500 strikes per year involved approximately 150,000 workers. By the 1890s there were from 1,000 to 2,000 a year,

During the Pullman strike of 1893–94, armed troops were called out to protect the interests of the rail companies. These members of the infantry are posed around an engine of the Rock Island Railroad Company in Blue Island, Illinois.

engaging as many as 700,000 protesting laborers. During these years a series of unprecedented efforts to form national workingmen's associations culminated in the formation of the enduring American Federation of Labor in 1886. As economic power became increasingly concentrated in the hands of giant industrial corporations, American workers began to join together to protect and advance their interests. There were great obstacles in their way, however, and only a small minority won significant protection.

SOURCES OF WORKING-CLASS DISCONTENT

The swelling of labor protest in the post-Civil War era is somewhat paradoxical, because it was a period of general prosperity for working people. The overall trend of real wages was upward, and rather strongly upward. Earnings in manufacturing (in constant dollars) climbed by half between 1860 and 1890, and by another 13 percent in the next ten years. The advance, however, was extremely uneven. Sharp rises in boom years were followed by abrupt falls in periods of depression. The increasingly pronounced cyclical economic fluctuations that accompanied industrialization produced fatter pay envelopes *some* of the time, but thinner ones or none at all at other times. The overall rise in wages over these four decades was impressive. But people must live from week to week and day to day, and for many American workers, stalked by the threat of unemployment, that was a struggle. The number of jobless reached record levels in the prolonged depression of the mid-1870s, and soared higher still during the collapse of the mid-1890s. Even in a quite ordinary year, about a third of all laboring men could expect to be without work for at least three or four months.

The Inadequacies of Poor Relief

In those days there was no unemployment insurance or other governmental programs designed to relieve or cushion the effects of unemployment. In the depression of the 1870s, President Ulysses Grant suggested a federal public works program to employ the jobless, but he soon renounced the scheme because "it is no part of the business of government to find employment for people." This was the orthodoxy of the day: that the natural operations of the free market would in time solve the problem. During the deepening economic crisis of 1874, one state legislature passed a remarkable resolution: "Recognizing in labor the true basis of a nation's wealth and prosperity," it read, "and recognizing its rights to obtain full and equitable remuneration, we extend to our fellow citizens now out of employment our sincere sympathies." That must have been very consoling to families on the verge of starvation.

Of course some assistance was available to the desperate. Caring for people unable to support themselves had been a responsibility accepted by the states and local communities since colonial times, and there were also voluntary charitable organizations. But just when unemployment was creating greater need, assistance

THE STRUGGLE TO SURVIVE, 1883

I have a brother who has four children, besides his wife and himself. All he earns is $1.50 a day. He works in the ironworks at Fall River. He only works about nine months out of twelve. There is generally about three months of stoppage, taking the year right through, and his wife and his family all have to be supported for a year out of the wages of nine months—$1.50 a day for nine months out of the twelve, to support six of them. It does not stand to reason that those children and he himself can have natural food or be naturally dressed.

—*Report of the Committee of the Senate on the Relations between Labor and Capital*, 1885

from public and private sources was becoming more difficult to obtain. Before the Civil War, American treatment of the poor was governed by a belief that a certain amount of poverty was inevitable. "The poor ye shall always have with ye" was the biblical phrase, and it was generally believed that it was in the nature of things that some people would be unable to support themselves at certain times, and to assist them was a matter of Christian duty. In the postwar decades, this attitude began to change as growing numbers of influential and affluent Americans attacked "the Old Charity." They saw poverty as the result of character weaknesses in the poor themselves, and held that to provide generous assistance only made the problem worse because it sapped the individual's determination to stand on his own two feet. "If it is known there is a loaf to be had for nothing, ten men will quit work to get offered the loaf," said Reverend William Ellery Channing of Boston. Another Massachusetts reformer offered an inventive plan for the treatment of paupers— placing them in cisterns, into which water flowed about as fast as a vigorous man could pump it out. "If he worked he was saved, and if he refused he was drowned." The Charity Organization Societies that were formed in most cities in the 1870s were based on these harsh doctrines. They campaigned against the distribution of free bread and soup to the needy by the police, established central record files to prevent seekers of aid from getting "excessive" aid by telling the same hard luck story to several different agencies, and in other ways reorganized the welfare system to make it far more difficult for the jobless to obtain aid. When the widow heroine of the best-selling children's book *Mrs. Wiggs of the Cabbage Patch* (1901) was tempted to register for aid with "The Organization," her thirteen-year-old son said:

Not yet, ma. It'd be with us like it was with the Hornbys; they didn't have nothin' to eat, an' they went to organization an' the man asted 'em if they had a bed or table, an' when they said yes, he said, "Well, why don't you sell 'em!"

The triumphant "New Charity" movement ignored the root cause of the growth of poverty—the soaring unemployment rate caused by unregulated capitalist industrialization. It claimed the authority of Science, and carried out pseudo-scientific studies "proving" that less than 10 percent of those who called themselves needy were truly "worthy paupers reduced to that condition by causes outside their own acts." It concluded that the dramatic rise in the number of requests for relief was a sign that the character of the American worker was deteriorating, not that the economic structure was flawed. The only way to arrest that deterioration was to cut off aid to the unworthy 90 percent. Consequently, in a time of serious and growing unemployment, relief funds shrank.

Employer–Employee Relations

A number of important changes in the organization of work and in employer–employee relations in the late nineteenth century had similarly distressing effects on the working class. The workplace was becoming larger and more impersonal. Before the Civil War, America's industrial production took place largely in units that in modern terminology would be described as small workshops. There were exceptions, notably cotton textile factories, but most firms numbered their work force in the dozens at most. Such companies were typically operated and supervised by their owners. In Lynn, Massachusetts, the shoe capital of the nation, the shoe "factories" were mere 10 by 14 boot sheds. As an aging shoemaker remembered those days, the owner "took in work and three, four, five, or six other neighbors came in there and sat down and made shoes right in their laps, and there was no machinery." The owner knew his men well, partly because of his self-interest in having a reasonably stable and contented group of employees. The intimacy did, however, encourage owners to show a degree of paternalistic concern that made workers less likely to view him as a member of an opposing class.

The postwar industrial transformation dramatically altered relations between workers and management. In Lynn "the immense factory, with its laboring steam engine and its busy hum of whirling wheels" quickly replaced the small shops, because shoes could be made much more cheaply with the newly invented McKay stitcher and other devices. Giant factories employing hundreds and even thousands of men appeared in many other industries as well. The owner could not possibly know a significant fraction of his employees. In any event, the individual owner was vanishing. The triumphant new form of industrial organization was the impersonal corporation, run by professional managers whose aim was to reap maximum profits for the thousands of stockholders who employed them. The social distance between employer and employee grew enormously. As it did, employers began to think of their workers less as individuals and more as an abstraction—as "labor," a mere factor in the cost of production. This spirit of the new era was well summed up by the manager who declared bluntly:

> I regard my people as I regard my machinery. So long as they can do my work
> for what I choose to pay them, I keep them, getting out of them all I can. What they

TECHNOLOGICAL CHANGE AND THE SKILLED WORKER

....In a little dark shop on a side street an old man had labored for years making axe handles. Out of seasoned hickory he fashioned them, with the help of a draw shave, a chisel, and a supply of sandpaper. Carefully was each handle weighed and balanced. No two of them were alike. The curve must exactly fit the hand and must conform to the grain of the wood. From dawn until dark the old man labored. His average product was eight handles a week, for which he received a dollar and a half each. And often some of these were unsaleable—because the balance was not true.

Today you can buy a better axe handle, made by machinery, for a few cents. And you need not worry about the balance. They are all alike—and every one is perfect. Modern methods applied in a big way have not only brought the cost of axe handles down to a fraction of their former cost—but they have immensely improved the product.

—Henry Ford, *My Life and Work, 1922*

do or how they fare outside my walls I don't know, nor do I consider it my business to know. They must look out for themselves as I do myself.[1]

Labor was only a commodity, to be bought, like any other, as cheaply as possible. Employers ceased to think of workers as people, as they rearranged the work process to maximize output and profits. The various tasks that had once been performed by a skilled artisan to make the whole product were divided and subdivided to take advantage of mechanization, and to make it possible to employ cheaper, less skilled workers. By the 1880s there were 40 different job titles for employees in the shoe industry, and older artisans who knew how to make an entire shoe were earning no more than "green hands" who had never served an apprenticeship but could operate a simple machine after only a few days' instruction. The untrained newcomers flooding into the cities from rural America and from abroad welcomed the new jobs, but the costs to the displaced craftsmen were heavy.

Mechanization did not altogether eliminate the need for skilled workers or reduce all work to routine machine tending. Instead it created demands for people with new, specialized skills, including a wide variety of machinists and engineers. But these new skilled jobs usually demanded a quite different kind of training than had previously been available, and often involved skills more closely related to other industries altogether. Shoemakers, for example, were accustomed to tanning

---

[1]Massachusetts Bureau of the Statistics of Labor, *Thirteenth Annual Report* (1883).

and sewing, but the new shoe factories also employed accountants and machinists. Opportunities for upward mobility appeared for some ambitious youths, but older artisans had little protection against downward mobility when a time-tested method of making a shoe, clock, or barrel became outmoded by machines that could turn out the same product faster and more cheaply. These artisans were victims of change, whether they continued to eke out a living by practicing their traditional crafts in isolated locations or gave them up and accepted lower wages for tending the new machines. The displacement and degradation of skilled labor was one of the deepest grievances of the working class. When coopers or carpenters saw the plight of the shoemaker, they could easily anticipate their own fate if it was left in the hands of their employers.

There was one seeming improvement in working conditions. The length of the average work week was shortened somewhat. In 1860, a typical worker labored eleven hours a day, six days a week; by 1900, the ten-hour day was standard. But this was offset—in many industries more than offset—by changes that forced the expenditure of more worker energy per day. Before the Civil War, the average work day had been very long, but periods of intense effort had been punctuated by frequent intervals of leisure—long dinner hours, visits to a nearby tavern, celebrations of "Saint Monday" (skipping work to sleep off the effects of the weekend's drinking), and a variety of other breaks sanctioned by pre-industrial custom. In the late nineteenth century, employers imposed new forms of discipline to stamp out the old practices. Strict work schedules were laid down, and overseers and foremen were empowered to enforce them with heavy fines and dismissals. The very appearance of the new factory buildings bespoke this purpose. Surrounded by high walls, with gates kept locked except when the shifts changed, they looked like prisons. Employees were required to punch a clock when they entered and left.

The lesson that time was money and that every moment had to be turned to productive advantage inspired the "time and motion" study methods pioneered by Frederick W. Taylor in the 1890s. After following the workers at a Bethlehem Steel coal yard with stopwatch and clipboard, Taylor had ordered changes in their work routines that increased their output spectacularly. Time study experts were hired thereafter in many other industries, establishing the production quotas needed to operate a new system of wage payment, the "piecework" system. When workers were paid not for putting in time but for work actually accomplished, they had every incentive to drive themselves mercilessly. Follow-up studies by the experts typically led to an upping of the quota and lower compensation for each unit produced, forcing them to work still harder.

The growing intensity of labor demanded by cost-conscious employers was not only draining but dangerous. The combination of inadequate safety provisions and fatigued workers resulted in an appallingly high accident rate. Some 35,000 American wage-earners were killed annually in industrial accidents in the late nineteenth century, and over half a million were injured severely enough to be incapacitated for more than three days. In a single year in the Pittsburgh steel mills alone there were 195 deaths from such causes as being hit by exploding metal or falling into vats of molten steel, and hideous burns were frequent. Inexperienced recent immigrants were particularly accident-prone. Some insight into why may be gleaned from an accident that took place at the Amoskeag Mill in Manchester, New Hampshire, the largest cotton mill in the world. A 23-year-old immigrant from Lithuania mangled his hand in a machine so badly that it had to be amputated. Investigation revealed that he didn't understand a word of English, and had no idea that the machine was dangerous. "He just used to give his head a nod," said the foreman who instructed him. "I used to explain to him what to do, but he didn't understand very well and I had to show him how to do it. When this fellow didn't understand, I took him by the coat, took him over to the picker and showed him what to do." With half of the industrial labor force composed of immigrants, the vast majority of them from non-English speaking lands, such careless training procedures were a recipe for disaster.

They were not disasters for the company, though, given the state of the law. The accident victim or his widow could expect little if any compensation, because no protective legislation had yet been enacted. Loss of life and limb were grounds for legal action, but that required money to pay a lawyer, and the courts of the day adhered to the ancient "fellow servant" rule of the English common law. Employers were liable only if clear proof of *their* negligence could be offered. If the accident was attributable to the mistakes of another employee—a "fellow servant"—then the company was not legally responsible. "Under our common law doctrine," said a corporate attorney, "the employee has not a chance of recovery" in more than two cases in a hundred. Perhaps the suffering of unfortunate workers and their families gave some company officials an uneasy conscience. "As humanitarians we might regret" the hardships endured by our employees, said a steel executive. But humanitarian considerations were quite irrelevant: "As managers we would not be justified in diminishing our employer's profits."

The growth of labor protest during this period of general prosperity is therefore not paradoxical. Despite the general upward trend of real wages from the Civil War to the end of the century, the bubble burst again and again, forcing crowds of jobless men into the city streets in search of work. Job security was going out the window, and relief funds were shrinking thanks to "the New Charity". The employer was becoming an ever more distant and ruthless figure, cutting his wage bill to the minimum, driving his workers to the point of exhaustion, and freely replacing skilled workmen with machines.

EFFORTS TO ORGANIZE

As American wage-earners became alienated from their employers, they also became accustomed to the idea that they must join together in defense of their common interests. Recognizing the *need* to organize, however, was not enough. There had to be agreement on such issues as how the organization was to be structured, who was to be eligible for membership, what its objectives were to be, and what tactics it would employ in pursuing those objectives. Some believed in the possibility of bringing together all "producers"; others were persuaded that the only practical course was to organize only the skilled craftsmen. Some hoped to achieve a sudden dramatic transformation of the entire socio-economic order; others had narrower pragmatic aims—a boost in pay or resistance to a cut, preventing a speedup of the work pace, keeping men from being fired without proper cause. Some thought that capturing political power and forcing the passage of reform legislation had the highest priority; others felt that the struggle could be won only by waging economic warfare—the strike—against their employers. As the labor movement emerged in the post-Civil War years, it was divided over all these issues. Not until almost the end of the century did one national organization—the American Federation of Labor—win clear ascendancy and give to the American labor movement a shape it would retain until the Great Depression of the 1930s.

Early Trade Unionism

Before the Civil War, labor organizations on a national scale were a rarity in the United States. Unions had existed since early in the century, but on a local basis. Similar craftsmen in one locality—the carpenters of Philadelphia, say—would join together to attempt to enforce a uniform wage scale or to prevent the hiring of workers who had not served a proper apprenticeship. Sometimes these local trade unions would band together with others in the city in a central labor union or trades assembly.

Local organization, however, proved an inadequate defense as production became increasingly geared to a national market. It didn't matter that the organized coopers of one community refused to make barrels for less than the union rate once an improved transportation and distribution network made available cheaper barrels produced by nonunion coopers somewhere else. An organization including all the coopers of the nation was obviously required.

The first such national craft union—the National Typographic Union—was formed in 1852. A meeting of delegates from printers' locals in twelve cities formed the body to fight for the nationwide adoption of wage scales and apprenticeship regulations then current in New York, to raise strike funds, and to circulate lists of printers who failed to comply with union rules. Five other national unions were established during the 1850s, and 21 more in the Civil War decade. On the eve of the depression of 1873–78, such groups as iron molders, cigar makers, telegraphers, shoemakers, railroad conductors, engineers, and firemen had all built national organizations. An estimated 300,000 wage-earners were unionized, 9 percent of the industrial work force. Most of these organizations, however, were weak; more than a third of them collapsed and disappeared during the depression. They were able to win some demands during prosperous years when skilled men were in short supply. But they failed to accumulate enough funds to hold their members through hard times, when union dues seemed expensive and the temptation to accept work at rates below the union scale was overwhelming. By 1878 membership in all American labor organizations had fallen to a mere 50,000 workers.

A broader organizational form seemed necessary, one that would embrace workers in many different crafts and industries and serve as a harness to make them pull together in the same direction at the same time. The first two efforts at such an overarching national organization of wage-earners—the National Labor Union and the Knights of Labor—failed dismally because their objectives and tactics were unrealistic.

The National Labor Union was formed in 1866 by men who adhered to the Jacksonian ideal of an economy of independent, small producers, and were horrified to see that the United States was fast becoming a nation of hired hands. They had a number of more immediate and practical ends as well, such as campaigning for state and federal laws mandating an eight-hour work day and for a ban on employer recruitment of immigrant contract laborers. But their central desire was to end "wage slavery" altogether, and to replace it with a system of worker-controlled producers' cooperatives. The "only way by which the toiling masses can protect themselves against the unjust claims and soul-crushing tyranny of capital," in their view, was for "themselves to become capitalists." The cooperative idea had support in many quarters in those years, but neither the National Labor Union nor anyone else found out how to translate it into reality. The NLU did manage to sponsor a few dozen cooperative workshops, but most quickly failed, and the few that prospered hired additional workers for wages as they expanded, thus perpetuating wage slavery for others. The National Labor Union sputtered out after an unsuccessful attempt to create a new political party, the National Labor and Reform Party, in 1872. Only seven people turned up at its final convention.

The Knights of Labor was, for a time, a far more serious and successful effort to mobilize wage-earners, but it too pursued visionary objectives that could not be realized. The Noble and Holy Order of the Knights of Labor was born in 1869, as a secret fraternal order with a strongly Protestant tone. The secrecy and religious character repelled many prospective members, especially Catholic workers, who by then made up at least half of the labor force in many industries. It had fewer than 10,000 members in 1879, when a Catholic, Terence V. Powderly, was elected its head. Prodded by Powderly, the organization then abandoned the principle of secrecy and much of the religious ritual. The Knights grew remarkably thereafter, and by 1886 claimed over 700,000 members. But its amazing growth was followed by almost equally rapid decline; by the 1890s, the organization was practically defunct.

Why did the star of the Knights burn so brightly and then fade so quickly? The distinctive philosophy and structure of the organization gave it wide appeal but little staying power. It had essentially the same fundamental objective as the National Labor Union—nothing less than the elimination of the gulf between labor and capital, the replacement of "the wages system" with an economic order organized on a cooperative basis. "The aim of the Knights of Labor," said Powderly, "is to make each man his own employer." But the approximately 140 cooperative workshops sponsored by the Knights were never enough to employ more than a tiny fraction of the membership, and they soon collapsed.

A second distinctive feature of the Knights of Labor was its organizational structure and open membership policy. Labor unions are normally either craft or industrial organizations; they bring together either all people with a common skill—carpentry or plumbing, say—or all those employed in a particular industry—such as coal mining or automobile manufacturing. The Knights, however, was structured along geographical lines, more like a political party than a labor union. Its basic unit was the local assembly, which mixed together all interested workers in a given locality. And membership was open to workers of every kind, whatever their skill, sex, or race. Ditch diggers, garbage collectors, janitors, and maids were as welcome as machinists and printers. Female workers and blacks, barred from most existing trade unions, were admitted on an equal basis. Membership was open not only to "any person working for wages but to anyone who had at any time worked for wages." The only exceptions were four groups whose occupations the Knights regarded as especially exploitative—bankers, saloonkeepers, lawyers, and gamblers. All others were fellow toilers, if they had ever been wage-earners and shared the Knights' vision of the good society.

The Knights sought to inspire a sense of solidarity and brotherhood among all workers. "An injury to one," they insisted, "is an injury to all." But the organization's structure and composition left it ill-equipped to carry out strikes against particular employers. The Knights in fact rejected the strike as an instrument for advancing labor's cause. The carpenters, shoemakers, ditch diggers, and maids who belonged to a mixed local assembly could not help the coopers of their town, whose wages were being driven down by external competition, by striking against their respective employers. Furthermore, those members of the Knights who lacked skills that were in short supply were in no position to carry out a successful strike, even if they could specify something reasonable that their own employers could do to help the coopers. Wage-earners with scarce skills find it extremely difficult to win demands from their employers because it is so easy to find substitutes for them. Unless all of the unskilled workers of the United States were loyal Knights—and at the peak of its influence hardly a tenth were—the ditch diggers and maids who refused to work until their demands were met could easily be fired and replaced with strikebreakers, or "scabs".

It is true that the Knights' principled commitment to mixed assemblies and rejection of the strike was stronger in theory than in practice. In fact, the tremendous growth in its membership in the early 1880s was due to the organization's increased willingness to abandon its principles and to operate more like a conventional trade union. The executive board began to tolerate the establishment of "trades assemblies" consisting entirely of workers from particular crafts or industries. And when these assemblies waged strikes against their employers, as did assemblies of railroad workers in the mid-1880s, the central body reluctantly went along.

But there were limits to the flexibility of the Knights. Its leaders sometimes compromised but never renounced their fundamental goal that all "toilers," regardless of skill, should join together in a crusade to eliminate the social divisions produced by industrialization and establish a harmonious, cooperative society. When a group of unionists with a radically different view of what the labor movement should be emerged in the 1880s, they felt compelled to form a rival organization, the American Federation of Labor. From its founding in 1886, the AFL grew rapidly, while the Knights declined and disappeared.

Samuel Gompers and the AFL

Unlike the Knights, the AFL was not an alternative to the existing trade unions but a coalition of them, a federation through which they could act in concert for certain purposes. Its membership was narrower and more exclusive than that of the Knights, consisting almost entirely of skilled craftsmen, for the simple reason that the established unions of the day were almost all organizations of the skilled. From the point of view of the Knights, the AFL represented the selfish interests of "the aristocracy of labor," and callously ignored the plight of the unskilled or semi-skilled majority. AFL leader Samuel Gompers offered a strong practical defense—namely that half a loaf was better than none. Only the skilled had the market power to organize against fierce employer resistance. Better to strengthen their hand than to pursue the impossible dream of organizing the entire working class and to lose all. A strong national labor organization, even a rather narrowly based one, would help significant numbers of wage-earners immediately. And in the future, when the time was right, less skilled workers would benefit from the precedent. The later failure of the Industrial Workers of the World (founded in 1905) to build an enduring organization of the unskilled indicates that Gompers had a point.

Gompers did not indulge in rhetorical rhapsodies about such ultimate objectives as the end of the wage system and the replacement of competition with cooperation. Gompers had been a socialist as a young man, and throughout his life remained sympathetic to the ultimate socialist goal of democratizing the economy. He broke with the socialists, however, on the question of how and when that objective could be achieved. For Gompers it was far in the future, and would come about by "a transition so gentle that most men will wonder how it all happened ." The immediate daily struggle consisted of labor's winning inch-by-inch advances through well-organized united effort. Most American workers, Gompers felt, would be unwilling to struggle and sacrifice for a goal as abstract and visionary as transforming the entire socio-economic order. That was "pie in the sky." But they could be reached by appealing to their immediate interests. Concentrating on such practical aims as better wages and working conditions was not surrendering the larger vision, Gompers believed. In fact, it was the only way to attain it—the only way to ensure that the power of labor would grow.

The AFL philosophy was not only severely practical; it was highly cynical: Power was all. The organizers of the National Labor Union and the Knights of Labor had been idealistic, optimistic, and vague about how to achieve their grand aim of ending the wage system, but sure that they had to persuade the general public. Winning sympathy for the sufferings of labor in the court of public opinion

SAMUEL GOMPERS
(1850–1924)

S amuel Gompers was an immigrant lad who made good—but as a captain of labor, not a captain of industry. He was born in London in 1850, the son of a Jewish cigarmaker who had recently migrated from Holland and who moved on again to New York City when Samuel was 13. Samuel left school at the age of ten, served an apprenticeship with his father, and went to work in a cigar shop, first in London and then in New York. At the age of 14, he joined the Cigarmakers' Union; in 1872, he became a naturalized citizen.

Although he was only five feet four, he was a strong, shrewd, vigorous worker with energy left over for night school and fraternal societies. Soon he was drawn into the affairs of his ineffective union local. His success in welding it into a more disciplined and powerful bargaining instrument elevated him to the presidency of the national Cigarmakers' Union at the age of 27. He was a principal figure in the first attempt to form a national federation of craft unions, the 1881 Federation of Organized Trades and Labor Unions of the United States and Canada, and when it was reorganized as the AFL in 1886 he was the natural choice as president, a position he held for all but one year thereafter until his death in 1924.

During World War I, President Woodrow Wilson formed the Council of National Defense with Gompers as one of its key members; Gompers himself organized the War Committee on Labor and attended the Versailles Peace Conference as an advisor for international labor legislation. His autobiography, *Seventy Years of Life and Labor* was published posthumously in 1925.

had been one of their principal objectives. But Gompers doubted that sympathy counted for much. "No matter how just a cause is," he declared, unless it "is backed up with power to enforce it, it is going to be crushed and annihilated." He illustrated the point by noting that when Britain had a dispute with a tiny country like Afghanistan, its rulers simply sent out the Navy to bombard the country. When it had a similar dispute with the United States, Britain said "let us arbitrate this question." The problem of labor was that it was in the position of Afghanistan.

Labor needed power, and power could be won only at the workplace, not in the court of public opinion or in the legislative halls. Gompers did not believe that politics was entirely irrelevant, however. Although the AFL refused to align itself with any one political party, and followed instead Gompers' advice to "reward your friends and punish your enemies," it did attempt to exert political influence on behalf of such measures as workmen's compensation laws and mandatory safety standards for industry. But favorable legislation was of secondary importance to the AFL.

What the wage-earner really needed was the ability to defend himself against a boss whose central interest lay in working him as hard, as long, and for as little pay as possible. "There are two classes in society—" said Gompers, "one incessantly striving to secure the labor of the other for as little as possible." The cardinal aim of the AFL, therefore, was to force employers to accept the union as their workers' legitimate spokesman, and to compel favorable settlements through collective bargaining between the union and management.

The chief weapon in labor's arsenal was the strike. "There is no tenderer or more vulnerable spot in the anatomy" of corporations, said Gompers, than "their dividend paying function." A strike at just the strategic moment, executed by a well-prepared, disciplined body of workers, would cut the flow of profits that was the lifeblood of business. The strike was by no means its invention, but the AFL employed it with a calculated sophistication. The temptation to strike, Gompers observed, was greatest in periods of recession, when wages were falling and workers were being laid off. But that was precisely the wrong time, both because employers often were happy to cut back production for a depressed market and because if they did want to keep producing they could easily find jobless men who would rather scab than starve. Strikes were easier to win in prosperous years, when labor was in short supply and employers were desperate to produce enough to fill the orders that were piling up. By exercising his authority to authorize strikes by the member unions of the AFL and providing support for strikers from the central treasury, Gompers ensured that the instrument was used in a more careful, calculating and effective manner.

Guided by Gompers' harshly realistic philosophy, the AFL became the dominant force in the American labor movement, while the more idealistic Knights of Labor passed into oblivion. But in noting the success of the AFL in besting its rivals, we should not ignore a more fundamental point: The AFL organized only a minority, a quite small minority of the country's workers. In 1900 there were fewer than 900,000 union members in the United States. That was triple the number in the early 1870s, but the industrial labor force had more than tripled in the interim, so that the percentage of organized workers had actually fallen slightly, from 9.1 in

1872 to 8.4 in 1900. The labor movement experienced further gains after the turn of the century and during World War I, but heavy losses in the 1920s. Why did organized labor remain so weak in the world's leading industrial power?

DETERRENTS TO ORGANIZATION

Narrow Craft Focus

There were limitations inherent in the AFL's principle of craft exclusivity. Gompers' hard-boiled "realism" was in one respect not so realistic after all. He was undoubtedly correct to concentrate initial organizing efforts on the most highly skilled trades; the skills of the artisan gave him market power. But Gompers did not think through the long-term implications of the crucial fact that technological advances were making it possible to replace skilled craftsmen with "green hands" who could perform the same work by machine. The strongest AFL unions involved trades that were least amenable to mechanization, such as carpentry and the other building trades. Elsewhere, the craft mode of organizing was dangerously vulnerable to attack by cost-cutting employers. The outcome of a bloody strike at the Homestead, Pennsylvania Carnegie Steel plant in 1892 was a vivid demonstration. The Amalgamated Association of Iron and Steel Workers, an AFL affiliate, was an association of proud artisans who failed to realize that recently introduced machines had made their services dispensable. When they protested a pay cut, the management threw them out and brought in strikebreakers guarded by 300 Pinkerton detectives. After a shoot-out that left 14 dead and hundreds seriously wounded, state troopers took charge and allowed the strikebreakers to enter the mill. The union men found themselves jobless, and the Amalgamated was crushed. In such circumstances, only a union organized along industrial lines—taking in all steelworkers instead of only the craft elite—might have been able to exert much leverage against management. Gompers was unwilling to sponsor such an effort.

Another effect of the narrow craft focus of the AFL was to make it an organization largely of white males of old immigrant stock. The newest immigrants, blacks, and women were barely represented, if at all, in the trades of the federation. In the early years Gompers urged that member unions accept blacks and women, but he had no power to force them to do so and eventually acquiesced to racial and sexual discrimination. Moreover, the AFL failed to extend a supportive hand to the eastern and southern European immigrants then beginning to arrive in such large numbers. Instead of attempting to organize them, it campaigned for immigration restriction to "safeguard America" from the dangers posed by the influx of such "inferior, unassimilable newcomers."

Repressive Tactics of Employers

Another reason for labor's weakness is that American employers fiercely resisted the organization of their employees, and were able to enlist the repressive power of local, state, and federal government on their behalf. Employers, not suprisingly,

A YELLOW DOG CONTRACT, 1890

In Consideration of employment by The Yale & Towne Manufacturing Company, and the covenants on the part of the latter herein set forth the person above-named hereby agrees with said Company as follows:....

(7.) To faithfully render the service which is undertaken and for which the Company pays.

(8.) To conform to the shop rules and carry out instructions received from the Foreman or the Officers of the Company.

(9.) In case any reasonable ground for complaint exists, to report the facts, first to the Foreman, and if no redress is thus obtained, to bring the matter, preferably in writing, to the notice of the Company, through the Paymaster or one of its Officers.

(10.) To take no action of any kind, individually, or with others, tending to cause disturbance of the relations between the Company and its employees, because of any grievance, until the matter has been first submitted to the Company in the manner indicated in Article 9, and, if said request, so presented, is not granted, to take no action tending to harass or injure the Company until at least fifteen days shall have elapsed after such request has been presented to the Company without its taking action thereon.

(11.) To withdraw and abstain, during the period of this contract, from membership in any organization whose rules would prevent the honorable carrying out of this contract.

(12.) To forfeit to the Company, as liquidated damages, a penalty or fine equal in amount to one week's wages or earnings, in event of any violation of Articles 10 or 11 of this contract.

wanted to maintain their absolute authority over the work force. They insisted on their right to bargain with each worker on an individual basis. Confronted with the enormous disparity in power between a giant corporation and an individual laborer, they retorted that a dissatisfied worker was perfectly free to leave and find another job elsewhere (conveniently overlooking the point that they would be equally powerless vis-à-vis their new employers). Employers claimed that they could be trusted to pay their workers precisely what they were worth. "The rights and interests of the laboring man," declared a railroad president, "will be protected and cared for, not by the labor agitators, but by the Christian men to whom God in his infinite wisdom has given control of the property interests of the country."

Not all wage-earners were wise enough to understand that management had their interests at heart. Consequently, business developed a variety of coercive devices to impede unionization. Workers were forced to sign "yellow dog" contracts, pledges that they would not join a union during the period of their employment (see box). Associations of employers were created to present a common front against unionization, and they compiled blacklists to insure that "unreliable" men—that is, men with prounion sentiments—would find no jobs. Private detectives from the Pinkerton Agency or similar firms were hired to ferret out disloyal employees and protect strikebreakers who were brought in to replace striking workers. The equivalent of a strike on the part of the employer—the lockout—was also widely employed to break existing unions. The factory gates would be shut, and when they reopened union men would not be rehired. The Homestead strike, which led to the demise of the Amalgamated Association of Iron and Steel Workers, began as a lockout on the part of an aggressive management.

Labor disputes that erupted into violence, like the Homestead strike, persuaded many Americans that organized labor was a threat to law and order. Sometimes strikers could not contain their rage at the scabs who were taking jobs they considered rightfully theirs, particularly when the strikebreakers were from despised new immigrant groups or were blacks. Sometimes the guards assigned to break the picket line were panicky and trigger-happy. Either way, the cause of labor suffered for being identified with bloodshed and anarchy. Popular novels like Thomas Bailey Aldrich's *The Stillwater Tragedy* (1880) and John Hay's *The Breadwinners* (1884) reinforced the impression by portraying innocent workmen duped by wily radical organizers with vicious purposes. The 1886 Haymarket riot in Chicago seemed to lend truth to such stereotypes. After a lockout at the McCormick Reaper Works triggered fighting that led to four deaths, a group of local anarchists organized a protest meeting at Haymarket Square. It was proceeding peacefully when city police arrived to break it up. A bomb exploded, killing seven policemen, and the officers opened fire on the mob. In the atmosphere of political hysteria that followed, eight anarchist leaders were tried for murder and convicted although no evidence to link them to the bomb was presented and a number were not even present at the meeting. Four were hanged, one committed suicide, and the others languished in prison until pardoned by a courageous governor, John Peter Altgeld, seven years later.

In such a climate, it was easy for employers to convince public officials to intervene on their side in labor disputes. A classic example was the Pullman strike of 1893–94. In the "model" company town of Pullman, Illinois, on the outskirts of Chicago, workers engaged in the construction of Pullman sleeping cars walked off their jobs to protest a 22 percent pay cut, and management's unwillingness to offer a corresponding reduction in the rents they paid for company housing. They persuaded the newly formed American Railway Union to support their cause by refusing to operate trains carrying Pullman cars. The railroads could have avoided trouble with the railway union by putting their Pullman cars on sidings until the dispute was resolved. However, the General Managers Association, which represented 24 railroads, sensed that a railroad strike might provide an opportunity to destroy the American Railway Union. They were right. When the strike broke out, the Association appealed to the U.S. Attorney General, who appointed as special counsel to the government a man who had been the attorney for one of the involved railroads for 25 years. He succeeded in getting an injunction outlawing the strike in a federal court. When ARU head Eugene V. Debs refused to order his men back to work, President Grover Cleveland—over the opposition of Illinois governor Altgeld—sent in the army to restore train service. The strike was broken. Debs was convicted of "conspiracy in restraint of trade" and obstructing the mails, and was sent to prison after an unsuccessful appeal to the Supreme Court.

The crushing of the strike was a mortal blow to the American Railway Union, and it dissolved. Debs was converted from a moderate trade unionist to a socialist, and went on to become leader of the American socialist movement for the next quarter of a century. Perhaps the most important legacy of the affair was that in upholding Debs' conviction the Supreme Court substantially enlarged the power of judges to interfere with planned strikes, making the injunction a potent anti-union weapon until federal legislation gave labor new rights in the 1930s. Most members of the judiciary approached labor-management conflicts in the spirit of the federal judge who said:

> It is idle to talk of a peaceable strike. None such has ever occurred. All combinations to interfere with perfect freedom in the proper management and control of one's lawful business, to dictate the terms upon which such business shall be conducted by means of threats, are within the condemnation of the law.[2]

THE LABOR MOVEMENT IN COMPARATIVE PERSPECTIVE

The determined resistance of employers and the hostility of public authorities obviously did much to retard the growth of labor organization in late nineteenth century America. But these factors do not explain why the American labor movement was notably weaker than the labor movements in industrial countries like Britain, France, Germany, and Sweden. In those countries, business also fought unionization tooth and claw, and was backed by government. And why did the socialist ideas so strongly supported by European workers meet with so little receptivity in the United States? There was a socialist faction within the AFL in the early years, and in one year—1895—it won a temporary majority and unseated Gompers from the presidency. But Gompers was back in the saddle the next year, and was never again seriously challenged. After the turn of the century, the Socialist Party of America that Eugene Debs organized had some minor electoral successes, but it never developed a solid working-class base. Both the relative weakness of the labor movement and the failure of American socialism stemmed from circumstances that distinguished American workers from workers in other lands, and made them less likely to engage in collective struggle.

First, laborers in the United States were better off in a material sense than workers elsewhere. Although relatively few had unions to defend their interests in the late nineteenth century, real wages were considerably higher in the United States than anywhere else in the world. "Socialist utopias have been defeated by roast beef and apple pie," observed the German social scientist Werner Sombart in his book *Why Is There No Socialism in the United States?* (1906).

This is too simple an explanation, however, for American workers might have

---

[2]Judge Jenkin, *Farmer's Loan and Trust vs. Northern Pacific* (1894)

Annual Consumption of Selected Foods by German and American Workers' Families, circa 1900

	Germany	U.S.
Bread (kg.)	582	113
Potatoes (kg.)	647	376
Meat (kg.)	112	382
Butter (kg.)	20	53
Eggs	612	1,022
Sugar (kg.)	31	121

expected more than workers anywhere else, in which case the gap between reality and expectations would have just as great here as elsewhere. But that was not the case. The unusually rapid pace of American industrialization spurred an exceptionally heavy volume of migration to the cities by both European immigrants and rural-born natives. This set in motion a cycle of migration and social mobility that dampened discontent. At any point in the late nineteenth century, the lowest paid jobs in the industrial sector were held by recent newcomers. And they were earning much more than they had been in the Old World or in the American countryside.

In time, of course, expectations did rise, and the tendency to judge by past standards diminished; however, as that happened, growing numbers found their way into more demanding and even better paid jobs, leaving openings at the bottom for the next wave of newcomers. Among immigrants working in a Pittsburgh steel plant at the turn of the century, for example, 85 percent of those with less than two years' service were unskilled, 15 percent were semiskilled, and not one was skilled. By contrast, among those with more than ten years' experience, almost a fifth (18 percent) were skilled, and another two-fifths (39 percent) were semiskilled. This special pattern of migration and social mobility dampened working-class dissatisfaction and led many workers to seek advancement through individual effort rather than collective action. The individualism of the American worker that foreign travelers often noted was naturally fostered in such an environment.

Other features of American society and American tradition also served to impede the growth of labor organization and class resentments. The political tradition associated with Jefferson, Jackson, and Lincoln was highly individualistic. And since universal suffrage (at least for white males) had been established in the United States well before it existed elsewhere, labor organizers could not, as they could in Europe, exploit grievances based on the denial of workers' political rights.

American society also had the distinction of being what Alexis de Tocqueville called "a democracy of manners." There was no hereditary aristocracy, and class differences in speech, manners, clothing and the like were much less marked than in Europe. American workers felt less constrained to "know their place" than their

European counterparts did; as a result, they were less inclined to blame the
capitalist system for their problems and more inclined to blame themselves. The
development of a universal, compulsory, tax-supported public school system,
again well in advance of Europe, reinforced the "democracy of manners." Scholars
are only now beginning to look critically at how public schools actually operated in
the American past; their preliminary findings invite skepticism about whether they
exerted the profound leveling and equalizing influence that folklore has attributed
to them. There is little doubt, however, that America's public schools propagated
the gospel of individual self-advancement with considerable success. They may
not have done a great deal to open up better career opportunities to youths from
working-class homes—the verdict on that question is not yet in. But they surely did
promote the *belief* that opportunity was available to the enterprising.

Ethnic Fragmentation

Another characteristic of American society that diminished the likelihood of its
wage-earners uniting against an oppressive class of employers was the extraordinary ethnic diversity of the population. The cleavage between labor and capital
was often obscured by the cleavages between different races and nationalities. The
problem was not unique to America. Ethnic hostilities between English and Irish
wage-earners, for example, impeded the growth of the British labor movement. But
no other industrial society depended so heavily on an immigrant labor force. A
study of the country's leading 20 industries shortly after the turn of the century
found that 58 percent of their employees had been born abroad, and another large
fraction were the offspring of immigrants. No other society drew newcomers from
such a wide range of lands. In the copper mines of Arizona, for example, a visitor
found workers of 26 different nationalities. Old World hatreds with deep historic
roots, differences in color, language, religion and cultural preferences, and the
tendency of employers to utilize the most recently arrived immigrants and non-

whites as strikebreakers all fragmented the working class into dozens of mutually suspicious, frequently warring, ethnic groups. Mutual benefit societies, social clubs, and churches organized along ethnic lines led immigrants and their children to identify first as Lithuanians, Poles, or Serbs, then as workers.

The presence of so many immigrants was not always a deterrent to labor organization, of course. Newcomers like Samuel Gompers, with trade union experience in the old country, in fact figured prominently in the building of the American labor movement. English, Scottish, Welsh, and Irish immigrants were prominent among labor's leaders. And when one ethnic group dominated a particular trade or industry—the Welsh in mining, the Germans in brewing, the Jews in garment making—the task of organizing was facilitated, because ethnic loyalties reinforced worker solidarity rather than undermining it. But that was the exception, not the rule.

SUGGESTED READINGS

The relevant chapters of Henry Pelling, *American Labor* (1960), Joseph G. Rayback, *A History of American Labor* (1966), and Melvin Dubofsky, *Industrialism and the American Worker, 1865–1920* (1975) provide good brief introductions. See also Milton Meltzer, *Bread and Roses: The Struggle of American Labor, 1865–1915* (1967) and Irwin Yellowitz, *Industrialization and the American Labor Movement* (1977). Stanley Lebergott, *Manpower in Economic Growth: The United States Record Since 1800* (1964) assesses living standards and unemployment. Changes in the character of work and workers' responses to them are analyzed in Herbert G. Gutman, *Work, Culture, and Society in Industrializing America* (1976), Daniel T. Rodgers, *The Work Ethic in Industrial America* (1978), David Montgomery, *Worker's Control in America* (1979), and David Montgomery, *Beyond Equality: Labor and the Radical Republicans, 1862–1872* (1967), David Brody, *Steelworkers in America: The Nonunion Era* (1960) and Robert Ozanne, *A Century of Labor-Management Relations at McCormick and International Harvester* (1967), Rowland T. Berthoff, *British Immigrants in Industrial America, 1790–1950* (1953), and Charlotte Erickson, *American Industry and the European Immigrant, 1860–1885* (1957).

On the clash between the Knights of Labor and the AFL see Gerald N. Grob, *Workers and Utopia: A Study of Ideological Conflict in the American Labor Movement, 1865–1900* (1961). Selig Perlman, *A Theory of the Labor Movement* (1928), is still stimulating. Harold C. Livesay, *Samuel Gompers and Organized Labor in America* (1978) is a good brief biography. See also Stuart Bruce Kaufman, *Samuel Gompers and the Origins of the American Federation of Labor* (1973). Terence V. Powderly, *The Path I Trod* (1940) and *Thirty Years of Labor* (1889) and Samuel Gompers, *Seventy Years of Life and Labor*, 2 vols. (1925) tell the story from the vantage point of the two major participants.

David Brody's essay on labor in Stephan Thernstrom, ed., *Harvard Encyclopedia of American Ethnic Groups* (1980) is penetrating. Victor Greene, *The Slavic Community on Strike: Immigrant Labor in Pennsylvania Anthracite* (1968) and Leon J. Wolff, *Lockout:*

The Story of the Homestead Strike of 1892 (1965) describe industrial conflict. John Jay's novel, *The Breadwinners* (1883) reveals the hysterical fears of "labor agitators" in middle-class circles. On the failure of socialists to attract mass support, see the variety of views presented in John H.M. Laslett and Seymour Martin Lipset, eds., *Failure of a Dream? Essays in the History of American Socialism* (1974). J.H.M. Laslett, *Labor and the Left: A Study of Socialist and Radical Influences in the American Labor Movement* (1970) and William M. Dick, *Labor and Socialism in America: The Gompers Era* (1972) are also illuminating.

Chapter Twenty-one

Politics and Diplomacy
in the Gilded Age

*L*ate nineteenth century American politics will disappoint anyone searching for statesmen of the stature of Jefferson, Jackson, or Lincoln. Ulysses S.
Grant was a great general, but a disastrously inept president. Thinking about
the course of American politics from President George Washington to President Grant, Henry Adams later remarked, was what first made him doubt the
truth of the Darwinian theory of evolution. The general's successors were not very
much better. Some were less mediocre than others, but none achieved anything
memorable. The student who has difficulty remembering the sequence of presidential administrations from the end of Reconstruction to the Depression of
1893 needn't worry too much. Chester A. Arthur and the rest really aren't very
important.

This is not to say, however, that there were no interesting and important
political developments in those years—only that the men who occupied the White
House did very little in office. Certainly the American people did not find the
political life of their era dull and irrelevant. In the typical election of the period,
almost 80 percent of adult males cast a ballot. If we exclude the South—where
efforts to disenfranchise blacks and poor whites were underway—the figure was 85
percent, notably higher than in any national election in recent decades. Popular
interest in politics was much greater than in our own time, as was attachment to
political parties. There were few independents who voted for "the best man"
regardless of party. Being a Democrat or a Republican was a much more important
component of personal identity than it is for most of us today. Consequently, it
took a political earthquake to shake large numbers of voters loose from their

William Jennings Bryan's declamatory style of oratory became obsolete with the passing of the Gilded Age of American politics.

traditional party allegiances and move them into the camp of what they had long regarded as the "enemy." After a long period of equilibrium and political stalemate in the 1870s and 1880s, such a political earthquake did take place. In the 1890s, the flaring up of the Populist movement, the capture of the Democratic Party by agrarian "free silver" forces, and the McKinley versus Bryan campaign in 1896 marked a fundamental turning point in American political history.

ERA OF EQUILIBRIUM: THE 1870s AND 1880s

America, it is commonly said, has a two-party political system. For most of our history we have really had something more like a one-and-a-half-party system. Normally, one party is ascendant over a long span of elections, while the other struggles to survive with a minority constituency, biding its time until a major crisis of some kind tilts the balance in its direction. From the Great Depression and the New Deal until recently, the Democrats have been the majority party. In the first three decades of the century, by contrast, the United States was a predominantly Republican country, and the Democrats were the "half" party with little prospect of winning power at the national level.

The 1870s and 1880s were a rare exception to this general rule. (The period of close Whig–Democratic rivalry from 1840 to 1854 is another.) The Democrats and Republicans had almost exactly equal strength. Never before or since have elections been as closely or as sharply contested. Three of the five presidential contests between 1876 and 1892 were won by the Republicans, but in two of them (1876 and 1888) the Republican candidate polled fewer popular votes than his Democratic opponent, and won only because of the peculiarities of the electoral college system. In the presidential races of 1880, 1884, and 1888, the Republican and Democratic shares of the popular vote did not fluctuate by even one percent, and in each election the margin between the two parties was under one percent as well.

The inability of either party to win the support of a solid and enduring majority of the electorate also extended to Congress. In only four of the ten Congressional elections held between 1874 and 1892 did one party manage to capture both the Senate and the House of Representatives at the same time. In no other period of American history has Congress been so often divided.

Political contests at the state level were equally close in these years. The Republicans won 49.5 percent of the races for governor between 1874 and 1892, the Democrats 48.9 percent, and third-party candidates 1.6 percent. It is hard to imagine a more perfect equilibrium of opposed political forces. As Lord James Bryce, a distinguished English observer of the American scene, said, it was almost as if "some queer mechanical balance holds the two parties even."

A Corrupt Issueless Politics?

Although Bryce's *The American Commonwealth* (1888) contains enduring insights, the author approached American public life holding his nose, and later historians

TABLE 21-1
Party Division of the Popular Vote for President, 1876-92

	Democratic	Republican	Other†
1876	51.0	48.0*	1.0
1880	48.1	48.5	3.4
1884	48.5	48.2	3.3
1888	48.6	47.9*	3.5
1892	46.1	43.0	10.7

*In these cases, the Republican won a majority of the electoral vote despite running behind in the popular vote total.

†Greenback in 1876, Greenback Labor in 1880, Greenback Labor and Prohibition in 1884, Prohibition and Union Labor in 1888, Prohibition and People's Party in 1892.

have too often done the same. Bryce saw monumental political corruption and little else. There were no significant differences between the parties, in his view. Neither had "any principles, any distinctive tenets. All has been lost, except office or the hope of it." Politics was a business and nothing more; it offered soft patronage jobs to thousands of party workers, and ample opportunities for enrichment for leaders with no scruples. This is the image of the era evoked by the familiar textbook label, the Gilded Age, first used by Mark Twain as the title of a satirical novel about business and political corruption. In a typical scene, the central figure, an amiable bandit, uses his connections to secure a Congressional appropriation of $200,000 for a fraudulent project. When the funds fail to arrive, he asks his agent in Washington for an explanation, and is presented with an itemized list of the bribes he allegedly paid out: $10,000 to $20,000 for a long string of senators and representatives, with "a high moral Congressman—the high moral ones cost more" getting $30,000. The whole appropriation went to pay the expenses incurred to obtain it.

Twain, of course, exercised some artistic license here, but corruption was widespread in American politics during the Gilded Age. Certainly "office or the hope of it" was a crucial incentive for many. Government was becoming an increasingly important source of jobs, because the growing complexity of economic and social life required a more elaborate apparatus of coordination and control. Fewer than 40,000 civilians worked for the federal government on the eve of the Civil War; some 240,000 did so in 1900. The number of federal employees had increased three times as fast as the population. Similar figures on state and local government payrolls are not available, unfortunately, but their expansion was probably even greater. As early as the 1870s, according to one estimate, 140,000 residents of New York City—one out of every 8 voters—were employees of the city, the state, or the federal government. These jobs were handed out through the "spoils system"—the principle that "to the victor go the spoils of office." Party loyalty rather than ability was the chief criterion employed in making appointments.

Reformers deplored this system and crusaded for the introduction of competitive examinations in which candidates could prove their ability. Once appointed on the basis of merit, they proposed, public officials should be protected against dismissal on political grounds. Civil service was the pet cause of the educated, prosperous, and genteel men who bolted from the Republican party in 1872 in protest against the corruption of the Grant administration. Professional politicians called them "mugwumps," and jeered at them for advocating "snivel service." The Mugwumps were determined, however, and met with some success. In 1883 Congress passed a civil service act covering a sizable number of federal jobs, and later measures extended its scope. Several state governments followed suit. But the legislation set only minimal standards that proved easy for the party faithful to meet, and they continued to enjoy an inside track when their party held the reins of government.

Party leaders reaped still greater rewards, of course, through the bribes and kickbacks they received from businesses seeking contracts, franchises, licenses, or subsidies. Some boasted of their skill in obtaining "honest graft" (see box). Political influence could be and was turned to financial advantage, with profits ranging from the tens of millions that went to the railroads down to the hundreds or thousands gained by the printers authorized to print the ballots for a municipal election. Both the Republican and Democratic parties were gigantic, cumbersome machines with an immense number of moving parts. They would have ground to a halt without the lubrication provided by the large amounts of cash that flowed through them.

Corruption was indeed rife in the Gilded Age. It does not follow, however, that "neither party" had "any principles." Although many party leaders and some followers proved quite willing to compromise principles for profit, there was nonetheless a distinctive Republican ideology and a quite different Democratic

A REPUBLICAN ORATOR WAVES THE BLOODY FLAG, 1876

Every State that seceded from the United States was a Democratic State. Every ordinance of secession that was drawn was drawn by a Democrat. Every man that endeavored to tear the old flag from the heaven that it enriches was a Democrat. Every man that tried to destroy this nation was a Democrat. Every enemy this great Republic has had for twenty years has been a Democrat. Every man that shot Union soldiers was a Democrat. Every man that loved slavery better than liberty was a Democrat. The man that assassinated Abraham Lincoln was a Democrat. Every man that sympathized with the assassin—every man glad that the noblest President ever elected was assassinated, was a Democrat. Every man that wanted the privilege of whipping another man to make him work for him for nothing and pay him with lashes on his naked back, was a Democrat. Every man that raised bloodhounds to pursue human beings was a Democrat. Every man that clutched from shrieking, shuddering, crouching mothers, babes from their breasts, and sold them into slavery, was a Democrat.

—Robert G. Ingersoll, *"Speech at Indianapolis"*

ideology. These ideologies shaped the perceptions and values of party loyalists. As a result, the two parties took different stances on public policy issues, and found their constituencies among different elements of the population.

The Republicans

The Republican Party identified itself above all with the cause of national unity. It was the party of the Union, the party of Lincoln. By waving the bloody flag, Republican orators sought to keep alive the passions that had been generated by the Civil War, and to induce men to "vote the way they had shot." The effectiveness of this appeal was bound to diminish in time, as the generation that fought the war began to die off. But that process was relatively slow. For example, returning home safely from combat in 1865, future Supreme Court justice Oliver Wendell Holmes, Jr. had a life expectancy of 36 years, and therefore a better than even chance of voting in the election of 1900. (In fact, he lived until 1935.) Furthermore, the family exerts a powerful influence on basic political attitudes (among other things) and party allegiances show a good deal of continuity from generation to generation. Images of the heroic war for the Union and of the martyred Lincoln could be deeply stirring, even to people too young to have experienced that time of crisis directly. Not surprisingly, then, the Republicans were especially strong in those areas of the country and among those elements of the population that had embraced the Union cause most enthusiastically during the war. And they were weak where passivity or opposition to the Union had been the dominant sentiment. Obviously Republicanism was stronger in the North than in the South, but it was also stronger in Northern Indiana than in Southern Indiana, stronger in counties with a free soil tradition than in those without it, stronger where there were large concentrations of black voters. The major veterans' organization, the Grand Army of the Republic, which had over 400,000 members in 1890, was virtually an arm of the Republican Party.

A second distinguishing trait of the Republican Party was its unmixed enthusiasm for economic growth, and for the use of federal power to stimulate growth. The party consistently sought to give a helping hand to business, and argued that the economic growth that would result would be of benefit to all Americans, whether businessmen, workers, or farmers. Republicans believed that the best way to aid American industry would be a higher tariff to protect it from foreign competition. The orthodox economic theory taught in most American colleges then celebrated the virtues of free trade, and insisted that tariffs on imports were in effect a tax paid by domestic consumers to producers in the form of higher prices than would prevail in a competitive international market. Republicans denied this, and asserted that the only competition checked by tariff barriers was "unfair" competition from industrialists in other countries who paid their workers starvation wages. Cutting tariffs might temporarily benefit consumers by driving down prices, but it would also lower profits and wages. Factories would be forced to shut down, unemployment would soar, and the blighting effects of depression in the industrial sector would soon spread throughout the entire economy. A Republican orator declared free trade "makes cheap labor; cheap labor is degraded labor; degraded labor makes tramps; tramps make criminals; criminals make Democrats."

Republicans also advocated that government encourage economic growth in other ways, to appeal to other interests in other spheres of the economy. They were eager to promote the development of a more extensive and efficient national transportation network. Accordingly, Republican Congresses granted immense tracts of Western land to the railroads during and just after the Civil War. Republicans were also responsible for a dramatic rise in federal expenditures to improve the nation's rivers and harbors. Congressional appropriations for these purposes averaged about a third of a million dollars per year in the 1850s; they exceeded $3,000,000 annually in the late 1860s, and $16,000,000 by the 1890s.

Especially attracted by the Republican commitment to improve transportation were farmers who needed to ship bulky commodities to distant markets. In addition, the Republican program included other measures beneficial to agriculture. The Homestead Act of 1862 (see pages 441–43) had been the fruit of Republican efforts, and for all of its deficiencies it was a great boon to farmers.

A closely related Republican measure passed that same year was also aimed at agrarian constituencies, but it rested on a principle that Republicans would soon attempt to extend further. The Morrill Act created the land-grant college system by offering generous federal subsidies to states that established colleges and universities offering instruction in agriculture, engineering, and military science. Education, Republicans believed, was an instrument that made for both economic progress and social betterment. It increased skills and opened up opportunities for self-advancement—therefore, the federal government had a duty to support it. The next step, proposed repeatedly by Republicans in the 1870s and 1880s but always defeated, was a general program of federal aid to elementary and secondary education. This program was designed to close the enormous gap in educational opportunities between children in prosperous Massachusetts and children in poverty-stricken Mississippi. Almost a century later, the idea of a truly national educational system was still considered radical and visionary in the United States, a dangerous infringement on "states' rights." The party's commitment to it in the late nineteenth century was an especially striking indicator of the strength of Republican nationalism, activism, and reformist zeal.

The reformist zeal of the Republicans was also manifest in the stance they took toward a series of cultural or lifestyle issues that divided American communities along ethnic and religious lines in the post-Civil War years. Like their Whig predecessors, Republicans generally lined up on the side of piety, purity, and cultural uniformity. They were more likely than Democrats, for example, to believe that drinking was sinful, and to favor laws regulating or even banning the sale of "the Demon rum." They were determined, too, that the Sabbath be observed according to their own strict standards, favoring "blue laws" prohibiting drinking, public recreation, or even ordinary shopping on Sunday. Another menace to American society, in the Republican view, was the effort made by Catholics and various immigrant groups to preserve their separate traditions by instructing their children in parochial rather than public schools, especially when the teaching was done in a language other than English. Most Republicans fiercely opposed proposals for public support of parochial education, and many believed that such schools should be outlawed altogether. Parochial schools perpetuated and accentuated cultural differences, they charged, and prevented assimilation to mainstream American culture.

These moral stands gave the Republicans a distinctive ethnic and religious constituency. They had a much stronger following among natives than immigrants, and far more support from Protestants than Catholics. Among Protestants they had particular appeal for members of sects marked by crusading evangelical zeal, and much less for communicants of churches that placed greater emphasis on formal ritual.[1] Although immigrants on the whole leaned more to the Democrats, there were important exceptions. The pietistic and temperance-minded Swedes and Norwegians were strongly Republican. German Catholics were overwhelmingly Democratic, whereas their Protestant fellow countrymen leaned the other way, German pietists particularly so. The outlines of the complex American ethnic and religious mosaic showed up clearly in the election returns.

---

[1]The South was the great exception to these generalizations about the political leanings of different groups. There, memories of the war and Reconstruction alienated most white voters from the Republican cause whatever their religious commitments.

TABLE 21–2
Ethnic Voting Patterns,
DeKalb County, Illinois, 1876

	Percent Republican
Native American	68
Immigrant	47
German Lutheran	57
German Catholic	0
Swedish	85
Norwegian	76
Irish Catholic	4

The Democrats

The Democratic Party took a quite different position on all of the preceding issues. The question of national unity and of the meaning of the Civil War, so central to the Republican appeal, was too delicate for there to be a single, unified Democratic position throughout the nation. In the eleven ex-Confederate states, the party denounced the war and its centralizing tendencies, and waved the bloody shirt as vigorously as Republicans did in the North. It had been the election of a Republican President, Democrats could argue, that provoked the South to secede; Republican denial of the right to secede that necessitated war; the armies of a Republican administration that conquered and devastated the South; Republicans who attempted to force the radical reconstruction of the southern social order. The reconstructed regimes had all been Republican, and it was hardly surprising that the "redeemers" who had returned to power everywhere in the South by 1877 were Democrats. Nor is it surprising that Republican presidential candidates failed to carry a single ex-Confederate state for decades after the war.

Revulsion against the Civil War and reverence for Jefferson Davis and Robert E. Lee, however, did not provide an adequate foundation on which to regain national political ascendancy. Southerners were a shrinking minority of the American population; other regions of the country were growing more rapidly. Outside the South, Democrats found the war issue an embarrassment, for most people had supported the Union, however grudgingly. The Democratic Party itself had split into northern and southern wings over the issues that had led to disunion; it could not reestablish itself in the North by taking a position repugnant to the vast majority of northern voters. It would have been suicidal to run against the memory of Lincoln.

However, once the passions generated by the war had begun to subside, and enthusiasm for the reconstruction experiment began to wane in the North, the Democrats devised a formula that had substantial appeal. Whereas the Confederates had carried the doctrine of states' rights to dangerous extremes, Northern Democrats argued, Republican radicals had erred in the opposite direction during Reconstruction, attempting to lodge unprecedented power in the central government at the expense of both states' rights and individual liberty. Here the Democrats tapped a popular suspicion of central authority and a faith in individualism that was deeply rooted in the American past.

Another powerful sentiment—racism—was successfully played up by the Democrats as well. Not only Reconstruction in the South but a variety of Republican proposals to extend basic rights to blacks in the North in the post-war years challenged the fundamental assumption of white supremacy. Although many Republicans in the late nineteenth century were far from being militant advocates of equality for blacks, it was only the Democratic Party that *boasted* that it was the white man's party. That slogan won votes in the South, obviously, but not only there. Northern workers who feared competition from low-cost black labor, for example, were often swayed by it.

Government assistance to business, in the Democratic view, was almost as reprehensible as assistance to blacks. Economic growth was, of course, desirable, but it was best achieved through unrestrained free competition. Government should not meddle in the workings of the marketplace, because it could never be truly impartial. Tariffs and subsidies benefited only "the special interests," and fostered the growth of a privileged class. To Democrats, the disappearance of small firms and the emergence of powerful national corporations in many sectors of the economy looked like the "unnatural" result of favoritism shown by Republicans to big business in the past. Democrats tended to be less complacent than Republicans about the problems created by industrialization, and more sympathetic to the unfortunate. In 1888, for example, Democratic President Grover Cleveland warned that "the gulf between employers and the employed is constantly widening, and classes are rapidly forming, one comprising the very rich and powerful, while in another are found the toiling poor." But Cleveland and other Democrats had few remedies to offer other than Jacksonian simplicities: Cut the tariff, pare the federal budget, provide no government aid to business, and somehow "the gulf between employers and the employed" would disappear.[2]

The Democrats in the late nineteenth century took a laissez faire stance not only toward economic policy but to cultural reform. The Republicans were crusaders, determined to shape up the unregenerate, and were willing to use the law to do so—to compel school attendance until children had reached a certain age, "proper" behavior on the Sabbath, abstinence from alcohol. They valued community righteousness, in a sense, above personal liberty. Democrats, the heirs of Jacksonian individualism, tended to be hostile to such coercive measures, and drew much of their support from the groups that the Republicans were trying to reform.

---

[2]Although the *parties* took clearly opposing stands on such issues as the tariff, other influences affected how any particular Congressman would vote. In a state like Pennsylvania, where high tariffs were extremely popular, Democratic candidates often deviated from the party stand. So did Republicans running in farming areas where the tariff was unpopular. And there was a lot of log-rolling behind the scenes in Congress, in accord with the "you scratch my back and I'll scratch yours" principle.

These were the principles and programs that divided the two parties in the 1870s and 1880s. They divided Americans into two camps of almost precisely equal size, and the result was a stalemate that precluded any dramatic changes of public policy. New measures that offended even a tiny minority of one party's normal supporters might be sufficient to tilt the balance to the opposition. In the 1888 election, a shift of 6,500 votes from the Republican to the Democratic column in the State of New York would have made Democrat Grover Cleveland, rather than Republican Benjamin Harrison, President.

The most important Republican legislative achievements—the establishment of a high protective tariff, the railroad land grants, the Homestead and land grant college acts, the creation of a national banking system—all came either during the war or in the early Reconstruction years, before Southern Democrats were a factor to be reckoned with in Congress. After that, the evenness of the party balance produced a legislative deadlock.

When public concern over the power of the railroads and the threat of monopoly reached a level that forced some legislative response, the Republicans and Democrats collaborated to devise bills that were so bland and vague as to be without practical force. The Interstate Commerce Act of 1887 sought to make railroad rates "reasonable and just," but provided no adequate mechanism of enforcement. The Sherman Antitrust Act of 1890, another measure backed by both parties, likewise promised much and delivered little. It passed the Senate by a vote of 52 to 1; voting for it was like voting for motherhood—and just about as effective. The Sherman Act banned monopolies and other combinations "in restraint of trade," but supplied no specific standards for determining what "restraint of trade" actually was. It was a gesture that appeased public nostalgia for the rapidly vanishing world of free competition between small entrepreneurs, yet did not seriously interfere with the growing concentration of production in giant corporate units.

Even if the Sherman Act had been given some teeth, it is doubtful that it would have mattered much, for the U.S. Supreme Court in 1895 reached the extraordinary conclusion that the act did not apply to manufacturing firms. The Court's decision was one sign of a vital new trend—the increasing assertiveness of the judiciary in defending property interests against legislative attack. In the immediate post-Civil War years, federal and state courts were tolerant of efforts to regulate business in the public interest. For example, *Munn vs. Illinois* (1877) upheld the right of a state to fix rates for railroads operating within its borders. In the 1880s, the courts became more solicitous about invasions of "the liberty of contract" of corporations, and developed a series of legal tools to void government regulation of business. Corporations were held to be "persons" protected by the Fourteenth Amendment; their right to "due process of law" was stretched to mean their freedom from almost all legislation that could be construed as threatening property interests. Most of the legislation voided was by states, but the Court scrutinized Congress with increasing care as well. Before 1864, only two acts of Congress had ever been declared unconstitutional; in the last quarter of the nineteenth century 11 were. The judiciary had become a vital bulwark of the status quo.

ERA OF INSTABILITY: THE DEMOCRATIC AND POPULIST SURGES

Political equilibrium prevailed from the end of Reconstruction until 1890. When the balance began to tilt, it tilted first toward the Democrats. The Congressional elections in the fall of 1890 yielded a smashing defeat for the Republicans, whose strength in the House of Representatives fell from 51 to 27 percent. It was the most dramatic political reversal suffered by any party since the Democrats' disastrous loss following the Kansas–Nebraska Act of 1854. The trend continued through 1892, when the Democrats won control of the Senate for the first time in 14 years, and Grover Cleveland defeated incumbent President Benjamin Harrison by more than a third of a million votes, the largest margin in 20 years. For the first time since 1856, the Democrats controlled both Congress and the White House.

This sudden alteration in the political mood of the country stemmed from three developments. First, just before the 1890 elections, the Republicans had managed to pass the McKinley Tariff, which raised the average level of import duties from 38 to 50 percent, the highest tariff America had ever seen. Such a major shift in policy in a very delicately balanced political situation can be dangerous, and so it proved to be.

A second source of the waning political fortunes of the Republicans was that in the late 1880s the party became unusually aggressive in pressing the cause of moral reform. It sponsored new prohibitionist measures in several states, and sought new means of forcing the "Americanization" of immigrant children. In 1889, for example, Republican legislatures in Illinois and Wisconsin passed laws making English the primary language of instruction in all private and public schools. In state after state, good Lincoln men or good high-tariff men found these assaults on their drinking habits and educational preferences intolerable. Swarms of them defected. America was not yet ready for the reign of purity. If Republicans continued to indulge in a politics of piety over such divisive cultural issues, they were in danger of becoming the party of the virtuous minority.

Rise of Populism

The third factor tipping the political balance was an immense surge of agrarian discontent. Although the industrial sector of economy was prosperous, the farmers of the Great Plains and the South were experiencing serious difficulties, and naturally blamed the party in power. (See Chapter 19 for an analysis of the real causes at work.) Threatened with bankruptcy due to falling crop prices, they began to form organizations called "farmers' unions," "wheels," or "alliances" in the 1880s. By 1890 there were two great national farmer organizations, the Southern Alliance and the Northwestern Alliance, with a total membership of close to two million. At first the alliances focused their energies on the creation of farmers' cooperatives—consumer cooperatives to purchase necessities for their members at bargain prices and producer cooperatives to market their crops without paying a middleman. But when the vast majority of the cooperatives quickly failed from lack of capital and managerial experience, the alliances turned to political action. In the South, fearful that running third party candidates would split the white vote and allow blacks to regain the power they lost with the collapse of Reconstruction, they sought to capture the Democratic Party. They were strikingly successful in the 1890 elections, winning control of eight state legislatures and electing four dozen Congressmen. In the Northwest and Great Plains states, where there was no racial issue to complicate matters, various independent or "people's" parties were organized, and they too made heady gains in 1890. By 1892 southern apprehensions of third parties had been overcome, and the alliances joined forces to create a national People's or Populist party. Its candidate for the Presidency that year, General James B. Weaver, won over a million popular votes, 8.4 percent of the total. It was a strikingly good showing for a brand new party.

Populism was a great folk movement. Populist orators—like Mary Elizabeth Lease of Kansas, who urged her listeners to "raise less corn and more hell"—had the missionary zeal of revivalist ministers. They saw the world in simple and lurid terms: A "conspiracy against mankind," organized by eastern financial and industrial interests, threatened the survival of American democracy. Continued business dominance of the government would mean "oppression, injustice, and poverty" for the common people. That was the message of the principal statement of Populist ideology, the Omaha Platform of 1892.

Although the organizers of the new People's Party were mostly farmers, they devised a platform with a broad-gauged social reform program designed to appeal to other groups. The people were to be given a greater voice in government, empowered to introduce legislation directly through the initiative and to pass on controversial measures by popular referendum. U.S. Senators were to be elected by the people rather than by state legislatures. To attract labor, the Populists called for a graduated income tax, immigration restriction, an eight-hour day on government projects, and limitations on strikebreaking agencies like the Pinkertons. As a long-range goal, they declared that "poverty should eventually cease in the land," thereby becoming the first significant American party to propose that eliminating want was a proper concern of the federal government.

At the core of the Populist program were various measures to benefit farmers. The railroads that carried their crops would no longer be free to charge what the market would bear; they were to be taken over and operated by the government. The mounting burden of farm debt was to be eased through a system of federal warehouses ("subtreasuries" they were called), which would provide one percent loans up to a year on the value of crops stored there. Finally, they demanded inflation through "free silver."

The silver issue, which became the central issue of American politics within a few years, was complex. But its essentials may be stated briefly. The level of prices in the United States had been steadily dropping since the Civil War, because production had been soaring and the money supply had grown much less. An economy that offers more goods without more money inevitably has declining prices. General deflation is not a problem for farmers more than for other groups; it reduces crop prices by no more than the prices of goods farmers buy. But in this era, wheat, corn, and cotton prices did in fact decline more than other prices, for quite different reasons (see Chapter 19). Most farmers failed to grasp the true causes at work, and placed the blame on a political decision taken in 1873—a law that "demonetized" silver, putting an end to the coining of silver dollars. In Populist folklore this came to be known as "the crime of '73," the conspiratorial work of wicked financiers. The decision was actually a simple recognition of the reality at the time. Silver prices were then so high that producers were not bringing it into the mint to be coined. The amount of silver in a silver dollar was worth $1.03 in the open market. A boom in silver production shortly after drove prices down, but no one had a crystal ball available to foresee that. When the changed circumstances became apparent, silver advocates in Congress won a small concession in the form of the Bland–Allison Act of 1878, which authorized the coinage of a fixed and modest amount of silver each year. A larger concession to the inflationary camp came in 1890, when the Sherman Silver Purchase Act substantially increased the federal commitment to silver; but even that could not satisfy farmers who were experiencing hard times and looking for a scapegoat. Nothing short of the "free and unlimited" coinage of silver, the Populists felt, would make up for "the crime of '73."

DEPRESSION AND DECISIVE POLITICAL REALIGNMENT, 1893–96

In 1893, a financial panic sent the economy sliding into the deepest depression of the nineteenth century. Its most obvious and immediate effect was to stimulate social unrest and political protest. Its deeper and more enduring consequence was that it ushered in a new era of American politics, an era of Republican ascendancy that lasted for a generation.

The depression had devastating effects on farmers and workers. Farm prices dropped to new lows; mortgage foreclosures on farm property reached new highs. Sharp wage cuts and mass layoffs took place in every industry. Unions that attempted to resist were defeated, and often wiped out altogether, as happened in both the Pullman and Homstead strikes of 1894 (see Chapter 20). That same year, a march on Washington, D.C. by "Coxey's Army"—a band of unemployed men led by Jacob S. Coxey—fizzled. The marchers were arrested for walking on the grass outside the Capitol, and Congress paid no heed to Coxey's demand for a federal public works program to alleviate mass unemployment.

The distress of the farmers and workers who were hardest hit by the collapse was acute. The question was whether the two groups could formulate a common program that would allow them to follow the same political banner. The Populists made strenuous efforts to enlist labor support. They stressed the various pro-labor planks in the Omaha Platform, and denounced Cleveland's decision to send in federal troops to break the Pullman strike. In Wisconsin, the State Federation of Labor endorsed the Populists, and a convention of the People's Party in turn adopted the AFL program.

The effort to forge a farm–labor coalition failed, however. Gompers and other labor leaders argued that farmers were capitalists, not wage-earners, and feared that the inflation of farm prices they sought would hurt workers already living close to the margin. Many Populists regarded the city and its largely immigrant

SAMUEL GOMPERS ON THE OBSTACLES
IN THE WAY OF A POPULIST-LABOR COALITION

To support the People's Party under the belief that it is a *labor* party is to act under misapprehension. It is not and cannot, in the nature of its make-up, be a labor party, or even one in which the wage-workers will find their haven. Composed, as the People's Party is, mainly of *employing* farmers without any regard to the interests of the *employed* farmers of the country districts or the mechanics and laborers of the industrial centres, there must of necessity be a divergence of purposes, methods, and interests.

In speaking thus frankly of the composition of the People's Party there is no desire to belittle the efforts of its members, or even to withhold sympathy due them in their agitation to remedy the wrongs which they suffer from corporate power and avarice; on the contrary, the fullest measure of sympathy and all possible encouragement should and will be given them; for they are doing excellent work in directing public attention to the dangers which threaten the body politic of the republic. But, returning to the consideration of the entire cooperation or amalgamation of the wage-workers' organizations with the People's Party, I am persuaded that all who are more than superficial observers, or who are keen students of the past struggles of the proletariat of all countries, will with one accord unite in declaring the union impossible, because it is unnatural. Let me add that, before there can be any hope of the unification of labor's forces of the field, farm, factory, and workshop, the people who work on and in them for wages must be organized to protect their interests against those who pay them wages for that work.

—*North American Review,* July, 1892

work force as an alien and evil presence. As a result, the People's Party began to back away from issues of primary concern to workingmen, focused their attention on the single issue American farmers cared about most, and exploited that issue to capture the Democratic Party. The issue was free silver. A Democrat, Grover Cleveland, was in the White House when the crash came. Like most Easterners in the party, Cleveland was a "Gold Democrat." He was convinced that even the moderate commitment to silver coinage made in the Sherman Silver Purchase Act of 1890 was dangerous. It had caused the panic of 1893, in his view, by raising doubts about the soundness of the country's money in the minds of investors; worse, it might soon drive the United States into bankruptcy. The market value of silver had fallen below the value of the gold for which it could be exchanged at the U.S. Treasury. Wealthy investors were therefore turning in silver for gold in large quantities, and the federal government's gold reserves were rapidly disappearing.

Using all of his political muscle and skill, and pulling every patronage lever, Cleveland succeeded in getting Congress to repeal the Silver Purchase Act late in 1893, thereby putting America solely on the gold standard.

The repeal of the Silver Purchase Act opened up a great fissure in the Democratic Party, alienating Congressmen from the Great Plains and Southern farming states and from the silver producing states of the Far West. Their disaffection grew more acute as the depression continued and deepened. If Cleveland was right in his claim that the silver purchase policy had caused the depression, reversing that policy should have prompted quick recovery. Nothing of the sort happened. Prices and wages continued to drop, and unemployment continued to rise. Bewildered and angry Americans became increasingly receptive to the argument that free silver was necessary for economic recovery. Populist tracts like W.H. Harvey's best-selling *Coin's Financial School* (1894) portrayed silver as the panacea for every ill that beset American society, and many found them convincing.

At the 1896 Democratic convention, the "Gold Democrats" were outnumbered by silver men from the West and South. Cleveland was unable to win renomination, the first time in American history an incumbent President was rebuffed by his own party. The nomination went to a dynamic young Congressman from Nebraska, William Jennings Bryan. Shortly after, Bryan was also endorsed by the Populists, and the Democratic and People's parties fused into one. Some of the more radical Populists were dismayed by Bryan's exclusive focus on the silver issue and lack of interest in other elements of the Populist program, but the majority were willing to drop those demands for the prospect of having a "Free Silver" President.

In the campaign that followed, Bryan traveled more miles and gave more speeches than any previous candidate in American history, and he preached the gospel of silver with passionate eloquence: "You shall not press down upon the brow of labor this crown of thorns, you shall not crucify mankind upon a cross of gold." But he lost to his stolid Republican opponent, Ohio governor William McKinley, by 600,000 votes.

The defeat of Bryan and the silver forces did not bring a return to the see-saw politics of the 1870s and 1880s. The crisis of the 1890s basically reshaped American politics. Millions of former Democrats left their party, never to return, making the Republicans the majority party. They carried the Presidency in 7 of the 9 Presidential contests from 1896 to 1928, and controlled both houses of Congress in all but 3 of 17 sessions. The Democratic Party was virtually wiped out in the Northeast, and badly hurt everywhere except in the South.

Causes of the Realignment

Why did it happen? One simple but absolutely fundamental explanation is that the depression came under a Democratic administration. Had the Republicans been in power, it would probably have happened anyway, but it was their good fortune not to be. When Cleveland was inaugurated in March, 1893, Republican orators had warned that "of this rich inheritance the Democratic party becomes the trustee for the people." Now they could charge that care of the country's "match-

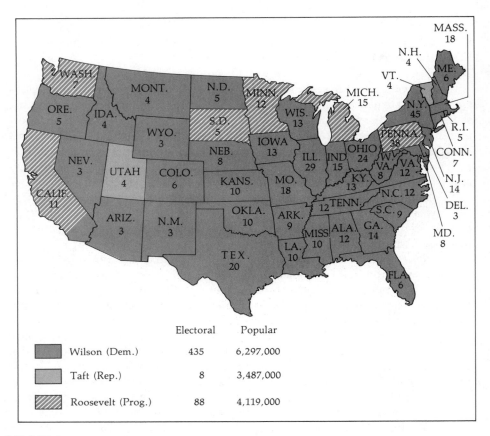

	Electoral	Popular
Wilson (Dem.)	435	6,297,000
Taft (Rep.)	8	3,487,000
Roosevelt (Prog.)	88	4,119,000

MAP 21-1
The 1896 Election

less prosperity" had been abused, and that the Democrats' threat of tariff reduction had destroyed the confidence of the business community. "We were told in the old times that the rich were getting richer and the poor poorer," a Republican spokesman said gleefully in 1894. "To cure that imaginary ailment our political opponents have brought on a time when everybody is getting poorer."

A second reason was that in the 1890s the Republicans retreated from the politics of piety that they had been practicing with such disastrous results at the polls. As party professionals shouldered aside amateur reformists within the state and local Republican organizations, less and less was heard about the burning need for moral reform. Many native Protestant Republicans continued to feel anxiety about the changing American social fabric, as is indicated by the sudden rise of an anti-Catholic secret society, the American Protective Association, which claimed some two and a half million members by the mid-1890s. But it is striking that Republican professionals successfully steered the party clear of association with the A.P.A. despite strenuous efforts by the Democrats to brand the G.O.P. as nativist and anti-Catholic.

WILLIAM JENNINGS BRYAN
(1860–1925)

William Jennings Bryan, the most eloquent spokesman for embattled American farmers in the industrial age, was not a farmer but a lawyer. He never even lived on a farm. He was born in Salem, Illinois in 1860, the son of a prosperous local judge and Democratic politician. Perhaps it took someone unfamiliar with the grinding daily realities of farm life to extoll the virtues of the yeoman farmer with Bryan's passionate simplicity. At college he first displayed his great rhetorical skills, taking second place in an intercollegiate oratorical competition attended by another contestant destined for later fame—social reformer Jane Addams. After studying at the Union College of Law in Chicago and practicing briefly in Chicago and Jacksonville, he moved on to Lincoln, Nebraska in 1887. Another irony: The greatest defender of the interests of the Great Plains region, the "boy orator of the Platte," had first laid eyes on the Platte River three years before he went off to Washington to represent Nebraska in Congress. Bryan's father had been an ardent inflationist, and a candidate for Congress on the Greenback ticket in 1878. His son took up the new inflationist remedy—free silver—and became one of its leading advocates. His sensational "Cross of Gold" speech at the 1896 Democratic convention made him the youngest presidential nominee in history. He was defeated in 1896, but remained the principal leader of the Democratic Party and ran again (and lost) in 1900 and 1908. He served as Secretary of State in the Wilson administration, resigning in 1915 out of the conviction that Wilson underestimated the danger of American involvement in World War I. After that he worked for prohibition and religious fundamentalism with the same righteous zeal with which he had supported free silver. He toured the country giving lectures arguing that only Christians should be permitted to teach on the faculty of any American university. Just before his death in 1925 he fought his last battle against the forces of modernity by serving as prosecutor at the Scopes trial, where he invited the ridicule of the educated class by supporting a Tennessee state law forbidding the teaching of the Darwinian theory of evolution in a public school.

TABLE 21-3
The Collapse of the Democratic Party
in the Big Cities, 1892–96

	Margin of Victory in Presidential Race		Net Shift to Republicans
	1892	*1896*	
New York	76,300D	21,997R	98,297
Chicago	35,625D	56,543R	92,168
Philadelphia	32,215R	113,999R	81,784
Brooklyn	25,595D	32,253R	57,848
Baltimore	14,606D	21,109R	35,715
Boston	10,376D	18,296R	28,672
St. Louis	859R	15,805R	14,946
Minneapolis	9,425D	5,454R	14,879
Total	138,853D	285,456R	424,309

Meanwhile, the Democratic Party itself was acquiring a crusading, rural, native Protestant tone, which eroded much of its traditional support from city dwellers. Bryan ran extremely well in rural areas, but the urban vote, divided fairly evenly between the two parties before that, tilted decisively toward the Republicans. Bryan was able to carry only 12 of the country's 82 cities with a population of more than 45,000, and 7 of the 12 were in the South. In the eight cities listed in Table 21-3, over 400,000 voters shifted from the Democratic to the Republican camp.

Although the Democrats portrayed themselves as the party of change in 1896, denouncing the Republicans as defenders of a bankrupt status quo, they were unable to win over many city dwellers. The only concrete change they demanded was free silver, and the urban workingmen most badly hit by the depression could not be convinced that currency inflation would solve their difficulties. Bryan's moralistic, evangelical style of campaigning, furthermore, was better attuned to rural audiences. He had little interest in city problems, and his insensitivity to urban needs was betrayed by his pronouncement that "the great cities rest upon our broad and fertile prairies. Burn down your cities and leave our farms, and your cities will spring up again as if by magic; but destroy our farms and the grass will grow in the streets of every city in the country." *Your* cities, *our* farms—no wonder Bryan's leadership of the Democratic Party weakened it at precisely the spot where most dynamic growth was occurring. It was a sure formula for defeat.

The events of the 1890s altered the images of the two parties and cut a substantial fraction of Democratic voters loose from their traditional moorings. The collapse of the economy during a Democratic administration, the Republican abandonment of a politics of piety, and the blindness to urban interests of the newly dominant Bryan Democrats produced a dramatic and enduring political realignment. McKinley's slogan—"a full dinner pail"—was hardly new. Republicans had been calling themselves the party of prosperity for decades. But by 1896 their claim became believable to many who had previously been skeptical. And, as if to confirm it, an economic upswing did in fact take place shortly after McKinley's victory. The recovery was not attributable to any actions of the new administration, but it nonetheless strengthened the identification of the Republican Party with good times.

Birth of the Solid South

The South was the only important exception to the new pattern of Republican ascendancy. There the direction of change was just the opposite of that for the rest of the nation: Opposition to the Democrats was eliminated altogether, and the one-party white South was born. The Democrats had won a controlling voice in every ex-Confederate state as early as the 1870s, when the Reconstruction regimes toppled. But it was not an unchallenged voice. Although Democrats had carried all of the South in every presidential race since 1880, in Congressional and state contests the Democrats had to contend with opponents running under many labels—Republican, Independent, Greenback, Populist and others. Despite the ruthless, violent campaigns of intimidation carried on by the Redeemers, blacks continued to vote after the end of the Reconstruction, and black voters were one key source of opposition to the Democrats. In 1880, for instance, a majority of black males went to the polls in 9 of the 11 Southern states. As late as the mid-1890s, black voting reached a peak of 64 percent in Alabama, 65 percent in Virginia, and 87 percent in North Carolina. Resentment against the planter-dominated Democratic party was also strong among poor whites, especially small farmers from outside the fertile black belt areas.

Poor whites and blacks together formed a majority of the southern population, but conflicting attitudes toward Reconstruction policies and white racism made it difficult for the two groups to join forces. The Populists made impressive attempts to win black support in some states. The Colored Farmers' Alliance was allied with the Southern Farmers' Alliance. Georgia's leading Populist, Tom Watson, called for bi-racial cooperation. There were black delegates at the Louisiana Populist convention of 1892, and a strong bi-racial Populist organization existed in East Texas. But in most parts of the South, the Populists failed to challenge the Democrats on the issue of white supremacy. Few blacks voted Populist, both because of their traditional loyalties to the Republicans and because the Populist program had little to offer a group made up largely of tenants and sharecroppers.

White Populists, therefore, did not oppose the campaign to deny blacks all political rights that gathered force in the late 1880s and 1890s. Every southern state restricted access to the polls through such devices as literacy tests, poll taxes, and a variety of registration requirements that were difficult for poor, uneducated blacks to meet. In Louisiana, for example, a new registration law passed in 1896 cut the proportion of Negro adult males eligible to vote from 93 to 9 percent. Two years later, a new state constitution whittled the proportion down to 3 percent. In South Carolina, new election laws reduced the percentage of blacks who voted from 70 percent in 1880 to 11 percent in 1896.

The denial of political rights to blacks was but one manifestation of a movement toward heightened racial separation and clearer subordination of blacks to whites. The number of Negroes accused of crimes who were denied due process of law and brutally lynched by mobs rose from an average of about 50 per year in the early 1880s (when the first statistics were kept) to two and three times that by the 1890s. Appropriations for black schools were cut to levels far below those for whites. Every state passed a body of "Jim Crow" legislation mandating racial separation on railroads and streetcars, in waiting rooms, theaters, restaurants, cemeteries, parks and other public facilities.[3] In Atlanta, there were special Jim Crow elevators for black passengers, and Jim Crow bibles for black witnesses to swear on in court. In Oklahoma, the law required separate phone booths, while in Florida and North Carolina white school children were protected from suffering contamination by handling textbooks previously used by black pupils. A politician in Macon County, Georgia, even proposed that the county maintain two separate systems of roads—one for whites and one for Negroes! In every sphere of life there were constant reminders that the two races were distinct, and that the white was superior to the black.

Denial of the right to vote on racial grounds, and enforced racial segregation of public facilities, of course, were difficult to square with the Fourteenth and Fifteenth Amendments. But interpretation of the meaning of the Constitution is the job of the Supreme Court, and the post-Reconstruction Court was more devoted to corporate property rights than to black rights. Its 1883 decision in the civil rights case declared the Civil Rights Act of 1875 unconstitutional, stripping the Reconstruction amendments of much of their meaning. In *Plessy vs. Ferguson* (1896) the justices gave a full go-ahead to Jim Crow attitudes. "If one race be inferior to the other socially," they said, "the Constitution of the United States cannot put them upon the same plane." Segregated facilities were perfectly acceptable, so long as they were "separate but equal." The "equal" in "separate but equal" was a fiction hard to take seriously. Implicit in the opinion was acceptance of the fact that the separate facilities for blacks would not indeed be "equal." If the Supreme Court of the United States branded blacks as "inferior," it could hardly object when a southern community decided to spend five times as much money on white schools as on black ones. The sole dissenter in the Plessy case, John Marshall Harlan, prophetically predicted that the decision would someday be considered just as "pernicious" as the Dred Scott ruling, but he was far ahead of his time. Most northern whites shared the racist assumptions of the Supreme Court, and were happy to leave southern whites a free hand to impose apartheid.

The poor whites who applauded the movement to tighten suffrage requirements to preserve white supremacy were in for a rude awakening. The backers of

---

[3]The term "Jim Crow" as an invidious synonym for blacks is of unknown origin, but was used well before the Civil War.

the voting restrictions were well-to-do men who regarded blacks *and* poor whites as unreliable members of the political community. It was rare for them to openly admit, as did a North Carolina newspaper in 1900, that they were worried about "the danger of the rule of Negroes and the lower classes of whites," but that was clear. They framed the disenfranchisement measures, therefore, so that they deterred lower-class whites as well as blacks from voting. The South Carolina reforms, which cut the proportion of blacks voting from 70 to 11 percent between 1880 and 1896, also reduced white turnout from 96 to 46 percent. The Louisiana measures that eliminated all but 3 percent of the state's Negroes from political participation also halved the white electorate.

By the opening of the twentieth century, the southern political system had two very obvious distinctions: the complete hegemony of the Democratic Party and the denial of political rights to most blacks (who formed a third of the region's population) as well as almost half of the whites—the poorer half. With no significant organized opposition, the Democratic Party, controlled by a white oligarchy, remained hostile to progressive social change. The South had undergone a reactionary revolution.

THE UNITED STATES AS A WORLD POWER

In 1880, the government of Turkey experienced minor financial difficulties and had to do some belt-tightening. After a careful review it decided to close down four of its diplomatic missions abroad. The countries judged too inconsequential to warrant the continued expense were Sweden, Belgium, Holland...and the United States!

Although the United States was the greatest economic power in the world—by then its fields and factories were producing more goods than those of its two closest rivals (Britain and Germany) combined—it was far from being a great power in the military or diplomatic sense. Although Americans had quickly built a great fighting machine during the Civil War, they had dismantled it just as quickly thereafter. The peacetime army was cut to less than 30,000, far below the strength of even such lesser European powers as Spain and Italy, and little more than a twentieth the size of the French or German army. Most of the American troops who went to war against Spain in 1898 carried Civil War rifles. By European standards, the U.S. Navy was not impressive either. It was small and very poorly equipped. More than half of the fleet had been scrapped after the Civil War, and what was not junked was allowed to rot. "Never was such a hapless, broken-down, tattered forlorn apology for a navy as that possessed by the United States," said an English naval publication in 1876.

The military weakness of the United States was obviously not the result of its inherently limited supply of manpower or material resources. Few Americans of the day saw a need for more than a token military establishment. Large standing armies seemed necessary to European countries separated from their neighbors by nothing more than lines on the map, but not to the citizens of a nation insulated

TABLE 21-4
Comparative Military Strength of United States
and European Countries, 1889

	Army	Navy and Marines
Austria–Hungary	327,100	8,019
France	541,365	53,960
Germany	491,677	15,573
Great Britain	149,667	62,400
Italy	253,900	12,728
Russia	809,973	29,245
Spain	144,664	21,671
United States	28,441	10,310

from powerful rivals by thousands of miles of ocean. Nature had provided defenses enough, it seemed.

Military might, of course, had more than defensive uses. The European powers in the late nineteenth century armed themselves not only to protect their existing boundaries, but to extend their influence over other nations. It was an age of fierce imperial rivalries, in which Britain, France, Germany, Portugal, Spain, Belgium, and Italy employed their superior power to impose colonial rule over the peoples of Asia, Africa, and the Middle East.

The United States, however, remained aloof from this struggle until almost the century's end. The enormous North American continent was large enough to contain the expansive energies of the American people during the first century of their national existence. While European powers pursued imperialistic policies, the United States engaged in "continentalism," shouldering aside the Indians, Spaniards, and Mexicans who stood inconveniently in their way. That didn't take many troops.

The preoccupation with internal expansion did not mean that Americans had no interest in developments in other parts of the world. As early as the 1820s, the United States claimed responsibility for preserving other countries in the entire Western Hemisphere from external interference under the Monroe Doctrine. Dismayed at the prospect of European intervention to crush the Latin American republics that had recently won their freedom from Spain, James Monroe announced in 1823 that attempts by European powers to "extend their system to any portion of this hemisphere" would be regarded as "dangerous to our peace and safety."

This was little more than a hollow gesture at the time, given America's military weakness. Intervention by the Holy Alliance was deterred not by American rhetoric but by the British Navy. But it was a precedent that would later be invoked when the United States had the power to back it up, as happened in Mexico in the 1860s. During the Civil War, Napoleon III of France sent troops into Mexico and established Archduke Maximilian of Austria as emperor. After Appomattox, the formidable Union Army and Navy was free for action, and a sharp American statement that France had violated the Monroe Doctrine forced a French withdrawal and the collapse of Maximilian's regime.

In the 1850s and 1860s commercial and colonial expansion became an issue on several occasions. President Millard Fillmore sent the U.S. Navy to Japan under Commodore Matthew Perry in 1853–54 in hopes of opening it up to American commercial penetration. Perry exacted agreements that gave foreign traders and diplomats access to Japan for the first time in centuries. In 1854, a proposal to seize Cuba from Spain, the Ostend Manifesto, was advanced by the Pierce administration, but it foundered because of northern opposition to opening a new frontier for slavery. In the flush of national pride and self-confidence following the Union victory in the Civil War, there was talk of taking over Canada, Cuba, the Dominican Republic, Haiti, and the Virgin Islands. But most of the designs of Secretary of State William Seward, an ardent expansionist, were frustrated. He made only two territorial acquisitions—the Midway Islands and Alaska. The tiny Midways, 1,000 miles west of Hawaii, had been discovered by the U.S. Navy in 1859; Seward ordered American occupation in 1867. His purchase of Alaska from Russia the same year was to prove far more significant in the long run, but to most Americans then it was "Seward's Folly." All Alaska offered, said one paper, was a bracing climate, an abundant ice crop, and cows that gave ice cream instead of milk.

Advocates of colonial expansion were unable to overcome the deep-rooted American conviction that, in the words of one journal, "We cannot have colonies, dependencies, subjects, without renouncing the essential conception of democratic government." Another less savory motive underlay opposition to empire—ethnocentrism. The areas in which colonies might be taken were inhabited by darker skinned, "backward" peoples, contact with whom might be "polluting." *Harper's Weekly* denounced plans for American annexation of Cuba in 1870 on the grounds that Cubans were "a people wholly alien from us in principles, language, and traditions, a third of whom are barbarously ignorant."

Changing Attitudes

There was no further agitation of consequence on behalf of imperial expansion until the 1890s. But a number of developments in the last quarter of the century prepared the way for the imperialist surge that then occurred. For one thing, advances in naval technology gave the strategic argument for imperialism greater force. Naval vessels powered by steam rather than sail could traverse the oceans with greater speed, carrying heavier armaments. But they could not operate long in remote waters without refueling. To be a great naval power, a nation had to have far-flung possessions as sites for coaling stations.

The case for building up the Navy and acquiring a chain of bases to support it was apparent to a small but influential group of Americans who saw the world as a Darwinian jungle in which only the fittest nations survived. In *The Influence of Sea Power Upon History* (1890), Alfred T. Mahan of the U.S. Naval War College developed this view persuasively. It was read with enthusiasm by Theodore Roosevelt, Senator Henry Cabot Lodge, and other members of the Republican foreign policy elite. "The great nations are rapidly absorbing all the waste places of the earth," said Lodge in 1895. "As one of the great nations of the world, the United States must not fall out of the line of march." Roosevelt agreed. Without a "large policy," he warned, "the bolder and stronger peoples will pass us by, and will win for themselves the domination of the world."

This ideology of conquest and domination, which echoed the expansionist "blood and iron" policies of Bismarck's German Empire, had too brutal a ring for many Americans. But similar policy conclusions could be derived from another concept that was gaining widespread currency in late nineteenth century America—the concept of America's mission to uplift the "backward" peoples of the world. The idea of a special American mission goes back to the first Puritan settlements in the New World; America was to be a city on a hill, an exemplar of godliness to the rest of the world. Later it reappeared in secular form, as the notion that the United States embodied the democratic ideal other countries should emulate, and that it was Manifest Destiny that American democracy expand across the continent. Late in the century, the notion that America's mission was to spread the blessings of its superior civilization to other corners of the globe began to gain currency.

Important support for this broadening of the concept of mission came from religious circles. By this time, American Protestants had developed an elaborate network of missions that sought to bring the Gospel to the "heathens" in nearly every part of the world. *Harper's Weekly* wanted nothing to do with the "barbarously ignorant" Cubans, but the missionaries had every confidence in their capacity to uplift "backward" peoples. It was necessary, said a leading missionary, to foster a "transition from heathenism to civilization; from utter and hopeless indolence to industry; from a beastly life to a Christian manhood." From the pulpits and the religious press, Americans were bombarded with the message summed up in Reverend Josiah Strong's best-selling *Our Country* (1885). The United States represented the finest flowering of Christian civilization, and it was "divinely commissioned" to spread its institutions over the entire face of the earth. "Coal and Christianity" were to the new expansionists what "Gold and Catholicism" had been to the conquistadores.

The new ideology of conquest and the expanded concept of the American mission in world history took hold partly because economic changes were forcing businessmen and commercial farmers to seek foreign markets. With its immense stock of raw materials and its enormous and rapidly growing internal market, the United States was not nearly as dependent on foreign trade as countries like Britain or Japan. The $845 million worth of goods exported from the United States in 1890 added up to less than 7 percent of the GNP. But between 1860 and 1890 exports tripled, a rate of growth substantially above that for the economy as a whole. Farm journals devoted increasing attention to the need to open foreign markets for American wheat, corn, cotton, and meat. Industrialists too began to worry about "overproduction" and looked abroad to sell surpluses. Fanciful visions of the rewards that would be won by tapping "the China market" enlivened sober trade newspapers. By the 1890s, more than half of America's refined oil, about half of its copper products, 40 percent of its wheat, and a quarter of its sewing machines were being sold abroad.

New Assertiveness—But Caution on Hawaii

In response to these currents, American foreign policy makers in the late 1880s displayed a new assertiveness—indeed, outright bellicosity. In 1888 a long-simmering dispute with Canada over fishing rights off Northern New England and Nova Scotia provoked President Cleveland to ask Congress to declare economic war against Canada, which it refused to do. The next year Congress backed President Harrison's aggressive stance in a quarrel with Germany over the Samoan Islands in the South Pacific, where both countries held naval bases. Were it not for a hurricane that sank the three German and three American warships that confronted each other in the harbor at Pago Pago—and a conciliatory gesture from Germany—the incident might have erupted into a full-scale war. Two years later, the United States nearly declared war on Chile on the mere grounds that it had been too slow to apologize properly for the deaths of some American seaman killed in a riot. Even mighty Britain became the object of American wrath in 1895 when it quarreled with Venezuela over the boundary of the colony of British Guiana. When the British rejected America's claim to the right to arbitrate the dispute on the grounds of its Monroe Doctrine responsibilities, President Cleveland threatened war and the British backed down promptly.

The United States was showing a new willingness to throw its weight around. But opposition to acquiring possessions outside the continental United States was still strong, as was shown in the failure to annex Hawaii in 1893. Hawaii had been an important base for American ships in the China trade from the early nineteenth century, and had attracted a substantial number of American missionaries, sugar planters, and merchants. Much of the land was in American hands, and American advisers controlled the government. Hawaiian sugar was allowed to enter the United States duty free under a special agreement, and in 1887 Hawaii gave America exclusive rights to use Pearl Harbor as a naval base. The succession of Queen Liliuokalani to the throne in 1890 was a blow to the American settlers; she launched a "Hawaii for the Hawaiians" campaign and proposed disenfranchisement of the whites. The 2,000 Americans staged a coup d'etat in 1893, with the support of the U.S. Minister, who ordered in the Marines on the pretext of protecting American property. The queen was forced to abdicate, and the Minister reported to Washington that "the Hawaiian pear is now fully ripe and this is the golden hour for the United States to pluck it." The political scene at home, however, was not "ripe" for the adventure. Grover Cleveland returned to the presidency before the Senate could ratify a treaty of annexation arranged by the outgoing Harrison administration. Cleveland was hostile to imperialism in principle, and questioned the morality of the American takeover. The treaty was defeated. The American rebel government remained in control but unaffiliated with the United States, like the Lone Star Republic of Texas from 1836 to 1845.

Hawaii became an American possession in 1898, in the midst of a war with Spain that gave advocates of imperialism the upper hand and led to the acquisition of colonies in both the Caribbean and the Pacific. The war arose over Cuba, which along with Puerto Rico had remained under Spanish control after the rest of the Spanish New World Empire had collapsed. In 1895 an insurrection aimed at overturning Spanish rule broke out, which Spanish General Weyler, "the butcher," sought to suppress with brutal tactics. American sympathies were all for the rebels. The creation of a "free Cuba" would expel European influences from an island at America's very doorstep. The revived anti-Catholic sentiments that were manifested in the rise of the nativist American Protective Association also promoted sympathy with the independence movement. American Protestants saw Spain as the home of the Inquisition. "Yellow press" editors such as William Randolph Hearst and Joseph Pulitzer viewed the Cuban struggle as a wonderful opportunity to boost circulation and, consequently, published superheated stories about alleged Spanish misdeeds.

As early as 1896, Congress responded to the inflamed public mood by passing a resolution directing President Cleveland to extend diplomatic recognition to the rebels, but he refused. The next year, the situation slowly cooled as the Spanish government made some positive responses to President William McKinley's request that the island be granted some political autonomy. McKinley, and the businessmen who bankrolled the Republican party, were fearful of war because they thought it would impede recovery from the depression. (People today often think war is good for the economy, but that was not commonly believed then.) But a shocking development early in 1898 suddenly transformed the situation. The American battleship *Maine* was anchored in Havana harbor, paying a "friendly" visit to remind Spain that American lives and property on the island had to be protected. On the night of February 15, it exploded, killing 252 American sailors.

What caused the explosion—a spark in the ship's powder magazine, a harbor mine that accidentally slipped its moorings, or sabotage—is still unknown. And if it was sabotage, the perpetrators were very likely rebels who hoped to provoke the United States into intervening. But the yellow press had no doubts, and hardly anyone in public life was willing to confess to any. It was "an act of dirty treachery," Assistant Secretary of the Navy Theodore Roosevelt fumed, a stain on the nation's honor that could only be expunged by blood. Marchers in the city streets chanted, "Remember the *Maine*, to hell with Spain." The terrified Spanish government quickly agreed to McKinley's demand for an armistice, but the clamor for war was overwhelming. McKinley asked Congress for a declaration of war—if he had not, Congress probably would have voted one anyway—and it passed overwhelmingly.

It was almost over before it began—a mere three months. The Secretary of State called it "a splendid little war," and many of the participants shared his enthusiasm. After resigning from the Navy, Theodore Roosevelt won the headlines he craved by leading his volunteer troop of Rough Riders, and later boasted that he had killed a Spaniard with his own hands. Only 460 soldiers and sailors died in battle, although more than 5,000 succumbed to tropical diseases. The most impressive feat of American arms was not in Cuba but half-way around the world, where Commodore George Dewey's Pacific fleet smashed the Spanish Navy at Manila Bay in the Philippine Islands with the loss of hardly a single man. It was announced that the assault was to prevent a Spanish attack on the West Coast, although the decrepit Spanish fleet probably couldn't have made it across the Pacific, much less inflicted any damage had it arrived.

The Debate Over Empire

How the fruits of victory were to be disposed of was settled by the Treaty of Paris, which provoked a heated debate between imperialists and anti-imperialists. The Spanish–American war originated as an explicitly anticolonial war. America's objective, said the war resolution, was a free Cuba. The Congress disclaimed "any disposition or intention to exercise sovereignty, jurisdiction, or control over" the island once the fighting was over. But the Treaty of Paris created an American empire. It honored the pledge to make Cuba independent, but it was little more than nominal independence. Spain's other Caribbean possession, Puerto Rico, was detached from Spain to become a possession of the United States. Both Guam and the Philippines were transferred into American hands. With Hawaii, annexed during the war, America now had a chain of islands across the Pacific to the Asian mainland.

The acquisition of the Philippine islands, nearly as large in area as Japan and some 5,000 miles from American shores and only 1,000 off the China coast, was particularly breath-taking. A heavy price had to be paid for it: A native uprising against American rule promptly broke out, and it took two years, more American troops than had fought against the Spaniards in Cuba, and brutally repressive tactics to put it down. An estimated 200,000 Filipinos lost their lives in their unsuccessful struggle to resist American rule.

Supporters of the Treaty of Paris marshalled the familiar strategic, economic, religious, and patriotic arguments. Control over Puerto Rico was crucial so that the United States Navy could guard the sea lanes to Central America, where American entrepreneurs hoped to build a canal across the isthmus to link the Atlantic and Pacific. Guam and the Philippines would provide havens for the Pacific fleet and secure access to Asian markets. McKinley argued, probably correctly, that if we let the Philippines go, they would be seized by France or Germany, "our commercial rivals in the Orient"; that would be "bad business." Instead, we should "take them all, and educate the Filipinos, and uplift and civilize and Christianize them." (Whether he didn't know it was a Catholic country or didn't regard Catholics as true Christians is unclear.) He believed that assuming "the white man's burden" would unify an American society, which had just undergone a period of acute social unrest, and encourage all citizens to rally round the flag. "No section any more," said Senator Albert J. Beveridge, "but a Nation. No, not *a Nation*, but the *Nation, The Nation*, God's chosen people."

The opponents of empire campaigned against it over the next two years. Most

Democrats, including Cleveland and Bryan, and a goodly share of the country's prominent professors and writers condemned the move. None questioned the importance of foreign markets, but they denied that having military outposts around the world was necessary for trade. To seize and subjugate other peoples was immoral and un-American. When "the desire to steal becomes uncontrollable in an individual he is declared to be a kleptomaniac and is sent to an asylum," said Bryan. "When the desire to grab land becomes uncontrollable in a nation, we are told that 'the currents of destiny are flowing through the hearts of men.'" American democracy itself was endangered, for "no nation can long endure half republic and half empire. Imperialism abroad will lead quickly and inevitably to despotism at home." Mark Twain suggested how to make an appropriate flag for our new colonies—take the Stars and Stripes, paint the white stripes black, and replace the stars with a skull and crossbones. Another critic rewrote a popular hymn:

> *Onward Christian soldiers,*
> *'Gainst the heathen crew!*
> *In the name of Jesus,*
> *Let us run them through.*

A southern Senator played on racist fears—expansion would mean "incorporating more colored men in the body politics."

It was a losing battle. The crisis of the nineties had unleashed anxieties that found release in war and imperial conquest. Adding to the shock of the deep depression was the widespread publicity given to the Census Bureau's announcement that the 1890 Census had registered a fundamental turning point in American history: There was no more open frontier within the country's boundaries, no more "Wests" to be conquered. Opportunity and adventure would have to be sought elsewhere, and it was younger Americans who would do the seeking. A study of the leading imperialists and anti-imperialists reveals one striking difference—age. Most important opponents of empire were in their sixties, with values shaped in the pre-Civil War years. The imperialists were two decades younger on the average. When Carl Schurz (age 69), a founder of the Republican party, spoke out against war with Spain, Theodore Roosevelt (age 39) rebuked him: "You and your generation have had your chance from 1861 to 1865. Now let us of this generation have ours!" War, and the empire it brought into being, gave Roosevelt's generation its "chance" for adventure, power, and glory.

PLATFORM OF THE AMERICAN ANTI-IMPERIALIST LEAGUE, 1899

We hold that the policy known as imperialism is hostile to liberty and tends toward militarism, an evil from which it has been our glory to be free. We regret that it has become necessary in the land of Washington and Lincoln to reaffirm that all men, of whatever race or color, are entitled to life, liberty, and the pursuit of happiness. We maintain that governments derive their just powers from the consent of the governed. We insist that the subjugation of any people is "criminal aggression" and open disloyalty to the distinctive principles of our government.

We earnestly condemn the policy of the present national administration in the Philippines. It seeks to extinguish the spirit of 1776 in those islands. We deplore the sacrifice of our soldiers and sailors, whose bravery deserves admiration even in an unjust war. We denounce the slaughter of the Filipinos as a needless horror. We protest against the extension of American sovereignty by Spanish methods.

We hold with Abraham Lincoln, that "no man is good enough to govern another man without that other's consent. When the white man governs himself, that is self-government, but when he governs himself and also governs another man, that is more than self-government—that is despotism." "Our reliance is in the love of liberty which God has planted in us. Our defense is in the spirit which prizes liberty as the heritage of all men in all lands. Those who deny freedom to others deserve it not for themselves, and under a just God cannot long retain it."

—Carl Schurz, *The Policy of Imperialism*, 1899

SUGGESTED READINGS

Samuel P. Hays, *The Response to Industrialism, 1885–1914* (1957), Robert Wiebe, *The Search for Order, 1877–1920* (1968), Alexander B. Callow, Jr., *From Hayes to McKinley* (1969), and H. Wayne Morgan, *Unity and Culture: The United States, 1877–1900* (1971) are brief syntheses from different vantage points. Morton Keller, *Affairs of State: Public Life in Late Nineteenth Century America* (1977) is excellent and comprehensive. Robert Kelley, *The Transatlantic Persuasion: The Liberal-Democratic Mind in the Age of Gladstone* (1969) makes interesting connections between American and British political developments.

David J. Rothman, *Politics and Power: The United States Senate, 1865–1901* (1966) and Robert D. Marcus, *Grand Old Party! Political Structure in the Gilded Age, 1880–1896* (1971) describe the evolution of institutions. Geoffrey Blodgett, *The Gentle Reformers: Massachusetts Democrats in the Cleveland Era* (1966) is a sensitive portrait. See also Gerald M. McFarland, *Mugwumps, Morals, and Politics, 1884–1920* (1975) and Arthur Mann, *Yankee Reformers in an Urban Age: Social Reform in Boston, 1880–1900* (1954), Sidney Fine, *Laissez Faire and the General-Welfare State, A Study in Conflict in American Thought, 1865–1901* (1956), and James Gilbert, *Designing the Industrial State: The Intellectual Pursuit of Collectivism in America, 1880–1940* (1972) trace shifting opinion about government and the economy.

Walter Dean Burnham, *Critical Elections and the Mainsprings of American Politics* (1970) is an excellent analysis of voting behavior. Further insight into electoral shifts may be gained from Paul Kleppner, *The Cross of Culture: A Social Analysis of Midwestern Politics, 1850–1900* (1970), Richard Jensen, *The Winning of the Midwest: Social and Political Conflict, 1888–1896* (1971), Samuel T. McSeveney, *The Politics of Depression: Political Behavior in the Northeast, 1893–1896* (1972), Frederick C. Luebke, *Immigrants and Politics: The Germans of Nebraska, 1880–1900* (1969), and J. Roger Hollingsworth, *The Whirligig of Politics: The Democracy of Cleveland and Bryan* (1963). R. Hal Williams, *Years of Decision: American Politics in the 1890's* (1978) is a good survey. On populism see Lawrence Goodwyn, *The Populist Moment: A Short History of the Agrarian Revolt in America* (1978), Peter H. Argersinger, *Populism and Politics: William Alfred Peffer and the People's Party* (1974), and Sheldon Hackney, *Populism to Progressivism in Alabama* (1969). William H. Harvey, *Coin's Financial School* (1894) uses bizarre arguments to make the case for "free silver." Richard Hofstadter's introduction to a 1963 edition lucidly unravels that murky issue. On the development of the one-party South and the rise of Jim Crow, see C. Vann Woodward's classic *The Origins of the New South, 1877–1913* (1951), Morgan Kousser, *The Shaping of Southern Politics: Suffrage Restriction and the Establishment of the One-Party South* (1974), H.N. Rabinowitz, *Race Relations in the Urban South* (1978), and John W. Cell, *The Highest Stage of White Supremacy: The Origins of Segregation in South Africa and the American South* (1982).

For conflicting views of the sources of America's rise to world power, see Ernest May's two studies, *Imperial Democracy: The Emergence of America as a Great Power* (1961), and *American Imperialism: A Speculative Essay* (1968), Walter LaFeber, *The New Empire: An Interpretation of American Expansion, 1860–1896* (1963), Milton Plesur,

America's Outward Thrust, 1865–1890 (1971), Robert L. Beisner, From the Old Diplomacy to the New, 1865–1900 (1975), and Charles S. Campbell, The Transformation of American Foreign Relations, 1865–1900 (1976). Edward P. Crapol, America for Americans: Economic Nationalism and Anglophobia in the Late Nineteenth Century (1973) and Rubin F. Weston, Racism in U.S. Imperialism: The Influence of Racial Assumptions on American Foreign Policy, 1893–1946 (1972) are stimulating. On the causes of the Spanish-American War, see H. Wayne Morgan, America's Road to Empire (1965) and David Healy, U.S. Expansion: Imperialist Urge in the 1890's (1970). Gerald F. Lindemann, The Mirror of War: American Society and the Spanish-American War (1974) is suggestive. On the experience of the war itself, see Frank Freidel, The Splendid Little War (1958). The brutal suppression of the Philippine rebels is described in Leon Wolff, Little Brown Brothers (1961). Robert L. Beisner, Twelve Against Empire: The Anti-Imperialists, 1898–1900 (1968) and E. Berkeley Tompkin, Anti-Imperialism in the United States: The Great Debate, 1830–1920 (1970) discuss the opponents of empire.

Child labor—as revealed in this Lewis Hine photo of a boy in a hosiery factory circa 1910—was not closely regulated until the 1920s.

Part Four

Regulation and Reform: The Consequences of Progressivism

Chapter Twenty-Two

The Progressive Era

The years between Theodore Roosevelt's accession to the Presidency in 1901 and America's entry into world war in 1917 are conventionally labeled "the Progressive Era." In this era of reform, many areas of American public life changed drastically. "Progressivism," however, was not a coherent, unified political movement. There was no single Progressive movement. There was, briefly, a single Progressive Party—formed by Republicans who could not swallow their party's choice of conservative William Howard Taft in 1912—but many of its opponents, followers of Democrat Woodrow Wilson, thought of themselves as progressives too. A wide variety of groups, with varying ends, marched under the reform banner in the early twentieth century. To understand their objectives and achievements it is necessary to examine reform at three levels—municipal reform, reform at the state level, and finally national political reform.

THE STRUGGLE FOR THE CITY

By the end of the nineteenth century, Americans were regarding their cities with an anxious eye. "The first city," wrote a leading minister in 1898, "was built by the first murderer, and crime and vice and wretchedness have festered in it ever since." "God created Adam and Eve in a garden," said another cleric; "cities are the result of the Fall." Books like Jacob Riis' *How the Other Half Lives* (1890), Stephen Crane's *Maggie* (1893), W.T. Stead's *If Christ Came to Chicago* (1894), Robert Hunter's *Poverty*

The backyard playground of the Henry Street Settlement House in New York City provided the subject matter for this Jacob Riis photo.

(1904), Lincoln Steffens' *The Shame of Our Cities* (1904), and Upton Sinclair's *The Jungle* (1906) revealed the poverty and misery, overcrowding and disease, and rampant political corruption of the urban scene. In response, a movement to "reform" the cities swept across the nation.

Spearheads for Reform: The Settlement Houses

A new institution—the settlement house—was a crucial source of information about urban problems and of ideas about how they might be improved. The first American settlement houses—New York's University Settlement and Chicago's Hull House—were established in the late 1880s, modeled on Toynbee Hall in the slums of London. A decade later, there were over 70, and by 1910 more than 400. They were creations of idealistic young men and women who chose to live with the poor and attempt to help them. The volunteers who staffed them were a privileged group; almost 90 percent had attended college, and over half had done graduate work—at a time when less than 4 percent of their peers had any higher education. Jane Addams, the founder of Hull House and the most extraordinary of them (winner of the 1931 Nobel Peace Prize), was one of less than 3,000 women in the entire country who received bachelor's degrees in 1881. A majority of the settlement volunteers were women who, refusing to believe that a woman's proper place is in the home, found most careers in business and the professions closed to them. Working with the poor offered them a chance to operate in the larger world in a role that was still in some sense maternal. The men were often former divinity students, influenced by the liberal "social gospel" message of Washington Gladden and Walter Rauschenbush. Lacking the faith to enter the ministry, they sought to serve God through immediate practical service to humanity.

Settlement house workers publicized the existence of widespread poverty in a land of abundance, and attacked the prevailing American tendency to blame the victim on the common assumption that poverty was the result of individual character failings. Other social critics were beginning to say the same, but the settlement house group conveyed the message not through tirades or sermons, but through careful empirical research. They conducted the first American "social surveys," mapping the slums and describing the lives of their inhabitants. Works like Jane Addams' *Hull House Maps and Papers* (1895), Robert A. Woods' *The City Wilderness* (1898), and Paul Kellogg's remarkable six-volume *Pittsburgh Survey* (1909–14)—milestones in the development of American sociology—helped to widen the sensibilities of a generation.

Not content to merely discover the extent of poverty, the settlement workers sought to alleviate it in a variety of ways. One means was education. Adult immigrants beyond the reach of the public school system, and working children who had dropped out of it, were offered classes in English, home management, and other basic skills. Some settlement leaders, like Boston's Robert Woods, were content with that. For them, the purpose of education was to promote individual economic advancement, and that was to be achieved by disseminating proper "American" values and elementary vocational skills. Others, like Jane Addams, were less condescending and more pluralistic. They had a faith that high culture could be imported into the slums, through dramatic and musical performances, poetry reading and the like. They respected immigrant cultures, and developed programs to encourage the preservation of some Old World customs and to bridge the cultural gap between immigrants and their American-born children.

The settlement functioned as a local social service center committed to defending and improving the neighborhood. The resident staff did what they could to help the particularly needy, which often wasn't much because the funds they could raise from donors were limited. They appealed for new facilities like public baths and playgrounds, and protested when the garbage wasn't picked up. They worked at the state and local level for social legislation, particularly laws to benefit women and children, and supported attempts at labor organization.

The empathy for the urban poor that the best settlement house workers developed broke down at one important point, however. They detested the political machines that dominated local politics, and believed fervently in "clean government." They could not comprehend why their impoverished neighbors supported the bosses so loyally. Consequently, they lent their weight to a municipal reform movement that may have done more harm than good.

The Nature of Machine Politics

Although reformers described city politics in conspiratorial terms, there was nothing very mysterious about it. The sinister "machine" was simply a party well enough organized to control a community on election day. To its supporters, it was merely "the organization." Machines were products of the late nineteenth century. The earliest specimen was Tammany Hall, which won control of New York City municipal politics in the late 1860s under Boss William Marcy Tweed. Tammany Hall soon had counterparts everywhere. They were elaborate hierarchical structures ranging from the city-wide boss on top to the thousands of grassroots party workers operating in their own neighborhoods, block by block. Their objectives were simple: to win elections, and then to govern the city in a manner beneficial to the organization and those who controlled it.

Before the Civil War, the tasks of municipal government were too limited to inspire highly organized political conflict. Local politics attracted mostly amateurs. City Hall became a bigger prize as the urban population grew from about 6 million in 1860 to 30 million in 1900. The need for government services increased even more than that because crowded living conditions made it impossible for people to fend for themselves as they had once done. The volunteer night watches that had kept the peace satisfactorily in communities in which most residents knew each other were inadequate in a more anonymous city environment, so uniformed professional police were needed. The volunteer fire companies could not cope with the growing fire hazard that accompanied higher density living; firemen had to be hired. Tossing one's garbage and trash out into the street posed a greater public health hazard when thousands of people were packed into a single block; municipal collection was the obvious answer. In these and many other ways, city government was expected to do a great deal more than it had in the past, and taxpayers were willing to support vast increases in municipal budgets to pay for it. The machines were organized to get these things done—and to reap the rewards.

The machines were run by professional politicians. They made their careers in politics as others did in business, and with essentially the same objective in mind—profit. "When a man enters politics," said a Tammany Hall boss candidly, "he should get something out of it." They did. Winning an election meant winning the authority to make crucial decisions: which contractor would build the new school or hospital and exactly where it would be situated, what company would operate the street railway system, whether or not the police would crack down on illegal gambling dens or houses of prostitution, what landlords would be prosecuted for violating the building code, who would get jobs teaching school, directing traffic, or sweeping the streets. The machine politician made such choices in accord with a simple criterion: Whatever brought the maximum economic and political benefits for himself and his organization was right. The contractor who offered a healthy "kickback" was preferred over his stingier (or more scrupulous) competitor; public employees who handed back a percentage of their salaries as "contributions" to the organization and worked diligently at election time were naturally selected ahead of the ungrateful (or disinterested). If possible, a new public facility was placed where it would increase the value of land held by the boss. If he didn't own the land yet, he would rush out and buy it cheap before the plans were made public. The issue was never who could erect the best building at the lowest cost to the taxpayers, what location would be most convenient for prospective users, who would be the most skillful and dedicated school teacher. The issue was what paid off, in money or votes.

Although the big city organizations that have retained significant strength until recently are chiefly Democratic, like Tammany Hall, a good many Republican machines dominated their cities in the late nineteenth and early twentieth centuries. The machine had little concern with the larger issues of national politics, little interest in ideology. Such matters as the tariff, the trusts, and free silver seemed utterly remote to them. The real action was in City Hall.

Machine politicians of both parties sometimes spoke in the language of class, posing as friends of the poor and calling their opponents wealthy snobs with no understanding of the common people and their problems. Some writers have even romantically portrayed the machine bosses as Robin Hoods, taking from the rich and giving to the poor. The machines were generally unpopular among the more affluent, but not because they threatened wealth. Some men of wealth, in fact, owed their prosperity to the profitable deals they made with the politicians. The bribes and kickbacks they paid came not out of their own profits but out of the public treasury, in the form of inflated charges for their services. So it was the taxpayer who paid, and the small taxpayer as much or more than the large one. The chief source of revenue for the American city in this era was the real estate tax, and it was not a progressive, graduated tax. The same percentage charge was levied on the owner of a shack and the occupant of a great mansion. Paying it was naturally harder for the former than for the latter. Even the tenement dwellers, most of them too poor to purchase homes of their own, helped to keep the machine well greased with cash as landlords raised the rent to pay the cost of tax hikes.

The machine, then, did not take from the rich in particular but from the community in general. Nor, contrary to legend, did it give much to the poor. The free turkeys passed out so lavishly at Thanksgiving, Christmas, and Easter—and the food and drink served up at party picnics and rallies—cost an insignificant fraction of the amount taken from the pockets of taxpayers. Of course there were jobs for the party faithful, but many of those were jobs that would have to be filled, whoever was in power. The garbage had to be collected and the streets repaired, and the same relatively uneducated and unskilled people did the work whatever the administration. To that extent, the machine did not give jobs to poor people, as a class, that they would not otherwise have had. It took jobs from poor people with no political connections and gave them to those who had some. Some jobs were added to the public payroll by machine politicians, either to improve public services or simply to increase the number of people dependent on their favor. Those jobs represented a net benefit to the poor as a class, but it is doubtful that the gain was very large compared to the costs of machine rule.

Although the machine boss was no Robin Hood when it came to distributing wealth, machine politicians did satisfy their constituents in other ways. The boss commanded an army of party workers. They made it their business to know who needed help, and the organization provided all sorts of emergency assistance—temporary shelter for those rendered homeless by fire or eviction, bail money and perhaps a good word to the judge, funeral expenses. As one of Boston's most skillful machine politicians said, "There's got to be in every ward somebody that any bloke can come to—no matter what he's done—and get help. Help, you understand, none of your law and justice, but help." The distinction between "help" and "law and justice" was well understood by an aspiring young Boston city council member and later mayor of the city, James Michael Curley. In 1902 Curley helped a constituent who couldn't pass the civil service exam by taking it in his name, and was caught and sent to prison. Proper Bostonians were outraged, but the incident gave a great boost to Curley's political career. His explanation—"I did it for a friend"—was language common Bostonians understood.

Machines were in effect social service and social welfare agencies. They performed the functions of specialized public and private bureaucracies that later replaced them, and possibly more humanely because they sought to provide not justice but mercy. The mercy, of course, was reserved for party supporters. But in their heyday the big city machines commanded the loyalty of most city dwellers on the lowest rungs of the social ladder.

One particularly needy element of the urban population—a special target of machine efforts—were the immigrants. It is commonly assumed, in fact, that there would have been no machines were it not for the massive influx of Europeans into American cities. But political machines grew up even in cities with a negligible foreign-born population. Certainly, however, the difficulties experienced by uprooted, bewildered immigrants in American cities presented abundant opportunities for the machine to win grateful, loyal support.

THE STRENUOUS DAY OF A TAMMANY DISTRICT LEADER

2 AM: Aroused from sleep by the ringing of his doorbell; went to the door and found a bartender, who asked him to go to the police station and bail out a saloonkeeper who had been arrested for violating the excise law. Furnished bail and returned to bed at three o'clock.

6 AM: Awakened by fire engines passing his house. Hastened to the scene of the fire, according to the custom of the Tammany district leaders, to give assistance to the fire sufferers, if needed. Found several tenants who had been burned out, took them to a hotel, supplied them with clothes, fed them, and arranged temporary quarters for them until they could rent and furnish new apartments.

8:30 AM: Went to the police court to look after his constituents. Found six "drunks." Secured the discharge of four by a timely word with the judge, and paid the fines of two.

9 AM: Appeared in the Municipal District Court. Directed one of his district captains to act as counsel for a widow against whom dispossess proceedings had been instituted and obtained an extension of time. Paid the rent of a poor family about to be dispossessed and gave them a dollar for food.

11 AM: At home again. Found four men waiting for him. One had been discharged by the Metropolitan Railway Company for neglect of duty, and wanted the district leader to fix things. Another wanted a job on the road. The third sought a place on the Subway and the fourth, a plumber, was looking for work with the Consolidated Gas Company.

Immigration contributed to the prevalence of machine politics in another way as well. Machine politics was ethnic politics. The pioneer machine-builders were the American-born offspring of Irish immigrants. The Irish were the largest ethnic group in most late nineteenth century cities, and they had a special flair for politics. When the second generation Irish came of age in the 1870s and 1880s, they found other avenues of social mobility blocked by Yankee prejudice and their own lack of education. They could climb the political ladder, however, through the sheer weight of numbers, if they could convince their fellow Irishmen that it was better to put Irish-American crooks than Yankee crooks in City Hall. Toward the end of the century, the Irish lost their numerical preponderance with the decline in immigration from Ireland and the large influx of Italians, Jews, Poles, and other "new immigrants." But Irish politicians were adept at forming alliances with the newcomers, providing them with just enough plums to win their allegiance but retaining the top spots in the organization for themselves. They shrewdly put together "balanced tickets" on election day, ethnic smorgasbords with a candidate

The district leader spent nearly three hours fixing things for the four men, and succeeded in each case.

3 PM: Attended the funeral of an Italian as far as the ferry. Hurried back to make his appearance at the funeral of a Hebrew constituent.

7 PM: Went to district headquarters and presided over a meeting of election district captains. Each captain submitted a list of all the voters in his district, reported on their attitude toward Tammany, suggested who might be won over and how they could be won, told who were in need, and who were in trouble of any kind and the best way to reach them. District leader took notes and gave orders.

8 PM: Went to a church fair. Took chances on everything, bought ice cream for the young girls and the children. Kissed the little ones, flattered their mothers and took their fathers out for something down at the corner.

9 PM: At the clubhouse again. Spent $10 on tickets for a church excursion and promised a subscription for a new church bell. Bought tickets for a baseball game to be played by two nines from his district. Listened to the complaints of a dozen pushcart peddlers who said they were persecuted by the police and assured them he would go to Police Headquarters in the morning and see about it.

10:30 PM: Attended Hebrew wedding reception and dance. Had previously sent a handsome wedding present to the bride.

12 PM: In bed.

—William L. Riordan, *Plunkitt of Tammany Hall*, 1905

or two for every group large enough to count. The Irish consequently stayed in command of the machines, even after they had become a dwindling minority.

The political structure of American cities in the era of machine politics was highly decentralized. It provided ample opportunities for political participation and upward social mobility to the common people, and was extremely responsive to neighborhood interests. The basic electoral unit was the ward. Large cities would have two to three dozen wards, each of which elected one or two local residents to the city council and to the school committee. Each neighborhood had spokesmen to defend it. Furthermore, given the pronounced class and ethnic segregation that developed in the late nineteenth century city, elections by ward tended to produce governing bodies that were fairly representative of the class and ethnic mix of the community. "Men of successful experience and ability large enough to do justice to public affairs," complained a leading Chicago businessman in 1911, "will seldom live and bring up their families in the poorer wards." He estimated that 27 of Chicago's 35 wards were unsuitable for habitation by the better sort; three-fourths of the seats on the city council were therefore reserved by default for people without "successful experience."

The Municipal Reform Movement

These circumstances allowed machines to develop and gave them their staying power. They did meet some genuine needs. But the costs were considerable. The money with which party leaders lined their pockets led to a soaring tax rate. Buildings constructed by incompetents using shoddy materials sometimes collapsed. When confronted with strong opposition, bosses were willing to steal elections by fraudulent tactics. Teams of "repeaters" followed orders to "vote early and vote often," moving from polling booth to polling booth, voting under the names of people who had recently moved away or died without being removed from the list of eligible voters. Civil service regulations were shamelessly evaded, either by the means used by James Michael Curley or the simple expedient of creating new job titles not on the civil service list. The payroll of the Boston Water Department in the year 1900 included a "ship caulker," several "miners," and an "expert swimmer" (stroke unspecified).

Such abuses provoked a drive for municipal reform that crested in the opening decades of the twentieth century. The earliest assaults on the machines typically took the form of simple campaigns to "throw the rascals out." Some scandalous misdeeds would be exposed and a fight to defeat the crooks and restore "clean government" would follow. The 1871 revelation of the monumental thefts by the Tweed Ring from the New York treasury resulted in a crushing loss for Tammany Hall in the next election. But the gentlemen amateurs aroused by scandal to fight the good fight lacked the stamina to do it time after time. The rascals always came back. Only a tightly organized and disciplined grassroots organization could keep the machine out of power—an opposing machine, in fact, that operated in much the same fashion. A Tammany boss at the turn of the century remarked that he couldn't remember exactly how many reform movements had appeared during his 40 years in politics, but he knew "how many have lasted for more than a few years—none." His high-minded opponents, he remarked, were morning glories. They "looked lovely in the morning and withered up in a short time, while the regular machines went on flourishing forever, like fine old oaks."

The fine old oaks would flourish and each new crop of morning glories would soon fade so long as the rules of the political game remained unchanged. But that seemed increasingly intolerable. At the very time that it was becoming "more and more imperative to have strong men, honest and experienced men, to manage the business of the great cities," said one frustrated reformer, it was becoming "more and more difficult to secure them on the basis of unrestricted suffrage." That is, had it been possible to disenfranchise those who were so misguided as to support the machine, reform might have had a chance. But this was politically impossible, except in the South where the supposed menace posed by black voters provided an acceptable pretext.

Municipal reformers soon discovered other, less blatantly undemocratic, ways to change the rules—modifications in electoral procedures and local government structure that sought to take power from "ignorant and irresponsible politicians" and place it in the hands of "honest and competent experts." Aided by sensational revelations of machine corruption by "muckraking" journalists, reformers organized campaigns for new city charters. With the solid backing of leading businessmen, professionals, and the newspapers, they frequently won majority support in local referenda. There was also another way to achieve their ends: Cities were creatures of the states and state legislatures could restructure their governments without consulting city residents. Because the state legislatures were typically dominated by rural and small town representatives of the same class and ethnic background as the reformers, it is not surprising that they were often persuaded to impose reform upon cities whose voters had resisted it.

One key change demanded by municipal reformers was the elimination of the ward system. They pressed for more centralized government, with smaller governing bodies elected on a city-wide rather than a neighborhood basis. Representatives who were responsible to the voters of the whole city rather than to those of their neighborhood alone, they argued, would have a larger vision of the public good than parochial ward politicians, and a greater understanding of how to further it. Such vision and understanding, they assumed, was not likely to be found among the common people. In a 1911 pre-election pamphlet, Pittsburgh's municipal reform association advised that:

> ...a man's occupation ought to give a strong indication of his qualifications for membership on the school board. Employment as an ordinary laborer or in the lowest class of mill work would naturally lead to the conclusion that such men did not have sufficient education or business training to act as school directors. Objection might also be made to small shopkeepers, clerks, workmen at many trades, who by lack of educational advantages and business training could not be expected to administer properly the affairs of an educational system requiring special knowledge, and where millions are spent each year.

Elections at-large rather than by ward increased the likelihood that people with "educational advantages and business training" would be returned to office. Once reform was accomplished, the kinds of candidates who had previously been elected from the low income, immigrant neighborhoods were seriously disadvantaged. They lacked the funds to blanket the entire city with posters and handbills, and the social status and contacts that could gain them wider visibility, and they were no longer protected from competition by the unwillingness of "men of successful experience" to live in the slums. A major barrier to elite dominance of community politics had thus been removed.

Other reforms that weakened the machines and diminished the political influence of the less affluent were aimed at "taking politics out of government." For example, forbidding the use of party labels in municipal elections and conducting

A CITY BOSS' VIEW OF THE STATE LEGISLATURE

This city is ruled entirely by the hayseed legislators at Albany. I've never known an upstate Republican who didn't want to run things here, and I've met many thousands of them in my long service in the Legislature. The hayseeds think we are like the Indians to the National Government— that is, sort of wards of the State, who don't know how to look after ourselves and have to be taken care of by the Republicans of St. Lawrence, Ontario, and other backwoods counties. Why should anybody be surprised because ex-Governor Odell comes down here to direct the Republican machine? Newburg ain't big enough for him. He, like all the other upstate Republicans, wants to get hold of New York City. New York is their pie.

Say, you hear a lot about the downtrodden people of Ireland and the Russian peasants and the sufferin' Boers. Now, let me tell you that they have more real freedom and home rule than the people of this grand and imperial city. In England, for example, they make a pretense of givin' the Irish some self-government. In this State the Republican government makes no pretense at all. It says right out in the open: "New York City is a nice big fat Goose. Come along with your carvin' knives and have a slice." They don't pretend to ask the Goose's consent.

—William L. Riordan, *Plunkitt of Tammany Hall,* 1905

them instead on a non-partisan basis was obviously a blow to the dominant party organization; the absence of party identifications made voters more likely to choose reformers endorsed by the newspapers.

A still more effective way to take politics out of government was to turn more decisions over to "experts" who were not directly accountable to the electorate. "Ignorance should be excluded from control," said one reformer in 1901. "City business should be carried on by trained experts selected upon some other principle than popular suffrage." Accordingly, independent commissions of appointed experts were given responsibility over matters that had previously been the concern of the city council. In some communities, the reformers' preference for selection by appointment rather than election went to the lengths of eliminating the office of mayor altogether, and substituting the city manager form of government. Reformers were fond of pointing out that major business corporations, such as Standard Oil, were operated by the best managerial talent, and the holder of a few shares of common stock was given no opportunity to interfere with the day-to-day operation of the business. City government, they held, should be similarly structured, with the ordinary voter as passive as the small stockholder.

Effects of Reform

The municipal reform movement did not meet with equal success in every city. There was greater resistance to change in the older eastern metropolises than in the newer western cities, more in giant cities than in smaller ones. In some places, structural reform had limited effects, because the machines there were sufficiently flexible and tenacious to manipulate the new system. But the overall national trend was clearly toward more centralized, non-partisan, businesslike municipal government.

This, in some ways, meant better government. The gross abuses of the public trust that had occurred under machine rule became rarer. The honesty and competence of the average public employee was greater than it had been before; citizens got better municipal service per tax dollar than they had in the heyday of the bosses. More efficient public administration was certainly in the public interest, and some reforms undoubtedly did promote efficiency. On the other hand, the structural reforms introduced in the name of efficiency served also to transfer power from the neighborhoods to the center, from the poor to the affluent, from the immigrants to the Yankees. In practice, taking the politics out of government seemed to mean taking the people out of government—at least the common people.

As the political influence of the urban masses declined and the reins of government passed into the hands of businessmen and their hired experts, public policy shifted correspondingly. Keeping the tax rate down was given the highest priority, even at the cost of cutting municipal services. Particularly drastic cuts were made in the inner-city neighborhoods, which now lacked the political defenders they had been guaranteed under the ward system. Reform regimes also engaged in strenuous efforts to impose uniform moral standards on the entire population. Machine politicians had traditionally been tolerant of minor vices and lawbreaking, such as gambling, prostitution, and keeping saloons open on Sunday or after the legal closing hour. The reformers, by contrast, were more moralistic and tended to enforce their own middle-class Protestant moral standards on others.

The costs of machine rule were so great that we should resist the temptation to mourn the passing of the boss or sentimentalize the charming scoundrels who plundered city treasuries. But it is true that the unreformed decentralized political system was more pluralistic and democratic, more responsive to the needs of ordinary working people than the centralized, business-dominated system introduced by municipal reformers.

STATE PROGRESSIVISM

Reformers active in state government during the Progressive era pursued two basic objectives—establishing "direct democracy" by giving the people more of a voice in the political process, and protecting "the public interest" from "the special interests." Much was achieved, but the effects were more ambiguous than reformers expected.

"The voice of the people," said Progressive editor William Allen White of Kansas, "is indeed the will of God." A series of changes in political procedures introduced in most states before World War I were designed to open up the political process along the lines first demanded by the Populists. Citizens were allowed to propose legislative changes (the initiative), to vote directly on controversial legislation (the referendum), and to remove unpopular officials without waiting until the next election (the recall). Direct primaries replaced party conventions as a means of selecting nominees for public office. And after it was ratified by enough states, the seventeenth Amendment to the Constitution (1913) mandated direct popular election of U.S. Senators.

"Direct democracy" proved rather disappointing in practice. Direct election of Senators seems to have made no difference in the kind of men sent to Washington, and the initiative, referendum, and recall procedures were rarely used. When they were it was no simple triumph for "the people," because raising the necessary number of signatures was such an expensive task that it tended to be well-financed pressure groups who undertook it. Direct primaries diminished the influence of established party leaders to some extent, but it is debatable whether the common man benefited except through an increased likelihood that he would vote for someone whose name signaled he was a member of the same ethnic group. Perhaps the most striking comment concerning these efforts to democratize the political system is that they did not increase the levels of voter turnout. Indeed, the percentage of eligible citizens going to the polls dropped sharply between 1900 and the 1930s. Historians are still uncertain about why so many people opted out of politics in these years. But the fact that they did certainly underscores the limitations of Progressive political reform.

Regulating the Economy

The other Progressive effort at the state level involved regulating the economy to make it operate more justly and humanely. By 1916, 32 states had enacted statutes providing compensation for injured workmen; 32 had laws regulating the hours worked by women and children; all exerted some control over child labor; and 11 specified minimum wages for women. The leading progressive states, like Wisconsin under Governor Robert "Fighting Bob" La Follette and California under Governor Hiram Johnson, created commissions to regulate the rates charged by railroads and public utilities and increased taxes on corporations.

Most of these measures accomplished less than their sponsors claimed, and some did very little good at all. State regulation of the railroads, for example, did not benefit "the public" in any simple sense. The chief beneficiaries, and the principal advocates, were the shipping interests—large merchants and commercial farmers—who set their own interests above those of railroad bond holders.

Laws banning child labor had mixed effects. At the opening of the century almost one out of every 5 youths aged 10 to 15 worked for wages; in 1930 it was less than one in 20. In 1900 only half a million students were enrolled in public high schools, a small minority of the age group. By 1930 more than 8 times that many students went on to high school, due to child labor and mandatory school attendance laws. Most young people were doubtless better off spending more years in school and fewer in the factory. But that was an unmixed blessing only in the eyes of middle class reformers who lacked an understanding of the pressures of poverty that had forced so many children into the labor market in the first place. To households that depended on the income of their children as the only source of savings to tide the family through a period of unemployment, the ban would have been beneficial only if it had been accompanied by other reforms that alleviated that core problem—unemployment insurance, for example. Child labor laws treated the symptoms and made the disease—poverty—worse.

State legislation making employers financially responsible for accidents incurred by their employees, and obligating them to carry insurance to cover the costs, were an advance from the dog-eat-dog era when the "fellow servant" rule made it so difficult for an injured worker to collect in court (see Chapter 20). But such laws weren't the great boon to downtrodden workers nor the blow to grasping employers that reformers thought they were. Businessmen actually found that they solved a serious problem. The legal profession had been growing very rapidly, and some hungry young lawyers had become "ambulance chasers" desperate for work. Although injured workers who sued their employers didn't have much chance of winning, given the prevailing doctrine that direct negligence by the employer had to be proven, they did have some. And ambulance chasers were finding it worthwhile to take such cases on a contingent fee basis—a large fee if they won, but no charge to the client if they lost. The volume of suits by workmen increased sharply as a result. When attorneys faced a sympathetic jury, they sometimes won alarmingly high damage awards. Although the new compulsory compensation system made it impossible for employers to get off scot-free, as often happened before, that disadvantage was more than offset by two benefits. The employer's losses from accidents became strictly predictable; he knew what his annual premium would cost. And the costs were kept quite low, because the award schedule specified by the typical compensation statute was well below what the more fortunate workmen had been winning in court. Far from being a menace to business interests, compulsory workmen's compensation introduced a new stability and rationality into an environment that had become dangerously unpredictable.

Progressive concerns over the plight of working women were reflected in a plethora of state laws governing hours, wages, and working conditions. They rested on the assumption, pervasive in American culture at the time, that women were fragile creatures who needed special protection. Restraints on the maximum work week for female employees, like child labor laws, hurt the very poorest families, who needed the income from as many hours of work as possible. Minimum wage laws boosted female earnings somewhat, but were declared unconstitutional by the U.S. Supreme Court in 1923 (a decision that was reversed in the 1930s).

There were inherent limits to the economic regulation that could be achieved at the state level. The corporations were national organizations, operating across state lines, with resources to hire expert legal defenders that few states could match. And a state that imposed regulations that seriously impaired business interests ran the risk of driving them out into other states where the climate for business was more favorable. Some of these problems, reformers came to perceive, required action by the federal government.

NATIONAL PROGRESSIVISM

The first steps in the direction of national progressivism were taken under Theodore Roosevelt, who entered the White House as a result of William McKinley's assassination in 1901. Roosevelt's twenty years in public life as a Republican regular gave little hint that his administration would set the nation on a new course. A Harvard-educated aristocrat, he believed that "the best men" should rule—and had no doubt he was among them. In his career as New York state assemblyman, New York City Police Commissioner, Assistant Secretary of the Navy, and Governor of New York, he had displayed no interest in reform causes, except in structural municipal reform measures aimed at his Tammany Hall opponents. But he was young—only 43—and represented a new political generation. All the Republican presidents from Grant to McKinley had been Civil War officers; Roosevelt saw Lincoln's funeral procession as a boy of seven. And he had boundless energy, zeal, and love of the limelight. It is hard to believe but true that he once was shot in the chest while on the campaign trail and refused to stop for medical assistance. "I will make this speech or die," he trumpeted. "It is one thing or the other. I have just been shot, but it takes more than that to kill a Bull Moose." Only after an hour's speech did he proceed to the hospital, where it was discovered that the bullet had fractured a rib but stopped just short of puncturing a lung. Roosevelt regarded the White House as "a bully pulpit" from which to preach his gospel of "the strenuous life." He certainly was a strenuous president, an aggressive leader in both domestic and foreign affairs.

Roosevelt took office in the midst of the greatest wave of business consolidation in American history. In the years 1897–1904, 4,227 firms merged into 257 corporate combinations. The most dramatic merger, which created the U.S. Steel Corporation, occurred just as he entered the White House. J.P. Morgan, the investment banker who raked in a profit of $150 million for organizing it, merged Carnegie Steel and its eight largest competitors into the world's first billion-dollar corporation, one that controlled two-thirds of the entire national market for steel castings and ingots. By 1904, one huge firm controlled half or more of the total output in no less than 78 industries. The 300 companies valued at $10 million or more owned over 40 percent of the private wealth in the United States. The six leading railroad corporations held 95 percent of the country's rail mileage. Two banking firms—those of J.P. Morgan and John D. Rockefeller—controled 341 directorships in 112 corporations with resources totaling $22 billion, more than the assessed value of all property in all states west of the Mississippi!

Roosevelt viewed these developments with some apprehension. He delighted in the prosperity that was the fruit of economic growth, but was concerned that the growing power of capital could be exercised irresponsibly. And he had an astute sense that public fear of the trusts could be exploited to win him public support. The bitterly contested anthracite coal strike of 1902 offered the opportunity. Roosevelt had never been a friend of organized labor, and during the Pullman strike had actually urged that the strikers be shot. But by the time of the coal crisis, he had concluded that stable trade unions might be necessary to prevent mass discontent of a more radical character. As the strike ground on, Roosevelt saw that a dangerous fuel shortage was not far off and decided to intervene. Instead of sending in federal troops to break the strike, as Grover Cleveland had done in the Pullman conflict, Roosevelt threatened the recalcitrant mine owners that he would send in troops to take over the mines unless they agreed to arbitrate the dispute. It was the first presidential intervention on behalf of labor's cause in American history—and it worked. The owners capitulated, and the result of the arbitration was concessions to the union.

Roosevelt's decision to indict the Northern Securities Company for violating the Sherman Antitrust Act that same year also surprised and dismayed big business. The company was a merger of two vast rail networks, the Northern Pacific and Great Northern railroads, engineered by J.P. Morgan. The Supreme Court upheld the Justice Department's case in 1904, dissolving the company and giving the Sherman Act at least a few teeth. This instance of "trust–busting" proved very popular with the public, and Roosevelt followed it up with several others, the most important being prosecutions of Standard Oil of New Jersey and the American Tobacco Company. The Supreme Court dissolved both firms in 1911, but the decision included an important new constraint on antitrust action—the "rule of reason." The Sherman Act, said the court, did not forbid all combinations in restraint of trade, but only those that exerted "undue" influence. It was up to the judiciary to determine what was reasonable restraint in each case.

Even more sobering for trustbusters than the rule of restraint was what actually happened after the dissolution of Standard Oil and the American Tobacco Company—practically nothing. Separating Standard Oil of New Jersey from its 37 subsidiary companies and breaking American Tobacco into three firms did not, it turned out, increase competition and force down gasoline and cigarette prices. Consumers were unaffected.

Federal Regulation

Although Roosevelt won headlines and votes for his assaults on a few trusts, he did not oppose economic concentration *per se*, only particular combinations that seemed in especially flagrant disregard of the public interest. In his view, there were "good trusts" as well as "bad trusts," and he thought it would be folly to interfere with the former simply because of their size and market power. "We draw the line," he said, "against misconduct, not against wealth."

Instead of breaking up giant corporations, Roosevelt proposed federal regulation to ensure responsible conduct. "Somehow or other," he said, "we shall have to work out methods of controlling the big corporations *without* paralyzing the energies of the business community." He succeeded in winning approval of several bills to that end. The Elkins Act of 1903 outlawed railroad rebates to favored shippers, and gave federal courts the power to enjoin railroads from discriminating against any customer. 1906 brought a burst of new laws—the Meat Inspection Act, the Pure Food and Drug Act, and the Hepburn Act, which strengthened the Interstate Commerce Commission and authorized it to set maximum railroad rates. A brief review of the Meat Inspection Act will clarify the point that can be made about all of them—that they were not simple victories of the public interest over the special interests but complex struggles in which the affected industries skillfully defended themselves.

The Meat Inspection Act was passed as a result of public outrage at the grossly unsanitary conditions in the meat-packing industry that had been publicized in Upton Sinclair's sensational muckraking novel, *The Jungle*. The compulsory inspection system it established did indeed eliminate those abuses and ensure cleaner and safer meat. But it was not a serious blow to Swift, Armour, and the other "Big Five" meat-packing corporations. They had long been receptive to some kind of federal regulation. Having the federal stamp of approval on their products would make them more salable in both the American and the foreign market, a particularly important consideration once the revelations of *The Jungle* had cut sales almost in half. Furthermore, the burden of meeting the higher sanitary standards would fall less heavily on them than on the proprietors of smaller firms who felt a greater temptation to sell diseased or spoiled meat to compete with the giant firms. The Big Five might have been somewhat hurt if each company had been forced to pay for the costs of inspecting its products, and to put a date on its canned meat. Efforts to incorporate these requirements into the bill, however, were defeated after energetic lobbying by the industry. On the other hand, the packers' efforts to write a guarantee of a broad court review into the bill to ensure that their property interests were not impaired was beaten down. On the whole, the final measure provided valuable new protection for the public, but in a manner quite tolerable to the corporate giants.

Conservation

Much the same can be said about the conservation movement. Perhaps Teddy Roosevelt's most far-sighted and most popular achievement was the imposition of new controls over the exploitation of America's natural resources. There had been precedents for federal action, beginning with the creation of Yellowstone National Park in 1872. But Roosevelt developed a national conservation program on an immense scale. More than 148 million acres were set aside as national forest land during his administration, and over 80 million acres of mineral lands were withdrawn from public sale. The U.S. Forest Service was established, and given supervision over 51 new wildlife reserves and several national monuments, including the Grand Canyon. Enormous tracts of forest were protected from indiscriminate cutting by lumber companies.

THE NEED FOR REGULATION OF THE MEAT PACKERS

When the whole ham was spoiled it came into the department of Elzbieta. Cut up by the two-thousand-revolutions-a-minute flyers, and mixed with half a ton of other meat, no odor that ever was in a ham could make any difference. There was never the least attention paid to what was cut up for sausage; there would come all the way back from Europe old sausage that had been rejected, and that was mouldy and white—it would be dosed with borax and glycerine, and dumped into the hoppers, and made over again for home consumption. There would be meat stored in great piles in rooms; and the water from leaky roofs would drip over it, and thousands of rats would race about on it. It was too dark in these storage places to see well, but a man could run his hand over these piles of meat and sweep off handfuls of the dried dung of rats. These rats were nuisances, and the packers would put poisoned bread out for them, they would die, and then rats, bread, and meat would go into the hoppers together.

—Upton Sinclair, *The Jungle,* 1906

The conservation movement, however, did not mark the beginnings of an ecological concern for preserving Nature unspoiled. The central aim of Progressive conservation policies was not to preserve the wilderness, but to exploit the country's resources in a way that would be more efficient in the long run. It was an effort applauded not only by the public in general but by the most powerful lumber companies as well.

Most of the land added to the public domain was not set aside for strictly recreational use, but was instead made available for selective cutting and systematic replanting. It was the large firms with good connections to the bureaucrats in the Forest Service who were allowed those privileges. The losers were the smaller operators who had previously been free to slash, grab, and move on to other virgin forests. Checking their operations was indeed in the long-term public interest, for it prevented the squandering of a precious resource. But it was likewise in the interest of the largest corporations in the industry.

Some Americans supported conservation on ecological grounds, to be sure—for example, the great naturalist John Muir and members of the Sierra Club (formed in 1892). But they were an impotent minority, as was demonstrated by the outcome of a major conservation dispute in 1913, during the administration of Woodrow Wilson. The city of San Francisco was short of water, and the best way of obtaining it was by constructing a dam that would submerge the spectacularly beautiful Hetch-Hetchy Valley 150 miles to the east. Hetch-Hetchy was part of Yosemite Valley National Park. Invading a national park for such purposes seemed an unconscionable outrage to true lovers of nature. But their numbers were too few. The dam was built and the valley disappeared under the water.

Roosevelt and the World

Although Theodore Roosevelt had been an ardent expansionist in 1898, he made no effort to seize other colonies during his two terms as President. His foreign policies were aggressive, however, and he scorned interference from Congress, setting an unfortunate precedent for later "imperial presidents." In 1907, for example, he ordered the "Great White Fleet," the Navy's new battleships, to sail around the world to demonstrate America's might, even though Congress had refused to appropriate funds to pay for the trip. Congress obviously could not leave the ships stranded in the middle of the Pacific. Roosevelt had lost his enthusiasm for oversea possessions, however, having discovered that colonial rule could be a difficult and costly business. Suppressing the Philippine insurrection of 1899–1902 required expenditures of $600 million, over twice as much as the war with Spain. And it quickly became evident that islands 5,000 miles from American shores could not be defended against an assault from another major power without defense expenditures on a scale no Congress would contemplate. The fruits of empire were not nearly as sweet as anticipated.

Theodore Roosevelt liked to boast that he "walked softly but carried a big stick." In the Western Hemisphere, he didn't walk very softly; in the rest of the world, he didn't carry a very big stick. He regarded the Caribbean as an American lake, and all the countries of Latin America as American client states. He (and his successor, Taft) followed policies that amounted to colonialism in everything but name. The United States did remove its troops from Cuba and allowed a native government to assume power. But the terms of withdrawal—specified in the 1901 Platt Amendment—gave the United States the right to veto treaties Cuba concluded with other countries, to intervene it its internal affairs "for the protection of life, property, and individual liberty," and to take any land it chose for naval bases (such as the one constructed at Guantanamo Bay). With that authority, Roosevelt put the island under American occupation from 1906 to 1909 in order to suppress an insurrection. "I am doing my best to persuade the Cubans that if only they will be good they will be happy," he explained. "I am seeking the very minimum of interference necessary to make them good."

The rest of Latin America had to be "good" too. Although the Platt Amendment applied to Cuba alone, Roosevelt put all of the Western Hemisphere under an American protectorate when he proclaimed the "Roosevelt Corollary" to the Monroe Doctrine in 1904. It declared that the United States would unilaterally exercise "an international police power" throughout the Western Hemisphere. Whenever political turmoil in a country reached a level that impaired its ability to pay its foreign debts, thereby offering a pretext for intervention by a European power, the United States instead would step in to restore order and ensure that the debt was paid. On these grounds, Nicaragua underwent American military occupation for 20 years, Haiti for 19, and the Dominican Republic for 8. The Latin

THE ROOSEVELT COROLLARY

Chronic wrongdoing, or an impotence which results in a general loosening of the ties of civilized society, may ultimately require intervention by some civilized nation, and in the Western Hemisphere the adherence of the United States to the Monroe Doctrine may force the United States, however reluctantly, in flagrant cases of such wrongdoing or impotence, to the exercise of an international police power. If every country washed by the Caribbean Sea would show the progress in stable and just civilization which with the aid of the Platt amendment Cuba has shown since our troops left the island, and which so many of the republics in both Americas are constantly and brilliantly showing, all question of interference by this Nation with their affairs would be at an end. Our interests and those of our southern neighbors are in reality identical. They have great natural riches, and if within their borders the reign of law and justice obtains, prosperity is sure to come to them. While they thus obey the primary laws of civilized society they may rest assured that they will be treated by us in a spirit of cordial and helpful sympathy. We would interfere with them only in the last resort, and then only if it became evident that their inability or unwillingness to do justice at home and abroad had violated the rights of the United States or had invited foreign aggression to the detriment of the entire body of American nations. It is a mere truism to say that every nation, whether in America or anywhere else, which desires to maintain its freedom, its independence, must ultimately realize that the right of such independence can not be separated from the responsibility of making good use of it.

American republics retained the freedom to govern themselves, but only as long as they did so in a manner acceptable to the United States.

These were not instances in which America's overwhelming power was employed to suppress social revolutions that would otherwise have benefited the peasant masses. Intervention was provoked not by genuine social upheavals but by repeated palace coups that brought no redirection of economic and social policy and benefited only their organizers. In the five years before American action in Haiti, for example, there had been five coups and three presidential assassinations. If the United States had not played this role, European imperial powers with economic interests in Latin America would doubtless have stepped in themselves. It was the blockade and bombardment of Venezuela by Germany, Britain, and Italy in 1902–1903 that prompted Roosevelt to launch the policy in the first place. The issue was not whether the small and weak republics of Latin America should be left truly free or forced to conform to the wishes of the United States. The issue

MAP 22-1
U.S. Involvement in the Caribbean

concerned *which* of the major world powers would oversee them, and there is no reason to believe that the people of these countries would have been better off if Britain, Germany, or Italy rather than the United States had played that role.

Still, America's treatment of her neighbors to the south was high-handed. The ugliest example was the land grab that preceded the construction of the Panama Canal. The best site for a canal lay within Colombia. Roosevelt's Secretary of State, John Hay, offered the Colombian government $10 million for the rights; the Colombians insisted on $20 million, plus guarantees of sovereignty in the canal zone. Roosevelt was furious at the "Dagoes" for holding out—they were "inefficient bandits," mere "jack rabbits" who could not be allowed to "bar one of the future highways of civilization." So he engineered a coup d'état. Phillipe Bunau-Varilla, the agent for a French company that claimed prior rights to build a canal through Panama, was given to understand that the United States would not interfere if he were to lead a struggle for Panamanian independence from Colombia. Indeed, it would recognize the new government promptly and would use American warships to prevent Colombia from suppressing the uprising. The Navy arrived, the new state of Panama was born, and it immediately granted the United States canal rights for the original $10 million. Another $40 million went to Bunau–Varilla's company for surrendering its rights in the area, $600,000 of which ended up in his pocket. Some Congressmen, it was rumored, were among the stockholders who benefited. Colombia got no compensation at all until 1921, when it was paid $25 million—but that conciliatory gesture was prompted less by guilt than by American eagerness to win concessions in newly discovered Colombian oil fields.

Outside the Western Hemisphere, Roosevelt was less prone to shake the big stick and more willing to walk softly. His administration was the first to regularly send American representatives to international conferences. Roosevelt watched the course of European affairs closely, but refrained from entangling commitments there. He did use his considerable persuasive skills as a mediator to good effect in 1906, when a war between Germany and the British and French threatened over territorial rights in Morocco. But it was not followed up by further attempts to use American influence to alleviate the tensions that exploded into an all-out European war in less than a decade.

The Far East was of special concern to Roosevelt, because a major rationale for acquiring colonies in the Pacific had been to open up Asian markets to American traders. The McKinley administration had articulated a policy to foster such trade, expressed in Secretary of State John Hay's 1899 and 1900 "open door" notes to the imperial powers that—in the wake of the Boxer Rebellion—were then carving up China into separate spheres of influence. The United States had sent 2,500 troops to China to help suppress the uprising, and tried to use its leverage to keep China from being dismembered by foreign powers. Roosevelt supported the Open Door policy, but realized that he had little power to enforce it. Japan and Russia in particular had a much stronger stake in the area than the United States, and were attempting to annex Manchuria. The riches that were supposed to flow from the Far Eastern trade in general and the China trade in particular never materialized. The volume of commerce with tiny Cuba alone was four times greater than that with China; exports to all of Asia were under 5 percent of the American total. About all that Roosevelt could do to preserve the Open Door principle without running the risk of a war that might have been unpopular was to encourage the Japanese to exert pressure against the Russians. He did what he could to keep China open when he persuaded Russia and Japan to end the Russo-Japanese War at a peace conference he arranged in 1905; the settlement left Manchuria part of China. And the Root-Takamura Agreement of 1908 affirmed Japan's commitment to the Open Door. But it also conceded de facto Japanese domination in northern China. The continuing weakness of China and the expansionist energies of Japan would be sources of grave trouble in the future.

From Roosevelt to Taft

As Roosevelt's second term in office approached its end, he advanced a number of new reform proposals. Denouncing "certain malefactors of great wealth," he called for taxes on large inheritances and high incomes, federal control over railroad securities, limits on the power of courts to grant injunctions against labor unions, a mandatory eight-hour day, and a national system of workmen's compensation.

There were still too many conservatives in Congress to push any of these bills through, but he had hopes for the future. Recent Congressional elections had returned a growing number of Senators and Representatives with progressive leanings, and there was every reason to believe that Roosevelt's successor would be dealing with a Congress more receptive to reform.

That was true. But Roosevelt's chosen successor, William Howard Taft, proved to be the obstacle. He was so resistant to progressive demands that his administration ended in political catastrophe—a split in the Republican party that made possible the election of a Democratic President, Woodrow Wilson. Theodore Roosevelt ranks among America's most energetic and forceful chief executives. William Howard Taft, who weighed in at over 350 pounds, was its fattest president. He was intelligent, but passive and painfully shy. "I don't like the limelight," he said.

The Congress returned in the election of 1908 was sharply divided between the Republican old guard, led by Speaker of the House "Uncle Joe" Cannon and Senator Nelson Aldrich, and a new progressive "insurgent" element, led by Senators Robert La Follette and William Borah and Representative George Norris. At first Taft attempted to keep on good terms with both groups, but he sided with the old guard on the issue of tariff reform and lost the respect of the insurgents. They were further alienated in 1910 when Taft fired Gifford Pinchot, Roosevelt's appointee as Chief Forester, after Pinchot had publicly criticized the Secretary of the Interior for releasing public land and reservoir sites to business.

As the fissure in the Republican Party widened, Roosevelt decided he could no longer remain in retirement from public life, and he leaped into the fray on the side of the insurgents. In a major speech at Osawatomie, Kansas in 1910 he called for a "New Nationalism," a government that recognized that "every man holds his property subject to the general right of the community to regulate its use to whatever degree the public welfare may require." He abandoned trust-busting altogether, on the grounds that "combinations in industry are the result of an imperative economic law. The way out lies not in attempting to prevent such combinations but in completely controlling them to the interest of the public welfare." He repeated his earlier endorsement of income and inheritance taxes on "the big fortunes," and attacked conservative judges for failing to value "human welfare rather than property." It was necessary to change "the present rules of the game" in order to "work for a more substantial equality of opportunity and of reward."

The 1912 Election

Taft and other conservatives who found these views dangerously radical dug in their heels. Roosevelt sought the Republican presidential nomination in 1912, denouncing Taft supporters as "men of cold heart and narrow mind, who believe we can find safety in dull timidity and dull inaction." But Taft had the votes, and Roosevelt stormed out of the hall to form a new party, the Progressive or "Bull Moose," party, so called after Roosevelt's claim that he felt as strong as a bull

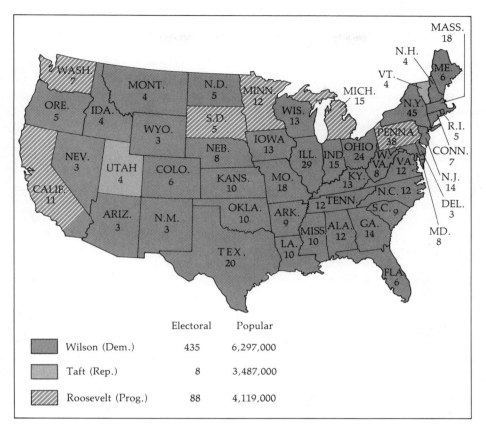

MAP 22–2
The 1912 Election

	Electoral	Popular
Wilson (Dem.)	435	6,297,000
Taft (Rep.)	8	3,487,000
Roosevelt (Prog.)	88	4,119,000

moose. The Progressive platform followed the outlines of Roosevelt's New Nationalism, with a long list of welfare measures called "industrial minimums," a proposal for popular overriding of judicial decisions, and a demand for women's suffrage. Even Jane Addams was won over, despite the clash between her pacifism and Roosevelt's muscular militarism. Conservatives were appalled. The *New York Times* warned that Roosevelt stood for "Socialism and Revolution, contempt for law, and doctrines that lead to destruction."

The split in the Republican ranks gave the Democrats their first serious crack at the presidency since the depression of the 1890s. Prospects seemed especially good because the Democratic party had been experiencing a resurgence in the cities. Massive waves of "new immigrants" from Eastern and Southern Europe were pouring into the cities, and the majority were Catholics or Jews who gravitated towards the Democratic camp. The Democrats they were sending to the state legislatures and Congress were "urban liberals," concerned with legislation to benefit working people. It was a trend that would lead to a near civil war within the party a decade later, when the northern urban progressive wing battled incessantly with the southern reactionary faction. But the party was sufficiently unified in 1912 under Woodrow Wilson, a Virginian who had long lived in the North and who had modest progressive credentials. Wilson won an easy victory, winning with 6.3 million votes to Roosevelt's 4.1 million and Taft's 3.5. Eugene V. Debs, the American Socialist Party's candidate, got 6 percent of the popular vote, the high-water mark for a Socialist candidate in American history.

Wilson, former President of Princeton University and governor of New Jersey, was an eloquent campaigner. The greatest menace to America, in his view, was "the curse of bigness," a pet phrase of his chief economic advisor, Boston attorney Louis D. Brandeis. The country needed not a New Nationalism but a New Freedom. Roosevelt's plans to harness the trusts through strong regulatory agencies manned by experts would compound the evil of big business by creating an even greater evil—big government. Appealing to traditional Democratic suspicions of concentrated power, Wilson pledged that he would restore opportunity for "the man on the make" by disentangling the "colossal community" of corporate interests, and would "pull apart, and gently but firmly and persistently dissect." Lest anyone be frightened by such sweeping promises, however, he added remarks of calculated ambiguity. "I am for big business and I am against the trusts," he declared inscrutably, without providing a clue as to the distinction between them. He did not "wish to upset business or interfere with any honest or natural process of it"; business underlay "everything in our national life, including our spiritual life." It was a winning combination, put together by a master politician.   .

The Wilson Administration

Wilson was a forceful and effective president, until the grave foreign policy miscalculations he made late in his second term (see Chapter 23). He was the first chief executive since John Adams to address Congress in person, and he expended great effort to pressure or cajole the legislators into action. Some of his activism was directed toward unfortunate ends. A Southerner committed to white supremacy, he ordered racial segregation in federal agencies and deprived blacks of all but the most menial government jobs. In other respects, however, his achievements were impressive.

Wilson's first priority was to lower the tariff. Every Democratic President since the Civil War had tried to do so; Wilson was the first to succeed. The Underwood tariff bill of 1913 lowered duties on imports by 25 to 40 percent. More important than the cuts was the provision of the law that generated funds to make up for the loss in tariff revenues—a graduated tax of up to 7 percent on high personal incomes and a 1 percent levy on corporate incomes. An earlier federal income tax, passed during the Civil War, had been abandoned in 1872. Another income tax bill had been passed by Congress in 1894, as part of a tariff measure, but the conservatives who dominated the Supreme Court called it a dangerous "assault on capital" that would be "a stepping-stone to others, larger and more sweeping," and declared it unconstitutional. The Sixteenth Amendment to the Constitution, proposed in 1909 and ratified just before Wilson took office in 1913, was necessary to break the judicial stranglehold over taxation policy. The new administration quickly took advantage of the opportunity. Taxing away 7 percent of J.P. Morgan's income and 1 percent of U.S. Steel's was not a great leveling act, of course, but establishing the principle of progressive taxation was a major step toward social justice.

A second key Wilsonian reform was the creation of the Federal Reserve system. The banking industry was in near chaos when he took office. Control over the size of the money supply, the availability of credit, and the location of banking facilities was entirely in private hands. There was pressure for change from western and southern farmers who wanted easier credit, from critics of Wall Street who believed that such vital decisions should be made by a public body, and from bankers who wanted a central bank that could pool reserves and shift them about readily in response to crises. After complex maneuvering, Wilson won a bill that struck a compromise between the contending forces. The Federal Reserve Act of 1913 created 12 district banks, two-thirds of whose directors were elected by private bankers in the region, under the supervision of a central Federal Reserve Board with quite limited powers. It provided an adequate reserve system and a flexible currency, and increased the supply of mortgage money for farmers. But it also gave Wall Street much of what it wanted, partly because Wilson gave three of the five seats on the first Federal Reserve Board to large bankers, partly because the New York Federal Reserve Bank quickly came to dominate the system, rather than the nominal controlling authority, the Federal Reserve Board. Politics, however, is the art of the possible, and Wilson had done all that was politically possible to create a system that allowed public input into economic decisions that had previously been made by the J.P. Morgans of the country.

When he came to deal with the problem of the "colossal community" of corporate interests, Wilson did an about-face. Initially he backed the trust–busting Clayton Antitrust Act, which closed several gaps in the Sherman Act.[1] By the time a watered down version was approved, Wilson was lobbying for the creation of a Federal Trade Commission, which was to police corporate conduct a la the New Nationalism. It was empowered to gather information from businesses and to prevent unfair competitive practices. It was a substantial extension of government power, although in practice it promoted corporate interests. The FTC protected firms from unexpected antitrust prosecutions by offering advice as to whether planned actions were "unfair." It showed considerable solicitude toward the companies it was supposed to regulate, partly because the men appointed to preside over it tended to be drawn from the affected industries, partly because conservative judges had review power over its actions.

A second wave of Wilsonian reform came with the approach of the 1916 election, in which Wilson was challenged by a progressive Republican, Charles Evans Hughes. The Progressive Party had collapsed and the Republicans had made

---

[1]The Clayton Act was hailed by Samuel Gompers as "labor's Magna Carta," because it exempted labor organizations from antitrust prosecutions and attempted to limit the granting of injunctions in labor disputes. Gompers' enthusiasm was misguided; loopholes in the language of the Act left anti-union injunctions in widespread use until the law was rewritten in the 1930s.

a strong comeback in the 1914 elections, so Wilson appealed to labor and other reform-minded groups. The La Follette Seaman's Act improved working conditions in the Merchant Marine. The Adamson Act provided an eight-hour day for employees of interstate railroads; federal employees were granted workmen's compensation. The peak income tax rate was raised to 15 percent, which meant that more than 95 percent of the revenue came from the tiny group earning over $20,000 per year. Agricultural credit terms were eased by the Federal Farm Loan Act. A federal ban on child labor was passed, although the Supreme Court promptly declared it unconstitutional. A final important gesture appealing to the left was Wilson's decision to appoint Louis D. Brandeis to the Supreme Court, the first Jew on the high court and a sharp critic of the conservative jurisprudence of the day. These steps, plus the advantage of being an incumbent, were enough to win him a victory over Hughes, although only by the thinnest margin. The time for further domestic experimentation was over, however. By the time of Wilson's second inaugural, the nation was on the verge of entering a war that would seriously alter the political landscape.

SUGGESTED READINGS

Richard Hofstadter, *The Age of Reform: From Bryan to F.D.R.* (1955) is a brilliant synthesis. Otis L. Graham, Jr., *The Great Campaigns: Reform and War in America, 1920–1928* (1971), William L. O'Neill, *The Progressive Years: America Comes of Age* (1975), and J.W. Chambers II, *The Tyranny of Change: America in the Progressive Era, 1900–1917* (1980) are more overviews of the era.

On the urban conditions that distressed reformers, see Robert H. Bremner, *From the Depths: The Discovery of Poverty in America* (1956), Allen F. Davis, *Spearheads for Reform: The Social Settlements and the Progressive Movement, 1890–1914* (1967), David Tyack, *The One Best System: A History of American Urban Education* (1974), Roy Lubove, *The Progressives and the Slums: Tenement House Reform in New York City, 1890–1917* (1962), and John D. Buenker, *Urban Liberalism and Progressive Reform* (1973). Jane Addams, *20 Years at Hull House* (1910) should not be missed. Zane L. Miller, *Boss Cox's Cincinnati* (1968), Melvin Holli, *Reform in Detroit: Hazen Pingree and Urban Politics* (1969), John M. Allswang, *A House for All Peoples: Ethnic Politics in Chicago, 1890–1936* (1971), John M. Allswang, *Bosses, Machines, and Urban Voters* (1977), Theodore J. Lowi, *At the Pleasure of the Mayor: Patronage and Power in New York City, 1898–1958* (1964), and Nancy Weiss, *Charles Francis Murphy, 1858–1924: Respectability and Responsibility in Tammany Politics* (1968) illuminate municipal political struggles. Frederick C. Howe, *Confessions of a Reformer* (1925) and William L. Riordan, *Plunkitt of Tammany Hall* (1905) present the views of a municipal reform leader and a machine boss.

Sheldon Hackney, *Populism to Progressivism in Alabama* (1969), Richard M. Abrams, *Conservatism in a Progressive Era: Massachusetts Politics, 1900–1912* (1964), and David Thelen, *The New Citizenship: Origins of Progressivism in Wisconsin, 1885–1900* (1972) examine state politics. On the level of national politics, see

Robert H. Wiebe, *Businessmen and Reform: A Study of the Progressive Movement* (1962), L.L. Gould, *Reform and Regulation: American Politics, 1900–1916* (1978), and L.J. Holt, *Congressional Insurgents and the Party System, 1901–1916* (1967), Samuel P. Hays, *Conservation and the Gospel of Efficiency: The Progressive Conservation Movement, 1890–1920* (1959) and James H. Timberlake, *Prohibition and the Progressive Crusade, 1900–1920* (1963). William H. Harbaugh, *Power and Responsibility: The Life and Times of Theodore Roosevelt* (1961), and John Morton Blum, *The Republican Roosevelt* (1954) are good biographies. Woodrow Wilson's life is the subject of five volumes by Arthur S. Link and of John Blum's stimulating essay, *Woodrow Wilson and the Politics of Morality* (1956). David Thelen, *Robert La Follette and the Insurgent Spirit* (1976) is another useful brief biography. On the failure of the left, see John P. Diggins, *The American Left in the 20th Century* (1973), David Shannon, *The Socialist Party in America* (1967) and Melvyn Dubofsky, *We Shall Be All: A History of the Industrial Workers of the World* (1969). Mary O. Furner, *Advocacy and Objectivity: A Crisis in the Professional-ization of American Social Science, 1865–1905* (1976), R. Jackson Wilson, *In Quest of Community: Social Philosophy in the United States, 1860–1920* (1968), James Gilbert, *Designing the Industrial State: The Intellectual Pursuit of Collectivism in America, 1880—1940* (1972), and Jean B. Quandt, *From the Small Town to the Great Community* (1970) probe the intellectual assumptions of American Progressives.

George F. Kennan, *American Diplomacy, 1900–1950* (1951) offers shrewd insights. The Roosevelt administration's conduct of foreign affairs is dealt with in Howard K. Beale, *Theodore Roosevelt and the Rise of America to World Power* (1956), Raymond A. Esthus, *Theodore Roosevelt and the International Rivalries* (1970), Frederick Marks III, *Velvet on Iron: The Diplomacy of Theodore Roosevelt* (1979), Dexter Perkins, *The Monroe Doctrine, 1867–1907* (1966), and Walter LaFeber, *The Panama Canal* (1978). See also Joan Hoff Wilson, *American Business and Foreign Policy, 1902–1933* (1971).

Chapter Twenty-Three

The Great War
and Its Aftermath

Woodrow Wilson had no taste for the saber-rattling "dollar diplomacy" of his Republican predecessors. He proclaimed himself a man of peace and an anticolonialist, and appointed pacifist William Jennings Bryan his Secretary of State. Bryan had faith that war could be prevented by legal pledges, and quickly negotiated treaties with 21 countries that bound them to submit disputes to impartial investigating committees and refrain from using force until a report was handed down. Wilson vetoed American participation in a multi-national banking consortium formed to build railroads in China, on the grounds that it represented undue external interference. When asked to intervene in Mexico when American property was endangered, he declared, "I am President of the United States, and not of a small group of American investors with vested interests in Mexico."

But the change from the Roosevelt and Taft administrations was more in rhetoric than in substance. After rejecting the China consortium, Wilson accepted another in 1917 that provided more favorable terms for the United States. He was as vigorous in policing the behavior of our neighbors to the south as his predecessors had been. He kept on the occupying forces Taft had sent to Nicaragua, and sent the marines to take over Haiti and Santo Domingo as well. He purchased the Virgin Islands to help protect the Panama Canal. And despite his earlier disavowal, he did meddle repeatedly in Mexican affairs, twice to the point at which war between the two countries was very narrowly averted. Wilson was motivated not only by a concern for the billion dollars in American investments there; he genuinely believed that it was his duty to assist in the formation of a

Woodrow Wilson departs for France, December 4, 1918. Beyond the gangplank, wearing a tophat, is then Secretary of the Navy, Franklin Delano Roosevelt.

liberal constitutional government, whether or not the assistance was requested. He probably saw nothing anomalous in the advice of the Congressman who said, "I'd go to Mexico with beans in one hand and hand grenades in the other, and God help them if they do not accept our well-intentioned and sincere friendship." A Mexican, we may surmise, would have wondered "with friends like this, who needs enemies?"

THE ROAD TO WAR

In August, 1914 the guns began to boom across Europe. Every major European country was by then part of a system of alliances carefully contrived to prevent war by guaranteeing that any use of military force would quickly draw in all the major powers. It would bring a war of catastrophic proportions—a risk that no rational and responsible government would run. (An uncomfortable analogue, perhaps, to the current assumption that nuclear war will be so destructive that no one will ever dare start one.) The rationality and responsibility on which the stability of the system depended, alas, was not in evidence during the crisis that erupted in the summer of 1914. Convinced (mistakenly) that the Serbian government had arranged the assassination of the heir to the Austrian throne by a Serbian nationalist, Austria–Hungary declared war on Serbia. Forceful action was necessary to intimidate the restless Czechs and South Slavic peoples within its polyglot empire, whose rebelliousness seemed a much more real danger than the possibility that Russia would actually back up its treaty with Serbia with fighting men. But Russia felt compelled to mobilize, rather than lose face in Southern and Eastern Europe, and Germany was committed to the defense of Austria. France felt it necessary to support its Russian ally, particularly against the hated Germans, and Britain in turn was implicated by its treaty with France. Turkey was allied with Germany, and ready to honor her pledge. Determined to win the advantage of striking the first blow, the German Army slashed through Belgium, whose independence and neutrality had been guaranteed by the great powers for almost a century, and penetrated deeply into northern France.

At that point, however, the German offensive ground to a halt, due to strategic blunders and to fierce resistance by French and British troops. Both armies dug into trenches in a line extending more than 300 miles across Belgium and France from the English Channel almost to Switzerland. There they stayed. The front moved no more than ten miles in the next three years. But it was not for want of trying. Although successful assaults on entrenched troops equipped with machine guns were well-nigh impossible, the generals of both sides ordered repeated attacks and spent lives with astonishing prodigality. In the first year of the war alone, almost half of the families of France suffered the death of a husband or a son. By the war's end more than ten million men had gone to their graves, killing on a scale far exceeding that in any war in all previous history.

Americans were astonished and appalled at the carnage. Sympathies tended to be with the Allies. There had been longer and more favorable cultural contacts and closer economic ties with the British and French than with the Germans, and a large proportion of the population was of British descent. Germany was, at least in the technical sense, the aggressor who had invaded the lands of others. The violation of Belgian neutrality seemed shocking, and the harshness of German treatment of civilians in occupied areas of Belgium and France even more so. (Britain had shrewdly cut the transoceanic telegraph cables between the United States and the Continent, so that the news came over British cables, ensuring that German misdeeds were played up and those of the Allies played down.)

American Neutrality

Such sympathy, however, was by no means strong enough to prompt any widespread support for American intervention on behalf of the Allies. In the early phases of the conflict, hardly anyone favored such action, because no vital American interest seemed to be at stake. Wilson announced that the United States would remain neutral, and his appeal to the country to remain neutral "in thought as well as in action" met with almost universal acclaim. When the President heard a rumor that the army was working on contingency plans for fighting Germany, he told the Secretary of War that if it was true he should "relieve every officer in the general staff and order him out of Washington."

Not least among the reasons for refraining from intervention was the fact that a great many Americans had ethnic allegiances that inclined them toward the Central Powers. There were over 9 million Germans, the country's largest immigrant group. There were also 5 million fiercely anti-British Irish, a key element in the Democratic party, and 3 million Jews, for whom the Allied camp was tainted because it included Czarist Russia.

Wilson, however, was a thorough Anglophile. The writers who shaped his thinking were all British; his first book, *Congressional Government*, urged that the American system be reshaped along British lines; his favorite vacation was a bicycle trip through the Lake District with the *Oxford Book of English Verse* in his pocket. "England is fighting our fight," he confided to a close cabinet member early in the war. "I will not take any action to embarrass England when she is fighting for her life and the life of the world." His advisers—right-hand man Colonel Edward House, Robert Lansing, who replaced Bryan as Secretary of State in 1915, and Walter Hines Page, his Ambassador to Britain—were of the same mind. Page was so committed to the British cause, indeed, that he once delivered an official State Department protest against a British violation of international law to the English Foreign Secretary and said, "I do not agree with it. Now let us sit down and see how we can answer it."

The result of these convictions and predispositions was that when difficult decisions had to be made in response to pressures from the contending belligerents, the Wilson administration usually tilted toward the Allies. The pressures mounted in intensity as the war dragged on. The stalemate in the trench warfare on the Western Front impelled the leaders of the two rival alliances, Britain and Germany, to attempt to starve each other out. They were the most highly urbanized

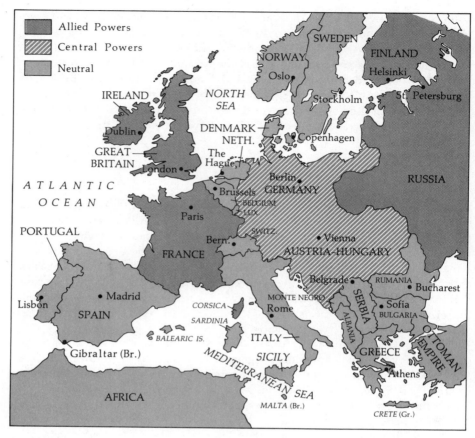

MAP 23–1
European Alignments, 1914

and industrialized countries of Europe, the ones most dependent on imports for food and industrial materials, the ones most vulnerable to economic strangulation. As the world's largest exporting country, the United States was bound to suffer from the efforts of Britain and Germany to strangle each other.

The first sign of a tilt toward the British involved loans to the warring parties. At the outset of the war, Wilson had banned foreign loans to prevent Americans from developing economic connections that would give them a vested interest in the outcome of the struggle. But it did not include interbank credits, a serious omission. In October, 1915, even that ban was lifted, because the Allies were running low on cash. Loans were permitted to both sides, so it was not a departure from neutrality, strictly speaking. But the United States had much stronger economic ties to Britain and France, and they grew still stronger as a result. By 1917, $2.25 billion had been loaned to the Allies, and only $27 million to Germany. Trade with the Allies rose from $800 million in 1914 to over $3 billion in 1916, while trade with

Germany and Austro-Hungary dropped from $169 million to a mere $1.15 million. The United States now had a stake—a large stake—in the war's outcome.

This redirection of trade was in part the result of wise British policies that encouraged it, in particular their government's decision to guarantee the purchase of enough American cotton to fix its price at its high 1913 level. But the crucial cause was the Wilson administration's decision to acquiesce in a British blockade of Germany that flouted international law, and its insistence that Germany scrupulously honor American rights on the high seas. At the onset of the war, Wilson asked the warring parties to allow neutrals to trade freely with both sides, with the exception of absolute contraband—war materials. The Germans were willing, because they were self-sufficient in munitions and armaments, but the British refused. They had to keep Germany from getting needed food and raw materials, and unilaterally declared a long list of such items contraband. Neutral merchant vessels suspected of carrying them were stopped and searched, and anything useful to Germany was confiscated. The Wilson administration lodged repeated protests, but the British regarded the blockade as a life or death measure. The British government, however, was careful never to push Wilson over the edge at critical moments, and Wilson was unwilling to threaten war. British actions, although disrespectful, infringed on property rights without threatening lives, and wrongs could be rectified by compensation negotiated after the war. Moreover, American foreign trade was flourishing as never before. The loss of $168 million in exports to Germany was not too painful to bear when sales to Britain and France had risen by over $2 billion.

Wilson was much sterner in dealing with Germany. The Germans were bent upon the same economic strangulation policies as the British, but they had only a very blunt instrument to work with—the submarine, a potent but undiscriminating weapon. A "U-boat" could not halt vessels suspected of carrying contraband; its crew was too small, and it could be sunk by a light gun or even by ramming. The first submarine crisis came in 1915 with the sinking of the *Lusitania*, a British vessel carrying 1,200 passengers, 128 of them Americans. Bryan thought it unwise to insist on the right of Americans to travel in the ships of belligerents, particularly ships carrying munitions, and urged a balanced response. Both Britain and Germany should be asked to respect neutral rights, and Americans should be barred from travel on their ships. But Wilson would not bend and demanded that Germany abandon submarine warfare altogether. Bryan resigned in protest. After a number of other incidents, in the spring of 1916, the Germans pledged that they would sink no more unarmed passenger or merchant vessels.

Their compliance, however, was due less to fear of American action than to a temporary lack of submarines and confidence that their coming summer campaign would knock the Allies out of the war. By his firm stand, Wilson had painted himself into a corner, and had in effect placed the decision for or against American intervention in the hands of the Kaiser. If he decided to unleash the submarines once again, Wilson would find it hard to do anything but declare war. Although one of his slogans in the 1916 campaign was "He kept us out of war," Wilson realized that a continued guarantee of peace was next to impossible. He confided to a friend, "Any little German lieutenant can put us into war at any time by some calculated outrage."

"There will be no war," Wilson said to Colonel House, on January 4, 1917. "This country does not intend to become involved in this war. It would be a crime against civilization for us to go in." He still hoped for a negotiated peace to stop the slaughter, and was pressuring both sides to state peace terms they would find acceptable. On January 22, he gave a great speech to the world outlining his conception of "a peace without victory," a "peace among equals." By then the chance for peace for America was virtually gone, although Wilson didn't yet know it. Two weeks before, the Kaiser had authorized a policy of unrestricted submarine warfare against neutral as well as enemy shipping, unarmed as well as armed, to be announced on January 31. Although this was almost certain to provoke war with the United States, it seemed an excellent gamble. The German High Command was convinced that it could win a decisive victory in Europe before America could mobilize. An all-out submarine campaign, the admirals assured the Kaiser, would reduce Britain to starvation and surrender within five months.

Wilson promptly broke off diplomatic relations with Germany, but hesitated over asking Congress for a declaration of war. His hesitations were overcome at the end of February, when a secret telegram from the German Foreign Secretary Zimmerman to his minister in Mexico was intercepted. It instructed the minister that if war erupted between Germany and the United States, he should invite Mexico to ally itself with Germany and should promise to see that the territory stripped from her after the Mexican War would be returned.

Another development—the overthrow of the Czar and the establishment of parliamentary democracy in Russia in March—removed a deterrent to intervention on the side of the Allies that had weighed heavily in Wilson's mind. The contest between the Allies and the Central Powers could not be regarded as a struggle between free and tyrannical governments so long as the Czarist regime, the most reactionary in Europe, was a partner of Britain and France. Now, Wilson told Congress in his April speech requesting a declaration of war, the "autocracy" had been "shaken off and the great, generous Russian people" had been added "to the forces that are fighting for freedom in the world." The world "must be made safe for democracy"—that was the rationale for American entry. It was another variation on the old theme of America's special mission, and a very expansive one.

The United States didn't really go to war to make the world safe for democracy. Theodore Roosevelt was closer to the mark when he said it was "because we had a special grievance"; we did it "to make the world safe for ourselves." Germany need not have become a threat to American safety, perhaps, had different policies been pursued before 1917. But after Wilson had defined American rights as he did, and after Germany decided to play for victory by torpedo, the safety of American citizens was indeed jeopardized. Wilson knew that the notion of "a war to end war" would appeal to the idealistic streak in the American people. Justifying it in those high blown terms, however, created expectations that were bound to be dashed.

Congress did not vote the war without debate. There was sharp opposition, led by veteran Progressives like Robert La Follette and George Norris, who charged

THE ZIMMERMAN NOTE

Berlin, January 19, 1917

On the first of February we intend to begin submarine warfare unrestricted. In spite of this it is our intention to keep neutral the United States of America. If this attempt is not successful we propose an alliance on the following basis with Mexico: That we shall make war together and together make peace. We shall give general financial support, and it is understood that Mexico is to reconquer the lost territory in New Mexico, Texas, and Arizona. The details are left for your settlement. You are instructed to inform the President of Mexico of the above in the greatest confidence as soon as it is certain there will be an outbreak of war with the United States. Please call to the attention of the President of Mexico that the employment of ruthless submarine warfare now promises to compel England to make peace in a few months.

that intervention would benefit only the international bankers and the munitions makers. Most skeptics came from Midwestern or Great Plains states with strong concentrations of German-Americans, or clusters of other groups attracted to German culture, like Scandinavians and Hollanders. Wilson denounced his critics as "a little group of willful men, representing no opinion but their own," and newspapers called them "decendants of Benedict Arnold." The war resolution finally passed, with 6 dissenting votes in the Senate and 50 in the House.

Within six months, a token force of American soldiers was fighting in the trenches of France, but not until the summer of 1918 was it possible to train and transport enough troops to play an important role in the fighting. Having entered the conflict so late, America's contribution was necessarily modest by some measures. Its total casualties—116,000 deaths—were only an eighth of those suffered by Britain, and a twelfth those of France.

The entry of the United States, however, came at a decisive moment, and it probably made the difference between victory or defeat for the Allies. U.S. Naval patrols played a key role in breaking the German submarine cordon. In early 1917, before America's involvement, 900,000 tons of shipping per month was lost to torpedos. By November, it was less than 300,000 tons, and by the next year under 200,000 tons. Without American destroyers, the Allies might well have strangled. Furthermore, American troops arrived in time to blunt and roll back the great German offensive in the summer of 1918. Lenin had seized power in Russia in the Bolshevik Revolution of November, 1917, and he accepted the harsh peace terms the Germans offered in the Treaty of Brest–Litovsk the following March. It gave Germany the rich food supplies of the Ukraine, and freed dozens of experienced divisions for service on the Western front. As a result, the German armies came very close to making a decisive breakthrough in the West. It was the hard fighting of the million American soldiers who had been landed in France by July, 1918, and the psychological lift their presence gave to the other Allied armies, that more than anything else served to turn the tide.

ON THE HOME FRONT

Woodrow Wilson was confident that American entry into the European war would help spread American democratic freedoms to the rest of the world. It certainly did not enlarge the freedoms available to the ordinary American at home. The zeal with which the Wilson administration silenced opponents of intervention virtually made the Bill of Rights a dead letter. These repressive efforts were successful—frighteningly so—but they soon boomeranged back at the President himself. Within a few years, in the midst of a national "Red Scare" triggered by wild statements by his own Attorney General, Wilson's book *The New Freedom* (1913) was banned in Nebraska. Superpatriots in the American Legion declared the book subversive in the name of the very "100 percent Americanism" Wilson had called for so stridently.

The war had many such unanticipated effects on American life, some of them temporary, some of them far-reaching. It brought important gains for blacks and women (as discussed in Chapters 25 and 26), and gave a strong but short-lived boost to the labor movement. It led the federal government into deeper involvement in the management of the economy than ever before. Most important, it unleashed waves of hysteria and xenophobia that drowned out dissent, and contributed to the triumph of two intolerant and repressive "reforms"—immigration restriction and national Prohibition.

Mobilization

The most pressing tasks for the administration after Congress had declared war against Germany were to raise an army and to regear the economy for war production—to shift from butter to guns. The troops were obtained by the first military draft since the Civil War. It worked more smoothly and met with less resistance than conscription under Lincoln because it was fairer; there were no provisions allowing the well-to-do to hire substitutes. By November, 1918, 4 million Americans were in uniform, 1.4 million of them at the front lines.

Most draftees spent their weeks at boot camp marching around with broomsticks, but economic mobilization proceeded rapidly enough to supply the needed armaments and equipment in time for use. Some economic planning had begun before America entered the war; in August of 1916, the Council of National Defense was created and charged with coordinating industry for national security purposes. As soon as the United States became a participant, Congress handed the President a wide range of powers over the economy. After the whirlwind passage of a measure giving Wilson broad authority to ignore statutory regulations and create new agencies at will, a senator jokingly suggested an amendment providing that "if any power, constitutional or not, has been inadvertently omitted from this bill, it is hereby granted in full." A War Industries Board was created to oversee the operations of defense plants, a Food Administration, a Fuel Administration, a War Labor Board, a Shipping Board, and other similar agencies. In response to an impending transportation crisis, Wilson ordered a federal takeover of the railroad, telegraph, and telephone systems.

Some considered it "war socialism" but it is better described as an unprecedented example of government-business partnership. The managers of the new coordinating apparatus were top businessmen like financier Bernard Baruch, who headed the War Industries Board, and engineer Herbert Hoover, chief of the Food Administration, unpaid "dollar a year" volunteers from the upper echelons of the corporate world. They relied on persuasion rather than coercion, encouraging business to engage in informal price fixing and collusive bidding under a "cost-plus" system of contracts that assured healthy profits. Although the railroads were in government hands, normal dividends continued to be paid to stockholders. Baruch did not share Wilson's prewar fears of "the curse of bigness", and encouraged economic concentration. "The great difficulty about the distribution of work among smaller manufacturers," he said, "is the difficulty of getting the work done. We have been trying to meet this situation by endeavouring to get a number of firms to consolidate."

Although corporations did not suffer, there were serious attempts to check war profiteering. The income tax was boosted steeply, with a base rate of 12 percent on incomes of $4,000 and a graduated surtax of up to 65 percent; excess corporate profits were taxed as well. Much of the cost of the war was paid for by deficit spending, which resulted in runaway inflation that doubled the price level between 1915 and 1920. Although that hurt poor people on fixed incomes, progressive taxation assured that a substantial part of the burden of financing the war fell on the well-to-do.

Organized labor benefited considerably from the tight labor market created by the drop in European immigration caused by the outbreak of the European war. It benefited still more from the administration's decision to avoid disruptive strikes by giving labor a voice in the planning effort. Samuel Gompers was appointed to the Advisory Commission to the Council of National Defense when it was first created. With his backing, a War Labor Board was created, with equal representation for industrialists and labor. It banned strikes in war industries, but pressured employers to grant wage hikes, shorter hours, and the right of collective bargaining. The organization drive was strikingly successful; between January, 1917 and the end of 1918, AFL membership climbed almost 40 percent.

Propaganda and Suppression of Dissent

The guarantees of free speech and freedom of the press written into the Constitution proved almost meaningless once America entered the war. Opinion on the intervention issue was divided, and the administration regarded any hint of continuing division as tantamount to treason. The Committee on Public Information,

PROPAGANDA IN A CIGAR ADVERTISEMENT

Did I bayonet my first Hun?
Sure! How did it feel? It *doesn't*
feel! There *he* is. There *you* are.
One of you has got to go.
I preferred to stay.

So when sergeant says,
"Smash 'em, boys,"—we do.
And we go them one better
like good old Yankee Doodle
Yanks. For bullets and bayonets
are the only kind of lingo that
a Hun can *understand!*

—*Saturday Evening Post*, August, 1918

the first federal propaganda agency, circulated 75 million pieces of patriotic literature, sponsored films like *The Kaiser—the Beast of Berlin,* and placed ads urging
citizens to report to the Justice Department anyone "who spreads pessimistic
stories, divulges—or seeks—confidential military information, cries for peace, or
belittles our efforts to win the war. Show the Hun we can beat him at his own
game." Nothing less than "100 percent Americanism" was required.

The CPI helped stir up popular hysteria against Germans, socialists, anarchists,
and pacifists. Everything German became anathema. The teaching of the German
language was outlawed in several states; countless cities and towns changed their
names from Berlin and Frankfurt, and German measles became "liberty measles";
a school teacher in Maine was fired for taking driving lessons from a German
immigrant; Beethoven was banned in Boston. In Los Angeles, three pacifist ministers were beaten by a mob. When the police arrived they jailed the clerics and
prosecuted them for expressing "thoughts and theories calculated to cause any
American citizen then and there present to assault and batter them." They were
sentenced to six months behind bars and $1,500 fines. A citizen who shot another
man to death for shouting "to hell with the United States" was acquitted by an
Indiana jury after two minutes of deliberation. The Industrial Workers of the
World, an anarchist group opposed to all capitalist wars, was a special target of
vigilante patriots. In Arizona, 1,200 Wobblie strikers were kidnapped and dumped
in the desert; in Montana, IWW organizer Frank Little was tortured and hanged by
a mob.

The federal government encouraged these indiscriminate assaults by the Espionage Acts of 1917 and 1918, which defined "obstructing the draft" so broadly as to mean almost any criticism of the war effort. Under the authority of these acts, the Postmaster General banned German, socialist, and pacifist papers from the mails. The head of the American Socialist Party, Eugene Debs, was given a 10-year jail sentence for urging socialists to "resist militarism, wherever found"; other socialist leaders were imprisoned for remarks no more incendiary. A film celebrating the American Revolution, *The Spirit of '76*, was suppressed, and its producer sentenced to ten years. References to British misdeeds a century and a half before, the court judged, might be harmful to the Allied cause. The Supreme Court reviewed the constitutionality of these repressive statutes after the war was over and upheld them. "When a nation is at war," it said, "many things that might be said in time of peace are such a hindrance to its effort that their utterance will not be endured so long as men fight." The First Amendment, Justice Oliver Wendell Holmes, Jr. declared, did not give anyone the right falsely to shout fire in a crowded theater. That reading of the Constitution can be defended; the wonder is that Holmes and his fellow justices could seriously think that war critics were doing anything remotely comparable to shouting fire in a crowded theater.

The Coming of Peace

As the German armies fell back in 1918, the question of peace terms became critical. The aims of the British, French, and Italians (who joined the coalition in 1915) were traditional in European power politics. They sought punishment and territorial aggrandizement, and were determined to strip Germany of all of her colonies and to redraw her European boundaries. A series of secret treaties between them spelled out in detail how the spoils were to be divided in the event of victory.

America's aims were fundamentally different. Wilson knew of the treaties, but did not inform the American public of them. He unwisely refused to make an issue of them when the Allies needed him, deferring the negotiations until after the war, when they would not. But he was genuinely committed to a just peace that would establish a new world order. Even his most bloodthirsty statements were intensely moralistic. Thus his call, in April, 1918, for "Force. Force to the utmost. Force without stint or limit, the righteous and triumphant force which shall make Right the law of the world, and cast down every selfish dominion in the dust." The Fourteen Points he spelled out in January, 1918 were idealistic principles—an end to secret diplomacy, the right of self-determination for subject European peoples, constraints against colonial exploitation in the underdeveloped world, disarmament, a new world organization to settle disputes peacefully. If Germany would accept these principles, Wilson believed, and would replace the Kaiser with a democratic regime, she could be restored to the community of nations on an equal footing.

When the Germans sued for peace, in November, they did so directly to Wilson on that basis. The abdication of the Kaiser and the establishment of a German Republic brought an armistice and the withdrawal of all German forces beyond the Rhine. The Fourteen Points, however, were a unilateral proclamation by Wilson. They did not commit the Allies. Whether the final terms of settlement would embody Wilsonian principles depended on the outcome of the bargaining at the Versailles Peace Conference. By then Wilson held a weak hand, because American power was no longer needed to stave off German advances.

Considering his limited bargaining power, Wilson was quite effective at Versailles. The final terms of the treaty were harsh, but considerably less so than the agreement the Germans had imposed on Bolshevik Russia the year before. Germany's colonies were taken from her, and handed to the Allies, with a vague stipulation for some supervision by a league of nations. Much of the European territory of the German state was left intact, but sizable slices along her eastern frontier went to a newly-created independent Poland, while France reclaimed Alsace–Lorraine (seized from it by the Germans in the Franco–Prussian War of 1870) and won permanent demilitarization of the Rhineland and the right to hold it under military occupation for 15 years. The German army and fleet were dismantled. Most galling, Germany was forced to accept full "responsibility for causing all the loss and damage" entailed by the War, and despite Wilson's pledge that she would not be expected to pay "punitive damages" was charged a vast sum in financial reparations. The peace terms would have been harsher without Wilson's efforts. He checked the more extreme territorial demands of the Allies. And he won what he regarded as the most important objective of all—agreement on the formation of a new world organization that could, he believed, eventually rectify the flaws and imperfections of the Versailles agreements—the League of Nations.

The Debate Over the Treaty

Wilson's political miscalculation lay not in his dealing with the Allied statesmen, but with his political opponents back home. The United States was still a Republican country. Wilson had slipped into office in 1912 only because the Republican Party split in two, and despite the advantage of being an incumbent he had narrowly escaped defeat in 1916. In the Congressional elections of 1918, he had unwisely appealed to the public to again return a Democratic Congress as a gesture of support for his leadership, insinuating that voting Republican was unpatriotic. It didn't work, largely because of domestic discontent over wartime inflation. The Democrats lost 26 seats in the House and 6 in the Senate, which produced a Republican Congress. The loss in the Senate was crucial for the ratification of the Versailles Treaty, because treaties require Senatorial approval by a two-thirds margin.

Intoxicated by his vision of a new world order, and by the experience of having wielded all the power the U.S. Constitution allows a President in wartime, Wilson failed to take the opposition seriously. Ignoring the implications of the 1918 election, he defied a number of precedents in choosing the American delegation to the peace conference. It contained not a single Senator, and only one Republican. It was headed by Wilson himself, the first American President to visit Europe while in office. He grudgingly accepted some of the criticisms of a draft version of the Covenant of the League of Nations that were pressed upon him during a brief return home midway in the peace conference, and won Allied acceptance of several minor amendments. But after his final return to the country in July of 1919, he was utterly unbending. The Senate would have to endorse the treaty exactly as written or not at all.

Fewer than 20 Senators were true "irreconcilables" completely opposed to any form of American participation in the League of Nations. They included La Follette, William Borah, and others who had rejected American intervention in the first place, and some hypernationalistic racists from southern and border states. James Reed of Missouri refused to even "think of submitting questions involving the very life of the United States to a tribunal on which a nigger from Liberia, a nigger from Honduras, a nigger from India, and an unlettered gentleman from Siam each have votes equal to the great United States."

The irreconcilables were too small a group to make a difference alone, but so too was the band of Senators who would follow Wilson without hesitation. The critical swing group was the "strong reservationists," led by Henry Cabot Lodge, Chairman of the Foreign Relations Committee. They were willing to accept American membership in the new world organization, but only on a number of conditions. The key condition involved Article X of the Covenant of the League of Nations, which they feared would commit the United States to send troops abroad in a future war. Article X didn't really do that; it only required members to "advise on the means by which" the League could meet its obligation to preserve "the territorial integrity and existing political independence" of member nations. It was at most a moral rather than a legal obligation. But it was more than Lodge and other reservationists would tolerate. They held out for an explicit statement that America would not be required to act under Article X until Congress debated the circumstances in each case and gave its approval.

Wilson was outraged at the opposition, with some justification. Lodge and many of his followers were clearly exploiting the issue for partisan advantage, offering strained and distorted arguments. But Wilson was wrong in thinking that he could win in a showdown over the treaty as written. He began a cross-country speaking trip to whip up public support for the treaty, but collapsed after three weeks with a stroke that left him partially paralyzed for the rest of his administration. When the treaty with reservations was put to a Senate vote, Wilson urged his backers to have none of it, and they joined the irreconcilables to defeat it. When the treaty without reservations came to a roll call, the reservationists and the irreconcilables together overwhelmed it. It drew only 40 percent of the vote. Four-fifths of the Senate wanted the United States to join the League of Nations, but the antipathy between the Wilson and Lodge camps was so great that they obstinately shot down each other's schemes for accomplishing it.

The defeat was a personal tragedy for Wilson, but probably not a tragedy for the United States and the world, as some have argued. The argument that American participation in the League would have given it the strength necessary to check the aggressive impulses of Germany, Italy, and Japan in the 1930s—and hence to prevent World War II—is highly questionable. World War II grew out of the efforts of those countries to alter the distribution of territory in accord with new power realities, and the determination of the powers satisfied with the Versailles settlement to preserve a status quo that was to their advantage. Vision, courage, and an ability to transcend narrowly conceived national interests were not much in evidence in European ruling circles in the 1930s—nor in the United States, for that matter. It is hard to believe that an American presence at Geneva could have altered these uncomfortable realities. Even if the treaty had passed the Senate without reservations, Article X was not a binding commitment, and the American public would not have tolerated any involvement abroad that might have led to another war. The vast majority believed that our entry into the "Great War" had been a colossal mistake, and drew the lesson "never again." With or without America, the League could be no more than a nice gesture toward the ideal of human solidarity transcending the nation state. After its formation, the countries that created the League demonstrated their true convictions by maintaining strong military establishments and employing force or the threat of force whenever it suited them.

BACKLASH

The return of peace did not put an end to efforts to stamp out dissent. A nationwide strike wave in 1919, a series of bombings thought to be the work of anarchists, and the formation of an American Communist Party pledged to Leninist goals inspired a new panic—the Red Scare. The strikers aimed at modest goals like higher wages, shorter hours, and union recognition. And the anarchists and communists were a tiny, impotent minority. But Wilson's Attorney General, A. Mitchell Palmer, declared frantically that "a blaze of revolution" was "sweeping over every American institution of law and order, eating its way into the homes of the American workman, licking the altars of the churches, leaping into the belfry of the school bell, crawling into the sacred corners of American homes." Other high officials were equally unhinged. The Army Chief of Staff, General Leonard Wood, demanded that all "Bolsheviks" be deported in "ships of stone with sails of lead, with the wrath of God for a breeze and with hell for their first port." Palmer didn't go quite that far, but he did appoint J. Edgar Hoover head of a new antiradical division of the Justice Department and ordered more than 6,000 suspected revolutionists arrested and held for questioning, in blatant violation of their consitutional rights. A Communist insurrection was so imminent, Palmer announced, that "no nice distinctions" could be drawn "between the theoretical ideals of the radicals and their actual violations of our national laws." It was a crime to hold ideas critical of the government, in short, even in peacetime. At his order, hundreds of aliens were deported, and American citizens with leftist views were turned over to state governments for prosecution under vaguely worded "criminal syndicalism" statutes. In the midst of this campaign to ferret out subversives, two Italian anarchists—Nicola Sacco and Bartolomeo Vanzetti—were arrested in Boston for murder during a 1920 bank robbery. At the trial, the prosecution did more to establish their dissenting political beliefs than it did to demonstrate their presence at the scene of the crime. But they were convicted and executed in 1927, after a long series of unsuccessful appeals.[1]

The labor movement was a prime victim of the drive to impose order and suppress dissent. With the end of the wartime no-strike pledge, labor was free to press for higher wages to offset raging inflation, and 1919 was a year of unprecedented labor unrest. It began with the Seattle General Strike in January, and spread to the coal mines, the steel industry, and the textile mills. Over 4 million workers participated, much the largest number in any year before 1937. But the strikes failed. The Wilson administration provided no support; indeed, federal troops were deployed to protect strikebreakers during the steel and coal walkouts. The lurid prophecies of revolution issued by Palmer and Hoover were damaging too, because they convinced many Americans that even the moderate business unionism of the AFL was dangerously "pink." The Boston Police Strike in September, 1919 fanned those fears. The officers walked off their jobs to protest the firing of several of their leaders for union activity, leaving the city without protection. Three days of looting and mob violence ensued before the mayor restored order with local militia. Screaming headlines about the outbreak of anarchy in Boston gave labor's cause the worst possible publicity. (The Boston Police Strike had another historical consequence of some significance: It put the name of the Governor of Massachusetts, Calvin Coolidge, on the front page around the nation. Coolidge didn't do anything to end the strike, but his pronouncement that "there is no right to strike against the public safety by anybody, anywhere, any time" gave him the visibility to win the Republican vice-presidential nomination in 1920.)

In the following decade, employers were able to take advantage of the anti-union feelings the Red Scare had stimulated. They waged a national drive for what they shrewdly called "the American plan"—"open shops" in which no union had the right to represent and collect dues from all employees. Strong, independent unions had no place in "the American plan"; by implication they were un-American. The campaign was a great success. Union membership declined steadily after 1920; by the end of the decade, the percentage of the work force that was organized was lower than it had been in 1914. All of the gains of the war years had been wiped out, and the future for organized labor looked bleak.

Immigration Restriction

Between 1917 and 1924, the United States Congress approved a series of immigration restrictions that reversed the nation's historic free immigration policy. A drive to limit immigration had been underway for a long time. It began well before the end of the nineteenth century and grew in strength during the Progressive era. But the war and the Red Scare provided the impetus for the final triumph

---

[1]It is possible, recent scholarship suggests, that Sacco was in fact guilty, although the evidence remains inconclusive. The important point is that the prosecution did not establish guilt beyond a reasonable doubt at the trial, and the judge was clearly prejudiced. Sacco and Vanzetti died because of who they were and what they believed.

of the restrictionist forces. Immigration law, as they reshaped it, branded many of the peoples of the earth as innately inferior and unsuitable for admission into the United States. An intricate system of national quotas was devised to keep the "inferiors" out and preserve the American people from contamination.

Nativist resentments against newly arrived immigrants spurred political action even before the Civil War. But the Know-Nothing movement did not press for limitations on *immigration*. They sought a tightening of *naturalization* requirements, to check the growing political power of Catholic newcomers. The first demands for the outright exclusion of certain groups thought to be inferior and incapable of learning American ways were made by California whites (many of them Irish immigrants) threatened by competition from Chinese laborers in the 1870s. They charged that the Chinese worked at starvation wages, undercutting white labor, that the coolie system that brought them to the United States was a form of slavery, and that they were dishonest and immoral. It was impossible to tell when Chinese were lying, went one argument; their yellow skins hid their blushes. Although the United States had shortly before negotiated a treaty with China that guaranteed free immigration, Congress in 1882 soothed the fears of Californians by excluding the immigration of Chinese laborers for ten years, and by declaring the Chinese already in the country "aliens ineligible for citizenship," on the grounds that they were non-whites and the Naturalization Act of 1790 had limited citizenship by naturalization to "free white persons." The exclusion was renewed repeatedly thereafter. The arrival of significant numbers of Japanese immigrants on the West Coast after 1900 revived anti-Oriental agitation, and ended with negotiations between the United States and Japan that closed the door to all but a few upper-class Japanese newcomers (the "Gentlemen's Agreements.") The Japanese, too, were held to be "aliens ineligible for citizenship." In Western states, both Japanese and Chinese were barred from owning or leasing land and from marrying whites, and were in other ways subjected to treatment comparable to that meted out to blacks in the Jim Crow South.

The Chinese and Japanese were physically distinctive and visibly non-white—and consequently were treated with some of the disdain and fear with which blacks and Indians were long familiar. Until almost the end of the nineteenth century, the European immigrants flocking into the country were regarded as members of the same white race as the dominant group. Thereafter, a growing number of Americans came to believe that some *whites* were genetically superior to others. A flood of popular literature appeared, arguing that the secret of American greatness lay in the intrinsic superiority of its "Nordic" population—the first Anglo-Saxon settlers and the "old immigrants" from the British Isles and Northern and Western Europe. The "old immigrants" supposedly had blended smoothly into American life, because they were of the same race. The "new immigrants," who came after 1890 from Eastern and Southern Europe, were considered another breed altogether, a lower race whose "immemorial hereditary tendencies" rendered them incapable of contributing anything positive to the nation. Indeed, they were a menace: If they inter-married with the Nordic stock, declared a leading anthropologist from the American Museum of Natural History, the result would be "many amazing racial hybrids and some ethnic horrors that will be beyond the powers of future anthropologists to unravel." But one thing was certain. In such a mix, Nordic man's "light colored eyes, his fair skin and light colored hair, his straight nose and his splendid fighting and moral qualities" would be bound to disappear. By allowing the free entry of people "from the lowest stratum of the Mediterranean basin and the Balkans, together with the hordes of the wretched submerged populations of the Polish ghettoes" true Americans were committing "race suicide." The monstrous consequences of a similar "master race" philosophy would later be revealed in Adolph Hitler's Germany.

These new racist views were promoted by the Boston Brahmins who founded the Immigration Restriction League in 1894. They could claim the support of the new science of genetics, which revealed the vital importance of heredity in plant and animal populations. (Advances in genetics since that time have thoroughly discredited such notions, but leading scientists then generally adhered to them.) After 1910, with the publication of a massive study of the immigration problem by the U.S. Immigration Commission, they could point to a massive body of social scientific evidence as well. The Immigration Commission, headed by Senator William Dillingham, began its work with the assumption that the new immigrants were racially inferior to their predecessors. It manipulated 42 volumes of statistical data in an attempt to establish evidence that Southern and Eastern Europeans were an unassimilable lump in the body politic and a threat to the social order. Upon careful reading, the evidence contradicted the conclusions on most issues, but few people detected that. The Dillingham Commission report was generally taken to be powerful social scientific proof of the case for restriction.

Although restrictionists argued their case on racist grounds, before World War I the policy change they called for was not overtly so. Their principal demand was a literacy test, to keep out newcomers who could not read. And it was a test of literacy in any language, not in English alone. Supporters of the change clearly assumed that most of the failures would be new immigrants, but they were not yet ready to defend openly discriminatory quotas for immigrants of varying nationalities. A ban on illiterates seemed fairer, and politically more salable. A bill mandating a literacy test passed Congress as early as 1896, but was vetoed by Grover Cleveland. Similar measures passed in 1913 and 1915, only to be vetoed by Taft and Wilson.

The xenophobic passions stirred up during almost three years of argument over the war in Europe gave the literacy test the final push it needed. In January, 1917, on the eve of American entry into the war, another literacy bill was approved by Congress. Wilson again vetoed it, but this time restrictionists had the two-thirds margin necessary to override the veto and make it law. The measure also reassured those worried about "the yellow peril"; it banned immigration from an "Asiatic Barred Zone" including India, Indochina, Afghanistan and most of the rest of Asia.

Although Wilson opposed the literacy test, his frequent charges that opponents of foreign policies had "divided loyalties" fed restrictionist sentiments. Wilson denounced "hyphenates"—people whom he said had hyphens in their name (German–American, Irish–American)—because only part of them had come over from Europe, leaving their hearts behind. Although Wilson and Roosevelt agreed on very little else, they were in perfect accord on the need for 100 percent Americanism. "The question," Roosevelt warned, "is whether we are to continue as a separate nation at all, or whether we are to become merely a huge polyglot boarding-house and counting-house, in which dollar-hunters of 20 different nationalities scramble for gain, while each really pays his soul-allegiance to some foreign power."

Wilson claimed to be impartial in his attacks on hyphenism. "A man who thinks of himself as belonging to a particular national group in America," he said in 1915, "has not yet become an American." But he behaved as if only the new immigrants, plus older groups with grudges against Britain like the Germans and Irish, were hyphenates. Americans of British stock (like Wilson himself) were free to back Britain without being accused of giving their "soul-allegiance to some foreign power." In 1917 Wilson's Ambassador to Britain, Walter Hines Page, unblushingly displayed his own form of hyphenism while denouncing another: "We Americans have to throw away our provincial ignorance, hang our Irish agitators and shoot our hyphenates, and bring up our children with reverence for English history and in awe of English literature."

To be 100 percent American meant being Anglo-American. The result was a drastic narrowing of the original cosmopolitan vision of the melting pot, in which all of the diverse groups included in the American population mixed together to form a new and better species. The war promoted a preservationist mentality; only those newcomers who fitted into an already fixed national pattern would be welcomed. It was the conception behind the Americanization classes conducted at Henry Ford's huge Dearborn plant. A gigantic wooden pot was erected on the stage for the graduation ceremony. Graduates would march into it wearing Old World costumes, singing native folk songs. The teachers stood on the edge stirring the pot with big spoons. And then the door would open, and out marched the immigrants in American dress, singing the Star-Spangled Banner. In the older version of the melting pot, the teachers would have been inside as well, being changed into something new. Now assimilation had become sheer Anglo-conformity. Perhaps the most amazing manifestation of this new parochialism was the fact that by 1919 no less than 15 states had passed laws forbidding instruction in any foreign language. Americans evidently had to be protected from corrupting contact with minds like Goethe, Dante, Cervantes, and Tolstoy.

The Red Scare reinforced popular fears that the new immigrants would never conform to American ways. Most of the targets of Palmer's "Red Raids" were aliens from Eastern or Southern Europe. The old immigrants, said the Secretary of Labor, were "the beaver type that built up America"; the new immigrants were "rat-men trying to tear it down," bomb-throwing revolutionaries striking at "the foundations of society." Manufacturers, traditionally firm supporters of the free immigration that provided them with low-cost labor, swung to the other side out of fear of the alien radical. "We have enough immigrants from Southern Europe to last us for the next 50 years if we are to maintain Americanism," said a coal company president.

The literacy test, it quickly became apparent, would not be enough to "maintain Americanism." It was completely ineffectual, in fact, because restrictionists had underestimated the literacy of Europeans seeking entry into the United States.

In 1920, half a million immigrants passed the test and gained entry; in 1921, over 800,000 did, about as many as in a typical pre-war year. Worse yet, the vast majority were from the despised new immigrant nationalities. Congress then moved to close the gates, decisively and with very little dissent. First, it set a firm limit on the total number of newcomers, however well-qualified, who could be admitted into the country. The 1921 Quota Act fixed the annual level at only two-fifths of the average that had prevailed before the war; a 1924 bill cut it to less than one-fifth. Even more significant, Congress apportioned quotas for specific countries in a manner that was nakedly discriminatory. Newcomers were admitted not in proportion to the number who wished to immigrate, or some other neutral standard. Instead, a formula was chosen that strongly favored applicants from Northern and Western Europe, and eliminated almost entirely those from Southern and Eastern Europe, precisely the countries in which economic and demographic pressures had produced the largest pools of people eager to leave. The 1924 act specified that immigrants from a given country could be admitted in accord with the proportion of their fellow countrymen living in the United States in *1890*, before the mass immigration from Southern and Eastern Europe had begun. The quotas for the British, Scandinavians and Germans turned out to be only slightly below the actual number of people who had chosen to come to the United States from those countries in the immediate pre-war years, but the number of Italians, Poles, Greeks, and East European Jews allowed to enter was slashed to a mere 3 percent of the pre-war average.[2]

Senator Albert Johnson, a principal sponsor of the legislation, was frank about its discriminatory purpose:

> *The United States is our land. If it was not the land of our fathers, at least it may be, and it should be the land of our children. We intend to maintain it so. The day of unalloyed welcome to all peoples, the day of indiscriminate acceptance of all races, has definitely ended.*

It had, at least for 40 years. Not until 1965 did the United States abandon a quota system that ranked the "races" of the world in the order of their desirability, with Nordics at the top and Eastern and Southern Europeans and Asians on the bottom.

It was not surprising that the United States at last erected barriers against the unfettered flow of people across its borders after decades of agitation. America was no longer an underpopulated country with an open frontier. During the Progressive era, the old nineteenth century faith in the beneficent workings of the free market began to give way to a belief that social regulation was sometimes necessary. Tariffs, after all, had for some time protected American manufacturers from the vicissitudes of the international market. It was natural that other Americans sought means of protecting their society from the vicissitudes of the international labor market. Organized labor in particular had strong reasons for supporting a

---

[2]The restriction acts had an important loophole. As a gesture of good will towards our hemispheric neighbors, no restrictions were applied to countries in the Western Hemisphere. Over half a million Mexican immigrants entered the U.S. in the 1920s, and a million French Canadians and British Canadians.

TABLE 23-1
The Effects of the Quota Acts on
the Volume and Sources of Immigration

	Immigrants from Northern and Western Europe	Other Immigrants, Chiefly Southern and Eastern Europe
Average annual inflow, 1907–14	176,983	685,531
Quotas under 1921 Act	198,082	158,367
Quotas under 1924 Act	140,999	20,847

tightening of immigration standards, because trade unionists were incensed at the frequent use of the greenest immigrants as scabs to break strikes. Even with the quotas, the United States had one of the most liberal immigration policies of any advanced industrial society—far more so than Britain or France, for example. Still, restriction was accomplished in an ugly and hysterical atmosphere, by discriminatory means that belied the older American faith that all people were capable of flourishing in conditions of freedom.

Prohibition

The long drive for immigration restriction finally triumphed because of the anxieties and hatreds stirred up by World War I. The same can be said for another reform movement with an even longer tradition—the crusade against the Demon Rum. The Eighteenth Amendment to the Constitution (1919), which banned alcohol from the land, was the culmination of almost a century of effort. The prohibitionist movement, born in the age of Jackson, had won 13 states to the "dry" cause by 1855. Most were recaptured by "wet" defenders of "personal liberty" a few years later, however. A second prohibitionist campaign, led by the Women's Christian Temperance Union (1874) and the Anti-Saloon League (1893), surged in the 1880s and 1890s before it lost force. A third and more powerful drive arose in the decade before America's entry into the war. By 1915 there were 15 dry states, by April of 1917, 26.

The roots of the final prohibitionist drive were in the small towns and farming areas of the Midwest, West, and South. The Northeast was solidly opposed to it. Of the 11 Northeastern states, only Maine and New Hampshire were dry in 1917, and they were uncharacteristic in having no large cities. The prohibitionist heartland was Bryan country. The maps of the vote for Bryan in 1896 and of states that had gone dry by 1917 are almost identical. Of the 22 states that Bryan carried, 20 were in the dry camp. It was a Bible Belt cause, its most ardent advocates evangelical Baptists, Methodists, and smaller fundamentalist sects. And it was very much a rural and small town cause. Not one of the 9 states that were at least

60 percent urbanized was dry; of the 19 states whose populations were less than 30 percent urban, all were dry. To the plain folk of Bryan's Nebraska, indulgence in alcohol was sinful. City dwellers with different cultural preferences could not be allowed to do something so plainly against the will of God. As Bryan put it, "this is a moral question. There is but one side to a moral question."

Until 1917 it seemed unlikely that prohibitionists could enlarge their base and enforce their morality upon the residents of New York or Chicago. The legislatures of heavily urbanized states could not regard drink as sinful; their members had too many constituents with quite different religious views. The WCTU and the Anti-Saloon League therefore developed other more secular arguments as to why alcohol should be banned. They stressed the mounting medical evidence that it was a dangerous drug, and argued that it was a primary cause of poverty. Some of them, including WCTU head Frances Willard, were active in other Progressive causes, and saw a natural affinity between banning child labor, regulating the hours women worked, preventing the sale of diseased meat, and prohibiting a beverage harmful to health and stable family life. And they made much of the ties between the brewers and distillers, the saloon-keepers, and the ward bosses. The "liquor interest" and the political machines, they charged, went hand in glove. From this vantage point, Prohibition was a classic example of "progressive" and "scientific" action to strike at "the special interests."

These arguments struck responsive chords among some city dwellers, particularly middle-class native Protestants. But it is doubtful that prohibitionists would have swept the nation as they did without American entry into the war. The war provided an immediate practical reason for at least a temporary ban on the manufacture of alcoholic beverages—it would allegedly free enough grain to produce 11 million loaves of bread a day to feed the boys in uniform and our starving allies. "Every man who works on the land to produce drink instead of bread," said a WCTU speaker, "is a loss in winning the war; and worse, he may mean a dead soldier." Congress quickly acted to ban the use of grain for the production of alcohol for the duration of the conflict.

That made some sense (though the 11 million loaves estimate was picked out of a hat by a dry economist.) A number of other nations barred or limited alcohol production during the emergency. The United States was unique, however, in going on to make the ban a permanent one. After a tremendous lobbying effort by the prohibitionist forces, Congress voted approval of the Eighteenth Amendment in January of 1918 and sent it to the states for ratification. In a year's time, 46 of the 48 states had said yes. It was the only war measure of the Wilson administration to become part of the Constitution.

Prohibition, it has been said, was "a measure passed by village America against urban America." This neglects the fact that village America was by then a dwindling minority; the Eighteenth Amendment was passed on the eve of the first U.S. Census to report to an urban majority. And it passed in almost every state; Connecticut and Rhode Island were the sole hold-outs. A great many people living in "urban America" obviously supported it too, They did so because of the great revulsion against German and other "alien" influences produced by the war. "Kaiser kultur," according to the Anti-Saloon League, "was raised on beer"; true

Americans stuck to cold water. The xenophobic feelings that led to the closing of the gates to the new immigrants were successfully exploited by advocates of Prohibition. The ban-the-bottle literature could have been written by the Immigration Restriction League:

> Besodden Europe sends here her drink-makers, her drunkard-makers, and her drunkards, with all their un-American and anti-American ideas of morality and government; they are absorbed into our national life, but not assimilated; through the ballot box, flung wide open to them by foolish statesmanship that covets power, their foreign control has become an appalling fact; they dominate our Sabbath over large areas of country; they have set up for us their own moral standards, which are grossly immoral; they govern our great cities; the great cities govern the nation; and foreign conquest could gain little more, though secured by foreign armies and fleets.

Prohibition was a grand renunciation of "besodden Europe," a national assertion that the "grossly immoral" standards prevailing in the great cities would no longer be tolerated. The roots of the movement were in village America, but it triumphed because the auspicious climate provided by the war allowed it to enlist the support of much of urban native Protestant America.

SUGGESTED READINGS

William E. Leuchtenberg, *The Perils of Prosperity, 1914–1932* (1958), David A. Shannon, *Between the Wars: America, 1919–1941* (1965), Otis L. Graham, Jr., *The Great Campaigns: Reform and War in America, 1900–1928* (1971), and Ellis W. Hawley, *The Great War and the Search for a Modern Order: A History of the American People and Their Institutions, 1917–1933* (1979) are good brief syntheses. David M. Kennedy, *Over Here: The First World War and American Society* (1980) is the fullest account of the impact of the War at home. Robert Cuff, *The War Industries Board* (1973) analyzes government–business relations. On the suppression of dissent, see William Preston, Jr., *Aliens and Dissenters: Federal Suppression of Radicals, 1903–1933* (1963), and Paul L. Murphy, *World War I and the Origin of Civil Liberties in the United States* (1979). The problems of the Germans are analyzed in Frederick C. Luebke, *Bonds of Loyalty: German–Americans and World War I* (1974), Philip Gleason, *The Conservative Reformers: German–American Catholics and the Social Order* (1968), and a probing essay on Chicago's Germans in Peter d'A. Jones and Melvin C. Holli, *Ethnic Chicago* (1981).

America's reluctant entry into the European war is examined in Ernest R. May, *The World War and American Isolationism* (1959), and *American Intervention: 1917 and 1941* (1960), John M. Cooper, Jr., *The Vanity of Power: American Isolation and the First World War* (1969), and Ross Gregory, *The Origins of American Intervention in the First World War* (1971). For the latest reflections on that problem by Woodrow Wilson's leading biographer, see A.S. Link, *Woodrow Wilson: Revolution, War, and Peace* (1979). Bradford Perkins, *The Great Rapprochement: England and the United States, 1835–1914* (1968) is essential to an understanding of the issue. On the

Wilson administration's aims after the war, see N. Gordon Levin, Jr., *Woodrow Wilson and World Politics: America's Response to War and Revolution* (1968), and Arno J. Mayer, *Wilson vs. Lenin: Political Origins of the New Diplomacy, 1917–1918* (1964), and *Politics and Diplomacy of Peacemaking: Containment and Counterrevolution at Versailles, 1918–1919* (1967). For a different analysis of America's stance toward the Bolshevik regime in Russia, see George F. Kennan's two masterful studies, *Russia Leaves the War* (1956) and *The Decision to Intervene* (1958).

The postwar fear of radicalism is treated in Robert K. Murray, *The Red Scare: A Study in National Hysteria, 1919–1920* (1955), and David Brody, *Labor in Crisis: The Steel Strike of 1919* (1962). On the movement to restrict immigration, see Oscar Handlin, *The American People in the Twentieth Century* (rev. ed., 1966), John Higham, *Strangers in the Land: Patterns of American Nativism, 1860–1925* (1955) and *Send These To Me: Jews and Other Immigrants in Urban America* (1975), and Barbara M. Solomon, *Ancestors and Immigrants: A Changing New England Tradition* (1956).

Andrew Sinclair's *Prohibition: Era of Excess* (1962) is highly critical of the temperance movement. Norman H. Clark, *Deliver Us From Evil: An Interpretation of American Prohibition* (1976) is more sympathetic.

Chapter Twenty-Four

The Auto Age

A strange new sight greeted the residents of Detroit, Michigan, one day in 1900. An obscure 37-year-old mechanic and tinkerer, the son of an Irish immigrant farmer, staged a public demonstration of a new "mechanical buggy" with a gasoline-powered engine. Henry Ford, the newspaper reported, "began by giving his steed three or four sharp jerks with the lever at the righthand side of the seat. Mr. Ford slipped a small electric switch handle and there followed a puff, puff, puff. The puffing of the machine assumed a higher key. She was flying along about eight miles an hour. The ruts in the road were deep, but the machine certainly went with a dreamlike smoothness. By this time the boulevard had been reached, and the automobiler, letting a lever fall a little, let her out. Whiz! She picked up speed with infinite rapidity. As she ran on there was a clattering behind, the new noise of the automobile."

Three decades later, the entire population could conceivably have gone whizzing down the road at the same time—there were almost 27 million cars registered, one for every five Americans. No single invention in previous American history had caught on so quickly or had such revolutionary impact on the lifestyles of ordinary people. None better symbolized the broader transformation of the American economy in the first three decades of the twentieth century—the shift to a high consumption consumer goods economy.

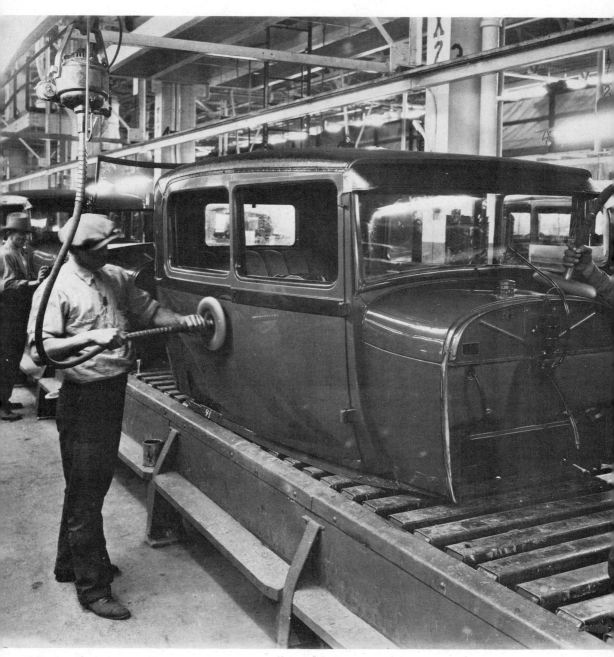

Henry Ford's assembly-line methods—shown here in a 1928 photo from Ford Motor Company archives—revolutionized American industry.

PROSPERITY AND THE MASS MARKET

After the depression of 1893–97, the growth of the American economy resumed and accelerated. Over the next 30 years, the Gross National Product (in constant dollars) nearly tripled. Population growth accounted for part of that rise in total output by increasing the labor force. But in fact production *per person* doubled. These overall trends do not mean that each year was more prosperous than the one before, of course. A table of per capita GNP for the period suggests peaks and valleys, and a business cycle in which the immediate future was always uncertain for businessmen and workers alike (see Table 24–1). In 10 of the years shown, output per person fell below the previous year's level, and in 14 years the unemployment rate rose. Moderately serious downturns occurred in 1907–1908, 1913–14, and 1919–21, in addition to other minor fluctuations. But most of the cyclical declines lasted less than two years, and only in 1921 did the unemployment rate exceed 9 percent.[1] On the whole, these were very good times compared to the nineteenth century and the 1930s. There were serious flaws in the American economic system, to be sure. In 1929 the bubble would burst and the country would slide into the most acute depression it has yet seen. But for a third of a century the economy lurched along confidently.

Electricity and Automobiles

The two most dynamic sectors of the economy by far were electrical power and automobile manufacturing. In the 1880s inventors like Thomas Edison, George Westinghouse, and Nicola Tesla had discovered how to generate electrical power cheaply, to transmit it over long distances, and to use it to power machinery and appliances. The mass adoption of electricity came in the opening decades of the new century. In 1902 Americans consumed 6 billion kilowatt hours of electricity; by 1929 it was 118 billion. Only 8 percent of the country's residences were electrified in 1907, the year of the first available statistics; but by 1929, over two-thirds were, and 85 percent of all dwellings in urban areas. By then 80 percent of the nation's industrial machinery was electrically powered, up from a mere 2 percent in 1902.

The growth of the auto industry was equally spectacular. In 1911, the year reliable data begin, some 200,000 cars were sold. In 1929, the figure was over 4.5 million, 23 times greater. Sales exceeded $3.5 billion, almost an eighth of total manufacturing output. Even these heady numbers understate the economic significance of the automobile, for as the industry grew it stimulated rising output across the economy. By the late 1920s, for instance, Ford, General Motors, Chrysler, and a few smaller automobile manufacturers were purchasing more than

---

[1]This is not intended to suggest that unemployment was not much of a problem for American workers in these years. It was. Note that the 11.7 percent rate for 1921 is for the entire labor force, including agricultural workers, who experience less joblessness than industrial employees. For non-agricultural workers, the 1921 rate was a much higher 19.5 percent. Furthermore, as explained previously, the percentage of people without jobs for a sizable number of months at some point during the year is always considerably larger than those out of work at any one time. But unemployment was less of a threat to the average worker in these years than it was in the late nineteenth century.

TABLE 24–1
Gross National Product Per Person (1958 dollars)
and Unemployment Rate, 1896–1929

	GNP per person	Percent unemployed		GNP per person	Percent unemployed
1896	875	14.4	1913	1331	4.3
1897	941	14.5	1914	1206	7.9
1898	944	12.4	1915	1224	8.5
1899	1013	6.5	1916	1377	5.1
1900	1022	5.0	1917	1328	4.6
1901	1109	4.0	1918	1449	1.4
1902	1107	3.7	1919	1446	1.4
1903	1141	3.9	1920	1403	5.2
1904	1105	5.4	1921	1344	11.7
1905	1164	4.3	1922	1404	6.7
1906	1275	1.7	1923	1562	2.4
1907	1271	2.8	1924	1578	5.0
1908	1144	8.0	1925	1593	3.2
1909	1259	5.1	1926	1674	1.8
1910	1246	5.9	1927	1667	3.3
1911	1266	6.7	1928	1668	4.2
1912	1305	4.6	1929	1849	3.2

a seventh of all the steel produced in the country, as well as more nickel, lead, and plate glass than any other industry. It was the automobile more than anything else that multiplied petroleum output 22-fold and rubber production 13-fold between 1900 and 1929. And of course it was the automobile that required the massive expenditures on concrete and other materials and labor to develop the modern system of public streets and highways that were authorized by the 1916 Federal Aid Roads Act, which provided states a 50 percent federal subsidy for building approved roads. By 1929, the country had over 600,000 miles of surfaced highways, an investment of $1.8 billion. Add to this the countless garages, salesrooms, gas stations, truck lots and warehouses and the basis for the estimate that one in four working Americans depended directly or indirectly on the auto for employment becomes clear.

Ford and the Assembly Line

The automobile industry pioneered new modes of producing and selling its products that quickly spread to other types of enterprise. The innovations in production methods came first, with Henry Ford's introduction of the assembly line system in 1913, the major breakthrough. In the old process, major parts had been

TABLE 24-2
Motor Vehicles Registered, 1910-29*

	Number	People per Vehicle
1910	458,377	201
1920	8,131,522	13
1929	26,704,825	5

*In 1975, for comparison's sake, registrations totaled 133,727, or 1.6 people per vehicle.

built in separate areas of the plant and then carried to one place for final assembly. The introduction of conveyer belts and automatic machinery eliminated a good deal of waste. Managers had more control over the pace of work as well; they determined the pace at which the line moved past the workers, and summarily fired those who couldn't keep up. The time required to put together a Ford automobile was cut by 90 percent! It was a perfect embodiment of Frederick W. Taylor's dream of a fully rationalized operation in which labor was coordinated with stopwatch precision.

The workers on the assembly line performed the same simple mechanical tasks time after time without relief, and they hated the boredom and regimentation. As the novelist John Dos Passos described it, it was "fifteen minutes for lunch, three minutes to go to the toilet, the Taylorized speedup everywhere, reach under, adjust washer, screw down bolt, shove in cotterpin, reachunder adjustwasher, screwdown bolt, reachunderadjustscrewdownreachunderadjust until every ounce of life was sucked off into production and at night the workmen went home grey shaking husks." Most employees couldn't take it and quit in a few months. A great German silent film of the twenties showed workers in a factory of the future in which workers who couldn't keep pace were fed into the machines; the lead actor closely resembled Ford. But there were no unions to protest. Ford was vigorously anti-union, and the company police were on the alert to keep organizers out of the plant. But there was a good reason to endure the wretched working conditions—high wages. The savings the company realized from assembly line production allowed Henry Ford to announce a $5 a day pay scale at his plant, almost double the national average for manufacturing workers. As a result, Ford was never short-handed.

Despite these high wages, production was so efficient that Ford was able to reduce prices steadily without cutting into company profits. For the first time, people with moderate incomes could afford automobiles. The Model T Ford, the famous "Tin Lizzie," sold for $600 in 1912, $490 in 1914, $360 in 1916, and $290 in 1924. In 1912 the price of Model T was more than the average American worker earned in a year; a dozen years later, a new Ford cost less than three months' wages. Producing an efficient automobile at the lowest possible cost opened up a mass

THE ASSEMBLY LINE

The first step forward in assembly came when we began taking the work to the men instead of the men to the work. We now have two general principles in all operations—that a man shall never have to take more than one step, if possibly it can be avoided, and that no man need ever stoop over.

The principles of assembly are these:

(1)   Place the tools and the men in the sequence of the operation so that each component part shall travel the least possible distance while in the process of finishing.

(2)   Use work slides or some other form of carrier so that when a workman completes his operation, he drops the part always in the same place—which place must always be the most convenient place to his hand—and if possible have gravity carry the part to the next workman for his operation.

(3)   Use sliding assembly lines by which the parts to be assembled are delivered at convenient distances.

The net result of the application of these principles is the reduction of the necessity for thought on the part of the worker and the reduction of his movements to a minimum. He does as nearly as possible only one thing with only one movement. . . .

—Henry Ford, *My Life and Work*, 1922

market for what had been a luxury far beyond the reach of ordinary people. The Tin Lizzie was an amazing bargain, a triumph of functional design, and it soon dominated the booming market. Ford produced fewer than 40,000 cars in 1911, a fifth of the national total. Ten years later, 845,000 Fords were sold, 55 percent of all the motor vehicles turned out that year. Henry Ford was the richest man in the world.

GM and the Auto as Status Symbol

Business success, however, depends on more than sheer productive efficiency, as Henry Ford soon learned to his sorrow. Ford's share of the auto market dropped from 55 percent in 1921 to 31 percent in 1929, while that of General Motors rose spectacularly, from only 13 to 32 percent. Ford sales increased 69 percent during the 1920s; those of General Motors soared 667 percent. General Motors employed essentially the same technology as Ford, with no greater efficiency. Its competitive advantage came from the innovations it made in its internal management, and in advertising and selling its products.

TABLE 24–3
Wage Levels and Ford Prices, 1912–24

	Average Annual Earnings, All Industries*	Price of Model T Touring Car
1912	$ 592	$600
1914	627	490
1916	708	360
1924	1,303	290

*These earning figures rise much more sharply than those for per capita GNP in Table 24–1 because the GNP figures are in constant 1958 dollars, whereas these are in current dollars, as are the Ford prices with which they are to be compared. This is appropriate, because the question at issue is not how much real wages were changing between 1912 and 1924, but whether the ability of an average worker to afford a Tin Lizzie was markedly improved.

The Ford Motor Company was a tightly centralized operation, with Ford himself making all key decisions. General Motors, by contrast, developed a decentralized administrative structure that made it more sensitive to the changing nature of consumer demand and more flexible in responding to it. General Motors began as an amalgam of the Buick Motor Company, Cadillac, and a number of other firms. Under the presidency of Pierre du Pont and Alfred Sloan, who succeeded him in 1923, GM gave the separate operating units wide autonomy, and developed a general office to ensure overall coordination. The general office gathered massive amounts of statistical information to allow them to make predictions about the auto market.

One key sign of GM's greater awareness of marketing considerations was that it took the lead in offering customers the opportunity of paying for their cars in installments over a period of years, while enjoying their use. The General Motors Acceptance Corporation, organized in 1919, was the first national consumer credit organization, the first major effort to cultivate the great American "fly now, pay later" spirit. By 1929 it was doing a billion dollars of business a year, and was the largest sales financing company in the world.

The same superior foresight and flexibility was evident in GM's response to the crisis that loomed ahead for the automobile industry in the late twenties: a sharp shift in the character of the market. Henry Ford had designed the ideal car for the purchaser buying an auto for the first time—inexpensive, simple to repair, and practically indestructible. In a sense, he succeeded all too well. By 1927 Ford had sold an astonishing 15 million Tin Lizzies, and a large proportion of them were still on the road. The number of families without a car had shrunk, and they now had the option of buying used cars instead of new ones. It was obvious to the managers of GM—though not to Ford—that if they were to continue selling large numbers of new cars, they would have to entice a different type of customer—someone who already owned one.

Why should someone with a perfectly serviceable Model T invest a large amount of money in a new Chevrolet or Buick? And how could he be persuaded to buy yet *another* GM car three or four years later? GM displayed a great deal of inventiveness in solving these problems. One was to produce a much wider range of cars, with an elaborate gradation of prices—"a car for every purse and purpose." In their basic mechanics they might not differ much from the Tin Lizzie, but they were to be packaged more attractively, with flashier lines, better springs and upholstery, more varied body styles, and so on. While Henry Ford remained puritanically adamant that all Model T's be black, GM began to offer a wide choice of colors.

By spending more than its rivals on sales efforts, GM developed the largest national network of automobile dealers. GM also spent more on advertising to persuade the public that a car was more than a means of transportation—it was a badge of social status. It was demeaning to drive a Ford if you could afford a Chevrolet, inappropriate to be seen in a Chevrolet if your income would finance a Pontiac, and so on up the ladder through the Oldsmobile and Buick to the Cadillac. Furthermore, why drive a four-year-old Chevrolet if you could afford a new one? Such a question would not occur to a Ford owner. It was very difficult to tell the age of a Tin Lizzie. Ford made only the smallest changes in the car over 19 years, but GM introduced the custom of restyling its products each year, and bombarded the public with information about the many "improvements" that distinguished this year's model from the last. Sales boomed, and so did those of the Chrysler Corporation, which followed the GM strategy of "a car for every purse and purpose" and aggressive promotion. In 1927 a desperate Henry Ford capitulated, dropping the Tin Lizzie for the more stylish and expensive Model A.

The automobile industry was the "push" industry of the early twentieth century, much as the railroads and the steel industry were in earlier phases of industrialization. But it was not just another push industry, the source of industrial spinoffs that stimulated growth in other sectors of the economy. Much more than the others, it wrought fundamental changes in American lifestyles. The automobile allowed city dwellers to take up residences far removed from streetcar and commuter railroad lines, creating urban sprawl, and permitted them to venture into the country for picnics and camping trips. It gave residents of rural areas new opportunities to taste urban delights. When an investigator from the U.S. Department of Agriculture asked a farm woman in the 1920s why her family had bought a Model T even though they lacked indoor plumbing, she answered, "Why you can't go to town in a bathtub!" The auto also helped to erode traditional restrictive sexual mores; the old porch swing could be kept under parental observation, but the car could be a mobile private bedroom.

Most important, the high pressure promotion of automobile sales altered people's relation to consumption. No one really *needed* any car but a Model T, or a new auto every few years, but they could and did learn to *want* them. Even in 1929, many poor people in the United States lived close to the margin of subsistence and had to devote their slender resources to meeting elemental needs—paying the rent and buying groceries and shoes for their kids. But a large and rapidly growing fraction of the population had incomes high enough to be consumers in this new sense.

ECONOMIC ADVANCES

Scarcely less characteristic of our period than unit-cost reductions is the rapid expansion in the production and sale of products little used or wholly unknown a generation or even a decade ago. Among consumers' goods, the conspicuous instances are automobiles, radios and rayon. But the list includes also oil-burning furnaces, gas stoves, household electrical appliances in great variety, automobile accessories, antifreezing mixtures, cigarette lighters, propeller pencils, wrist watches, airplanes, and what not. Among producers' goods we have the truck and the tractor competing with the horse and the mule, reinforced concrete competing with brick and lumber, the high-tension line competing with the steam engine, fuel oil competing with coal, not to mention excavating machines, belt conveyors, paint sprayers, and "automatics" of many sorts competing with manual labor.

—National Bureau of Economic Research,
Recent Economic Changes in the United States, 1928

As a result, the most dynamic sector of the economy was the "consumer durables" sector. Unlike such producers' goods as steel, they are sold directly to the consumer, yet are relatively expensive and long lasting, as opposed to nondurable consumer goods like food and clothing. The opening of a mass market for consumer durables like automobiles, refrigerators, washing machines, and radios, accomplished by heavy advertising and liberal credit, was a new stage in American economic development. The consumption frontier was open to anyone willing to pay "a dollar down and a dollar a week—forever."

Increased Leisure, Improved Diets

Prosperity gave people more money to spend on pleasure, and more time to devote to it. At the end of the nineteenth century, the typical worker toiled 10 hours a day, 6 days a week. By 1929, the work week was 5 nine-hour days. Working people had 15 more hours each week for other activities.

Much of that time was devoted to sports. Between 1900 and 1929, expenditures on sporting equipment rose 641 percent. The number of organized bowling teams rose from 150 to 27,000. Professional baseball became an addiction for big city residents from the playing of the first World Series in 1903. A new kind of mass entertainment—the motion picture—quickly became astonishingly popular. By the late 1920s 90 million people a week were going to the movies, in a country whose population was 124 million. It appears that everyone, except infants, shut-ins, and those living in the remotest rural areas, saw a film a week!

THE CREDIT ECONOMY COMES TO MIDDLETOWN, INDIANA

When the fathers of the present generation in Middletown wanted to buy a piece of land they were likely to save up the money and "pay cash" for it, and it was a matter of pride to be able to say, "I always pay cash for the things I buy." Today Middletown lives by a credit economy that is available in some form to nearly every family in the community. The rise and spread of the dollar-down-and-so-much-per plan extends credit for virtually everything—homes, $200 over-stuffed living-room suites, electric washing machines, automobiles, fur coats, diamond rings—to persons of whom frequently little is known as to their intention or ability to pay.

—Robert and Helen Lynd, *Middletown*, 1929

People spent some of their new leisure time, of course, at home. Electrification meant brighter and safer lighting. Telephones allowed instant communications with friends and relatives miles away. By 1929, more than 20 million phones were in operation. The radio produced music, news, and other diversions, well-spiced with commercials, with the twist of a dial. Commercial broadcasting began in 1921; within ten years, almost 15 million radios and radio–phonograph combinations had been sold. Once the modest investment had been made in a set, the radio brought free entertainment into the livingroom—and offered a powerful instrument of persuasion to advertisers and politicians. Few innovations have done more to nationalize American culture. During these same years, the electric stove, refrigerator, washing machine, vacuum cleaner, and electric iron appeared in the American household. Now that we take such amenities for granted, it is hard to appreciate how much easier and pleasanter they made life, but these changes in domestic technology were thrilling to live through.

Prosperity, health, and longevity went hand in hand. Most people could stop living on bread and potatoes: Between 1910 and 1929 per capita consumption of wheat flour fell 21 percent, of corn meal 47 percent, of potatoes 29 percent. The average family in 1929 ate twice as much fresh citrus fruit and four times as much canned fruit as twenty years earlier. In the 1920s alone, per capita consumption of fresh vegetables rose 45 percent, that of canned vegetables 35 percent. A source of increased eating enjoyment, if not better nutrition, was the cultivation of the national sweet tooth. In the first three decades of the twentieth century, per capita consumption of sugar soared 75 percent; ice cream production multiplied tenfold.

Partly because of an improved diet, and partly because of advances in medicine and public health programs, the average citizen had a better and better chance of living to a ripe old age. Until nearly 1900, the sources of disease were little known and the quality of medical training was poor. A sick person who consulted a physician was as likely to be harmed as helped. Then a number of discoveries and educational advances increased the effectiveness of medical intervention. In the four decades before 1890, life expectancy at birth in Massachusetts (the only state which gathered accurate information) had increased by only three years, from 39 to 42. In the next four decades, it rose by 17 years! Although striking improvements in medicine have occurred since 1930, they have yet to add another 17 years to average life expectancy.

THE CHANGING COUNTRYSIDE

Farmers benefited least from the material advances of the early twentieth century. Few farm families could delight in refrigerators and washing machines. In 1920, less than two percent of rural households had electricity. Even in 1930, the proportion was only one in 10.

The most obvious fact about the farm population in this era was that it was shrinking. That in itself was nothing new, of course. It had been declining relative to the urban population since well before the Civil War. But its rate of decline was especially rapid in these years. The portion of the labor force employed in agriculture fell from 40 percent in 1900 to barely half that—21 percent—in 1930, a larger drop than had taken place in the entire second half of the nineteenth century. Moreover, for the first time in American history, the number of farmers declined not only relatively but absolutely. Although the population of the nation as a whole grew by more than 60 percent in these years, the number employed in farming actually fell 10 percent.

This shrinking group was able to feed the rapidly growing urban population, as well as many people abroad, because the productivity of the average farm worker was rising. The federal government promoted scientific agriculture through its network of agricultural experiment stations linked to the land-grant colleges. New crops, improved hybrid seed strains, and new cultivation techniques were rapidly developed and disseminated. The use of chemical fertilizers and of labor-saving machinery became increasingly widespread. Both the value of farm implements and machinery and the amount of commercial fertilizer sold rose more than fourfold. By 1930, 920,000 tractors and 900,000 trucks were in use on American farms.

The soaring output that these innovations permitted, however, was no guarantee of prosperity for the average farmer. Profits followed productivity only when farm product prices were reasonably high. The years from the end of the depression of the 1890s through World War I were a golden age for American agriculture. Farm prices were rising faster than other prices. It was not because farmers had gained any new control over the market in which they sold their products—it simply happened that the international agricultural market was much stronger in these years than it had been in the 1880s and 1890s. Furthermore, the establishment of new farms—a key source of surplus production and depressed prices in the crisis of the 1890s—had come to a halt. By 1900, most suitable farmland had already

TABLE 24-4
Changes in Agriculture, 1900–30

	1900	1910	1920	1930
Number of farm workers in thousands	11,680	11,770	10,790	10,560
Percentage of the labor force in farming	40	31	26	21
Farm output as percentage of Gross Domestic Product	23	16	12	10

been settled. Until after World War I, the demand for farm commodities matched the supply and prices held up nicely.

The Agricultural Slump

In the 1920s, farmers ceased to share in the prosperity of the American economy overall. The brief depression of 1919–21 hit them especially hard. Farm income fell from over $10 billion to only $4 billion. And although recovery was rapid in other sectors of the economy and the income of nonagricultural producers soon climbed well above the 1919 level, farmers remained in a depression throughout the decade. In 1929, farm income was still 30 percent below its 1919 peak. Many farmers sold out in despair; the number of farm owners dropped by almost half a million during the decade. But it was a very poor time to sell, because the value of the average acre of farm land declined by 28 percent. Most sellers consequently were forced to settle for less than they had originally paid for their properties.

The depression in the countryside stemmed from the fact that crop prices in the twenties lagged behind the prices farmers paid for manufactured goods (see Table 24-5). Two circumstances were responsible. First, foreign markets stopped absorbing such a large share of American farm output following World War I, when European nations erected tariff barriers in response to America's failure to provide them with the credit necessary to finance further heavy importing. More than a billion dollars worth of American wheat and flour was exported in 1919; ten years later, less than a third of that went abroad. Foreign meat sales in 1929 amounted to only one-ninth of the $700 million recorded 10 years earlier.

Second, while foreign demand was shrinking, the supply of U.S. farm products continued to grow, partly because of increases in yields per acre, partly because the switch from work animals to machinery expanded the number of acres available for commercial production. Until 1920, about a quarter of the nation's farm land was employed to grow crops to feed horses and mules. As tractors, trucks, and automobiles reduced the need for work animals in the 1920s, 25 million cultivable acres were freed for other uses. Devoting them to the production of cash crops

TABLE 24–5
Farm Income and Prices, 1910–29

| | Income to Farmers (billions) | Index of Prices (1910–14 = 100) | |
		Received by Farmers	Paid by Farmers
1910	$ 4.7	104	97
1911	3.9	94	98
1912	5.0	99	101
1913	4.3	102	101
1914	4.7	101	103
1915	4.8	99	105
1916	5.1	119	116
1917	9.0	178	148
1918	9.7	206	173
1919	10.1	217	197
1920	9.0	211	214
1921	4.1	124	155
1922	5.1	131	151
1923	5.9	142	159
1924	5.7	143	160
1925	7.6	156	164
1926	6.8	145	160
1927	6.6	140	159
1928	6.8	148	162
1929	7.0	149	160

did not benefit farmers *as a group*. On the contrary, the resulting increase in supply relative to demand simply drove prices down. But it seemed in the *individual* interest of each farmer to use all the land he had, for he knew that his neighbors would use all the land available to them. There was, as yet, no way in which the decisions of millions of individual farmers could be coordinated to control production and maximize prices.

Despite low farm prices, the largest commercial farms yielded their owners a comfortable living in the 1920s. The trend toward more mechanized and scientific agriculture did not affect all farmers equally. Instead, it split the farm population. Operators with large land holdings and the capital to invest in tractors, combine harvesters, and other equipment were producing more of the total output and reaping more of the profits. In 1930, the largest and most productive half of the country's six million farms turned out 89 percent of the total cash crop. It was these farmer-businessmen who organized and dominated the American Farm Bureau Federation, the major pressure group exerting powerful political pressure for federal assistance for farmers in the 1920s. Their demand for a federal guarantee of farm prices was unsuccessful—the McNary–Haugen bill was twice passed by Congress but vetoed by President Calvin Coolidge—but they did win legislation providing easier credit to farmers and facilitating the formation of farm cooperatives.

The successes of the Farm Bureau, however, did very little to help small farmers. There were many of them, unorganized and easily forgotten. The half of the farms that produced only 11 percent of the crop marketed in 1930 received an average income of less than $200, less than a sixth of the average earnings of nonfarm employees that year. In addition to these three million desperately poor marginal producers, many of them tenants or sharecroppers, another two and a half million farm laborers worked for extremely low wages on farms owned by others. The misery of urban poverty was known to most Americans through a flood of books and articles about how "the other half lived." The farm population's other half, by contrast, were hidden away in dilapidated shacks and cabins along back roads. They were America's invisible poor.

Transportation and Communication

Some aspects of rural life were changing for the better, even for many of those in the other half. The historic isolation of country living was breaking down as a result of improved transportation and communication. By 1930 almost two-thirds of the nation's farms had automobiles, and half had telephones. At the close of the nineteenth century, improved postal services and mail order houses like Sears Roebuck had given farmers new consumption opportunities. The Sears catalogue was dubbed "the farmer's Bible." Now the car made it feasible to visit the city to shop. In 1930, four out of five Americans lived within an hour's drive of a city of 25,000 or more, and it was there that major purchases were made.

The spread of automobiles—and buses—also narrowed the glaring differences between educational opportunities available to rural and urban children. The old one-room country schoolhouses gradually closed down once pupils could be transported to larger schools with better educated teachers. These consolidated schools, along with radio, phonographs, and the movies, blurred the traditional cultural differences between country and city people. By the late 1920s even a quite small country town usually had a motion picture theater where farmers and their children could marvel at the same heroes and heroines worshipped by city dwellers. Thanks to the new electronic media, urban–rural differences in accent, humor, musical tastes, and values were disappearing in the crucible of a new national culture.

URBAN DEVELOPMENT

The U.S. Census of 1920 marked a watershed in American history. It was the first to report that city dwellers were a majority of the population. Some 40 percent of the

TABLE 24-6
Urbanization, 1900–30

	1900	1910	1920	1930
Urban population (millions)*	30.2	42.0	54.2	69.0
Percentage of U.S. population	40	46	51	56
Number of principal standard metropolitan areas†	52	71	94	115
Population of principal standard metropolitan areas (millions)	24.1	34.5	46.1	61.0
Percentage of U.S. population	32	38	44	50

*Urban communities defined as those with populations or 2,500 or more.

†Defined as a central city with at least 50,000, and a total population of at least 100,000 when the suburbs are included.

American people lived in urban communities in 1900; in 1930, the proportion was 56 percent. The total population of the United States increased by 48 million during these three decades; 40 million of the gain occurred in urban areas.

The Census Bureau defines an "urban" place generously, as one with a population of 2,500 or more. This is somewhat misleading on two counts. For one, the residents of a Podunk with a population of 2,800 probably have less in common with the people of Pittsburgh or Philadelphia than with those of a village of 1,500 or 2,000, who are not classified as "urban." On the other hand, the 2,500 dividing line fails to record as urban the residents of suburbs smaller than that, even though they live within a metropolitan area with a population of half a million. A better measure of urbanization is the concentration of people in "principal standard metropolitan areas," which are defined as clusters including a city of at least 50,000 and having a total population of at least 100,000 in the central city and outlying towns and villages that are socially and economically integrated with the central city. In 1900, there were 52 principal standard metropolitan areas, with a bit less than a third of the country's population. By 1930, the number had grown to 115, and they accounted for half of the total population. The 1930 Census was the first to disclose an urban majority in this more meaningful sense of the term, the first to show a majority clustered in units with populations numbering at least six figures.

The Major Metropolises

In 1900, the United States had only three cities with more than a million residents—New York, Chicago, and Philadelphia. By 1930, it had ten giant metropolises. New York, the country's major seaport and financial and communications capital, remained number one, having added a stunning five million to its popula-

TABLE 24-7
The Ten Biggest Population Centers, 1900 and 1930*

1900	1930
1. New York—4,023,000	1. New York—9,423,000
2. Chicago—1,768,000	2. Chicago—3,870,000
3. Philadelphia—1,458,000	3. Philadelphia—2,399,000
4. Boston—905,000	4. Detroit—1,837,000
5. Pittsburgh—622,000	5. Los Angeles—1,778,000
6. St. Louis—612,000	6. Boston—1,545,000
7. Baltimore—543,000	7. Pittsburgh—1,312,000
8. San Francisco—444,000	8. San Francisco—1,104,000
9. Cincinnati—414,000	9. St. Louis—1,094,000
10. Cleveland—402,000	10. Cleveland—1,048,000

*Figures are for the entire metropolitan areas, including suburbs.

tion. Chicago, the focus of the national rail network and the center of the Midwestern manufacturing belt, doubled in size and remained the second city. Philadelphia grew at a somewhat slower pace, but continued in third place. Numbers four and five, however—Detroit and Los Angeles—were newcomers whose remarkable growth reflected basic changes in the economy. Detroit had little more than 300,000 inhabitants in 1900; only thirty years later, its population was approaching two million. Detroit's fivefold population increase in a mere three decades was overshadowed by the even more spectacular rise of Los Angeles, whose 1900 population (114,000) increased by over 1,400 percent during the period.

Detroit and Los Angeles were products of the automobile age. Detroit was quite obviously so. It was "motor city," the home of the industry and a host of other auto-related spinoff industries like metal-working and glass manufacturing. No other major American metropolis has ever depended so heavily on a single industry.

A number of circumstances contributed to the meteoric rise of Los Angeles. The agricultural potential of the area was enormous if the water for irrigation could be found, and the city fathers had the vision and daring to obtain it by constructing a gigantic 225-mile aqueduct to tap the water of the Owens River, completed in 1913. The city had a superb natural harbor, as well as excellent rail connections. The climate made it possible to shoot motion pictures year round; hence Hollywood. Hollywood not only supplied jobs; it disseminated an image of the good life in Southern California on screens across the nation. The most important single industry powering the growth of Los Angeles, however, was directly linked to the auto. The demand for petroleum to fuel gasoline engines led to the opening of the rich Southern California oil fields, and made Los Angeles America's greatest refining center.

Los Angeles was a product of the auto age in another sense as well: Its distinctive spatial organization depended on widespread private ownership of automobiles. Los Angeles was a decentralized and fragmented metropolis, sprawling across the desert landscape over an area of 400 square miles. It was a city without a real center. The downtown business district did not grow apace with the city as a whole, and the rapid transit system designed to link the center with outlying areas withered away from disuse. Some 800,000 cars were registered in Los Angeles County in 1930, one per 2.7 residents. Some eastern visitors were dismayed at the endless urban sprawl, and dismissed Los Angeles as a mere collection of suburbs in search of a city. But the freedom and mobility of a city built on wheels attracted floods of migrants to the City of the Angels.

The same decentralizing trend was at work in other American metropolises. Los Angeles only displayed it in exaggerated form because almost all of its growth took place in the auto era. Urban growth in the railway age had been a centralizing process. Of course there were streetcar suburbs whose residents commuted to a nearby downtown each day. But the inner cities grew more rapidly than the suburban "ring" around them. After 1900, that was no longer the case. In the first decade of the new century, the population of the urban ring grew 17 percent more rapidly than the central city; in the next decade, 36 percent more; in the 1920s, more than twice as fast (44 percent vs. 20 percent). Industry began to disperse too; most new factories built after 1900 were in the suburbs.

The automobile and the electric motor were primarily responsible. Autos allowed people to satisfy their taste for lower-density, single-family housing in neighborhoods far from a streetcar line, where land prices were still low. And industry now no longer needed to crowd into the center, where land was expensive, in order to be near the rail terminal. Trucks could bring in needed raw materials and carry away the finished product. Of course trucks cannot compete with railroads in carrying bulky products like coal, the main source of industrial power in the nineteenth century city. But the switch from coal-burning steam engines to electrical motors eliminated that reason for centralized location. The emergence of what has been called the "electric-oil-auto complex" was consequently as great a turning point in national life as the railroad revolution of the middle of the nineteenth century.

THE POLITICS OF PROSPERITY

The Republicans swept back into power in the national elections of November, 1920, and remained in control of the White House and Congress for the next dozen years. The Republican victory was expected; the electorate still leaned Republican in normal circumstances. Wilson had been, in a sense, an accidental President. And he left office an extremely unpopular one. An atmosphere of sour disillusionment with the war, the League, and spiraling inflation allowed Warren G. Harding and

Calvin Coolidge to win over the Democratic team of James M. Cox and Franklin Delano Roosevelt by the most lop-sided margin in a century. The Republicans won Congress overwhelmingly, too, taking more than two-thirds of the seats in the House and almost two-thirds in the Senate.

Harding was a handsome, convivial man, and a surprisingly tolerant one. Righteous and vengeful Woodrow Wilson refused to pardon the aging Eugene V. Debs, despite his ill health; Harding did so and invited him to dinner at the White House. His heart, however, was better than his mind. He strained for eloquence but attained only vague pomposity. Thus his famous campaign assertion that America needed "not heroism, but healing, not nostrums but normalcy, not revolution, but restoration, not agitation but adjustment, not surgery but serenity, not the dramatic but the dispassionate, not experiment but equipoise, not submergence in international duty but sustainment in triumphant nationality." Complex issues were too much for him. "I can't make a damn thing out of this tax problem," he confided to his secretary. "I listen to one side and they seem right, and then—God!—I talk to the other side and they seem just as right, and here I am where I started. I know somewhere there is a book that will give me the truth, but hell, I couldn't read the book." He couldn't read people very well either; he gave high offices to corrupt cronies who abused his trust by taking bribes and kickbacks. The worst of the many scandals of his administration, Teapot Dome, broke in 1923. The Secretary of the Interior, a Congressional investigating committee discovered, had signed leases giving drilling rights on land set aside as U.S. Navy oil reserves at Teapot Dome, Wyoming, and Elk Hills, California, in return for a satchel containing $100,000. Harding's only good fortune was that he did not have to face the storm; he died on a vacation trip shortly before.

His successor, Calvin Coolidge, was as dour as Harding was genial, and a doctrinaire conservative. In his first address to Congress, he stressed that the American system of government was designed to protect *minority* rights. He did not mean blacks, Indians, or other oppressed groups but men of large fortunes. "The business of America," he said, "is business"; the role of government was to protect and promote business interests. He retained Harding's Secretary of the Treasury, millionaire banker Andrew W. Mellon. Although the war had created a huge national debt, Mellon believed that lower taxes were necessary to stimulate the "man of energy and initiative. When initiative is crippled by a tax system which denies him the right to receive a reasonable share of his earnings, then he will no longer exert himself and the country will be deprived of the energy on which its continued greatness depends." Mellon accordingly sliced income and inheritance taxes, particularly in the upper brackets. By 1926, the income tax rate was as much as two-thirds below the 1918 level (see Table 24–8). The increasingly unequal distribution of wealth produced by Mellon's policies contributed significantly to the depression that began in 1929 (see Chapter 27).

Coolidge's solicitude for business did not extend to what was still the nation's largest business—farming. The persisting hard times in the countryside through the twenties brought to Congress a strong farm bloc that pressed for a federal subsidy to boost farm prices. The McNary–Haugen Bill, a scheme for federal purchase of crops to prop up prices, passed Congress twice, in 1927 and 1928. But

TABLE 24–8
Percentage Tax Rates for High Income Earners
1918–26

	$25,000–49,999	$50,000–99,999	$100,000–999,999	$1,000,000 and up
1918	15.4	22.3	35.2	70.3
1921	7.9	13.1	22.7	41.3
1926	4.9	9.9	16.1	24.1

Coolidge vetoed it both times. "Farmers have never made enough money," he said coldly. "I don't believe we can do much about it."

Harding and Coolidge sometimes spoke as if they believed "that government is best that governs least." But the scope of the federal government did not contract during their administrations; it expanded. In 1928 25 percent more people were on the federal payroll than had been in 1914, and a host of new federal agencies and commissions had been created—the Federal Power Commission, the General Accounting Office, the Budget Bureau, and the Federal Radio Commission (later broadened into the Federal Communications Commission). The complex interdependencies of an advanced industrial society required more government management, and no important Republican wanted to turn the clock back to the days of McKinley. These agencies were not hostile to business, and indeed proved extremely useful to business. The Commerce Department under Herbert Hoover's leadership was extremely active in gathering data useful to American corporations in domestic and foreign markets. The men appointed to staff these agencies could not be accused of radicalism. Coolidge's choice to head the Federal Trade Commission promised that the FTC would no longer be "a publicity bureau to spread socialist propaganda." It never had been, nor had any other of the regulatory bodies created in the Progressive era. But Wilson and Roosevelt could at least conceive of a distinction between the public interest and business interests, as the appointment of men like Chief Forester Gifford Pinchot showed. Harding and Coolidge could not.

The Supreme Court, with four justices appointed by Harding and one by Coolidge, also took on a more strongly conservative cast in the 1920s. William Howard Taft, chosen Chief Justice by Harding, had said before his appointment that it was crucial to maintain the Court "as a bulwark to enforce the guarantee that no man shall be deprived of his property without due process of law." Under his leadership the Court struck down a federal law banning child labor, a statute fixing minimum wages for women and children in Washington, D.C., and other protective social legislation as violations of "freedom of contract." And it interpreted Section 6 of the 1914 Clayton Antitrust Act, intended as a guarantee that labor organizations were exempt from the Sherman Antitrust Act, so narrowly as to deprive it of meaning. Legal injunctions against strikes, and antitrust prosecutions became commonplace, contributing significantly to the decline in trade union membership throughout the decade. The Supreme Court, Coolidge said contentedly in 1924, had become the chief obstacle to the "deliberate and determined effort" then being made to "break down the guarantees of our fundamental law." The question was whether "America will allow itself to be degraded into a communistic and socialistic state, or whether it will remain American"; the Court was the patriot's strongest weapon in the battle to defend the American way of life.

The Divided Democrats

The flourishing economy of the 1920s helped to secure the ascendancy of the Republican party. But even if the economic picture had been less rosy, it is doubtful that the Democrats would have been able to make much capital from it. The Democrats drew the bulk of their support from two constituencies that had antithetical views on the central issues of the day—native white Protestants in the South and West, and predominantly Catholic immigrants and their children in the eastern cities. Throughout the decade, these two wings battled incessantly for control of the party, spilling enough blood to enfeeble it on election day.

The two great issues over which they fought were Prohibition and the Ku Klux Klan. Most southern and western Democrats, the products of village America, were ardent Prohibitionists, and saw the Eighteenth Amendment as a noble device to purge their civilization of a corrupting European influence. Eastern Democrats represented urban, immigrant America and resented the attempt to force the restrictive moral code of the village on cosmopolitan city dwellers. They worked to commit the party to a constitutional amendment overturning the Eighteenth Amendment.

The extraordinary growth of a new national secret organization—the second Ku Klux Klan—divided the Democrats along essentially the same lines. The original Klan, founded in 1866, was a purely Southern organization with a single aim—to deprive blacks of the liberties they had won during Reconstruction and reestablish white supremacy. The second Klan had broader aims and more of a national base. It was formed in 1915 and grew like wildfire. Precise estimates of the membership of a secret organization cannot be made, naturally, but some authorities believe that at its peak in the mid-twenties about a quarter of the adult white male native Protestant population of the entire country belonged. Although much of its support came from the South, the Klan was also strong in a number of midwestern and western states, including Indiana, Oregon, and California.

The second Klan was as committed to white supremacy as the first, and struck out against blacks who failed to abide by the Jim Crow code. But it had the much broader aim of establishing 100 percent Americanism and imposing fundamentalist Protestant morality on society as a whole. "We are a movement of the plain people," said the Grand Wizard of the Klan in 1926. "We are demanding, and we expect to win, a return of power into the hands of the everyday, not highly cultured, not overly intellectualized, but unspoiled and not de-Americanized, average citizen of the old stock." Immigrants, Catholics, Jews, socialists, bootleggers, gamblers, atheists, adulterers—all were targets of the economic boycotts, beatings, whippings, lynchings, and cross-burnings carried out by the hooded men. Catholics, a very large and increasingly powerful group, inspired the most audible vehemence. "Who assassinated Garfield?," asked a Klan paper. "A Catholic. Who assassinated McKinley? A Catholic. Who has recently bought a huge tract of land opposite West Point, and another overlooking Washington? The Pope."

The chasm between dries and wets, and between Klansmen and enemies of the Klan was unbridgeable. The 1924 Democratic convention left the party in a shambles. The eastern wing, led by Catholic Alfred E. Smith, Governor of New York, insisted that the platform support repeal and condemn the Klan. The leaders of the southern and western wing, William Jennings Bryan and Woodrow Wilson's son-in-law, William Gibbs McAdoo, would have none of it. Both resolutions were narrowly defeated after bitter argument. Then Smith and McAdoo battled it out for the presidential nomination, with neither able to win the necessary two-thirds margin. After 9 abrasive days, and 103 roll calls, the exhausted convention settled on a compromise dark horse, John W. Davis, a New York corporation lawyer with West Virginia origins.

Davis was too obscure to have much chance of defeating Coolidge. Moreover, his extreme conservatism alienated liberals who couldn't stomach "silent Cal." In the election they defected to Robert La Follette, running as the candidate of a revived Progressive Party formed by discontented farmers and labor leaders. La Follette pulled an impressive 17 percent of the vote, and Davis only 29 percent, concentrated almost entirely in the solid South. Coolidge was an easy victor.

For Democrats, the 1928 election was only a variation on the 1924 theme, with the same dismal results. The same conflicts erupted at the convention, only this time Al Smith's supporters had enough muscle to secure him the nomination. The choice of Smith was only a jump from the frying pan into the fire. He was a Catholic, and many Protestants thought that meant his first loyalty was to the Pope rather than to his country. His election, they charged, would make the United States "the tail of the Roman Catholic kite." He was an unabashed wet, and sure to use his influence to throw open the saloon doors once again. As a leader of Tammany Hall, he was a symbol of machine politics. And he spoke with a heavy "New Yawk" accent that grated on the ears when heard over the radio in a living room in Mississippi, Missouri, or California. Hundreds of thousands of normally Democratic voters found Smith unbearable, and defected to the Republicans. Herbert Hoover carried 40 of the 48 states, including 7 in what had been for half a century the solidly Democratic South.

Al Smith's campaign was a disaster for the Democrats, but not an unmitigated disaster. Hidden in the election returns was one ray of hope for the future—Smith ran better in the cities than had any Democratic candidate for a generation. In the great political realignment of the 1890s, the Republicans had won over a solid majority of city dwellers. They remained dominant in most urban communities outside the South down into the 1920s, piling up 1.6 million votes more than the Democrats in the 12 largest cities in 1920 and 1.3 million in 1924. Smith broke the Republican stranglehold on the big cities in 1928, and actually defeated Hoover

THE KLAN AT WORK, 1921

March 13, 1921, Houston, Texas

J. Lafayette Cockrell, Negro dentist, irreparably mutilated by masked men.

April 10, 1921, Houston, Texas

J.S. Allen, Houston attorney, taken from crowded downtown street into the country and given coat of tar and feathers. He was then returned to the city and dumped from an automobile in the middle of the business section. Nude, except for tar and feathers.

June 10, 1921, Shreveport, Louisiana

A number of propaganda spreaders of the National Association for the Advancement of Colored People, fresh from Tulsa, Oklahoma, were run out of Shreveport, Louisiana by the Ku Klux Klan.

June 12, 1921, Daytona, Florida

As a result of the open defiance of the Knights of the Ku Klux Klan, threats were made through the mails to editor H.C. Sparkman of the Journal that the Klan would deal with his case and intimating that he was in danger of bodily harm, perhaps death at their hands.

July 8, 1921, Pensacola, Florida

Night of July eighth, white-robed masked men drove up to the restaurant owned by Chris Lochas, a Greek, and in the presence of the Chief of Police of the city handed him this warning: "You are an undesirable citizen, you violate federal Prohibition laws, the laws of decency, and are a running sore of society. Several trains are leaving Pensacola daily. Take your choice, but do not take too much time. Sincerely, in earnest."

July 12, 1921, Enid, Oklahoma

Walter Billings, movie operator, whipped and given coat of cotton and crude oil.

—*New York World*, September 19, 1921

there by a slight margin (38,000 votes). The shift was especially marked in cities with the heaviest concentrations of new immigrants. They had been the targets of the backlash by the "plain people of the old stock" in the Klan, the victims of immigration restriction, Prohibition, and 100 percent Americanism. Many had been too preoccupied with earning a living to give much thought to politics before, and had failed to naturalize and register. During the twenties, partly as a result of these attacks, they began to mobilize politically. Only 49 percent of the immigrants listed in the Census of 1920 had taken U.S. citizenship; by 1930 the proportion had risen to 59 percent. And their native-born children, educated in American schools, were citizens by birth. These second generation immigrants were a rapidly growing group, and were more attuned to the American scene than their parents. Hundreds of thousands of them reached voting age during the twenties. The vote of the awakening ethnics was a source of great potential strength for the Democrats, particularly because it was concentrated in populous states with large numbers of electoral votes. Al Smith proved that it could be won by a candidate who spoke their language.

The claim that 1928 brought an "Al Smith Revolution," making it possible to forge a Democratic national majority in the 1930s is excessive, however. It took much more than the mobilization of the urban ethnic masses to produce a new national majority. Smith, after all, carried only two states outside the South. Furthermore, his appeal within the cities was largely a personal one that did not help Democratic candidates for other offices. But the 1928 election returns did suggest new possibilities for the Democrats in the future. If some crisis were to shake the normal Republican allegiances of other important elements of the population, and if the Democrats could choose a candidate with some of Smith's appeal in the cities but without the traits that repelled voters elsewhere, a major political realignment like those that occurred in the 1850s and the 1890s might take place.

Culture in Transition

George F. Babbit, the hero of Sinclair Lewis' best selling 1922 novel, has often been taken as a representative American of the twenties, a symbol of the coarse and vulgar materialism that pervaded the entire society. Babbitt was a real estate salesman whose only talent was "selling houses for more than people could afford to pay"; his god was "Modern Appliances." He was an utter conformist, with a provincial certainty that his civilization was the grandest the world had ever known.

There were real life counterparts to the fictional Babbitt in the 1920s. President Calvin Coolidge sounded much like him in his infrequent public statements. And there was Bruce Barton's appalling book, *The Man Nobody Knows* (1925), which portrayed Jesus Christ as the world's greatest salesman, "the founder of modern business" (see box). But the striking thing about the culture of the period was not the prevalence of boosterism, but the beginnings of a serious challenge to it. Sinclair Lewis was not pilloried for his scathing satire of the businessman; *Babbitt* was a runaway best-seller that made him rich. It was read not only by educated cosmopolites in the large metropolises, but by people in smaller cities and towns like those the book held up to ridicule. The same can be said for Lewis' earlier exposé of the stifling complacency of small town life, *Main Street* (1920). What was new about the twenties was not the ascendancy of George F. Babbitt and the folks on Main Street, but the fact that they were on the defensive. Millions of Americans were questioning traditional verities and experimenting with new modes of behavior.

The spirit of revolt, the quest for liberation from stultifying tradition that characterized the decade, was expressed most clearly and enduringly in a rich outpouring of creative literature. Sherwood Anderson's *Winesburg, Ohio* (1919) portrayed small town life even more bleakly than *Main Street*. The American success ethic was subjected to searching criticism in F. Scott Fitzgerald's brilliant *The Great Gatsby* (1925) and Theodore Dreiser's elephantine but powerful *An American Tragedy* (1925). Disillusionment with war and distrust of all large-scale institutions were at the core of John Dos Passos' *Three Soldiers* (1921), E.E. Cummings' *The Enormous Room* (1922), William Faulkner's *Soldier's Pay* (1926), Ernest Hemingway's *The Sun Also Rises* (1926), and Ezra Pound's long poem, "Hugh Selwyn Mauberly" (1920).

Writers of "the lost generation" like Hemingway, Fitzgerald, and Cummings were so despairing of American civilization that they lived in exile in Paris for most of the decade. But there were many observers who remained at home to subject American society to critical scrutiny. Foremost among them was Sinclair Lewis. His works have not worn well, because his characters are cardboard figures and his point of view was confused; although he was awarded the Nobel Prize for Literature in 1930, Lewis was a journalist rather than an artist. But his sociological novels skillfully and entertainingly exposed some of the absurdities of the society of the twenties. Two new magazines, H.L. Mencken's *American Mercury* (founded in 1924) and the *New Yorker* (1925) took on the same mission. Mencken waged war on what he called the "booboisie," denouncing the "yokels" and "half-wits" who marched with the Klan, supported Prohibition, believed in the literal truth of the Bible, and opposed the teaching of the Darwinian theory of evolution in the public schools. In their cooler, buttoned-down way, E.B. White, James Thurber, and other *New Yorker* writers commented wryly on the vulgarity of the American scene. The *New Yorker* announced that it was for "the caviar sophisticates," and not for "the old lady in Dubuque."

It would be perilous to judge how the masses of Americans were leading their daily lives on the basis of a few novels and magazines. These works were the product of middle and upper middle-class people, by and large. The immense class, regional, ethnic, and religious diversity of the American population defies easy generalizations. But the mood of revolt and experimentation clearly affected the behavior of many people, especially the young. The twenties were "the Jazz Age," the era of the flapper, the speak-easy, and bathtub gin. The young woman of the decade was freed from the long skirts and flowing petticoats her mother had worn; the typical woman's costume in 1913 required 19½ yards of cloth; the flapper of 1925 wore only 7 yards' worth. And some women felt liberated from restrictive Victorian sexual mores as well. A survey of college-educated women born between 1890 and 1900 revealed that 74 percent were virgins at marriage, but only 31 percent of those who graduated in the 1920s made that claim. "If all the girls at the Yale prom were laid end to end," quipped humorist Dorothy Parker, "I wouldn't be surprised." Prohibition certainly didn't lead the young to enlist in the cold water army; it probably stimulated overindulgence in alcohol. Enforcement was extremely lax in most communities, and the relish of tasting forbidden fruit only added to the appeal. Workingmen may have been denied their evening mugs of beer; beer was too bulky and cheap for bootlegging to be profitable. But college youths could easily keep flasks of gin full.

The "flaming youths" of the twenties, of course, were a distinct minority of their age group, confined largely to the few million mostly middle-class young people attending college. But some cultural changes in the era cut deeper. Prosperity, the increase in leisure time, and the new mass media were undermining the traditional work-centered, self-denying Protestant Ethic and encouraging a new "fun morality." An imaginative study of biographical essays appearing in the *Saturday Evening Post* since 1901 revealed a striking change. At the opening of the twentieth century the subjects were almost all "idols of production," people who had achieved success in the world of work—immigrant scientists, corporate leaders, serious artists, political leaders. By the twenties they had been replaced, for the most part, by "idols of consumption"—professional athletes like Babe Ruth and Jack Dempsey, and Hollywood stars like Mary Pickford and Charlie Chaplin. This shift did not result from a change in the editorial biases of the magazine, which remained constant over the period. It seems to indicate a basic change in the values of the mass, albeit middle-class, audience to which it was directed. The old Protestant Ethic of self-denial and disciplined pursuit of a productive calling was giving way to a consumption ethic that sanctioned self-indulgence and the hedonistic

HENRY FORD: (1863–1947)

Henry Ford was born on a farm outside Detroit, but detested the drudgery and monotony of farm work, and took off for Detroit when he was 16. After an apprenticeship as a mechanic, he built his first automobile in his barn in 1896, while working as an engineer for Detroit Edison. He had plenty of help from his friends. In the 1890s many young men of a mechanical bent were piecing together horseless carriages of various kinds. Ford's genius was not in devising machinery of a type no one else had ever envisioned, but in conceiving of the automobile as a product that could be tailored for a mass market.

At first Ford was handicapped by the need to cooperate with partners who had a similar vision; but after the organization of the Ford Motor Company in 1903, he was in a position to call the shots. After years of experimentation, he perfected the "Tin Lizzie"—the Model T-Ford—in 1908. It was inexpensive, it was simple to repair, it would wear forever —and it was light enough and rode high enough above the ground to travel freely over a country that as yet had few decent roads. Ford had enough insight into the American character to perceive that "everybody wants to be someplace he ain't. As soon as he gets there, he wants to go right back." He made a colossal fortune by providing the common man with a way of satisfying that itch to move. The Model-T, along with the assembly line method of producing it (introduced in 1913) and the Five-Dollar Day (1914), made Ford a household word.

For a time Ford was the most popular man in America and the most famous American in the world. He was spoken of as a prospect for the White House and clearly had aspirations. In 1916 he commissioned a "Peace Ship" in which he sailed to Europe, hoping to convince belligerents to call off World War I. In 1918, without making a single campaign speech, he ran for the Senate from Michigan and was defeated. In light of his views, his silence was perhaps wise. He once said, "I don't like to read books; they muss up my mind." In 1919 he began to publish the Dearborn *Independent,* a rabidly anti-Semitic weekly that blamed the Jews for the evils of the Great War, Bolshevism, Darwinism, short skirts and lipstick, jazz, and bootleggers. Millions of Americans of the day believed in these bigoted simplicities, but never enough to put Henry Ford into public office.

Although Henry believed that "history is bunk," in his declining of rural America in the horse and buggy days before the Model-T. He rebuilt his father's farmhouse as he remembered it from his boyhood, and assembled a whole village of museums stuffed with antique ploughs, wagons, waterwheels, and the like. No one had done more to kill the culture he looked back on with such nostalgia.

pursuit of individual happiness. From this vantage point, the twenties may be seen as the crucial decade in which modern America was born.

SUGGESTED READINGS

Thomas C. Cochran, *The American Business System: A Historical Perspective, 1900–1955* (rev. ed., 1957), and *American Business in the 20th Century* (1972) offer succinct introductions. Harold V. Faulkner, *The Decline of Laissez Faire, 1897–1917* (1951), and George Soule, *Prosperity Decade: From War to Depression, 1917–1929* (1947) are detailed accounts. See also Jim Potter, *The American Economy between the Wars* (1974), Siegfried Giedion, *Mechanization Takes Command: A Contribution to Anonymous History* (1948) is a brilliant discussion of technological change. Alfred Chandler, Jr., *Strategy and Structure: Chapters in the History of American Industrial Enterprise* (1962), and the final section of his *The Visible Hand: The Managerial Revolution in American Business* (1977) are outstanding. The achievements of Henry Ford are portrayed admiringly in Allen Nevins and F.E. Hill, *Ford: The Times, the Man, and the Company* (1954) and *Ford: Expansion and Challenge* (1957), and sardonically in Keith Sward, *The Legend of Henry Ford* (1948). See also Reynold M. Wik, *Henry Ford and Grass-Roots America* (1972) and Stephen Meyer III, *The Five Dollar Day: Labor Management and Social Control in the Ford Motor Company, 1908–1921* (1981). Other aspects of corporate development are considered in Louis Galambos, *Competition and Cooperation: The Emergence of a National Trade Association* (1966), A.A. Berle, Jr. and G.F. Means, *The Modern Corporation and Private Property* (1932), Albro Martin, *Enterprise Denied: Origins of the Decline of American Railroads* (1971), Otis Pease, *The Responsibilities of American Advertising* (1958), J.W. Prothero, *The Dollar Decade: Business Ideas in the 1920's* (1954), Morrell Heald, *The Social Responsibilities of Business: Company and Community, 1900–1960* (1970), and Louis Galambos, *The Public Image of Big Business in America, 1880–1940: A Quantitative Study of Social Change* (1975).

The best account of how economic change in the Auto Age altered living patterns is to be found in a classic sociological community study, Robert S. and Helen M. Lynd, *Middletown: A Study in Modern American Culture* (1929). In *First Person, America* (1980) edited by Ann Banks, 80 anonymous Americans tell their life histories from their childhoods to the late 1930s. See also John Rae, *The Road and the Car in American Life* (1971), and James J. Flink, *The Car Culture* (1975). David Montgomery, *Workers' Control in America* (1979), David Brody, *Workers in Industrial America: Essays on the 20th Century Struggle* (1980), Tamara K. Hareven, *Family Time and Industrial Time: The Relationship between the Family and Work in a New England Industrial Community* (1982), Albert Camarillo, *Chicanos in a Changing Society: From Mexican Pueblos to American Barrios in Santa Barbara and Southern California, 1848–1970* (1979), and Irving Bernstein, *The Lean Years: A History of the American Worker, 1920–1933* (1960) illuminate the lives of workers.

For farmers, see Don S. Kirschner, *City and Country: Rural Responses to Urbanization in the 1920's* (1970), Grant McConnell, *The Decline of American Democracy*

(1953), John D. Hicks and Theodore Saloutos, *Twentieth Century Populism: Agricultural Discontent in the Middle West, 1900-1939* (1964), and J.D. Black, *Agricultural Reform in the United States* (1930). On the exploding metropolis, see Olivier Zunz, *The Changing Face of Inequality: Urbanization, Industrial Development, and Immigrants in Detroit, 1880-1920* (1982), Robert M. Fogelson, *The Fragmented Metropolis: Los Angeles, 1850-1930* (1967), William H. Wilson, *Coming of Age: Urban America, 1915-1945* (1974), and Beverly Duncan and Stanley Lieberson, *Metropolis and Region in Transition* (1970).

Paul Carter, *The Twenties in America* (rev. ed., 1982) is a thoughtful overview of the decade. Ethnic tensions in the period are explored in David Burner, *The Politics of Provincialism: The Democratic Party in Transition, 1918-1932* (1968), Samuel Lubell, *The Future of American Politics* (1951), Oscar Handlin, *Al Smith and His America* (1958), David Chalmers, *Hooded Americanism: The History of the KKK* (1965), Kenneth Jackson, *The Ku Klux Klan in the City, 1915-1930* (1968), Edward R. Kantowicz, *Polish–American Politics in Chicago, 1880-1940* (1974), and John N. Allswang, *A House for All Peoples: Ethnic Politics in Chicago, 1890-1936* (1971). Henry F. May, *The End of American Innocence* (1959) and Roderick Nash, *The Nervous Generation: American Thought, 1917-1930* (1970) cover intellectual and cultural developments. Loren Baritz, ed., *The Culture of the Twenties* (1971) is a useful collection of primary documents.

Chapter Twenty-Five

The Color Line

A s the twentieth century began, almost nine million Americans—a ninth of the population—were Negroes. By 1930, the number had grown to over twelve million. A color line that relegated them to a separate and inferior social position was drawn most rigidly in the Jim Crow South. But the mass migration of southern blacks to "the Promised Land" of the northern city during and after World War I did not result in the smooth and speedy integration of blacks in the American mainstream. As the black population of the North swelled, so did white racist hostility. Prejudice forced blacks into ghettoes set apart from the larger society. In these segregated enclaves, they struggled to develop forms of organization and cultural expression to give coherence to their lives.

THE PLIGHT OF THE SOUTHERN BLACK

In 1900, a generation after Emancipation, nine out of ten black Americans still lived in the South, almost the same proportion as in 1860. The overwhelming majority, desperately poor, scratched out a living in the cotton fields. Three out of four black farmers were tenants or sharecroppers, often chained by debt to the land. Nine out of twenty Afro-Americans in the country as a whole, and well over half of those in the rural South, could not read or write. Blacks by then had entirely lost the battle to retain the basic political and civil rights granted them during Reconstruction. A Supreme Court eager to appease southern white opinion had stripped the Four-

The usually nocturnal Ku Klux Klan made daylight appearances to threaten Negroes after a 1956 boycott of city buses in Montgomery, Alabama.

GEORGIA JUSTICE, 1915

The man who had killed the officer submitted to arrest by the mob, which by this time numbered about 400. Placing a rope around his neck he was led to the center of the town and in the presence of women and children they proceeded to hold a conference as to the kind of death that should be meted out to him. Some yelled to hang him; some to burn him alive. It was decided in a few minutes. Willing hands brought a large dry-goods box, placed it in the center of the street; in it was straw on which was poured a tub of oil; then the man was lifted with a rope around his neck and placed in this box head down, and then another tub of oil was poured over him. A man from the crowd deliberately lit a match and set fire to the living man. While in this position the flames shot up at great height. The crowd began to yell as the flames shot upward. In an instant the poor creature managed to lift himself out of the box, a mass of flames. He was fighting the flames with his hands in an effort to shield his face and eyes, and in this condition attempted to run. The crowd allowed him to run the length of the rope, which was held by willing hands, until he reached a distance of about twenty feet; then a yell went up from the crowd to shoot. In an instant there were several hundred shots and the creature fell in his tracks. The crowd deliberately walked up to the prostrate form and shot the remainder of their guns into his lifeless body. With the flames still leaping into the air, he was pulled back into the fire that was now roaring with boxes and oil brought out of the different stores by men and boys. Every time they would throw on more oil and boxes the crowd would yell as though they were at a bull fight. Standing about fifty or seventy-five feet from the scene I could actually smell the flesh of the poor man as it was being burned. Not a voice was raised in the defense of the man. No one attempted to hide their identity. I looked into the faces of men whom I knew to be officers of the town lending a willing hand in the burning of this man. No wonder the coroner who held the inquest returned a verdict that the Negro came to his death "at the hands of an enraged mob unknown to the jury," because to get a jury in that town they had to get some who participated in the burning.

—Thomas F. Gosset, *Race,* 1963

teenth and Fifteenth Amendments of their meaning and freed southern legislators to deprive blacks of the right to vote, hold political office, or serve on juries. All were bound by Jim Crow codes that confined them to separate and inferior schools and public facilities of every kind. A hundred horrible lynchings a year reminded the potentially rebellious of the consequences of challenging white authority (see box). In the first two decades of the century, more men were lynched in the South than were legally executed by the courts in all the 48 states, the vast majority of them southern blacks.

Two events in 1895 symbolized the transition to the Jim Crow era: the death of Frederick Douglass and the sudden rise to eminence of Booker T. Washington, a new kind of black leader. Douglass, a runaway slave who became a great abolitionist orator, had been the most eloquent black defender of Radical Reconstruction. He had bitterly criticized the drive for segregation and white supremacy that gathered force throughout the South in the closing decades of the century. Washington first won national prominence by giving an address at the Atlanta Exposition in the year of Douglass's death, an address which outlined a philosophy of black accommodation to Jim Crow. Washington had been born in slavery and raised in poverty. Although he was sent to work at a West Virginia salt mine at the age of nine, he managed to educate himself at night school and then the Hampton Normal Agricultural Institute. In 1881 he founded the Tuskegee Institute in Alabama, and made it into a leading black educational center. Unlike Douglass, who never returned to the South from which he had fled, Washington had a painful first-hand knowledge of powerful forces behind the segregationist drive. Open, militant protest in Douglass fashion, he was certain, would be futile and counterproductive. His Atlanta Exposition address declared that segregation was not necessarily degrading to blacks. In all things that were "purely social," the two races could be "as separate as the fingers, yet one as the hand in all things essential to mutual progress." What was truly "essential to mutual progress" was not social equality or even political rights, but economic advancement for blacks. Achieving it would require fair treatment by white employers and others with economic power. Washington professed optimism about the opportunities: "It is in the South that the Negro is given a man's chance in the commercial world."

Why, then, were most blacks crowded on the lowest rung of the economic ladder? Because, said Washington, they had not developed the skills, ambition, and drive it took to climb higher. They needed to pull themselves up by their own bootstraps, and that they could do through education. By education he meant not abstruse book learning, but practical studies of the sort emphasized in the curriculum of the Tuskegee Institute—basic literacy plus crafts like carpentry, masonry, and agricultural science. The aim was to produce black workers so skilled and diligent that nothing could hold them back. This would uplift the race in a way that could only benefit whites as well: "There is no defense or security for any of us except in the highest intelligence and development of all."

Washington, of course, knew full well that blacks were not really given "a man's chance in the commercial world" in the South of his day. But he was an extremely subtle and devious man, who believed that saying so would soothe the powerful whites he sought to placate, and permit him to carry on his educational mission. Consequently, he maintained public silence about black disfranchisement, lynchings, and Jim Crow, and insisted that it was up to blacks to earn their rights by becoming more productive workers. Some northern blacks denounced the "Atlanta Compromise" as a sell-out, and dismissed Washington as an "Uncle Tom." They still believed that the ideals of Radical Reconstruction could be realized. Washington knew the South much better. He did oppose disfranchisement and segregation, but believed that militant protest on behalf of an impossible dream would be simply suicidal. It might have been literally so; at least until he became a nationally known figure at the age of 40, it is probable that any southern white who chose to could have shot Washington to death without running much risk of being brought to justice. But behind the scenes, Washington maneuvered as best he could to preserve black rights through political bargaining and legal action. In one revealing and symbolic incident, he publicly refused refuge at Tuskegee to a wounded black lawyer fleeing a lynch mob. To flout local white opinion, he felt, would imperil the very existence of an institution central to the welfare of southern blacks. But after publicly spurning the potential lynching victim, Washington quietly saw to it that he was hidden, given medical care, and safely guided out of the community.

Washington was indeed an accommodationist, but the accommodation was frequently more apparent than real. He was a shrewd politician making the best of a very bad lot, a poker player with few chips in a crooked game. Given his priorities—his belief that education was the indispensable prerequisite for the advancement of his race—he played it skillfully. When told that some American Negroes were radical and some conservative, a Russian visitor laughed. "What on earth," he exclaimed, "have they got to conserve?" But Washington believed they *did* have much to conserve. State and local appropriations for black schools under the South's dual system were well below those for white students, but they probably would have been lower still if not for the efforts of conservatives like Washington and his followers. The bulk of the funds that kept alive the struggling southern black colleges came from northern white philanthropists carefully cultivated by Washington. These colleges trained the next generation of southern Afro-American leaders. Washington's fawning manner before white audiences seems repellent by today's standards, but we have to ask whether or not these real achievements could have been attained in any other way.

Although Washington's base of operation down to his death in 1915 was the Tuskegee Institute, his influence extended into the small black enclaves in northern cities as well. He had good connections with wealthy white benefactors and with key figures in the Republican party; in 1901 Theodore Roosevelt had him to dinner at the White House, an invitation which outraged southern white racist congressmen. Blacks appointed to civil service jobs had to be cleared by Washington; no black schools received contributions from Carnegie, Rockefeller, and other large donors without Washington's approval; several editors of black newspapers received subsidies from him and followed his ideological direction. In 1900 the "Tuskegee Machine," with funds from Andrew Carnegie, established the National Negro Business League to encourage black business. Despite Washington's apparent accommodationism, the National Negro Business League's "buy black" campaigns were an early expression of black nationalism. It appealed to rising black entrepreneurs who saw little prospect of competing successfully in white markets. Most of them were migrants from the South who shared Washington's separatist views and overriding concern with economic goals. They sought to take "advantage of the disadvantages" of segregation, by servicing the captive black market. Aspiring politicians in the North, where blacks could vote,

THE RATIONALE FOR JIM CROW

As governor of my State I am sure that I exerted myself as much to protect the negro in the enjoyment of his life, his liberty, the pursuit of happiness, and the products of his own toil as any executive in America has ever done. He does not vote much in Mississippi, but I really think that he votes more than he ought to vote, if he votes at all. I do not think it was ever intended by the Creator that the two races should live together upon equal terms—enjoy equal political and social advantages. One or the other must rule. The people of the South tried to share with the negro in the government of the country after the war, but the negro declined to share with the white man. Black heels rested cruelly upon white necks for many years after the close of the war. The white man endured the negro's misrule, his insolence, impudence, and infamy. He suffered his criminal incapacity to govern until the public domain had been well-nigh squandered and the public treasury looted. We saw the civilization reared by the genius of our fathers, glorified and cemented by their sacred blood, vanishing from the earth, and by means, I will not say in this presence, fair, but by means sufficient, we invoked the law of self-preservation; we arose in the might of an outraged race and as the Savior scourged the money changers from the temple, so the southern white man drove from power the scalawag, the carpetbagger, and the incompetent negro. . . .

God Almighty never intended that the negro should share with the white man in the government of this country; and you can not improve upon the plans of God Almighty or defeat His purposes, either, by legislative enactments. Do not forget that. It matters not what I may say or others may think; it matters not what constitutions may contain or statutes provide, wherever the negro is in sufficient numbers to imperil the white man's civilization or question the white man's supremacy the white man is going to find some way around the difficulty. And that is just as true in the North as it is in the South. You need not deceive yourselves about that. The feeling against the negro in Illinois when he gets in the white man's way is quite as strong, more bitter, less regardful of the negro's feelings and conditions than it is in Mississippi. And that is true of every other Northern State.

—James K. Vardaman, *Congressional Record*, February 1914

also saw advantages in segregation. The concentrated votes of the ghetto could catapult them into office.

Washington spoke for a majority of blacks, both in the South and in the North. But after the turn of the century, he met with a significant challenge from one stratum of the northern black community—educated members of the traditional elite, many of them descendants of the antebellum free black community. W.E.B.

DuBois, Harvard's first black Ph.D., and William Monroe Trotter, the first black to win a Phi Beta Kappa key at Harvard and editor of the militant Boston paper, *The Guardian*, were leading critics of the separatist and accommodationist philosophy. In 1905 they organized the Niagra Movement, which took a strong integrationist stance and demanded "the abolition of all caste distinctions based simply on race and color." It fought a few legal battles against segregation in the schools and on the railroads, but was significant chiefly as the precursor of a more powerful integrationist organization which grew out of it in 1909, the National Association for the Advancement of Colored People. The NAACP included most members of the Niagra Movement, but its principal leaders in the early years were white Progressives like Oswald Garrison Villard, publisher of the *New York Evening Post*, Jane Addams, and attorney Clarence Darrow. All of its chief officers except Du-Bois, editor of the association's journal, *Crisis*, were white at first. But the core membership consisted of the college-educated black middle class. The NAACP concentrated its efforts on legal challenges to segregation and disfranchisement. It won its first great victory in 1915, just before Washington's death, when the U.S. Supreme Court ruled unconstitutional a "grandfather clause" in the Oklahoma state constitution (a measure exempting from the poll tax and literacy tax those whose ancestors were qualified to vote in 1860—that is, all whites).

THE GREAT MIGRATION

Washington and his Tuskegee machine and DuBois and the white liberals of the NAACP struggled in their different ways to change the position of black people in American society. The major transformation in the life of the nation's black community in the period, however, was not the result of organized effort. The Great Migration that transferred millions of blacks from the South to the North, from farm to factory, began during World War I in response to changing economic circumstances.

Before World War I, there seemed little place for blacks in the United States except in the southern countryside. The South had few cities and little industry. Afro-Americans who did make their way into southern cities had very restricted employment opportunities. The vast majority worked for abysmal wages at menial service tasks—as waiters, janitors, porters, laundresses, or servants.

There was, of course, the possibility of moving to the North. In many ways, northern cities were freer and less oppressive to blacks than anyplace in the South. "I just begin to feel like a man," wrote a recent migrant to Chicago to a friend back in Mississippi. "It's a great deal of pleasure knowing that you have got some privilege. My children are going to the same school with the whites and I dont have to umble to no one. I have registered—Will vote in the next election." Despite that, relatively few Afro-Americans moved northward. The proportion of the American black population residing in the North in 1910 was only 11.1 percent, up only slightly from the 9.3 percent there at the end of the Civil War. The root cause was the lack of jobs. In New York and Chicago as much as in Atlanta and Charleston, black men and women were confined to traditional "Negro jobs." The greater industrial development in these northern cities might have meant greater opportunities for blacks to do unskilled or semi-skilled factory work at higher wages, but employers filled these posts with recent immigrants. Nor did the greater demand for skilled industrial workers spell opportunity for Afro-Americans in the North. Few had been able to obtain the necessary training in the South before migrating, racially restrictive trade union policies barred them from apprenticeship programs in the North, and blacks who somehow managed to acquire skills were hired reluctantly or not at all. Blacks in 1910 comprised only 2 percent of the population of Boston and Chicago, 1.9 percent in New York, 1.5 percent in Cleveland, and 1.2 percent in Detroit—because, in the last analysis, there were only that many "Negro jobs" in those cities.

The tight labor market created by World War I suddenly changed all that. The outbreak of the European war brought flush times for American manufacturers. Orders soared, and the in-flow of immigrant manpower was blocked. America's entry into the fighting in 1917 added to the labor scarcity, by putting 4 million men in uniform. The only way to increase production was to tap the black community for labor. That triggered a massive relocation of the black population that continued unabated through the 1920s. By 1930, the number of Afro-Americans living in the North had tripled. There were a third of a million in New York alone, almost a quarter million in both Chicago and Philadelphia. In 1910 census takers found only 6,000 blacks in Detroit; in 1930 they counted more than 20 times as many.

Of course there were other good reasons for blacks to flee the South—disfranchisement, tightening segregation, fear of lynch mobs. But these were old conditions and were not growing worse. The number of lynchings per year was falling before the war, not rising. Some contemporary observers attributed the flight to the devastation wrought by the boll weevil, a quarter-inch insect that devoured cotton plants. But, again, the timing is wrong. That pest had invaded the South from Mexico in the early 1890s; by World War I, reasonably effective defenses against it had been developed. Nor did fluctuations in cotton prices drive blacks from southern farms. Once the flight began, it continued through years of high and low prices alike.

The Great Migration was not precipitated by any new push from the South. The impetus was a pull from the North—the opening up of better jobs. Before the war, fewer than 3,000 black men worked in Chicago's factories, less than a sixth of the black labor force. By 1920 there were more than five times that number. A third of all black males worked for firms like International Harvester, Pullman, Swift, and Armour—in jobs once restricted to whites. The proportion in traditional service jobs had dropped from over half to little more than a fourth. For black women, however, there was less of a change; 61 percent of them were domestic servants in 1920. But even that was a substantial drop from the 77 percent before the war, and the proportion employed in manufacturing had increased from 11 to 22 percent.

The extent of this breakthrough should not be exaggerated. Afro-Americans in northern cities remained very heavily clustered at the lower levels of the occupational structure. In the Chicago of 1920, for example, only 9 percent of the city's black males were professionals, business proprietors, clerks, or salesmen—less than a third of the proportion among whites. Only a tenth worked in skilled trades, compared to over a quarter for Chicago's whites. Not only were four out of five black men unskilled or semi-skilled laborers; they were usually found in the dirtiest, most dangerous, most insecure, and lowest-paid jobs.

Still, blacks advanced. Within the industrial sector they were largely confined to the back of the bus, as it were, but before World War I they had not been allowed on the bus at all. If they had the worst factory jobs, at least they were in the factories. And some were moving up the occupational ladder. Although the number of blacks in unskilled manufacturing jobs in Chicago rose fivefold between 1910 and 1920, the number in semiskilled posts increased tenfold. Paychecks, too, were much fatter than in the South. The $4 to $5 a day commonly paid manufacturing workers in 1920 compared well with the 75¢ a day southern farm laborers collected. The cost of living was much higher too, of course: "They give you big money for what you do, but charge you big things for what you get," warned one migrant in a letter back home. Nonetheless, a study of Detroit that accounted for the difference in costs of living showed that real earnings for blacks there were 81 percent higher than in the South.

The gain in personal independence was significant, too. The foreman or supervisor was usually white, but his relationship to the black laborer did not have the paternalistic character of that between planter and tenant or master and servant. In the factory, if you did your job adequately you got your pay and your private life was your own business. On the other hand, the strict work discipline, the tyranny of the clock was difficult to bear for people accustomed to the slower and more irregular rhythms of rural life.

Adjustment to crowded urban conditions was difficult in other respects as well. The tenements of Harlem and Chicago's South Side were better than the shanties the migrants had left behind in Mississippi, but high density urban living had its hazards. Because of infectious disease, the death rate in Harlem was 42 percent higher than that for New York City as a whole in 1923–27. A high incidence of poverty, crime, juvenile delinquency, vice, and marital breakdown was also to be found in the neighborhoods in which black migrants concentrated. Reformers worried that the black ghettoes were becoming sites of pathological social conditions like the immigrant ghettoes that preceded them.

The Last of the Immigrants?

The apparent analogy between the problems of black migrants and those of earlier newcomers from abroad led some observers to suggest that blacks were only "the last of immigrants." W.E.B. DuBois' pioneering social study, *The Philadelphia Negro* (1898) recognized the special difficulties posed for blacks by the prevalence of white racism, but nonetheless portrayed Philadelphia's blacks as peasants temporarily unprepared to cope with an urban industrial environment. If this was the core of the problem, an optimistic conclusion followed. With prolonged residence,

A LETTER FROM A MIGRANT TO PHILADELPHIA, 1917

Well Dr. with the aid of God I am making very good I make $75 per month. I am carrying enough insurance to pay me $20 per week if I am not able to be on duty. I don't have to work hard. dont have to mister every little white boy comes along I havent heard a white man call a colored a nigger you no now—since I been in the state of Pa. I can ride in the electric street and steam cars any where I get a seat. I dont care to mix with white what I mean I am not crazy about being with white folks, but if I have to pay the same fare I have learn to want the same acomidation. and if you are first in a place here shoping you dont have to wait until the white folks get thro tradeing yet amid all this I shall ever love the good old South and I am praying that God may give every well wisher a chance to be a man regardless of his color.

—*Journal of Negro History*, July, 1919

blacks and their children would blend into the American mainstream as successfully as the Irish and Italian peasants before them.

The analogy between black and foreign newcomers was accurate in some respects. The incidence of both alcoholism and marital breakup among Irish immigrants in the late nineteenth century, for example, was even higher than among blacks in the post-World War I metropolis. The concentration of Afro-Americans in jobs on the lowest rungs of the occupational ladder was no greater than that of the Irish, Italians, Slavs and others when they first arrived in the American city. All these predominantly rural people had much in common. Their lack of education, capital, or industrial skills, and their bewilderment at the scale and tempo of urban life put white and black rural migrants alike in the worst jobs and the most dismal slums.

There were crucial differences, however, between the black and the white immigrant experience. After the initial pangs of adjustment to the urban scene, European newcomers and their children typically moved ahead, albeit in differing ways and at varying rates. The avenues they followed remained closed almost entirely to urban blacks for decades to come. Black assimilation was blocked in at least three of these avenues—jobs, neighborhoods, and marriage. After 10 or 15 years, the average European immigrant had climbed a notch or two up the occupational scale. His children—second generation Americans—moved up still further. Opportunities for occupational mobility were far more constricted for urban blacks. World War I opened up a good many unskilled or semiskilled factory jobs to them, but ten years later it was evident that no self-sustaining mobility cycle was drawing blacks upward. And second generation urban blacks were not finding it possible to advance beyond the position their fathers had attained. They obtained a good deal more schooling than their parents, on the average, but education did not pay off for Afro-Americans as it did for other groups. None of the immigrants encountered a job ceiling like that which forced some Negro college graduates to settle for positions as Pullman porters or luggage-carriers in railroad terminals. Indeed, to be a Pullman porter, barber, or postal clerk carried considerable status in the black community, because there were so few physicians, attorneys, and substantial businessmen to exercise leadership. After the great economic collapse in 1929, a black journalist explained bitterly, "The reason why the Depression didn't have the impact on the Negroes that it had on the whites was that the Negroes had been in the Depression all along."

Blacks were also more strongly clustered in ghettoes than European immigrants, and their residential concentration resulted from external prejudice more than group preference. Before World War I, the relatively small urban black population typically lived in neighborhoods that were heavily but far from overwhelmingly black, much as immigrant Jews or Italians lived in neighborhoods heavily but not overwhelmingly Jewish or Italian. A small but important minority, mostly from the business and professional elite, were dwelling outside the ghetto in largely white areas. By the time the war was over, most cities were much more sharply segregated residentially, with their black citizens confined almost entirely to ghettoes like Harlem and Chicago's South Side Black Belt. This strict segregation meant that blacks had little chance for the informal inter-group contacts that undermine unfavorable racial stereotyping.

More important, the white immigrant ghettoes resulted largely from the choice of those groups to live with others of their culture, and they gradually disappeared as the Europeans and their children became assimilated and moved into more spacious housing in mixed areas away from the city center. Blacks, too, displayed some preference to live near other blacks, but there is no parallel in the immigrant experience to the campaigns of intimidation and terror that were waged against Afro-Americans during and after World War I. Blacks were expelled from largely white neighborhoods and forced back into the ghetto. The Sweet case in Detroit in 1925 revealed the general pattern. After Dr. Ossian Sweet bought a home in a prosperous white neighborhood and moved in with his wife, a howling mob stoned their house and then tried to break in. Sweet fired a gun, killing one member of the crowd. Then the Detroit police, which had been infiltrated by the KKK, arrested not the mob members but Dr. Sweet—and charged him with murder. Sweet eventually was freed, after a brilliant defence by Clarence Darrow, who had been retained by the NAACP. But the mayor of Detroit reflected prevailing white opinion when he said, "I deprecate most strongly the moving of Negroes into districts in which they know their presence may cause riot or bloodshed. Any colored person who endangers life and property simply to gratify his pride is an enemy of his race." In city after city, middle-class blacks who attempted to follow the immigrants' "tenement trail" into outlying areas were barred from so doing. That constraint in the housing market meant that blacks, unlike other groups, paid a "color tax" in the form of inflated rentals and sale prices. The unwillingness of whites to rent or sell to blacks outside ghetto areas arbitrarily limited the supply of black housing and forced prices above fair market levels.

THE "COLOR TAX" PAID BY BLACKS FOR HOUSING

A study of 4,000 Negro families of Harlem in 1920 revealed that one-half the income of the heads of these families ($102 per month average) was expended for rent. To supplement this income, over 80 percent of mothers worked away from home; 65 per cent resorted to taking in of lodgers.

Restriction to definite areas and denial of opportunities to work at the more remunerative jobs were the main contributing factors. A study just completed by the New York Building Congress divides Manhattan into four rental zones. Although the majority of the Negro population falls within the lowest-income group, 75 per cent of them live in the fifty- to one-hundred-dollar-per-month rental zone—the third highest rental section for the city.

Negroes have usually taken over declining areas, houses abandoned as undesirable in the general forward movement of whites to other sections and supply tenants for houses that would otherwise remain unoccupied. Strange as it may seem, these newcomers have been compelled to pay from 10 to 40 per cent more for these houses than was paid by white tenants who preceded them. In Chicago, Negro tenants paid from $8.00 to $20.00 for the same room for which white tenants fomerly paid $4.00 to $5.00. In New York, Negroes were found paying, in some instances, $110.00 per month for the same apartments for which whites had previously paid $55.00. Similar conditions were found in Philadelphia and Buffalo.

—Proceedings of the National Conference of Social Work, 1933

Assimilation through intermarriage with whites was nearly impossible as well. Critics of the new immigrants warned that the Nordic race was committing suicide by intermarrying with others, but not a single state passed statutes banning unions between Swedes and Italians. Most states, by contrast, forbade marriages between whites and Afro-Americans. And even where the law did not forbid such mixed marriages, public opinion was vehement and extraordinary courage was needed to defy it. The result was a radical contrast in rates of intermarriage. With most European nationalities, from 80 to 90 percent of first generation newcomers married other immigrants from the same country, but only half to two-thirds of their children, and less than half of those in the third generation. They did not necessarily vanish into a single American melting pot. Most intermarried with people of the same religion, preserving separate Protestant, Catholic, and Jewish melting pots. But lines of nationality quickly blurred.

The rate of marital mixing between blacks and whites in the early twentieth century was infinitesimal in comparison. Only 3 percent of blacks marrying in

Boston had white partners, 2 percent in New York, 1 percent in Los Angeles. Nor did these few interracial marriages result in assimilation. The offspring of a marriage between a German–American and an Irish–American could identify themselves as German, Irish, German–Irish, or simply American. The children of a black–white union had no such choice; they were regarded as black by the white majority, as were their children and their children's children.

Race Riots

The blacks who migrated northward may have breathed a sigh of relief that they had put themselves beyond the reach of the lynch mob. But the race riots that greeted them in the North were nearly as hazardous. In this respect, too, the black experience in the city differed from that of the immigrants. Ethnic tensions accompanying an influx of immigrants erupted into violence often enough in earlier phases of American history. In the mid-nineteenth century, before effective professional police forces had been organized in most cities, native Catholics clashed bloodily with native Protestants. As late as 1871, a battle between Irish Catholics and Scotch–Irish Protestants in the streets of New York left 33 dead. But by the twentieth century, such clashes between whites were a thing of the past. Those most fearful of the new immigrants contented themselves with political action, fighting for municipal reform that would diminish immigrant influence in local affairs and national legislation to block the entry of more newcomers. The great influx of blacks into northern cities during World War I, by contrast, provoked a series of murderous race riots.

In 1917 in East St. Louis, Illinois, 39 blacks and 9 whites lost their lives in the bloodiest American racial conflict of this century. (By way of comparison, 43 were killed in the Detroit riot of 1967, the worst one of the 1960s.) The savagery of the white crowd was almost indescribable. A ten-year-old black boy whose mother had been shot down was running around sobbing and looking for her; some members of the mob shot him too, and threw him into a fire while still alive. The Chicago race riot two years later was nearly as horrible, with 23 black and 15 white deaths. Other major outbursts took place that year in Nebraska, the District of Columbia, South Carolina, and Texas. The precise cause varied from place to place. In East St. Louis, fighting broke out after blacks who had been beaten by a white gang shot two white detectives they mistook for the culprits. In Chicago, a black boy was drowned by whites for swimming off a section of the Lake Michigan beach they regarded as turf for whites only; blacks began to riot after a policeman on the scene refused to arrest the killers. But the general pattern was the same. Whites, angered by the influx of black newcomers, seized upon some incident and stormed into black neighborhoods to kill, loot, and burn, while white police forces averted their eyes or in some instances joined in. Often the full-scale riot was the climax of a campaign of white-initiated violence designed to force blacks out of "contested areas." In the two years before the Chicago riot, 27 black-occupied dwellings on the fringes of the ghetto had been bombed. Unlike the major race riots of the 1960s, the racial disturbances of this era were not essentially black assaults on white-owned ghetto property; they were white assaults on black people, an expression of hatred designed to terrorize them into isolation and submission. Although white ethnics often encountered ugly nativist prejudices against their group, none met with resistance as fierce and brutal as this.

Blacks, in short, were not simply another ethnic group. They had cultural handicaps in common with immigrant newcomers of peasant origins, but they constituted a separate caste, regarded as inferior by the white group and restricted from contact with it to an unparalleled degree. More strictly segregated in low-ranked jobs and slum neighborhoods, and barred almost entirely from the opportunity to leave their caste through intermarriage with others outside it, they could not escape from the caste, but only improve their position within it. The lines of caste were more sharply drawn in the South than in the North, to be sure, but the system was national rather than regional in scope.

Black Organization and Cultural Life in the Twenties

The Great Migration stimulated black organization and cultural expression, and accentuated cleavages within the black community. The NAACP made impressive gains in membership and became the principal black political organization. It provided counsel for blacks treated unjustly by law enforcement officials, lobbied for a federal anti-lynching law, and pressed military authorities for fairer treatment of black troops. It protested against showings of D.W. Griffith's enormously popular film, *Birth of a Nation* (1915), which portrayed blacks as subhuman rapists and celebrated the Ku Klux Klan. The NAACP won a major decision outlawing municipal residential segregation statutes, and began a legal struggle against southern all-white primaries that would succeed much later. Progress at whittling away the mountain of discriminatory legislation and practices on a case by case basis, however, was obviously slow.

Divisions within the black community as well as prevailing white racial attitudes impeded the efforts of the NAACP. Some of the aims of the organization benefited all blacks, but its principal goal was to resist segregation and move blacks into the American mainstream. That was primarily of interest to the black middle class; the masses of working people were preoccupied with more immediate bread and butter matters. And it was not an unambiguous issue for many members of the middle class, because they had achieved some success within the ghetto world and might lose out if the barriers surrounding it were removed. Should the NAACP fight on behalf of black doctors who sought staff appointments at white hospitals, or agree to plans to build a new segregated hospital within the black community? Should it protest when black youths were kept out of the YMCA or raise funds to establish a black YMCA in the ghetto? Should it object when northern school boards redrew district lines to create almost all-black schools with black teachers, when winning genuine school integration would probably mean that fewer black teachers would be hired? These cruel dilemmas often divided the black middle class

into warring factions. The NAACP generally held firm in pursuit of its long-term
goal of an integrated society, but on such issues it could not speak for the black
community as a whole, or even for the black middle class.

To the left of the NAACP, a small but vocal radical fringe was led by socialist
A. Philip Randolph. Randolph's journal, the *Messenger*, denounced the NAACP for
neglecting the core problems of poverty and unemployment experienced by the
black proletariat, and called for working-class unity in the struggle against capitalist oppression. Few members of either the white or the black proletariat responded
to his call. Randolph did win a significant victory for at least some black workers,
however. In 1925 he successfully organized the Brotherhood of Sleeping Car
Porters and Maids, the country's strongest all-black union.

Neither the legal niceties of the NAACP nor the socialist slogans of Randolph
stirred the hearts of the masses of black migrants like the preaching of a new

prophet of black nationalism, Marcus Garvey. Garvey was a bold and flamboyant West Indian who moved the headquarters of his Universal Negro Improvement Association to New York in 1916 and quickly gained an immense popular following. Garvey was a great admirer of Booker T. Washington, and shared his belief in racial separation and self-help. But New York in 1916 was not Atlanta in 1895, and Garvey was free to express the racial pride and resentment at injustice that Washington was forced to conceal. He denied that "white is right," insisted that God and Christ were black, and accused the NAACP of wanting "us all to become white by amalgamation." Garvey's slogan was "Back to Africa," but it is hard to know if he meant that literally; his paeans to the glories of African civilization may have been intended primarily to awaken black pride and self-assertion within the United States. The strength of the Garvey movement is hard to gauge. He claimed five million followers; the skeptical DuBois put the number at less than 100,000; some historians suggest half a million as an upper bound estimate. But it was unquestionably the first black mass movement in American history.

At first, the UNIA bore impressive fruits in the form of a series of business enterprises—a chain of groceries, laundries, and restaurants, a hotel, a printing plant, a doll factory, and a steamship company to carry on trade between Africa, the West Indies, and the United States. At least 25,000 people attended the month-long convention of the UNIA in New York in 1920, where Garvey was grandly named "Provisional President of the African Republic." The UNIA foundered within a few years, however. "Back to Africa," if it was ever seriously intended, proved an empty dream due to the hostility of the colonial powers then occupying the continent, and the understandable reluctance of American blacks to leave their homeland for the privations of life in the bush. The incompetence and dishonesty of some of Garvey's principal associates in the organization were damaging as well. Eventually Garvey himself was convicted of fraudulent business dealings (that appear actually to have been the work of his subordinates) and deported from the United States. It may be that the government and the jury regarded his black nationalism as the real crime. His assertive separatism, in any event, remained as a legacy remembered by many, and it contributed directly to the rebirth of black nationalism in the 1960s.

The freer atmosphere of the northern city offered new opportunities for cultural expression. The "Harlem Renaissance" of the 1920s produced such important black American writers as James Weldon Johnson, Langston Hughes, Countee Cullen, and Jean Toomer, as well as some painting and sculpture. A few blacks of exceptional talent—Paul Robeson, Roland Hayes and Ethel Waters, for example—were able for the first time to pursue serious careers in the theatre and concert hall. Black musicians made a major contribution to American popular culture—jazz. This innovative musical form, derived from African traditions, emerged in the South early in the twentieth century and came North with the migration. Blacks and whites mingled in Harlem's night clubs to hear Louis Armstrong, Count Basie, Duke Ellington, Jelly Roll Morton, and blues singer Bessie Smith. Most whites, however, were exposed in jazz as played by white popularizers like Paul Whiteman, or as adapted by George Gershwin, who used jazz themes in several of his major compositions.

The church was the central ghetto institution. A 1926 survey counted no less than 140 of them in a 150 block area of Harlem. About a third were located in regular church buildings. These belonged to the large nationally organized Christian denominations, and were generally attended by the more established and affluent families. The remaining two-thirds were "storefront churches," which offered a more highly emotional and expressive religious experience that appealed to many of the same blacks who admired Marcus Garvey. Radical critics deplored the black churches for offering otherworldly compensations and blinding their communicants to the evils inflicted on them in this world. Nevertheless, fundamentalist Christianity provided a source of hope that allowed its followers to endure an oppressive environment thay were powerless to alter. Life in the North was undoubtedly better for blacks in many important respects, but they still had an abundant share of sufferings to endure.

Other Nonwhite Peoples

Afro-Americans were the largest but not the only group of people whose skin pigmentation created difficulties for them in the late nineteenth and early twentieth centuries. As the color line between whites and Afro-Americans grew sharper, the question of how to react to groups who were neither black nor white became more pressing. The influx of Chinese immigrants into California at mid-century marked the beginning of the expansion of the "nonwhite" category. The racist anti-Chinese movement secured a ban on further immigration from China and the branding of the Chinese already in the country as "aliens ineligible for citizenship" on racial grounds in 1882. The same thing happened to Japanese immigrants of the early twentieth century (see Chapter 23). The few thousand Hindu immigrants from India who arrived on the West Coast at the same time received similar treatment. The authors of the Naturalization Act of 1790, which limited citizenship by naturalization to "free whites," would have considered all of these Oriental groups as whites, but the courts and legislators of the period had a more restrictive conception. These groups represented "the Yellow Peril," and were denied political privileges and subjected to various other disabilities.

The arrival of other seemingly exotic groups raised similar fears of racial dilution. No uniform policy was arrived at, but immigration officials and the courts at various times barred the naturalization of Hawaiian natives, Filipinos, Koreans, Armenians, Palestinians, Syrians, Persians, and Turks. In Michigan, a court revoked the citizenship of an Arab immigrant from India. He argued that his ancestors had not intermarried with Indians and had "kept their Arabian blood line clear and pure," but the judge was not moved by that argument. He declared that Arabs, too, were a prescribed nonwhite race. The Quota Acts of 1921 and 1924 barred the entry of all but a handful of people from groups such as these.

Another group that was rapidly growing in numbers posed problems for those drawing the color line—Mexicans. The Quota Acts did not cover newcomers from other countries within the Western Hemisphere, partly as a gesture of good will to our neighbors, partly because southwestern growers lobbied for the exemption to secure needed migratory agricultural workers from south of the border. The spread of commercial agriculture from Texas to California created large numbers of jobs so onerous and ill-paid that neither European immigrants nor blacks were willing to take them. By 1910, over 200,000 Mexicans were living in the Southwest. The tight labor market produced by the war doubled the number in the following decade, and another half a million more came during the 1920s. (These figures are only for those who entered legally. The 2,000-mile border was unfenced and largely unpoliced, and a great many Mexicans slipped into the country without abiding by the formalities.) The work was hard and the wages were low, but conditions were notably better than in impoverished Mexico.

Mexican immigrants defied racial classification. Some were of pure Spanish or pure Indian origin, but the great majority were of mixed Spanish, Indian, and, to a lesser degree, African, background. Most had distinctly darker skins than American whites. The U.S. government made no effort to bar them from citizenship as nonwhites. Only a small fraction took out naturalization papers, but that was because they retained close ties to their homeland and moved back and forth across the border with relative ease. But in other ways they were treated as a separate, subordinate caste. They concentrated in areas in which whites were already fearful of blacks and Orientals, and were frequently barred from public facilities, refused burial in white cemeteries, sent to separate schools, turned away from white primaries, and so on. The treatment of Mexicans was much more varied than that of blacks and Orientals. It depended on the social class, education, and skin color of the Mexicans involved, and varied between urban and rural areas and from city to city and state to state. But many were subjected to prejudice and discrimination. The 1930 Census attempted to clarify their ambiguous position by defining a Mexican "race" consisting of all those who were not definitely "white" in appearance and life-style. Protests from Mexican–American organizations and the Mexican government led the Census Bureau to abandon the practice. But the very attempt revealed the disabilities that flowed from having a darker skin in a white society.

The first natives of the New World, the American Indians, were in the most ambiguous position of all. They were physically distinctive, and the census takers considered them as a separate nonwhite race, tabulating them with Asiatics. Courts ruling on naturalization applications from Indian immigrants born in Canada and South America also put them on the wrong side of the color line; they were held ineligible for citizenship as nonwhites. On the other hand, federal policy from the Dawes Act of 1887 to the New Deal of the 1930s rested on the premise that America's Indians would lose their distinct identity and merge into white society. The Dawes Act dissolved tribal political structures and transferred tribal lands into individual hands. The climax of this assimilationist drive came in 1924, when full U.S. citizenship was granted to all Indians. An unknown number of Indians in these years did disappear into the larger society, especially those who moved to cities. But most did not want to and were not permitted to. In the Southwest, where the bulk of the Indian population was concentrated, local mores branded Indians as "colored," and little mixing took place. No other element of the American population was so painfully exposed to conflicting assimilationist and separatist pressures. It was hard to escape being branded an Indian, yet no space was permitted them for a group life of their own.

American rhetoric of the opening decades of the twentieth century celebrated the promise of American life and portrayed the United States as the land of unparalleled opportunity. It was a fluid, dynamic, and diverse society in which inherited wealth and social position counted for less than in the Old World. That claim, although exaggerated, had much truth to it. But it was a mockery to those on the wrong side of the color line. Blacks, Orientals, and Indians—and to some extent Mexicans, Arabs, and other darker skinned peoples—did not have the freedom of choice available to other Americans. They had to accommodate themselves as best they could to positions determined not only by their individual talents but their "racial" characteristics.

SUGGESTED READINGS

For the life of a southern black sharecropper, as told to a young historian, see Theodore Rosengarten, *All God's Dangers: The Life of Nate Shaw* (1974). Charles S. Johnson, *Shadow of the Plantation* (1934) deals with the subject more broadly. Roger L. Ransom and Richard Sutch, *One Kind of Freedom: The Economic Consequences of Emancipation* (1977) stresses persisting black poverty. Robert L. Higgs, *Competition and Coercion: Blacks in the American Economy, 1865–1914* (1977) sees signs of economic advance. Booker T. Washington's autobiography, *Up From Slavery* (1901) is a fascinating tale. It must be remembered that it was written for a white audience in a virulently racist era, and reveals more of what they wanted to hear than what Washington truly thought. For the "real" Washington, see Louis Harlan's superb *Booker T. Washington: The Making of a Negro Leader, 1856–1909* (1972). George M. Frederickson, *The Black Image in the White Mind, 1817–1914* (1971), Jack Temple Kirby, *Darkness at the Dawning: Race and Reform in the Progressive South* (1972), Morgan Kousser, *The Shaping of Southern Politics: Suffrage Restriction and the Establishment of the One-Party South* (1974), H.N. Rabinowitz, *Race Relations in the Urban South* (1978), and John W. Cell, *The Highest Stage of White Supremacy* (1982) reveal the constraints within which Washington had to operate. August Meier, *Negro Thought in America, 1880–1915: Racial Ideologies in the Age of Booker T. Washington* (1963) and William Toll, *The Resurgence of Race: Black Social Theory from Reconstruction to the Pan-African Conferences* (1979) are excellent accounts of black thought in the period.

J.M. McPherson, *The Abolitionist Legacy from Reconstruction to the NAACP* (1975), Charles F. Kellogg, *NAACP: A History of the National Association for the Advancement of Colored People, 1909–1920* (1970), and Nancy Weiss, *The National Urban League, 1910–1940* (1974) analyze the struggle to build effective organizations to defend black interests. Francis L. Broderick, *W.E.B. DuBois: Negro Leader in a Time of Crisis* (1959) and Elliot M. Rudwick, *W.E.B. DuBois: Propagandist of Negro Protest* (1960) are perceptive studies of the leading northern black intellectual. DuBois, *The Souls of Black Folk* (1903) and James Weldon Johnson, *Autobiography of an Ex-Colored Man* (1912) are classics. On the Great Migration, see Henri Florette, *Black Migration:*

Movement North, 1908–1920 (1975). Gilbert Osofsky, *Harlem: The Making of a Ghetto, 1890–1930* (1966), Allan H. Spear, *Black Chicago* (1967), Thomas L. Philpott, *The Slum and the Ghetto* (1978), and Kenneth Kusmer, *A Ghetto Takes Shape: Black Cleveland, 1870–1930* (1976) are valuable studies of particular communities. The latter is especially so because of the attention it pays to the ethnic differentiation of the white population. Arthur F. Barbeau and Henri Florette, *The Unkown Soldiers: Black American Troops in World War I* (1974) covers blacks in the military services. Elliott M. Rudwick, *Race Riot at East St. Louis, July 2, 1917* (1964), William Tuttle, Jr., *Race Riot: Chicago and the Red Summer of 1919* (1970), and Robert V. Haynes, *A Night of Violence: The Houston Riot of 1917* (1976) examine three terrible race riots in chilling detail. For cultural developments in the 1920s, see Nathan I. Huggins, *Harlem Renaissance* (1971). Theodore Vincent explores *Black Power and the Garvey Movement* (1972). Ira Katznelson, *Black Men, White Cities* (1973) treats black political activity.

Chapter Twenty-Six

The New Woman

I n 1915 the *Literary Digest* asked if "the 'old-fashioned girl' with all that she stands for in sweetness, modesty, and innocence," was "in danger of becoming extinct?" Certainly some of the restrictive customs of Victorian times were going out of fashion. The novelist William Dean Howells had described American middle-class society in the Gilded Age as "a hospital for female invalids." By World War I that could hardly be said. The popular advice columnist Dorothy Dix informed her readers that "the type of girl that the modern young man falls for" was "a husky young woman who can play golf all day and dance all night, and drive a motor car, and give first aid to the injured if anybody gets hurt, and who is in no more danger of swooning than he is."

Indeed, major changes in the role of women in American society had taken place between the Gilded Age and the Progressive Years, and still more after World War I, when females won a Constitutional amendment securing their right to vote. There were important continuities, too, however. Although assumptions about what was appropriate behavior for females shifted in many respects, a clearcut sexual division of labor remained in force. Some feminists chafed at these restrictions and struggled to win full equality for women in every sphere. They were victorious on many fronts, but failed to bring about the revolution that would have been required to eliminate sexual barriers altogether.

Suffragettes—such as these demonstrating in New York City in 1905—won the right to vote in 1920. Although Congress proposed an Equal Rights Amendment in 1972, 10 years later the States had failed to ratify it.

CHANGES AND CONTINUITIES IN WOMEN'S ROLES

One great advance for women involved the realm of education. Before the Civil War, few American women obtained anything but the most elementary education in reading, writing, and arithmetic. Girls dropped out of school at an earlier age than their brothers to help around the home and acquire the domestic skills needed for marriage. In some communities, women were barred from school except in the summer, when the departure of boys to work in the fields created vacant places. Oberlin College admitted women in 1837, Antioch College in 1852, and the Elmira Female College in 1855; other than that, American higher education was an all-male affair. The only other avenues of continued education for women were female academies and state normal schools (teacher training institutions), neither of which offered much intellectual stimulus.

In the late nineteenth century, the situation changed dramatically. Several first-rate women's colleges were founded—among them Vassar (1861), Smith (1872), Wellesley (1875), and Bryn Mawr (1885). By 1901 there were 128 private women's colleges in the country. Even more important in terms of total enrollments, women by then had won admission to almost all state universities, and most private institutions in the Midwest and West. By the turn of the century, approximately 80 percent of the nation's colleges, universities, and professional schools were coeducational. The number of female college students rose from 84,000 in 1890 to 450,000 in 1924. By 1929, 40 percent of all bachelor's degrees awarded were going to women, approximately the proportion that prevails today. A rung down the educational ladder, the advances of females were even more striking; 163,000 women were enrolled in secondary school in 1890, and almost two million, twelve times as many, in 1925. In 1929, 369,000 women and only 283,000 men graduated from high school. The traditional pattern was reversed; now, in order to take a job, boys were more likely to drop out of high school than girls.

Employment

Work opportunities for women were broadening as well. The evidence about working females in the nineteenth century is spotty, but the best estimate is that only 15 percent of women 14 or older worked in 1870. (Of course all women but the few in the leisure class "worked," some of them exceedingly hard. But the figures are for those who earned wages.) The proportion rose to 18 percent in 1890, and 25 percent by 1910.

More important than this increase in the female labor force participation rate was the penetration of women into many spheres of the economy that had traditionally been closed to them. About two-thirds of all working women in 1870 were performing the tasks of a housewife only for someone wealthy enough to hire a substitute; they were domestic servants. Twenty-five percent worked in manufacturing, primarily at semiskilled tasks related to work they had customarily carried out at home—spinning thread and weaving cloth, sewing clothing and stitching

TABLE 26-1
The Occupational Distribution of
Women Workers, 1900–30

	1900	1930
Professional and technical workers	8	14
Managers, proprietors, and officials	1	3
Clerical and sales workers	8	28
Skilled artisans	1	1
Operatives and laborers	26	19
Domestic servants	29	18
Other service workers	7	10
Farmers	6	2
Farm laborers	13	6

shoes, processing foods. The only other occupation available to women was school-teaching; two-thirds of the nation's school teachers were female.

By 1900 women's employment had become considerably more diversified. The servant class was shrinking rapidly; the proportion employed as domestics was down from two-thirds to well under one-third (29 percent). About a sixth of working women held white collar, non-manual jobs of some kind. Most of the 8 percent who were professionals were elementary and secondary school teachers, librarians, or nurses, but a determined few had penetrated professions such as medicine, law, architecture, and university teaching. Another 8 percent were salesclerks in shops and department stores or office clerks. Over the next three decades, employment opportunities for women broadened still further. The proportion working as domestic servants dropped to below a fifth (18 percent), and the fraction engaged as farm workers, factory operatives, and laborers also fell. The shift of women into white collar occupations was striking; the proportion in non-manual jobs soared from 17 to a remarkable 45 percent. The fraction of women professionals nearly doubled, and the number of women managers and proprietors, though still very small, grew significantly. The greatest change, however, was in the clerical and sales category. By 1930 there were almost three million female secretaries, typists, file clerks, and salesclerks. Those were the principal jobs available to the army of young women who graduated from high school each year.

These were important advances, but historians who call them a "feminine employment revolution" exaggerate their significance. The jobs that became available to women in these years did not put them on an equal economic footing with men. Within each occupation, females were clustered in the least skilled and most poorly paid jobs, and they generally received lower wages than men performing the same tasks. In 1914, male manufacturing workers brought home an average wage of $13.65 for a 52-hour week; females toiled 50 hours for an average of $7.75, 42 percent less. Clerical and sales work was certainly more attractive than domestic service or factory work for educated young women with middle-class origins or aspirations. But they were dead-end jobs that offered low wages, little independence, and few opportunities for long-term career advancement. The upper ranks of management remained a male preserve. Most of the impressive growth of the female professional class came in school teaching, nursing, and library work— "women's jobs," within administrative structures controlled at the top by male administrators. The gains made by women in the "higher" professions around the turn of the century were not consolidated and extended. The proportion of women employed as architects and attorneys remained constant after 1910; they accounted for only 3 percent of workers in both professions. Due to stricter licensing requirements, the number of female physicians dropped from more than 9,000 in 1910 to fewer than 7,000 in 1930.

The prejudices of males with the power to block the advancement of women were part of the reason that career opportunities for females were constricted. Although most law and medical schools, for example, admitted female students, they typically set quotas on the number—often as low as five percent. Colleges and universities were biased in favor of male professors; in the 1920s, women received about a third of all graduate degrees in the arts and sciences but held only four percent of the full professorships. It is doubtful, however, that eradicating all male prejudice against career women would have changed the situation of female workers very much. Two basic assumptions deeply imbedded in the culture and widely held by women and men alike determined employment opportunities.

The first assumption was that women should marry and have children. The second was that married women should devote their primary energies to rearing their children. Almost all American women did marry; of those aged 65–69 at the time of the 1910 Census, for example, only 7 percent were spinsters. The rate was significantly above that for the select group of highly educated women; 30 percent of female college graduates in their forties were still single, and the percentage was even higher among graduates of elite women's colleges like Bryn Mawr. These were the pioneering women who chose careers over marriage and broke the sex barrier in law, medicine, journalism, and social work. In 1920, 88 percent of women professionals were single. But they were rare, though important, exceptions.

Once married, women normally dropped out of the labor force, and by the time their children were raised found it difficult to resume their careers. That was the principal reason for both the low wages and the patterns of occupational specialization of female workers. In 1890, 41 percent of the single women in America held jobs, but less than 5 percent of those who had married. By 1930, married women worked somewhat more often, but they were still a very small minority—12 percent. (Today the figure is well over 50 percent.) Furthermore, very few of these wives worked to pursue gratifying careers. They worked because they had to; their families were so poor that they needed the income to survive. Only 4 percent of the married white women in New York City had jobs, but almost a third (31 percent) of the black wives worked. In 1930, women whose husbands earned less than $400 per year were four times as likely to work as those whose spouses earned over

$3,000. Men, in short, pursued careers over a lifetime, and frequently climbed several rungs up the occupational ladder. The average woman held a temporary dead-end job for a few years before marriage and motherhood.

That cultural pattern was firmly entrenched throughout the United States in the opening decades of the twentieth century. The idea that women should remain in the sheltered domestic environment and devote all their energies to childrearing became the middle-class ideal during the great industrial transformation of the first half of the nineteenth century. Thereafter, the affluence that accompanied continuing economic growth allowed that ideal to spread more widely throughout the society. The exceptions were at the opposite ends of the social spectrum—the mostly unmarried career women educated at elite schools and the larger number of married women from families below the poverty line, often immigrants or blacks.

The predominance of single, short-term employees in the female work force had another signficant consequence: It made it difficult to organize them into trade unions. To wage a strike requires painful sacrifices in the here and now, if future benefits are to be won. Female workers were less willing to pay that price because their careers were measured in years rather than decades. Efforts were made to unionize women. The AFL was not very keen on the idea; there were few women in the skilled trades, and male artisans did not welcome their entry as competitors. But it did provide some funds for the Women's Trade Union League, founded at an AFL convention in 1903. The WTUL, led by Margaret Dreier Robins, a wealthy New York philanthropist, sought to enlist middle-class women in support of the organization of female workers. Progress was slow, because the job turnover rate was high for women and because most female workers held low-skilled jobs which are always difficult to organize. The greatest success was in the garment industry, where workers were largely East European Jews with radical leanings. The International Ladies' Garment Workers Union became the strongest largely female trade union in the country. The Industrial Workers of the World, whose leaders included Mary "Mother" Jones and Elizabeth Gurley Flynn, also reached out to women. In the major IWW-led strike in the Lawrence, Massachusetts textile mills in 1912, women fought management as vigorously as their male co-workers. But these were the exceptions to the general pattern of female exclusion from the labor movement.

Wives and Mothers

Despite increased schooling and the growth of employment opportunities outside, the great majority of American women continued to think of themselves as first and foremost wives and mothers. The nature of domestic life, however, was altering in several significant ways. For one thing, women were gaining increased control over their reproductive lives. The average American mother at the time of the Civil War gave birth to 5.2 children, and families of eight, ten, or more were not at all uncommon. At marriage a woman could expect a 15-to-20 year cycle of conception-birth-nursing-weaning-conception that often would break her health. Birth was hazardous for women, in the absence of medical techniques to prevent puerperal fever and to cure prolapsed uteruses, a chronic complaint of mothers who bore several children. The most frequent medical treatments for gynecological problems were bleeding, blistering, and strong potions, which only made things worse.

Medical advances in the late nineteenth century diminished those hazards. Life expectancy at birth for females rose from 40 to 51 years between 1850 and 1900, and another 12 years by 1925. Simultaneously, women began to devote less of their allotted life span to bearing children. By 1900, the average was down to 3.6 births; by 1930, it was only 2.5, only a shade above the fertility level required to maintain a stable population. Very little is known about *how* women managed to restrict their families so sharply. Mechanical modes of contraception were not widely available, and dissemination of birth control information was illegal under the 1873 Comstock Law, designed to advance "social purity." The greatest advocate of birth control, Margaret Sanger, was widely regarded as the most dangerous and depraved of radicals when she began her public campaign for planned parenthood on the eve of World War I. It is probable, therefore, that restriction was accomplished via either abstinence from sex or by *coitus interruptus.* Of course, husbands, too, had reasons for desiring smaller families; children were less of an economic asset in an urban environment, and educating them for careers was becoming more costly. But the sharp drop in family size brought improved health and increased happiness to women, and it may be an indicator that women were gaining power within the family circle. "It is a woman's right, not her privilege," said a marriage manual in strikingly modern language, "to control the surrender of her person; she should not allow access unless she wants a child."

Having smaller families did not mean that women rushed back into the labor market when their children reached school age; that was quite uncommon. Instead, they devoted more attention to each child as an individual, as well as to organizations concerned with children's issues, like the PTA. They devoured books and articles that told them of the latest "scientific" methods for bringing up the young. The methods proposed by the experts were sometimes strict, such as adherence to rigid feeding schedules (see box). But the aim was different from the nineteenth century objective of producing disciplined, obedient, virtuous youths. Parents were to strive to bring up happy and well-adjusted youngsters who got on with their peers. Persuasion was to replace punishment. "Do you punish" your child, asked a government pamphlet for mothers, "because *you think* he is naughty and you want to make him good? Are you sure he is really naughty and not just playing some game or trying to help?"

Some historians have argued that the job of the housewife became much less arduous because smaller families were the trend and because a series of economic changes occurred at the same time. Rising prosperity, in their view, freed wives from the necessity of baking their own bread and making the family's clothing. Appliances such as washing machines, vacuum cleaners, gas stoves, and refrigerators eased and speeded up many household tasks. There was less and less for a woman to do at home, and still hardly any opportunity to work outside it. The result was boredom, frustration, and diminished self-respect for wives. This ar-

THE U.S. CHILDREN'S BUREAU'S ADVICE
ON HOW TO RAISE YOUR CHILD, 1928

Mrs. Guerra had her first baby at home.

A neighbor came in to help her.

The doctor told her to feed the baby every four hours.

The baby cried.

Mrs. Guerra and her friend said, "The baby is hungry; we must feed him."

The baby cried soon again. Mrs. Guerra fed him again.

She fed him many times.

Soon the baby got sick and cross.

His stomach was tired of working.

The mother said, "What is the matter with my baby?"

The baby cried all the time.

Mrs. Guerra had her second baby at the hospital.

The nurses took care of him.

They fed him every four hours.

They bathed him at the same time every day.

They kept him clean and comfortable.

They did not pick him up when he cried.

They knew that babies get exercise when they cry. Babies need exercise.

This baby was well and happy.

The nurses said to Mrs. Guerra, "When you go home, do as we do. Then your baby will be well and happy and good."

Mrs. Guerra went home in two weeks. She did what the nurses told her.

The baby was always good and happy. He was always well.

She said: "I made a mistake before. The nurses are right. Now, I will see what I can do with my big baby to keep him well, too."

gument is highly questionable. It was indeed easier and faster to do laundry by machine, for example, but families with washing machines generally found that they "needed" to change clothes more frequently, so that wives who had the new appliance tended to spend as much time on laundry as they had before. They simply did much more of it. The introduction of the vacuum cleaner likewise raised expectations about how clean homes should be. And the decline in the size of the family generated new expectations about the intensity of the mother–child relationship. Perhaps time hung heavy on the hands of a tiny minority of wives from the leisure class, but these changes did not affect the average woman that way.

MADISON AVENUE'S VIEW OF FEMININE PSYCHOLOGY

The advertiser must use his own imagination to arouse the imagination of the reader. Analysis shows that of the total volume of merchandise bought at retail annually in the United States, nine-tenths is bought by women.

Woman is a creature of the imagination. We pay her a compliment when we say this, for imagination comes from the feelings, feelings come from what we call the heart, and the heart type of mankind is the highest of all.

And so the advertising appeal, to reach women, must not disregard the first great quality of the heart, which is love. Love is a product of the imagination; we love each other because we see things in the same light; we have the same ideals.

Most advertisers do not disregard the quality of love. There, unmistakably, in almost every advertisement is a reference, in word, or picture, to mother love, to the home, to children, to sentiment.

While it might be unwise to mix too much sentiment and imagination with reason in an advertisement to reach men, there can scarcely be too much sentiment or too much imagination in an advertisement to reach women. In fact, many advertisements for women should be pointed directly at the heart side of their nature.

Even vanity comes from the heart and vanity buys many articles of merchandise.

—J.H. Appel, *Growing Up with Advertising*, 1940

In 1929, when the typical male wage-earner worked a 42-hour week, the average urban housewife spent 51 hours weekly on domestic tasks; farm wives worked 62 hours a week.

Few wives labored for wages outside the home, therefore, because there was so much hard work to do within it. The family was a partnership to accomplish a variety of equally essential tasks. That the division of labor assigned to the father the role of breadwinner and to his wife the role of mother and housekeeper was not viewed by most women as a sign of their dependence and inferiority. How well or badly the wife played her role made as much difference to the family's welfare and happiness as the size of the paycheck brought home by the chief wage-earner. Wives were the primary purchasers of goods and services the household needed. Although advertisers demeaningly portrayed the female consumer as an easily manipulable creature of the heart (see box), there is no reason to doubt that women were as careful and rational in their purchasing as males. And wives did much productive labor that would otherwise have been a costly drain on the family—

cooking, cleaning, laundering, canning, tending the garden. Most working-class households took in boarders to help make ends meet, adding further to these burdens. All this had to be done in addition to the exhausting job of caring for children. The home was truly as much a part of "the real world" as the factory and office, and women had reason to take pride in managing it well. In certain ways, husbands were as dependent on their wives as wives were on their husbands in others.

This may help to explain why these historic assumptions about appropriate "masculine" and "feminine" roles have persisted so obstinately in American culture down to recent times. Part of the answer may be that homemaking and childrearing were both more demanding and gratifying than today's critics would allow. That they are no longer so regarded by increasing numbers of American women may be all to the good. But we do a real disservice to the women of another era when we dismiss them as mere victims because the pattern of their lives fails to measure up to some contemporary ideological standard.

THE DRIVE FOR EQUAL RIGHTS

Such basic social changes as the opening up of male colleges and universities to female students did not occur by happenstance. They took place, in considerable measure, because restless women (and some men) demanded them. A women's movement took shape in mid-nineteenth century America and gained strength thereafter. The Seneca Falls Declaration of 1848 called for equal educational opportunities, an end to laws that made married women mere appendages of their husbands, "equal participation in the various trades, professions, and commerce," and the right to vote.

The first two were gradually achieved, as the result of patient campaigns waged by women and male sympathizers across the land. Four-fifths of the nation's colleges and universities had female students by the end of the century; by 1929, over 40 percent of the college population was female. Similar success came in the struggle against legal discrimination. By 1900, wives could own and control their separate property in three-fourths of the states, and dispose of their property by will in all. In two-thirds of the states, their earnings from a job were their own, and in the great majority they could make contracts and file legal suits. Over the next three decades, these rights became almost universal. Of course, women might not be able to exercise those rights in the face of opposition from a domineering husband, but other legal changes provided a measure of new protection from domineering and brutal men—liberalization of the divorce laws in most states, and custody and alimony arrangements more favorable to wives.

The third objective—economic equality—was not won in the period considered here, of course, nor indeed has it been yet. In the late nineteenth and early twentieth centuries, women gained access to a good many professions and trades that had been all male bastions. But they remained a small minority in positions that offered status and power. Some radical feminists saw this as the core problem. Charlotte Perkins Gilman's *Women and Economics* (1898) argued that women would never be truly free until they were economically independent from men and could relate to them as economic equals. She urged the development of new family institutions (such as day-care facilities and central kitchens) to free housewives to pursue careers. But hers was an isolated voice. Most men and women regarded careers for women as incompatible with marriage and motherhood, and the vast majority of women opted for the latter.

The Suffrage Campaign

The other chief demand made by the reformers gathered at Seneca Falls was the right to vote, and other civic rights associated with it—to hold political office and to serve on juries. Those rights were finally won and written into the Constitution in the Nineteenth Amendment, which took effect in 1920. From our vantage point, nothing seems more logical and inevitable than the granting of the ballot to women. But it took 70 years of struggle to persuade the male electorate of its wisdom and justice.

A second national meeting to pursue the goals set forth at Seneca Falls was held in Worcester, Massachusetts in 1850, and such conventions met annually thereafter. A network of committed women's rights activists developed. The Civil War temporarily halted feminist activity as women turned to work in support of the war effort. Elizabeth Cady Stanton and Susan B. Anthony, however, contributed to the death of slavery by organizing a national petition drive for the passage of the Thirteenth Amendment. "Women," they declared, "you cannot vote or fight for your country. Your only way to be a power in the government is through the exercise of this one, sacred, constitutional 'right of petition,' and we ask you now to use it to the utmost." Some 400,000 women put their names to the document. Debate over the issue of enfranchising the freedmen during Reconstruction provided an opportunity to argue that sexual as well as racial barriers to voting should be lifted. The American Equal Rights Association, formed by Stanton and Anthony in 1866 with black abolitionist Frederick Douglass as a vice-president, demanded that the Fifteenth Amendment open the polls to women as well as the freedmen. Many of the most ardent Radical Republican supporters of votes for blacks, however, were not in favor of women's suffrage, and some who were sympathetic were unwilling to press the case for fear that it might bring the whole amendment down to defeat.

The women's movement itself divided over the issue. The uncompromising Stanton and Anthony formed a new organization, the National Woman Suffrage Association and, in their newspaper *The Revolution,* campaigned against the amendment because it left out women. A more conservative faction, led by Lucy Stone and her husband, Henry Blackwell, formed the rival American Woman Suffrage Association. Stone and Blackwell supported the Fifteenth Amendment on the grounds that half a loaf was better than none, argued that winning women's

ELIZABETH CADY STANTON ON THE CASE FOR WOMEN'S SUFFRAGE, 1869

While poets and philosophers, statesmen and men of science are all alike pointing to woman as the new hope for the redemption of the race, shall the freest Government on the earth be the first to establish an aristocracy based on sex alone? to exalt ignorance above education, vice above virtue, brutality and barbarism above refinement and religion? Not since God first called light out of darkness and order out of chaos, was there ever made so base a proposition as "manhood suffrage" in this American Republic, after all the discussions we have had on human rights in the last century. On all the blackest pages of history there is no record of an act like this, in any nation, where native born citizens, having the same religion, speaking the same language, equal to their rulers in wealth, family, and education, have been politically ostracised by their own countrymen, outlawed with savages, and subjected to the government of outside barbarians.

—Susan B. Anthony, *A History of Women's Sufferage*, 1869

suffrage on a state by state basis was more practical than concentrating on a change in the nation's Constitution, and were more careful not to challenge traditional sexual stereotypes. Stanton and Anthony were bolder and associated themselves with a variety of radical causes, even working for a time with the flamboyant Victoria Woodhull, an outspoken advocate and practitioner of free love, and the Presidential nominee of the Equal Rights Party in 1872. Anthony experimented in civil disobedience, leading a group of women in Rochester, New York to the polls in 1872 and insisting that they be let in. At her trial she urged women to "rebel against your man-made, unjust, unconstitutional forms of law that tax, fine, imprison, and hang women, while they deny them the right of representation in the government." All women, she said, should heed "the old revolutionary maxim that 'resistance to tyranny is obedience to God.'"

The small and divided women's movement had little political clout. In 1874, a California Senator introduced a constitutional amendment drafted by Anthony. The "Anthony" amendment, which would eventually be ratified in 1920, declared that "the right of citizens of the United States to vote shall not be denied or abridged by the United States or any state on account of sex." Subcommittees reported favorably on the measure on several occasions, but it was far ahead of its time. The only vote taken on the floor was a fiasco; only 6 of the 76 Senators were willing to back it.

The remarkable proliferation of women's associations, clubs, and societies in the late nineteenth century gradually broadened support for extension of the ballot. The most important new national organization was the Woman's Christian Temperance Union (1874), which soon attracted a membership of a quarter million. The WCTU's first concern was Prohibition, but its dynamic leader Frances Willard was a wide-ranging reformer and a strong supporter of suffrage. The formation of the General Federation of Women's Clubs in 1890, and the reuniting of the women's movement in the National American Woman Suffrage Association that same year were also auspicious. A great many more women than ever before were playing a role in public life. In 1893, Frances Willard published a biographical dictionary of 1,470 American women leaders from every state in the union. The NAWSA, dominated by followers of Lucy Stone, concentrated on winning the ballot by state action, and by 1896 had been successful in four western states— Wyoming, Utah, Colorado, and Idaho.

After that, the movement stagnated for 15 years. The NAWSA abandoned the Stanton strategy of pressing Congress for a national amendment, and Congressmen were delighted to be left alone. Campaigns in the states, after the first four victories, got nowhere. The NAWSA obtained popular referenda on suffrage in only six states; worse yet, they lost in every single one.

The final and triumphant phase of the drive began after 1910 and crested with ratification of the Nineteenth Amendment in 1920. An infusion of new leaders with innovative tactics, a shift in the ideology of the movement, and America's entry into World War I all contributed to victory. Carrie Chapman Catt, who became president of the NAWSA in 1915, was a shrewd organizer who made it a true grassroots organization for the first time, with two million members by 1917. She carefully coordinated work in the states with lobbying in Washington, compiling dossiers on every Congressman that revealed "everything that could be discovered about his stand on woman suffrage" and suggested means of pressuring him. Contrasting with an complementing Catt's moderate, practical tactics was the more militant and flamboyant strategy of Alice Paul and Lucy Burns, younger women who had lived in England and admired the direct action methods of the Pankhurst sisters, English suffragettes who heckled candidates for Parliament, spat on policemen who attempted to quiet them, and engaged in hunger strikes when arrested. Paul and Burns worked briefly with the NAWSA but broke off to form the Congressional Union, which employed such tactics. They organized suffrage parades, and in 1917 began round-the-clock picketing of the White House to pressure Wilson into backing the Stanton amendment. The administration blundered in sending them to jail; press coverage of the harsh treatment they received, including force feeding when they went on a hunger strike, made them martyrs.

The success of these new tactics in part depended on a shift in the kind of arguments offered on behalf of suffrage. Elizabeth Cady Stanton defended it as a "natural right," on the same egalitarian basis on which she supported black suffrage. NAWSA spokesmen argued the case for enfranchisement on almost opposite grounds. Emphasizing the inherent differences rather than the similarities between the sexes, they claimed that it was necessary to give a political voice to

A U.S. SENATOR SPEAKS AGAINST THE ANTHONY AMENDMENT, 1874

This is an attempt to disregard laws promulgated by the Almighty Himself. It is irreverent legislation in the simplest and strongest sense of the word. Nay, sir, not only so, but it is a step in defiance of the laws of revealed religion as given to men. If there be one institution which it seems to me has affected the character of this country, which has affected the whole character of modern civilization, the results of which we can but imperfectly trace and but partly recognize, it is the effect of the institution of Christian marriage, the mysterious tie uniting the one man and the one woman until they shall become one and not two persons.

Under the operation of this amendment what will become of the family, what will become of the family hearthstone around which cluster the very best influences of human education? You will have a family with two heads—a "house divided against itself." You will no longer have that healthful and necessary subordination of wife to husband, and that unity of relationship which is required by a true and real Christian marriage. You will have substituted a system of contention and difference warring against the laws of nature herself, and attempting by these new-fangled, petty, puny, and most contemptible contrivances, organized in defiance of the best lessons of human experience, to confuse, impede, and disarrange the palpable will of the Creator of the world. I can see in this proposition for female suffrage the end of all that home-life and education which are the best nursery for a nation's virtue. I can see in all these attempts to invade the relations between man and wife, to establish differences, to declare those to be two whom God hath declared to be one, elements of chaotic disorder, elements of destruction to all those things which are, after all, our best reliance for a good and a pure and an honest government.

—Senator Thomas Bayard (Del.) in *Congressional Record*

women to "protect the home" by introducing a higher morality into public life and countering the coarse materialism common to males. That argument appealed particularly to middle-class native white males who hoped that the women's vote would offset that of elements of the male population they regarded as inferior and dangerous. In the South, that meant blacks. Abandoning their earlier commitment to black rights, suffragists in the South contended that "there are more white women who can read and write than all Negro voters." Enfranchising females would help ensure white supremacy. On similar grounds, middle-class city dwellers who hoped to overturn the immigrant-based machines looked favorably

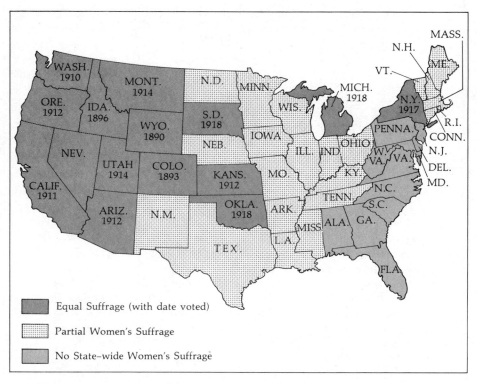

MAP 26-1
Progress Toward Women's Suffrage before the Nineteenth Amendment

on the suffrage cause. Uneducated immigrant women, suffragists argued, would be less likely to turn out at the polls than educated, native, middle-class females; the female vote would boost the reform cause and harm the bosses. Catering to racial, ethnic, and class prejudices in this manner compromised the moral intregrity of the movement, but it proved politically expedient.

Without American entry into World War I, however, the extension of the suffrage to women might well have been further delayed. After heartening victories in Washington, California, Oregon, Kansas, Arizona and Illinois between 1910 and 1913, suffragettes were rebuffed several times. They lost referenda in five major states in 1914, and won only in two thinly populated Western ones. In 1915 they were defeated in four more large Eastern states. The need to mobilize mass support for the war effort was the catalyst responsible for the breakthrough at the national level. How could the United States wage a war to make the world safe for democracy when half of its population was denied elemental civic rights? Woodrow Wilson, who had responded evasively to suffrage advocates for years, was at last won over on these grounds. In September of 1918, he took the extraordinary step of appearing before the Senate to argue that passage of the amendment was essential to "the winning of the war and to the energies alike of preparation and of battle." Jane Addams said later that suffrage was "a direct result of war psychology." It was true not only in the United States. Between 1917 and 1920, females won the franchise in Britain, Austria, Germany, Poland, Czechoslovakia, Russia, Holland, Sweden, and Canada.

The Fruits of Victory

The Nineteenth Amendment, as it turned out, did not uplift and purify American politics, as proponents had hoped. Nor did it destroy the family or do any other of the terrible things opponents had predicted. It was a significant step forward, but one that did little to disturb other aspects of the status quo. Women, it soon became clear, were less likely to exercise their newly won freedom than men. In Illinois, for example, three-fourths of the adult males but less than half of the females voted in 1920. Furthermore, most women who did vote voted the same way as their husbands. To the extent to which females differed from males politically, they were somewhat more inclined to support the candidates who seemed least threatening to the established social order. The triumphant women's movement splintered into competing factions when the cause that united them was won. Alice Paul's Woman's Party lobbied for an Equal Rights Amendment to the Constitution, first put forward in 1923; the party attracted only 8,000 supporters. The successor to the NAWSA, the League of Women Voters, and most other women's organizations opposed the ERA, fearing that it would deprive women of special protective social legislation that worked in their interest.[1] Activists who had marched together for the Nineteenth Amendment found new priorities. Jane Addams and Carrie Chapman Catt devoted their energies to the pacifist cause, the League concentrated on non-partisan voter education, and others worked for legislation favorable to women and children or for consumer causes.

Over the seven decades after Seneca Falls, a majority of American women came to share the belief that their sex should not disqualify them from having a political voice. When that battle was won, they spoke with not one voice but many, voting less as women than as Southerners, Catholics, blue collar workers, supporters of the KKK, opponents of the machine, or advocates of Prohibition. Few American women conceived themselves as a distinct social group with political interests different from men. Their primary identification was not with their sex but with their family, and the larger social groupings—class, ethnic, religious, and regional—to which their family belonged. What women had in common was that they were expected to play certain roles and not others. But that did not make them a group or coherent interest in the same sense as blacks, Italians, Catholics, big businessmen, or farmers. Perhaps they were united in the "oppression" inflicted

[1]The concern was justified. The Supreme Court had a long record of striking down regulatory legislation that covered male workers, but regarded some bills pertaining to women as constitutional. Not until 1941, in the *U.S. vs. Darby,* did it uphold protective legislation for both sexes.

on them by a sexual division of labor that shaped their lives differently from those of men, as contemporary feminists would say. But American women of that generation, with rare exceptions, did not perceive it that way.

SUGGESTED READINGS

Good general introductions to the topics considered in this chapter may be found in the relevant sections of William H. Chafe, *The American Woman: Her Changing Social, Economic, and Political Role, 1920–1970* (1972), Lois Banner, *Women in Modern America* (1974), Sheila Rothman, *Woman's Proper Place: A History of Changing Ideals and Practices, 1870 to the Present* (1978), Mary P. Ryan, *Womanhood in America from Colonial Times to the Present* (2nd ed., 1979), and Carl Degler, *At Odds: Women and the Family in America from the Revolution to the Present* (1980). Louise Tilly and Joan W. Scott, *Women, Work and Family* (1978) is an incisive discussion of modern Europe which contains rich implications for American history. Other valuable discussions of work and family patterns may be found in David Katzman, *Seven Days a Week: Women and Domestic Service in Industrializing America* (1978), Leslie W. Tentler, *Wage-Earning Women: Industrial Work and Family Life in the United States, 1900–1930* (1979), Winifred D. Wandersee, *Women's Work and Family Values, 1920–1946* (1981), and Tamara Hareven, *Family Time and Industrial Time: The Relationship between Family and Work in a New England Industrial Community* (1982).

On changing sex roles and sexual mores, see David Kennedy, *Birth Control in America: The Career of Margaret Sanger* (1970), Paula S. Fass, *The Damned and the Beautiful* (1977), Joseph Kett, *Rites of Passage: Adolescence in America, 1790 to the Present* (1977), Peter Filene, *Him/Her Self: Sex Roles in Modern America* (1977), James Reed, *From Private Vice to Public Virtue: The Birth Control Movement and American Society since 1830* (1978), William Leach, *True Love and Perfect Union: The Feminist Reform of Sex in Society* (1980), Elaine Tyler May, *Great Expectations: Marriage and Divorce in Post-Victorian America* (1980), and Lary May, *Screening Out the Past: The Birth of Mass Culture and the Motion Picture Industry* (1980).

The struggle for equal political rights is examined in Eleanor Flexner, *Century of Struggle: The Woman's Rights Movement in the United States* (1959), Aileen Kraditor, *The Ideas of the Woman Suffrage Movement, 1908–1920* (1965), William O'Neill, *Everyone Was Brave: The Rise and Fall of Feminism in America* (1967), Alan P. Grimes, *The Puritan Ethic and Woman Suffrage* (1967), Anne Firor Scott, *The Southern Lady: From Pedestal to Politics, 1830–1930* (1971), and David Morgan, *Suffragists and Democrats: The Politics of Woman Suffrage in America* (1972).

For other social movements in which women played a crucial role, see Stanley J. Lemons, *The Woman Citizen: Social Feminism in the 1920's* (1973), Gwendolyn Wright, *Moralism and the Model Home: Domestic Architecture and Cultural Conflict in Chicago, 1873–1913* (1980), Donald J. Pivar, *Purity Crusade: Sexual Morality and Social Control, 1868–1900* (1973), Estelle B. Freedman, *Their Sisters' Keepers: Women's Prison Reform in America, 1830–1930* (1981), and Ruth Rosen, *The Lost Sisterhood: Prostitution in*

America, 1900–1918 (1982). The best discussions of the settlement house movement are to be found in Allen F. Davis, *Spearheads of Reform: The Social Settlements and the Progressive Movement* (1967) and *American Heroine: The Life and Legacy of Jane Addams* (1973). Addams' own autobiography, *Twenty Years at Hull House* (1910), should not be missed.

Tethered to the Gemini-4 space capsule, astronaut Edward White floats above the Earth during the first "space walk" of 1965.

Part Five

Modern Times:
From Depression to Detente

Chapter Twenty-Seven

The Great Depression and the New Deal

I n the presidential campaign of 1928, Herbert Hoover expressed supreme confidence that all was right with America. The future looked bright to him—at least if the voters had the wisdom to keep a Republican in the White House. "We in America today," he declared, "are nearer to the final triumph over poverty than ever before in the history of any land. The poorhouse is vanishing from among us. We have not yet reached the goal, but, given a chance to go forward with the policies of the last eight years, we shall soon with the help of God be in sight of the day when poverty will be banished from this nation."

Hoover was given his chance. He defeated Al Smith by a landslide. By the time he left office four years later, tens of millions of his fellow countrymen were uncertain where their next meal was coming from. The country was in the depths of the worst depression in its history, and Herbert Hoover was the most hated man in America. In the 1932 presidential contest, Franklin D. Roosevelt trounced Hoover even more soundly than Hoover had defeated Al Smith four years before. He proceeded to launch a bold legislative program, the New Deal, and created an electoral coalition that dominated American politics for a generation.

THE COMING OF THE DEPRESSION

Herbert Hoover was not a fool, just a poor prophet. His optimism in 1928 was not at all unusual. During the twenties, a preposterous slogan of the French faith-healer, Emile Coué, became a popular fad in the United States: "Every day in

Displaced from their Midwest homes, thousands of families became migrant workers in California's fruit and vegetable fields, their living conditions even more squalid than suggested in this 1939 photo by Dorothea Lange.

every way I'm getting better and better." Sober economists and financiers were saying that about the economy, in only slightly more restrained terms, and not without reason. All economic indicators were pointing upward, and the standard of living was soaring. Between 1921 and 1929 the Gross National Product (in constant dollars) rose a heady 27 percent. The take-home pay of a worker in the steel mills of Pittsburgh, the stockyards of Chicago, or the Ford Motor Company increased in these years at an annual rate three times as high as the average for 1870–1920. For some groups—farmers, New England textile workers, and coal miners, for example—the twenties were lean years. But they were exceptions. Overall, unemployment averaged below 4 percent, a record low for America before or since. Even in the great economic boom of the 1960s, after the federal government assumed responsibility for keeping joblessness down and employed a staff of professional economic advisers who claimed to know how to do it, unemployment levels were higher than in the twenties. For most Americans, this was an epoch of unparalleled prosperity.

The boom, however, ended with a crash in 1929, and in the depression that followed the economy plunged to unprecedented depths. Industrial production began to sag gradually in the summer of 1929, but popular consciousness of trouble awaited the stock market panic that fall. The stock market had been booming. Between December of 1927 and September of 1929, average prices rose more than 60 percent. New fortunes were being made every day, and old fortunes were growing larger. Some 513 Americans reported an income of a million dollars or more in 1929, more than in the 1960s, when the GNP was six times larger. The bubble burst on October 24, 1929, "Black Thursday." Almost 13 million shares were sold by fearful investors, at a loss of $3 billion. The nation's leading financiers agreed to pool their resources to prop up the market, but it brought only temporary relief. Panicked shareholders were determined to sell out before prices dropped again, and the flood of sell orders exerted a relentless downward pressure on prices. The next Tuesday, October 29, was far blacker than "Black Thursday." By its close, the value of stocks on the New York exchange was $14 billion less than it had been at the start of the day. The downward spiral continued. Stock prices had plummeted 50 percent before the year was out; by 1933 they stood at less than a fifth of their September, 1929 levels. By then $74 billion in paper wealth had melted away.

After the collapse of the stock market, funds for investment in productive activity dried up. Factories shut down. The building of new factories ceased; the purchase of new equipment diminished; workers were laid off. The level of private investment fell even more precipitously than stock prices, from over $16 billion in 1929 to hardly 2 percent of that ($.34 billion) four years later. Industrial production plunged almost 50 percent between the summer of 1929 and the end of 1932. Wages fell sharply, and more and more people could find no jobs at all. In 1929 only one nonagricultural worker in 20 was unemployed; a year later it was one in 7; the next year one in 4; the next year more than one in 3. Moreover, many of those who still had jobs were working for lower wages and only part-time. Total labor hours worked by the end of 1932 were only 40 percent of the 1929 level.

These dry figures hint at personal tragedies of appalling magnitude. Half of the

TABLE 27-1
Stock Prices, Private Investment,
Industrial Production, and Unemployment, 1929–33

	Stock prices (1941–43 = 10)	Private Investment (billions of 1929 dollars)	Manufacturing Production (1957–59 = 100)	Percent of Nonagricultural Workers Unemployed
1929		16.23		5.3
July–Sep.	30.0		40.1	
Oct.–Dec.	23.3		37.0	
1930		10.45		14.2
Jan.–Mar.	22.9		34.9	
Apr.–June	23.6		33.6	
July–Sep.	20.9		30.3	
Oct.–Dec.	16.7		28.1	
1931		6.75		25.2
Jan.–Mar.	16.9		27.7	
Apr.–June	14.7		27.6	
July–Sep.	13.4		28.8	
Oct.–Dec.	9.7		22.9	
1932		.84		36.3
Jan.–Mar.	8.3		21.7	
Apr.–June	5.5		19.2	
July–Sep.	6.2		18.8	
Oct.–Dec.	7.0		20.3	
1933		.34		37.6
Jan.–Mar.	6.5		19.1	

nation's families had no savings accounts to fall back on; the half who did possessed an average of only $339, not much of a cushion. There was no national unemployment insurance or relief for the poor, and local communities and private charities lacked the funds to meet the staggering demands placed on them. Americans lost their jobs, their savings, their homes, and their pride. Jobless families faced a brutal struggle for survival, and some did not survive. An aged man thrown out of work came home and turned on the gas. His dazed widow sat alone for three days and then did the same. People unable to pay their mortgages or rent were driven into the streets, to take refuge in shacks pieced together out of tar paper, old packing cases, and junked car bodies. Such areas were referred to sardonically as "Hoovervilles." In Oakland, California people lived in sewer pipes lying unsold outside the factory that made them. Emaciated people thronged the

THE HOOVERVILLE PRAYER

Hoover is my shepherd; I am in want.
He maketh me to lie down on park benches:
He leadeth me beside still factories.
He restoreth my doubt in the Republican Party:
He leadeth me in the path of destruction for his party's sake.
Yea, though I walk through the valley of the shadow of destruction, I fear
   evil:
For thou art with me; the politicians, and professors, they frighten me.
Thou preparest a reduction in my salary before me in the presence of
   my Creditors: Thou anointest my income with taxes; my expenses
   runneth over.
Surely unemployment and poverty will follow me all the days
   of the Republican administration; And I shall dwell in a mortgaged
   house forever.

garbage dumps of Chicago and other cities. One family lived for 11 days on nothing but stale bread, purchased with a borrowed fifty cents at 3½¢ a loaf. Some families subsisted on potatoes, some even on dandelions. A teacher in a mining town asked one despondent pupil if she was sick, and was told that she was only hungry, because "this is Sister's day to eat."

Farmers were hit especially hard by the Depression. Even during the prosperous twenties, farm prices had been depressed relative to other prices. After the crash, the gap widened. By 1932 the prices of farm products had fallen 55 percent, as compared to 27 percent for nonagricultural products. At least 40 percent of the nation's farms were mortgaged, and hundreds of thousands of farmers lost homes and fields their families had worked for decades when they could not keep up payments and the banks foreclosed. Between 1930 and 1933, almost a third of all the farms in the country changed hands. In a single day, a quarter of the acreage in the entire state of Mississippi was auctioned off for nonpayment of debts. Throughout the South, landowners ran out of funds to finance the next crop, and expelled their tenants and sharecroppers from the land.

Although the nation's banks took back the property that served as collateral on the mortgages they foreclosed, many of them were in dreadful financial shape. No less than 5,500 banks failed between October of 1929 and the end of 1932—at a loss of over $3 billion. In the year 1931 alone, more banks went under than in the entire period 1900–29. Many had lost heavily on their investments in corporate stocks, and they suffered further losses when they attempted to resell foreclosed property in the acutely depressed market. That made them vulnerable to "runs." Banks make money by lending out all but a fraction of their deposits and collecting interest from borrowers, on the assumption that not too many of their customers will want to withdraw their funds all at once. That assumption failed to hold when rumors spread that a particular bank might fail; everyone rushed to get their money out before it was too late. (There was as yet no federal insurance on savings, a key New Deal reform that largely eliminated such "runs.") The rumors became self-fulfilling prophecies; even relatively strong banks could not withstand the pressure. By 1933, the savings of nine million Americans had been wiped out, and the level of popular panic placed the future of the remaining banks very much in doubt.

Basic Causes of the Depression

What caused the calamity? Economic historians are not yet entirely sure of the answer. The most recent study, by an outstanding scholar, concludes rather disconcertingly that "the Depression was started by an unexplained event." The crash was due to "some combination of factors which cannot be disentangled."[1] There is little doubt, however, that some key weaknesses in the economy were bound to cause trouble. The orgy of stock market speculation was certainly a key factor. No one knows exactly what pinprick burst the balloon on "Black Thursday," but the rubber was clearly stretched so thin that it would have happened some time soon. In the late twenties, stock prices were climbing wildly, at a rate far exceeding advances in worker productivity, technology, and corporate earnings. Investment in the stock market was always (and remains) a form of gambling, a bet on the future performance of stock. But in the 1920s it was a considerably riskier game than it has become since, because so many investors were playing with borrowed money. One could buy stocks on "margin," paying a broker as little as 25 percent of the purchase price in cash (a 25 percent margin) and borrowing the rest. The interest charges were high, and the balance of the loan could be "called" at the broker's discretion. There was no difficulty—so long as the price of the stock continued to climb. Suppose you purchased $4,000 worth of shares in General Motors, paying $1,000 down and covering the balance with a broker's loan of $3,000 at 9 percent interest. If you held the shares a year and they doubled in value—by no means unheard of in the period—you could dispose of them for $8,000. After the broker had taken his $3,000, plus $270 in interest, you would be left with $4,730, a profit of $3,730 on an original investment of only $1,000.

But what if the stock did not continue to rise? Even a moderate drop in price would wipe out your cash outlay, and force your broker to call in his loan before the value of your shares fell below what you owed him. In this case, a 20 percent decline in GM stock would bring your assets below the $3,270 he could demand of you, and you would be forced to sell your stock—or to supply him with more cash, more "margin"—before it dropped further. Because many other holders of GM stock would be similarly obligated to pay off their brokers, a slight break in price would lead to a flood of sell orders sending the stock on a continuing tailspin. That is what began to happen in October of 1929.

---

[1] See Peter Temin, *Did Monetary Forces Cause the Great Depression?* (New York: Norton, 1976).

The speculative fever affected businesses as well as individuals. The huge utilities empire of Samuel Insull, a great complex of holding companies and interlocking directorates, was capitalized all out of proportion to the value of its assets, and could not begin to pay off its debts when the crunch came. Many corporations and banks had made heavy speculative investments. When prices broke, they lacked the cash to repay and folded, dragging down those who had made them loans as they fell.

The great bull market of the twenties was a house of cards, bound to topple. But the market crash and the Great Depression are not the same thing. Other stock market collapses in history were not followed by depressions so deep and long-lasting. And, as mentioned earlier, the economy was actually beginning to decline some months *before* "Black Thursday." The crash greatly accelerated a drop that had already begun. Investment and output in some key sectors of the economy were sliding because the market had been saturated; supply exceeded demand (more precisely, supply was in excess of demand at current prices, an imbalance eventually bound to cause diminished output, falling prices, or both). Residential construction had been slowing since 1927. Tire production began to fall sharply in 1928, and there was "excess capacity" in both automobiles and textiles.

There are various explanations as to why these soft spots developed, but the most important reason consumer demand lagged was that income distribution had shifted to cut into the relative purchasing power of the average family. Although the income of most Americans was rising, a growing share of the wealth was going into the pockets of upper income groups. Real wages increased 21 percent between 1923 and 1929, but corporate dividends rose by three times as much (64 percent). Legend has it that virtually everyone was playing the market in the 1920s, but stock ownership was in fact largely confined to the well-to-do, and they were the recipients of these fat dividends. In 1929, 83 percent of all corporate dividends went to the richest 5 percent of Americans; over 70 percent, in fact, went to the richest 1 percent. During the decade, the share of national income after taxes accruing to the top 1 percent climbed from less than 12 to almost 19 percent; the share of the upper 5 percent went from less than 25 to over 33 percent.

Of course, the affluent constituted a market for producers. But on the average they spent a smaller fraction of their incomes on consumer goods than the less well-to-do. Furthermore, rising demand for Cadillacs, mink coats, and caviar was not sufficient to offset the shrinking demand for Fords, washing machines, and kitchen stoves. The high consumption economy developing in the 1920s depended on continued sales of such mass-produced "consumer durables." The trend toward the concentration of wealth in the upper income brackets gradually undermined this mass market. Successive Republican administrations did nothing to arrest this trend. In fact, they speeded it by sharply cutting back taxes on high incomes and large inheritances, which probably would have led to trouble even if the stock market had not been so vulnerable.

The Great Depression hit Europe as well as the United States; the decline in the European economy had negative effects in America (and vice versa). During the 1920s, America sought two incompatible objectives. It insisted on being repaid its large wartime loans to the Allies, yet it maintained high tariff barriers that kept the European powers from selling enough in American markets to finance such re-payment. For most of the decade, the contradiction was obscured because of the heavy flow of American investment capital into Europe, especially Germany. That capital was supposed to allow Germany to pay the reparations inflicted on her by the Versailles treaty, and those reparations in turn to permit the Allies to repay the United States. But the whole scheme depended on a high level of American capital exports. When those fell off in 1928 and more sharply in 1929, the entire European economy began to slow down. (There were other reasons, too, internal to the history of Germany and other European nations, but this was a significant dampening influence.) The unfolding depression forced the major European countries to suspend payments on the war debt; more important, their demand for American manufactures and foodstuffs shrank, further depressing American prices.

Policies of the Hoover Administration

For three years the Hoover administration struggled unsuccessfully to find a way to reverse the slide. By 1932, when he was whipped by Franklin D. Roosevelt, a majority of Americans were convinced that Hoover was callous and inept, a do-nothing leader who offered only hollow promises that prosperity was "just around the corner." He was indeed rather insensitive. "No one is actually star-ving," he declared, which wasn't true. When he noticed jobless men reduced to peddling apples on the streetcorner, his amazing explanation was that "many persons left their jobs for the more profitable one of selling apples." His handling of the Bonus March in the summer of 1932 left the worst impression. 20,000 veterans encamped on the outskirts of Washington to demand immediate payment of a bonus Congress had promised them in the future, over Hoover's veto. The Army, under the direction of General Douglas MacArthur, marched on the camp with tanks, machine guns, and tear gas, drove the veterans out, and burned down the camp. Two infants died from the gas. The assault was contrary to Hoover's orders, but he accepted responsibility and defended it on the grounds that the veterans were "insurrectionists" who sought to overturn the American system.

Herbert Hoover, nevertheless, deserves a better reputation for the vigor and boldness of his actions. Certainly he did more to combat the crisis than any preceding American president had during an economic downturn. The failure of his efforts stemmed not from lack of concern or ability, but from his attachment to the orthodox economic beliefs of the day. Hardly anyone in American public life—or indeed in the whole Western world—had a clear idea of how to cure the economic paralysis that was spreading on both sides of the ocean. We cannot fault Hoover for that. The bankruptcy in ideas was general.

Hoover moved on three fronts. First, he attempted to restore business confidence by offering public assurances that the system was essentially sound and that new investment would set the economy on the road to recovery. Those assurances may seem to us today like naive whistling in the dark, because they didn't work and the depression only deepened. But Hoover was not naive. Conditions might have deteriorated even more rapidly had the President of the United States been openly pessimistic, and he realized that.

Second, Hoover tried energetically to persuade business leaders not to cut wages and lay off employees. The cutbacks made sense for individual firms facing hard times, but Hoover understood that the resulting decline in purchasing power would depress the economy still further. He pleaded with corporations to act in accord with the public interest and their own collective interest by keeping wage payments up so that consumers would have the funds to buy their products. The reasoning was sound, but Hoover attempted to carry it out by persuasion rather than coercion. This was doomed to failure. No firm would follow his advice unless it was assured that all competing firms would do likewise. Otherwise, purchasing power would decline anyway, and the public-spirited companies would have wasted a great deal of money on unnecessary wage payments. Hoover managed to exact wage-maintenance pledges from most of the leading corporations in the early phases of the Depression, but by the end of 1931 they had been repudiated. Wage levels sank further and the jobless rate climbed to new heights. Only direct government controls could ensure the success of the President's scheme, and Hoover could not bring himself to flout American traditions by interfering with private business.

The Hoover administration did make a number of attempts to assist producers and stimulate economic revival. Expenditures on public buildings during his four-year term, for example, were triple those for the entire 28 years preceding, and investments in new roads and national parks also reached new heights. The creation of the Federal Farm Board brought half a billion dollars in federal loans to maintain cotton, wheat and wool prices. The Reconstruction Finance Corporation provided similar aid to banks, insurance companies, and other financial institutions, on the theory that such aid would "trickle down" to the general public. (A progressive economist said that it was like putting fertilizer on the branches of a tree instead of the roots.) Finally, Hoover's taxation and spending policies in the early years of the Depression had expansionist effects; federal expenditures exceeded revenues, yielding a substantial budget deficit, just what most economists advise today during an economic downturn.

These efforts, although unprecedented, were on too small a scale to counteract a crisis of the magnitude of the Great Depression. And no one, Hoover or his Democratic opponents, understood the value of "counter-cyclical" deficit financing—perhaps the most powerful single tool for promoting recovery. The basic principles of modern Keynesian economics were just being worked out in these years, and did not gain general acceptance in the United States until after World War II. The idea that the federal government, like a family, should spend no more than it earned (except in a wartime emergency) still had a powerful hold on the American mind, and certainly on Herbert Hoover's mind. His administration ran a deficit in 1930 and 1931, which had a stimulating effect. Realizing their "error," they rectified things by cutting expenditures by 10 percent and raising taxes by a third—the largest peacetime tax increase in the history of the nation. It was a dose of arsenic for a sick patient. So was the Smoot–Hawley Tariff of 1930, which set record high import duties. European nations predictably passed retaliatory tariffs of their own, which caused a 50 percent drop in American overseas sales by 1932.

Despite the steadily mounting toll of unemployment—an average of 4 million in 1930, 8 million in 1931, 12 million in 1932—the Hoover administration remained remarkably rigid about one matter. Direct federal assistance to the needy was unacceptable. Hoover did not take the extreme conservative view that unemployment was strictly the fault of the individual, a sign of bad character. He recognized that it was a social problem. But he believed passionately that relief was the responsibility of private donors or local authorities. Passing out "handouts" from Washington, he felt, would sap individual initiative and create a bloated welfare bureaucracy.

Hoover's fear of concentrated power, his preference for voluntarism and decentralized decision-making had deep roots in American tradition. It commanded the respect of many thoughtful people. The leaders of the American Federation of Labor, for example, shared his opposition to a national relief system until 1932. But it was becoming increasingly plain with each passing day that private donations and the limited taxing powers of local governments were grossly inadequate to the overwhelming task at hand. Cities depended on local property taxes, and could not begin to support their citizens when a third or more had no other income. Philadelphia, by 1932, could afford to give each of its 55,000 destitute families no more than $4.25 per week, enough for the most Spartan of diets but without any provision at all for rent, fuel or clothing. By summer, there was no money left at all.

Communities on the verge of bankruptcy turned in desperation to the states. Some received substantial assistance. New York state, under Governor Franklin D. Roosevelt, was a pioneer in assisting local communities. Most states, however, were constricted by constitutions that sharply limited their taxing powers—forbidding state income taxes, for example—and therefore could do little. The Hoover administration continued to maintain that the crisis could be surmounted if local and state authorities would only try harder. Only at the last minute, in 1932, did Hoover reluctantly authorize the Reconstruction Finance Corporation to loan the states $300 million for unemployment relief. But that was too little too late. By then most Americans recognized that they were in the midst of a national crisis that required much more vigorous action by the national government.

FDR AND THE FRAMING OF THE NEW DEAL

The economic policies of the Hoover administration did not cause the Depression. It almost surely would have occurred, even had voters made Al Smith President and returned a Democratic Congress in 1928. Still, the calamity had befallen the nation under Republican leadership. It was natural for the electorate to penalize the party in power. The Republicans suffered heavy losses in the 1930 Congressional elections, after only a year of economic decline; two more years of deteriorating conditions inevitably cost them more. With the Depression deflecting attention away from all other issues, the Democratic party was able to unite around a single presidential candidate—Franklin Delano Roosevelt.

FDR had a golden voice and a radiant smile, and he exuded concern and confidence—qualities that seemed notably lacking in Herbert Hoover after his four discouraging years in office. A distant cousin of Theodore Roosevelt, he shared his predecessor's love for the rough and tumble of politics. He had served as a New York state senator and as Woodrow Wilson's assistant secretary of the Navy. After going down to crushing defeat as the Democratic nominee for Vice President in 1920, he had been stricken with polio, which confined him to a wheelchair for the rest of his life. After his recovery, bored with the life of a gentleman farmer, he had reentered public life, winning the New York state governorship in 1928 and 1930. He was an active and extremely popular governor, and by 1932 had put together a strong and balanced team of advisers. There were hardboiled politicians like James A. Farley and Louis Howe to line up party support, millionaires like Bernard Baruch and Joseph P. Kennedy to supply funds, "brain trust" professors like Rexford Tugwell and Raymond Moley of Columbia to suggest ideas and write speeches.

FDR waged the 1932 campaign with vigor and zest, defeating Hoover by 7 million votes. But the vote was really less an endorsement of Roosevelt and his program than a vote of no confidence in the opposition. It couldn't have been an endorsement of his program, because he didn't offer one. He called for "bold, persistent experimentation," but gave few clues as to the character of these experiments. He did endorse federal funds for relief and increased aid to farmers. Beyond that, he resolutely avoided specifics, and devoted much of his energy to attacking Hoover for excessive federal spending. His administration would do more for the people, FDR pledged, but would at the same time cut total federal expenditures by 25 percent. The campaign, declared a liberal journal, was "an obscene spectacle". The gulf that divided Hoover and Roosevelt, someone remarked, was the gulf between Tweedledum and Tweedledee.

Keeping his plans blurred made good political sense for Roosevelt, to be sure. Under the circumstances, about the only way a Democratic candidate could conceivably have lost to Hoover would have been by committing himself to a highly detailed program that was so controversial as to frighten away masses of voters. At the close of the Democratic convention, his running mate, John Nance Garner of Texas, quipped: "All you have to do is to stay alive until election day." FDR kept popular attention focused on the need for change, rather than on the tougher and riskier question of what kind of change.

The wisdom of that strategy was confirmed by the dismal showing of two candidates who did propose clearly defined alternatives. Both the Socialist and Communist parties were confident that the unprecedented economic collapse would expose the capitalist system as bankrupt and win the masses of people over to the socialist cause. But even in the darkest days of 1932, few Americans favored fundamental social transformation. Socialist Norman Thomas polled barely two percent of the vote, and Communist William Z. Foster only .2 percent. Given the circumstances, the political mood of the country was strikingly cautious and conservative. The poor were not so much angry as fatalistic. "Always going to be more poor folks than them that ain't poor," said an impoverished southern farmer. "I ain't saying that's the government's fault. It's just downright truth, that's all."

Roosevelt proved a more forceful leader than anyone could have guessed from his campaign. He was a master of the art of persuasion. The first chief executive to recognize the potential power of radio as a political weapon, FDR announced his major decisions in broadcast "fireside chats" that brought his mellow voice directly into the American living room. Herbert Hoover had needed one White House staff member to answer his mail; FDR needed 50! At last, it seemed, someone was in charge and knew what had to be done. The reassuring impression so skillfully conveyed by Roosevelt was somewhat misleading. He had no clear understanding of the causes of the crisis or of the remedies to be applied. There were sharp policy differences among his advisors, and the President was reluctant to take a clearcut stance, sharply calculating the political costs and benefits. Accordingly, public policy was eclectic, erratic, and sometimes contradictory. But FDR's unfailing optimism and utter unflappability gave millions of Americans new faith that things would improve. The most famous line in his inaugural address—"We have nothing to fear but fear itself"—was catchy nonsense. In 1933 there was plenty for Americans to fear in addition to fear itself. But FDR's magic made people believe it.

Finance and Relief

Roosevelt's inaugural speech pledged "action, and action now"—and action aplenty there was. No less than 15 major new bills were passed in the frantic first 100 days of the New Deal, and a good many others shortly after. No Congress in American history passed so much innovative legislation; no President in American history exerted such vigorous legislative leadership in peacetime. His first and most urgent task was to prevent the nation's banking system from collapsing, a very real possibility in early 1933. Banking failures reached epidemic proportions in the four months between the election and the inauguration, partly because FDR coolly refused Hoover's pleas for joint action. New Dealers justified the failure to cooperate on the grounds that policy differences between the two were too deep. Republicans charged with some justice, that it was politically motivated; letting the economy slide further under a lame duck Republican president would make anything Roosevelt could do alone look better. FDR, in any event, did act dramatically when he seized the reins. He closed all banks by executive order, and requested that Congress immediately pass an Emergency Bank Act that would assist the solvent banks and reorganize the shaky ones. The House of Representatives unanimously approved the Act within seven hours of its introduction, without even having seen the actual text of the bill! People who were denied access to their savings accounts found the bank holiday traumatic, a disruption of the kind they wouldn't expect even in wartime. But it worked. Although the federal government lacked the personnel to launch thorough investigations of several thousand financial institutions across the land, its hastily-awarded stamp of approval restored popular confidence and prevented a further wave of runs when the banks were reopened a few days later. Later in the same session, Congress approved the Federal Deposit Insurance Corporation to guarantee the safety of all bank deposits up to $5,000 (raised to $100,000 today). It was the most powerful step the federal government ever took to support the banking system. FDR also took the United States off the gold standard, in order to be free to pursue inflationary policies; when the dollar's value is tied to gold, inflation could lead investors to exchange enough dollars for gold to drain away all the gold in Fort Knox. And he won a series of other basic financial reforms during the first 100 days or not long after—the creation of the Securities and Exchange Commission to police the stock market, a law increasing the powers of the Federal Reserve Board, and a Home Owners Loan Corporation to refinance mortgages at attractively low rates.

More than one out of every three nonagricultural workers in the land was jobless, so feeding the hungry was a pressing necessity. Roosevelt shared Hoover's feeling that this was a matter ideally left to the states and local communities, but was quicker to recognize practical realities. He won authorization for a grant of half a billion dollars in emergency relief funds to be distributed by the states and local communities through the Federal Emergency Relief Administration. It spent over $3 billion before it expired in 1935. A temporary work relief program, the Civil Works Administration, provided further aid through the hard winter of 1933–34. Young people from families on relief were provided an income and an opportunity for social service by the Civilian Conservation Corps, which employed two and a half million of them on reforestation and flood control projects, a boon for the environment as well as for their struggling families. Some eight million households, 22 percent of the population, were receiving federal assistance by the end of 1934.

Agriculture

Roosevelt sought to aid the nation's embattled farmers through a variety of means. The Farm Credit Administration supplied federal funds to refinance mortgages on easy terms, and a 1934 law assisted farmers in recovering property previously lost to the banks. The Rural Electrification Administration brought hundreds of thousands of rural homes into the twentieth century by extending power lines into the countryside. The largest and most important public work of the New Deal, the Tennessee Valley Authority (TVA), provided cheap power and flood control protection in the area through which the Tennessee River flows. The disastrous effects of the prolonged droughts that turned most of the southern Great Plains states into a massive dustbowl between 1934 and 1941 were mitigated by large-scale assistance from the Soil Conservation Corps.

The keystone of the New Deal's agricultural program was a scheme to control production and subsidize prices through the Agricultural Adjustment Administration. The AAA paid farmers to devote less acreage to specified crops selling below "parity"—a price that would restore the favorable ratio between farm and industrial goods that had prevailed between 1909 and 1914, the golden age of farm prosperity. Subsidy payments for such acreage restrictions would continue until prices climbed back up to parity. Cutting back on output at a time when many Americans were ill-fed seemed anomalous, and doubly so because the bill went into effect after the 1933 crops had been sown. To keep within the new quotas, a third of the South's cotton crop had to be plowed under and six million baby pigs were slaughtered. Roosevelt, one critic said, was solving the paradox of want amid plenty by doing away with plenty. But farm prices did rise sharply, from 52 percent of parity in 1932 to 88 percent in 1935. The gains were partly the result of the great droughts and windstorms that turned many wheat fields into little Saharas, reducing output more certainly than any government edict. But the AAA was at least in part responsible. Some element of order had been introduced into the chaotic competition that had prevailed in agriculture. The Supreme Court ruled the AAA unconstitutional in 1936, but later bills that achieved the same end through a somewhat different mechanism were allowed to stand, and the farm subsidy program continued.

The AAA did not help farmers in general—it helped the larger commercial growers and harmed the poorest marginal operators who produced only a small share of the marketable crop. It clearly worked to the disadvantage of tenants and sharecroppers, because the acreage restrictions allowed owners to dismiss many, and the subsidies often financed new farm machinery that displaced others. Some three million people were displaced from the land between 1932 and 1935 alone. A federal Resettlement Administration created in 1935 sought to assist them, and the Farm Security Administration (1937) had similar aims. But neither program had enough funds to do anything much for them. The small farmers were largely unorganized and invisible, despite the efforts of the radical Southern Tenant Farmers Union. The larger operators had political clout. They dominated the American Farm Bureau Federation and the local producer's committees that administered the program. For them, the AAA was unquestionably a boon, and they had enough political muscle to keep the subsidy system in place down to today.

Industry

The other major measure passed in the first 100 days, the National Industrial Recovery Act, was a flop. The NIRA created a National Recovery Administration to restore prosperity by imposing controls over industrial output and prices. The bill suspended the antitrust laws and sought to create codes to coordinate the activities of producers in each industry and eliminate "unfair" competition. It was to replace competitive chaos with rational planning. Was the NRA supposed to bring the corporations under democratic control, to establish a closer government-business partnership, or to delegate government authority to dominant corporate interests? Differing elements of the administration held conflicting views and the legislation was ambiguous. In practice, however, the main effect was to give more power to big business. The codes that were negotiated, one historian has concluded, were "bargains between business leaders on the one hand and businessmen in the guise of government on the other"—and they served to protect the most powerful firms from price competition by smaller producers. After the early codes were criticized, personnel changes brought in government representatives who were more independent and demanding, leading to increasing business disaffection from the NRA.

These were by no means the only flaws of the NRA experiment. The amount of bureaucratic red tape used in suddenly imposing order in an extraordinarily complex economy proved frustrating even to those firms that had most enthusiastically supported the plan. Most important, the basic premise of the entire effort was misguided. The crisis had not been created by excessive competition; therefore, limiting production and raising prices was not the solution. The price increases mandated by the NRA simply depressed consumer demand further. Lifting prices could stimulate recovery only if income was rising as well, which it was not. By the end of 1934, fewer workers had jobs in private industry than in the previous year. In May of 1935, the Supreme Court unanimously declared the NRA unconstitutional. Most New Dealers had mixed feelings. They were troubled by the indication that executive and legislative branches would not be allowed a free hand to intervene in the economy as they saw fit, but they welcomed the chance to liquidate this particular venture without admitting that it had been a dismal failure.

POPULAR DISCONTENT AND THE TURN TO THE LEFT

The early New Deal program was a *potpourri* that offered something for everyone— at least for everyone well organized enough to make himself heard. As the rosy glow of the first 100 days faded, however, it became clear that economic recovery was occurring only very slowly. Critical voices began to be heard. Some charged that the New Deal had gone too far, that its excessive interference in the economy had destroyed the business confidence on which prosperity depended. The Republican National Committee took this line, declaring that FDR was trying to replace "the American system of government with a socialist state honeycombed by waste and extravagence, and ruled by a dictatorship that mocks at the right of the states and the liberty of the citizen." The American Liberty League, organized in March, 1934, was a supposedly nonpartisan effort that enlisted disaffected conservative Democrats as well. It did win the support of the Democratic party's two preceding presidential candidates, Al Smith and John W. Davis. Not many voters were swayed, however. In the November Congressional elections of 1934, the Democrats did not lose seats, as the party in power normally does in an off-year contest. They gained a good many instead, dominating the incoming House and Senate by margins of almost three to one. Few Americans wanted to see a rollback of the New Deal.

A good many, indeed, were eager to see more far-reaching reforms. Roosevelt was encountering an increasingly serious political challenge from the left—not from the Socialist Party, the Communist Party, or other traditional radical sects, but from some new spokesmen of popular discontent. They did not sing precisely the same tune, but they all reached a national audience with demands for more drastic action to improve the condition of the poorest Americans. One was Father Charles Coughlin, a Roman Catholic priest from a Detroit suburb, who drew a weekly radio audience as large as 40 million and received more mail than any American, including the President. On Sunday afternoon in tenement neighborhoods so many radios were tuned to Coughlin's program that you could walk for blocks without missing a word. He was a crank on money matters who claimed that a conspiracy of international bankers was responsible for the Depression, and urged that capitalism be replaced with something like the fascist corporate state that had been imposed on Italy by dictator Benito Mussolini. At first, Coughlin backed Roosevelt—to the point of saying that the New Deal was "Christ's deal." But by 1934 he had begun to identify FDR with the "godless capitalists, the Jews, the communists, international bankers, and plutocrats" who Coughlin's Union for Social Justice was determined to oppose. Another new protest leader was Dr. Francis Townsend, a retired California physician who burst into national prominence in September, 1933 with a panacea to cure the Depression. The Townsend Plan was a scheme to give all citizens over 60 a pension of $200 a month (the equivalent of over $1,000 a month in current dollars) on the condition that they stop work and spend the full amount each month. Just how the whopping costs could be financed could not be explained to the satisfaction of critical observers, but the good doctor's followers were uninterested in such details. The movement mushroomed; within a year there were over 1,000 Townsend clubs, and more than 2,000 by 1935.

A third radical critic of the New Deal, politically the most dangerous of all in Roosevelt's eyes, was Senator Huey P. Long of Louisiana. In January of 1934, he formed a national political organization, Share Our Wealth, which claimed more than 25,000 chapters and a mailing list of over 7 million within a year. Long asserted that confiscation of the great fortunes would make it possible to guarantee every family a "homestead allowance" of $5,000 plus an annual income of at least $2,000 per year. His arithmetic was grossly deficient, and his earlier conduct as governor of Louisiana had revealed his dictatorial instincts. But the extent of economic deprivation, and the glacial pace of recovery in the first two years of the New Deal were enough to make many Americans blink at those flaws. A secret poll conducted by the Democratic National Committee in the spring of 1935 revealed that if Long carried out his threat to run for the presidency as a third party candidate in 1936, he might draw six million votes—even more if he joined forces with Coughlin and Townsend—in which case, the election might easily be thrown to the Republicans.

A PRIMITIVE PUBLIC OPINION POLL BY THE COLUMBUS, OHIO CITIZEN, 1934

	What do you need for future happiness?	What money means to them	What is your chief fear?	Do you think the government owes you a living?	Whom do you hold responsible for the present condition?	Would you farm a tract if the government gave it to you?	Has your religious faith helped you weather the storm?	Do you want the government to plan the future for you, or would you prefer to go it alone?
Waitress Age 25	Money	Joys the rich have	Loss of job	No	The bankers and building and loan men	Yes, if I knew how	When things were worst, yes	Thinks the government can plan without restricting
Housewife Age 43	Money	Chance to educate children	Poverty	No	Drift away from the church	No	Almost by itself	Will abide by the plan that offers a better day
C.W.A. Worker (Molder) Age 54	Money	No more relief orders	Things will never get better	Thinks U.S. owes all a job	Capitalism's greed	Yes	No	Wants help not advice
Unemployed Man, former Retail-store Owner Age 51	Money	Can make a new start Business of his own	Old age	No	We are all responsible	Yes, but doesn't know how	Very little	Prefers to be let alone
Bank Teller Age 33	Security		Loss of vision	No	War and inflation	Not if he can help it	Very little	Prefers to be let alone
O.S.U. Graduate '34 Female Teacher Age 22	Money	To help younger brother at college	Fewer teachers will be needed	No	Guilt and fear of big money	No	Greatly	Wants some government regulation of schools

	What do you need for future happiness?	What money means to them	What is your chief fear?	Do you think the government owes you a living?	Whom do you hold responsible for the present condition?	Would you farm a tract if the government gave it to you?	Has your religious faith helped you weather the storm?	Do you want the government to plan the future for you, or would you prefer to go it alone?
O.S.U. Graduate '33 Civil Engineer Unemployed Age 23	Money	To restore lapsed insurance	No jobs or good pay in his line	Decidedly not	Unholy deals of politicians and money lenders	No	None	Wants U.S. building program free from graft and politics
Gas Company Bookkeeper Age 34	Money	To pay debts and buy a home	Ownership by the state of utilities	No	Politicians	No	None	Wants U.S. to cease interference with all business
Hotel Clerk Age 27	Money	To buy a farm	Low salary and loss of job	Yes, if he can't find a job	Everyone—all spent too much	Yes	Very little	Wants U.S. to open the lands to all who'll take them
City Detective Age 50	Money	To make sure an old-age fund	Poverty	No	High living by everyone	Yes	Greatly	Wants federal law to supplant most all state functions
Housewife Age 60	Money	To pay debts	Poverty	No	The war, wild spending afterward	Yes	Yes	Yes, if it is wisely done
Professor Age 38	Money	To free self of worry for study	Financial worry affecting work	No	Collapse of capitalism	Not unless he had to	Greatly	Wants government rule to supplant all state functions
High-school Student Age 17	Money	To get through school	None	No	The war	No	Some	Wants helpful laws applying to all

The Second New Deal

The Roosevelt administration needed to do more, obviously, to alleviate the discontent that fed Long, Coughlin, and Townsend. In 1935, it began to do so, launching what some historians call "the Second New Deal." One step was simply to spend a great deal more on emergency relief and public works programs. The new Congress approved an Emergency Relief Appropriation of almost $5 billion, by far the largest single appropriation in American history. The greatest share of it went to a new agency headed by Harry Hopkins, the Works Progress Administration (WPA), which employed two to three million people and spent over $10 billion before it was phased out in 1941. Republicans complained that the administration was in effect buying elections by keeping a substantial fraction of the electorate on the public payroll, and publicized an alleged statement of Hopkins that New Dealers would "tax and tax, spend and spend, and elect and elect." The program, however, was small in comparison with the need; it never employed more than 40 percent of the people seeking work, and paid an average monthly wage of only $52, less than half the pre-depression wage level. But putting Americans to work on public projects was better for their morale than giving them cash for relief, and the nation benefited from the post offices, roads, bridges, and airports they constructed.

A second response of the administration to the threat from the left was a frank appeal to class resentments. Certain privileged elements of the population, it argued, were profiting from the miseries of the masses. By the time of the 1936 campaign, FDR spoke with a more radical accent than he had ever used before. He called his opponents "economic royalists," and compared them to "the eighteenth century royalists who held special privileges from the crown." Political tyranny had been banished by the American Revolution; now political equality had become "meaningless in the face of economic inequality." The targets of his attacks responded venomously. "That madman in the White House," they said, was "a traitor to his class." Some even spoke of "that cripple in the White House." They had little understanding of popular sentiment. "The women who come in here to have their hair done knock Roosevelt," said a Fifth Avenue hairdresser. "That's because they've got money and they're afraid he's going to take some of it away. We let 'em talk and say nothing ourselves, but I'll bet every girl in this shop votes for Roosevelt."

FDR did not in fact do much to take money away from the wealthy, but three controversial measures passed in 1935 appealed to the common people and dismayed conservatives. The Wealth Tax Act proposed by the administration would have sharply increased taxes on upper income groups. FDR was reluctant to do it, but wrote a friend that he was "fighting Communism, Huey Longism, Coughlinism, Townsendism," and that "to combat crackpot ideas it may be necessary to throw to the wolves the 46 men who are reported to have incomes in excess of one million dollars a year." By the time the amended bill got through Congress, it was so watered down that it threw no one "to the wolves." The tax increase was relatively innocuous. But it made Roosevelt appear a friend of the common man, which paid political dividends in the next election.

The Social Security Act of 1935 had much more substance—it launched the American welfare state, establishing our present national system of unemployment insurance, old age pensions, and aid for special needy groups like the crippled, the blind, the deaf, and dependent children. It was not a truly national system. Preserving the tradition of American federalism, the framers of the bill provided that all of these programs except the old age pensions were to be administered by the states. The level of the benefits paid was left to the states, so long as they reached a certain minimum. There were great discrepancies in the amounts provided, depending on the resources of state governments and whether they were humanitarian or stingy. Most states provided only the barest minimum.

The retirement program was inequitable as well, even though it was administered directly from Washington. For one thing, about a quarter of the labor force—farm workers, domestic servants, public employees, and others—was not covered at all. For another, the size of the pension was determined not by need but by the amounts workers and their employers had previously paid into the system (with a federal supplement for those whose earnings fell below a certain minimum). It was a compulsory insurance scheme, rather than a full commitment to the welfare state principle that government should guarantee all citizens a decent minimum standard of living during their waning years. Another flaw was that the first pensions would not be paid out until 1940. Until then the payroll taxes on employees and employers would accumulate in Washington, reducing overall purchasing power in an economy desperately in need of stimulation.

The Social Security program was limited in these respects, and it was very late in coming by the standards of other advanced countries, striking testimony to the persistence of American individualism and fear of big government. By contrast, German's national social insurance scheme dates back to 1888, France's to 1905, Britain's to 1908. But the 1935 act was an immensely popular great step forward. Conservative politicians long after—Barry Goldwater in 1964 and Ronald Reagan in 1976—learned that criticizing the Social Security program was politically as wise as criticizing motherhood.

The Rise of Labor

The most controversial of all the 1935 measures was the National Labor Relations Act, the Wagner Act, which spurred the greatest organizing drive in the history of the American labor movement. Organized labor had been on the defensive throughout the prosperous twenties; total union membership dropped almost a third in the decade. The drop continued through the Hoover years, and bottomed out in 1933. Membership rose in 1934 and 1935, but only modestly. The National Industrial Recovery Act of 1933 included language that seemed favorable to unionization—Section 7A assured labor of the right to organize and bargain collectively, and created a National Labor Board to enforce it. Not much happened, however, because employers hostile to independent trade unions instituted "employee representation plans," carefully controlled company unions, and the National Labor Board deemed them adequate substitutes for independent unions. By

1935, 2.5 million workers were enrolled in company unions, almost three-fourths as many as there were in the AFL and other independent labor organizations. The trade union movement had virtually no foothold in the giant industrial firms that occupied the commanding heights of the economy. Of the hundreds of huge firms employing more than 3,000 workers, only 4 percent recognized independent unions, whereas 82 percent had company unions and 14 percent had no workers' organizations of any kind. In the great auto plants of Detroit, the steel mills of Cleveland, and the tire factories of Akron, management held absolute sway over labor.

Business opposition to labor organization was not the only reason. Most leaders of the AFL had too little vision and daring to take up the challenge of organizing the mass production industries. They still held to Samuel Gompers' vision of how labor should be organized—on a craft by craft basis, with separate unions for carpenters, printers, machinists, painters, electricians, and so forth. That had made some sense in the days of Gompers, but the concentration of production in giant establishments since then required a new form of organization—industrial unions that would include all workers in a given industry, regardless of their skill level. When rubber workers in Akron started a union covering an entire plant, an AFL organizer split it into 19 separate craft locals, from Blacksmiths through Metal Workers to Teamsters. One big union of rubber workers obviously could speak with a more powerful voice than 19 small ones that could be played off against each other, but the autonomy of each craft had always been the guiding philosophy of the AFL, and its aging leaders were unwilling to abandon it. As they saw it, giant unions in which skilled craftsmen shared power with unskilled and semiskilled workers, most of them of new immigrant stock or blacks, could never work. A few successful industrial unions were already within the AFL—most notably John L. Lewis' United Mine Workers and the Amalgamated Clothing Workers—but the leadership wanted no more. The time was ripe for a surge of industrial organization; 1.5 million workers, mostly in the mass production industries, went on strike in 1934. But the AFL was too hidebound to seize the opportunity.

The Wagner Act increased the prospects enormously. It gave unprecedented federal encouragement to union organization. The law set up a permanent National Labor Relations Board to supervise elections by secret ballot to determine whether or not the employees of a particular firm wished to affiliate with a union. Organizers were guaranteed the right to place their case before the workers, and employers were barred from influencing the elections. The Wagner Act was the work of Senator Robert Wagner of New York and other Congressional liberals; FDR was extremely reluctant to tilt so far on the side of labor, and finally backed it only when it seemed sure to pass anyway. But then he jumped on the bandwagon and declared it a "must bill," claiming the credit with his customary political agility.

Three months after the passage of the Wagner Act, the AFL's national convention waged an acrimonious debate over the organization of the mass production industries on an industrial base. The traditionalists refused to move, and John L. Lewis and other members of the industrial–union bloc walked out. They formed the Committee for Industrial Organization, soon renamed the Congress of Industrial Organization. The CIO created ad hoc organizing committees of veteran union

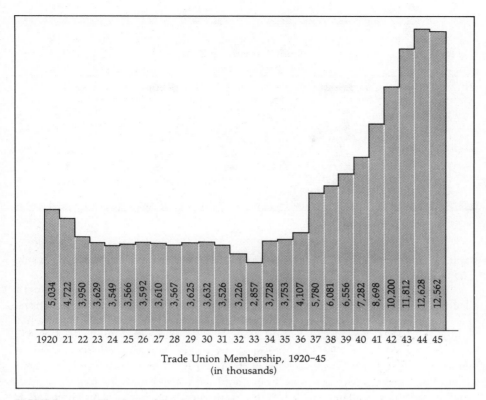

| | | | | | | | | | | | | | | | | | | | | | | | | | |
|5,034|4,722|3,950|3,629|3,549|3,566|3,592|3,610|3,567|3,625|3,632|3,526|3,226|2,857|3,728|3,753|4,107|5,780|6,081|6,556|7,282|8,698|10,200|11,812|12,628|12,562|

1920 21 22 23 24 25 26 27 28 29 30 31 32 33 34 35 36 37 38 39 40 41 42 43 44 45

Trade Union Membership, 1920–45
(in thousands)

FIGURE 27-1   The Rise of Trade Unions

members to preach the cause to workers in steel, textiles, petroleum, rubber, automobiles, and other unorganized industries. They won victory after victory, sometimes by simply winning an NLRB-sponsored election, sometimes by strikes that forced recalcitrant employers to grant union recognition. A key turning point came in early 1937, when the United Automobile Workers compelled General Motors to begin collective bargaining by a radical new tactic, the sitdown strike. Local militants, without authorization by the CIO leadership, stopped working, barricaded themselves within the plant, and refused to leave until management came to terms. It was far more effective than picketing outside the gates to keep scabs from entering. It was also illegal, however—the workers were confiscating corporate property, at least temporarily, and rendering it valueless to the owners. General Motors at first held firm, and demanded that state troops forcibly remove the sitdown strikers. In an earlier era of American history, such a request would undoubtedly have been granted. Roosevelt was dismayed by the sitdowns but refused to intervene, declaring "a plague on both your houses." By 1937 the cause of labor gained a new legitimacy, and neither the national administration nor the governments of the most industrialized states were willing to align themselves with

TABLE 27-2
Union Growth, 1936-41
(in thousands)

	Total Membership	AFL	CIO	Unaffiliated
1936	4,107	3,516	—	591
1937	5,780	3,180	1,991	609
1938	6,081	3,547	1,958	575
1939	6,556	3,878	1,838	840
1940	7,282	4,343	2,154	785
1941	8,698	5,179	2,654	865

capital and against labor. The strikers were left undisturbed, and after six weeks GM capitulated.

Other great CIO victories followed. U.S. Steel, Firestone Rubber, General Electric, and even one of the most fiercely antiunion of all American corporations, the Ford Motor Company, gave in. By 1941 the CIO had more than two and a half million members. Equally important, competition with the CIO shook the AFL from its torpor at last. The AFL mounted strenuous recruiting efforts of its own. Between 1936 and 1941, the strength of the labor movement as a whole doubled. 4.5 million workers whose wages, hours, and working conditions had previously been determined unilaterally by their employers now had an organization to defend their interests. It was the most far-reaching social change to occur in the entire Depression decade.

1936: The Roosevelt Coalition Takes Shape

The defections from the Democratic party that FDR had earlier feared did not occur in the 1936 election. Huey Long was dead from an assassin's bullet, and wouldn't have been much of a threat if he had been around to challenge Roosevelt. FDR was established as the idol of "the forgotten man." He swept all but two states (Maine and Vermont), winning five million more votes than he had in 1932. In the new Congress, the Democrats controlled over three-fourths of the seats in the House and nearly four-fifths of those in the Senate.

The Democratic party became as never before the party of the urban masses. FDR won an astonishing 104 of the nation's 106 cities of 100,000 or more. He had carried the twelve largest metropolises by nearly 1.9 million votes in 1932; in 1936 the margin was almost double that, 3.6 million. FDR appealed to foreign stock city dwellers, as Al Smith had, without repelling traditionally Democratic rural voters, and he brought two new elements into the Democratic camp—northern blacks and the labor unions.

The New Deal won a majority of black Americans away from their traditional allegiance to the party of Lincoln. Only 29 percent of the votes in the most heavily black ward in Cincinnati went to Roosevelt in 1932; in 1936 it was 65 percent. The shift of blacks into the Democratic party was not a result of anything the New Deal did to advance black civil rights directly. FDR, for example, did not courageously back the federal antilynching bill the NAACP called for. Antagonizing powerful southern white Congressmen, in his view, was too heavy a political price to pay. Blacks were attracted to the New Deal primarily because its relief programs benefited them disproportionately since they were an especially impoverished element of the population. It helped, too, that Roosevelt appointed more blacks to significant public offices than ever before. Harry Hopkins, Secretary of Interior Harold Ickes, and First Lady Eleanor Roosevelt were strong supporters of equal rights. Hopkins and Ickes worked to ensure that a fair share of relief funds and public works jobs went to the black community. (By contrast, the AAA's system of administration through local control meant white control in the South; not a single black served on an AAA county committee.) Eleanor Roosevelt struck a well-publicized blow at Jim Crow customs when she resigned from the Daughters of the American Revolution after it had refused to permit black singer Marian Anderson to perform in its hall; the First Lady and Harold Ickes arranged to have Anderson sing from the steps of the Lincoln Memorial instead.

The events of the 1930s also brought organized labor into partisan politics. The AFL in Gompers' day had endorsed and financially backed particular candidates from time to time, but it had never tied itself to either party, in part for the good reason that neither took stances that were especially enlightened from labor's point of view. The New Deal program in general, however, and the Wagner Act in particular, changed all that, and gave the labor movement a much greater stake in the outcome of electoral contests. In 1936 the CIO was the largest single contributor to the Democratic campaign fund. Although the AFL made no official endorsement, it is estimated that over 80 percent of all union members voted for Roosevelt.

The usual regional and ethnic lines that had governed most voters' political choices in the past were blurred in 1936. Although there were many exceptions— rich Democrats and poor Republicans—most "haves" opposed Roosevelt and most "have-nots" backed him. In a 1936 poll, 58 percent of those classified as "prosperous" were anti-New Deal; 74 percent of the "poor" favored it. Many of the additional five million votes Roosevelt pulled in that election must have come from people on the bottom who hadn't bothered to turn out at the polls previously. The choice between FDR and his opponent, Kansas Governor Alfred E. Landon, was the first one that seemed likely to make a difference in their lives.

THE STALEMATED SECOND TERM

The high-water mark of the New Deal was 1936. After that smashing triumph, resistance began to mount. The evidence of the election returns is clearcut. Through 1936, the Democratic tide was rising steadily. The party's share of seats in

TABLE 27–3
Voting Patterns, 1932–40

	Percent Democratic Popular Vote for President	Seats in House of Representatives	Seats in Senate
1932	57.8	71.8	62.5
1934	NA	73.8	71.8
1936	60.8	76.6	79.2
1938	NA	60.8	71.8
1940	54.8	61.6	68.9

the House of Representatives rose from 72 percent in 1932 to 74 percent in 1934, and then to 77 percent in 1936. In the Senate, the gain was even more marked—from 63 percent to 72 percent and then 79 percent. Roosevelt's popularity was growing, too, as his record victory in 1936 indicated.

After 1936, that trend was reversed. In the 1938 contest, the Democrats lost 70 seats in the House, and several in the Senate as well. In 1940, they gained back only 7 of the House seats, and suffered further losses in the Senate. Roosevelt's strength was waning, too. His margin of victory, although substantial, was less than in either of his two previous races. He was, of course, defying long-established custom in running for a third term as President. Some voters may have feared that he might pull the United States into the European war that had broken out the year before. The war, however, probably worked to his political advantage, with voters preferring an experienced captain in the stormy seas. Clearly the balance of forces was tipping back in a conservative direction.

The conservative swing would be even more apparent if the figures identified Congressmen not simply as Democrats or Republicans, but instead distinguished Democrats who were loyal supporters of the New Deal from conservative Democratic legislators who believed that the New Deal had gone far enough already. The 1938 elections decimated the ranks of the most reform-minded Democrats. Conservative Southern Democrats who had previously been pressured into supporting the administration were emboldened to join the Republicans in frustrating further reform efforts. Roosevelt personally campaigned against some of these conservative Democrats in the party primaries, but the voters did not respond.

The Sluggish Economy

Why did the New Deal encounter mounting resistance after the resounding triumph of 1936? One reason is that the New Deal's many innovative programs, its arm-long list of alphabet soup agencies from the AAA to the TVA and WPA, did very little to solve the core problem that brought about Roosevelt's election in the first place—the Depression. There was an economic turnaround of sorts when FDR

TABLE 27-4
Gross National Product and Unemployment, 1929-40

	GNP per capita (1958 dollars)	Percent of nonagricultural workers unemployed
1929	1,784	5.3
1930	1,565	14.2
1931	1,442	25.2
1932	1,234	36.3
1933	1,208	37.6
1934	1,301	32.6
1935	1,413	30.2
1936	1,591	25.4
1937	1,664	21.3
1938	1,573	27.2
1939	1,690	25.2
1940	1,818	21.3

came to power. From 1929 to 1933, national income per person dropped and the unemployment rate rose each year. For the next four years, unemployment declined steadily and output per capita grew almost as rapidly as in the boom years of the 1920s. The growth in output, however, was not accompanied by a proportionate decline in joblessness. In 1937, after four years of hectic activity in Washington, more than a fifth of the nonagricultural labor force was still out of work. It was still crisis level unemployment, a rate four times above that for 1929. The jobless, of course, were better off than in the Hoover years, but that was an achievement of relief, not recovery.

Even more discouraging, the partial recovery achieved from 1933 to 1937 was abruptly halted by another severe downturn in the winter of 1937–38. Production fell off again and the unemployment rolls grew longer. This setback was fortunately brief, but as Roosevelt's second term drew to a close, the GNP was only a shade higher than in 1929, and unemployment was still four times higher.

Whether a different set of policies would have yielded better results is debatable. Some Keynesian economists argue that adroit manipulation of the federal budget could have done the job. In depressions, a government should spend more than it collects in taxes to put money in the pockets of consumers who will spend it; the deeper the depression, the larger the budget deficit needed to stimulate expansion. The Roosevelt administration didn't follow that policy. FDR was a thoroughly conventional economic thinker. His pledges in the 1932 campaign to cut the federal budget were perfectly sincere; one of his first acts in office was to cut war veterans' pensions in half and reduce the salaries of federal employees. These steps did a good deal to offset the stimulating effects of increased spending for relief and public works.

TABLE 27-5
Federal Income and Expenditures, 1932–39
(billions of current dollars)

	Expenditures	Revenue	Balance
1932	4.7	1.9	-2.7
1933	4.6	2.0	-2.6
1934	6.7	3.1	-3.6
1935	6.5	3.7	-2.8
1936	8.5	4.1	-4.4
1937	7.8	5.0	-2.8
1938	6.8	5.6	-1.2
1939	8.9	5.0	-3.9

FDR never quite managed to bring the federal budget fully into balance, and the deficit each year provided some stimulus. But that was a fortunate accident, the result of a commitment to costly spending programs and the political difficulty of raising taxes during a depression. The deficits were accordingly quite small—smaller in 1933, for example, than during Hoover's last year in office. Even the $4.4 billion deficit for 1936, much the largest of the period, was less than double that for 1932, hardly a revolutionary increase. If we look at the fiscal picture in the entire public sector, including state and local revenues and expenditures, the deficit vanishes altogether. State and local authorities ran surpluses that more than counterbalanced the federal deficit, exerting a depressing effect on the economy. Disturbed at being so much in the red in 1936, FDR cut back expenditures sharply in 1937, bringing on the slump of 1937–38. As a result of that lesson, the government boosted expenditures again, the deficit climbed back up to nearly its 1936 level, and economic conditions began to improve. The federal deficit, however, still was not enough to counteract the deflationary effect of the surpluses taken in at the state and local levels.

This is true, but there are two flaws in this Keynesian "might have been" scenario. One is that the strategy recommended by such critics—much larger federal deficits—was politically impossible. Even if Roosevelt had been persuaded of its wisdom, it would have been a heroic task to convince the Congress. A public opinion poll in 1939 showed that less than a fifth of the public believed in deficit financing; the fraction of Congressmen who did was probably even less. A second crucial point is that in capitalist economies key investment decisions are made by private investors and institutions. Deficit spending will *not* stimulate a sagging economy if investors regard it as dangerous and respond by withholding their own funds. The decline in private investment will offset the stimulus supplied by the deficit, leaving conditions unimproved. That probably would have happened if Roosevelt had had the will and political support for a much more drastically unbalanced federal budget. In the 1960s the American business community had enough economic sophistication not to panic at the counter-cyclical deficit financing of the Kennedy administration, but a generation earlier it did not. Indeed, many business leaders were infuriated and terrified by some of the mildest New Deal measures. The beliefs that prevailed throughout the United States in the 1930s, in short, precluded the application of Keynesian remedies. Full recovery came only when the threat of impending war spurred massive increases in defense spending. Without that, the Depression might have dragged on even longer.

War on the Court

The continuing sluggishness of the economy was perhaps the most important reason why the drive for further reform failed following FDR's sweeping victory in 1936. But a major political blunder by Roosevelt early the next year—his attempt to "pack" the U.S. Supreme Court—contributed significantly. New Dealers were naturally frustrated by repeated vetoes of key reform measures handed down by the conservative majority on the Supreme Court. The NRA and AAA had already been stricken down, and in 1937 the justices were to rule on the constitutionality of the Wagner and Social Security Acts. Five conservatives among the "nine old men" might well say no, undermining the keystones of the second New Deal. It was a real problem, but FDR dealt with it in an underhanded manner that backfired. He said nothing of his plans in the 1936 campaign. Then, safely elected, he forwarded to Congress a bill authorizing him to appoint a new justice for each one presently serving past the age of 70. It was necessary, he said, to clear up the overcrowded court docket. The explanation that aged judges were unable to work with proper efficiency was duplicitous, and transparently so. The most trusting observers could see that the President's real aim was to add enough new men with his political views to the Court to create a pro-New Deal majority.

The problem with the Court was not the age of its members. Six of the nine were in fact over 70, but the oldest—81-year-old Justice Louis D. Brandeis—was among the most flexible and sensible, while two of the youngest—Justices Pierce Butler and Owen J. Roberts—were among the most rigid. Nor was the docket overcrowded, as Chief Justice Charles Evans Hughes demonstrated in devastating testimony at Congressional hearings on the court-packing bill. Had FDR been candid with the public about his dilemma, it is at least conceivable that he could have won support for a less extreme solution. Congress, after all, has the power to alter the number of seats on the Court, and had done so on no less than six occasions in the past. There was nothing sacred about the number 9. But Roosevelt on this occasion was too slippery for his own good. If he felt that the nation was in a crisis so severe as to require that the principle of a politically independent judiciary be compromised, he should have said so and laid out a compelling case. The proposal left a rotten taste in the mouths of some of his strongest supporters. Although the Democratic party had huge majorities in both houses of Congress—and the administration twisted arms as hard as it could—the bill was defeated.

While the fight over court-packing was raging, the Court itself moved in a direction that undermined the unspoken rationale for it. It approved the Social Security and Wagner Acts, and reversed a 1936 decision banning state minimum wage laws. It is not clear what motivated the two justices who broke from their previous pattern to form a new majority, but it was not fear of the court-packing plan alone; the minimum wage decision had been made, although not announced, before Roosevelt had announced his plan. The retirement of a conservative judge in May, and of 4 more in the next 4 years, gave FDR ample opportunity to shape a Court that would take a broader view of government powers and a narrower one of property rights. The nineteenth century tradition of reading into the Constitution strict limits on government intervention in the economy was finally dead.

The underhanded assault on the Supreme Court revealed Roosevelt at his worst, and lost him a good deal of political support. Moderates who had backed the economic reforms of the New Deal saw the court-packing plan as a cynical attempt to subvert basic constitutional arrangements—as indeed it was. Such fears had special emotional power in the late 1930s, when new revelations of the crimes of dictators like Hitler, Stalin, and Mussolini were appearing almost daily. In 1936, the charge that "the New Deal is to America what the early phase of Naziism was to Germany" seemed far-fetched except to the Republicans and Liberty Leaguers who made it. Court-packing made it seem appreciably less so. Roosevelt's evasive "plague on both your houses" response to the CIO sitdown strikes the same year also fanned such fears. A president impatient of constitutional restraints, it appeared, was aligned with aggressive labor leaders who violated the law to gain their ends.

This perception never became so widespread as to shatter the New Deal coalition completely. Roosevelt remained a hero, a figure of extraordinary adulation, for millions of Americans who kept his picture in their living rooms. The Republicans were unable to escape the onus of having been the party of Hoover. But the loss of confidence was enough to bar the door to further innovation. The engine of reform had stalled. With the 1938 Congressional elections, control shifted to an alliance of Republicans and conservative Southern Democrats. The New Deal was essentially over.

SUGGESTED READINGS

John K. Galbraith, *The Great Crash* (rev. ed., 1972) is a scintillating introduction to the boom and bust of the late 1920s. Robert Sobel, *The Great Bull Market* (1968), Jim Potter, *The American Economy between the Wars* (1974), Peter Temin, *Did Monetary Forces Cause the Great Depression?* (1976), Broadus Mitchell, *Depression Decade* (1947), Murray Rothbard, *America's Great Depression* (1963), Herbert Stein, *The Fiscal Revolution, 1931–1963* (1969), and Charles Kindelberger, *The World in Depression, 1929–1939* (1973) examine the economic history of the period more thoroughly from varying vantage points.

The pain and misery of the Depression is well conveyed in Edmund Wilson, *American Earthquake* (1958) and Caroline Bird, *Invisible Scar* (1965). Alfred Romasco, *The Poverty of Abundance: Hoover, the Nation, and the Depression* (1965), and Joan Hoff Wilson, *Herbert Hoover: Forgotten Progressive* (1975) trace the unavailing efforts of the Hoover administration.

For estimates of the New Deal, see William Leuchtenberg, *Franklin D. Roosevelt and the New Deal* (1963), Paul C. Conkin, *The New Deal* (2nd ed., 1975), Otis L. Graham, Jr., *Toward a Planned Economy: From Roosevelt to Nixon* (1976), and Gerald D. Nash, *The Great Depression to World War II: Organizing America, 1933–1945* (1979). Arthur M. Schlesinger's three-volume series on "The Age of Roosevelt" is a vivid if uncritical narrative. Frank Freidel's four volumes on FDR, the definitive biography, only take the story to mid-1933. James MacGregor Burns, *Roosevelt: The Lion and the Fox* (1956) is lively and penetrating. Ellis Hawley, *The New Deal and the Problem of Monopoly* (1966), Arthur S. Miller, *The Modern Corporate State: Private Governments and the American Constitution* (1976), Elliot A. Rosen, *Hoover, Roosevelt, and the Brain Trust: From Depression to the New Deal* (1977), Donald Worster, *Dust Bowl: The Southern Plains in the 1930's* (1979), Roy Lubove, *The Struggle for Social Security, 1900–1935* (1968), and James T. Patterson, *America's Struggle Against Poverty, 1900–1980* (1981) assess various New Deal Policies.

Alan Brinkley, *Voice of Protest: Huey Long, Father Coughlin, and the Great Depression* (1982) describes the discontent that led the administration to move to the left in 1935. James T. Patterson, *Congressional Conservatives and the New Deal* (1967) and Leonard Baker, *Back to Back: The Duel between FDR and the Supreme Court* (1967) reveal the strength of conservative political forces. Labor protest and organization are considered in Irving Bernstein, *The Turbulent Years: A History of the American Worker, 1933–1941* (1969), Sidney Fine, *Sit-Down: The General Motors Strike of 1936–37* (1969), John W. Hevener, *Which Side Are You On? The Harlan County Coal Miners, 1931–1939* (1978), David Milton, *The Politics of U.S. Labor: From the Great Depression to the New Deal* (1980), and David Brody, *Workers in Industrial America* (1980). The successes and failures of the traditional left are analyzed in Irving Howe and Lewis Coser, *The American Communist Party* (1957), Frank A. Warren, *Liberals and Communism: The "Red" Decade Revisited* (1968), Richard Pells, *Radical Visions and American Dreams: Culture and Social Thought in the Depression Years* (1973), and Bert Cochran, *Labor and Communism: The Conflict that Shaped American Unions* (1977).

A number of oral histories reveal how the American people coped with the Depression. See in particular James Agee, *Let Us Now Praise Famous Men* (1941) with extraordinary photographs by Walker Evans, Federal Writers Project, *These Are Our Lives* (1939), Studs Terkel, *Hard Times: Oral Histories of the Great Depression* (1970), and Ann Banks, ed., *First-Person America* (1980). Robert and Helen Lynd, *Middletown in Transition* (1937) and Alfred Winslow Jones, *Life, Liberty, and Property: A Story of Conflict and a Measurement of Conflicting Rights* (1941) are pioneering sociological studies that illuminate popular inertia. The experience of blacks is assessed in Dan T. Carter, *Scottsboro: A Tragedy of the Modern South* (1969), Harvard Sitkoff, *A New Deal for Blacks: The Emergence of Civil Rights as a National Issue* (1979), John B. Kirby, *Black Americans in the Roosevelt Era: Liberalism and Race* (1980), and James M. Jones, *Bad Blood: The Tuskegee Syphilis Experiment* (1981). For other non-white groups, see Abraham Hoffman, *Unwanted Mexican Americans in the Great Depression: Repatriation Pressures, 1929–1939* (1974), Donald L. Parman, *The Navajos and the New Deal* (1975), and Kenneth Philip, *John Collier's Crusade for Indian Reform, 1920–1954* (1977).

Chapter Twenty-Eight

From Isolation
to Intervention

On May 20, 1927, Charles Lindbergh took off from Long Island in "The Spirit of St. Louis." Thirty-three hours and thirty minutes later he touched down on the outskirts of Paris, the first man to fly alone across the Atlantic. A wave of adulation for "Lindy" swept the land. Americans saw his flight as a great victory of man and machine over the barriers of nature, and a symbol of the progress that further technological advances would bring.

A pessimist might have drawn other lessons from the Lindbergh flight. Planes that could carry an adventurer over vast distances at high speeds could also soar across national boundaries loaded with bombs. The shrinking of the ocean would not be an unmixed blessing for the United States, because it meant a new vulnerability to developments elsewhere around the globe and dictated deeper involvement in the affairs of other nations. When conflicts in Europe and Asia erupted into violence, America would face difficult and divisive choices as to where her own interests lay. The voyage of "The Spirit of St. Louis" had implications few Americans, including Lindbergh himself, were prepared to acknowledge. Before long the United States would be torn by a fierce debate between "interventionists," who believed America should accept new global responsibilities, and "isolationists," who did not. It was ironic that Charles Lindbergh became a leader of the isolationist forces. The debate came to a sudden end after a stunning demonstration of what it meant to live in an age of air power. Early in the morning of December 7, 1941, 275 Japanese bombers and 50 Zero fighters swooped down from the sky over Pearl Harbor, breaking the backbone of America's Pacific Fleet within two hours, and drawing the United States into a world war even more destructive than that of 1914–18.

In this Robert Jacobsen photo, the farewell of Pfc. John Winbury to his son is emblematic of the anguish suffered by soldiers and civilians during World War II.

But Lindbergh's flight provoked no nightmare visions of death raining from the sky. Instead, it helped in a small way to bring about perhaps the silliest international agreement of all time—the American-inspired Kellogg-Briand peace pact of 1928. In early 1927 a representative of French Foreign Minister Aristide Briand arrived in Washington seeking an American promise of aid to France in the event of a future German attack. Secretary of State Frank Kellogg was cool to any bilateral agreement. Things were stalemated until the upswelling of friendly Franco-American feeling that followed Lindbergh's triumph. Kellogg then made a counter offer: The United States would back an effort "to obtain the adherence of all the principal powers of the world to a declaration renouncing war as an instrument of national policy." The Kellogg-Briand Pact was initially signed by 15 nations, including Japan, Germany, and Italy; eventually 62 countries endorsed it. This pious pledge lacked only one small thing—a mechanism for enforcing it whenever a signer concluded that war would be in its interests. Advocates argued that it was harmless at worst, and that at best it might somehow encourage peaceful resolution of disputes. It was not altogether harmless, however. In the United States, at least, it created a naive complacency about the international scene that vanished only under the shock of many painful events. To *hope* for an end to war was natural. To *believe* that permanent peace had been secured by an agreement each party was free to interpret as it saw fit was misguided and dangerous. It left Americans ill-prepared to grasp the unpleasant things happening in the world around them in the years ahead.

REPUBLICAN DIPLOMACY

The three Republican Presidents who occupied the White House between 1921 and 1933—Harding, Coolidge, and Hoover—followed similar foreign policies. They sought to expand America's foreign trade without becoming entangled in foreign commitments that might draw the country into another great bloodbath like World War I. The war had brought an immense change in America's role in the international economy. The pre-WWI United States was a debtor nation; foreign investments in America exceeded American investments abroad by almost $4 billion in 1914. But enormous wartime loans to the Allies reversed the situation, making the United States the world's largest creditor, with overseas investments of over $12 billion. Over the next decade foreign indebtedness rose to $21 billion. America was at the center of the world economy, shipping out a sixth of total world exports and absorbing an eighth of the world's imports.

Although the United States had a solid and rapidly growing economic stake in world trade, it was unwilling to use its influence in ways that might possibly entrap it in another foreign war. It refused to join the international peace-keeping body, the League of Nations, or the World Court. Democrats pressing for American entry into the League in the 1920 campaign met with crushing defeat, killing the issue forever. There were other expressions of a narrow and xenophobic nationalism, particularly the very high Fordney–McCumber tariff of 1922, the immigration restriction acts of 1921 and 1924, and America's continuing insistence that the hard-pressed Allies pay off their war debts. The guiding principle of American policy was to remain free of foreign entanglements. It was well summed up by Herbert Hoover in 1931, when he rejected Italy's request to send an American representative to a world disarmament conference in Geneva. Hoover's view, as reported by Secretary of State Henry L. Stimson, was that:

> For a hundred and fifty years we had kept out of Europe; then in 1917 we had been dragged into a great war. We had spent forty billions of dollars in the war and we had added ten billions more in the shape of loans after the war. And yet Europe was in a worse condition than she was before the war. This led to despair as to Europe and European affairs on the part of the ordinary American citizen, and now he just wanted to keep out of the whole business.

The Western Hemisphere, of course, was something of an exception because of America's Caribbean interests, and the Panama Canal. Harding, Coolidge, and Hoover, however, were reluctant to send in the marines whenever political turmoil in Latin America appeared to threaten American interests. They gradually backed away from Teddy Roosevelt style unilateral military intervention. The marines were withdrawn from Santo Domingo in 1924, and from Nicaragua in 1933. When Mexico's revolutionary government sought to impose strict controls over land, oil, and mineral deposits owned by American investors, the issue was settled by peaceful negotiation. The Mexican Revolution proceeded without American interference. In 1928 an official State Department paper, the Clark Memorandum, redefined the Monroe Doctrine and repudiated the Roosevelt Corollary. The Monroe Doctrine, it declared, was "a case of the United States versus Europe, and not of the United States versus Latin America." America's right to keep European powers out of the Western Hemisphere did not give it similarly broad authority to take over other countries in the hemisphere whenever they failed to be "good" by American standards. The United States still regarded itself as a big brother to the Western Hemisphere, and expected the smaller Latin nations to follow its lead. But there was less shaking of the big stick and more give-and-take in the relationship. The Good Neighbor Policy Franklin Roosevelt laid down for Latin America was only the logical extension of the steps taken by his Republican predecessors.

Economic Policy Toward Europe

The renunciation of heavy-handed intervention in the Western Hemisphere was all to the good. Republican policies, vis-à-vis Europe and Asia were seemingly successful in the short run as well, but were seriously deficient when viewed in longer perspective. A grave underlying weakness of the economy of war-torn Europe in the 1920s stemmed from selfish and short-sighted American policies. The Allies requested that the United States write off the $10 billion debt that they had incurred during the war, on the grounds that they had suffered such heavy physical and human losses in the joint cause. The United States would have none of it, and insisted that they repay the debt in full, with interest that inflated it to $22 billion. At the same time, America perversely kept its tariff barriers high enough to keep out imports from Europe that could have supplied the earnings for repayment. The only way the Allies could keep up on their stiff payments was by exacting from Germany the large reparations specified in the Versailles Treaty, which were too great a burden for Germany to bear without assistance. In the decade after Versailles, this critical problem remained hidden from view, because Germany did get the necessary external assistance—in the form of American private investment in Germany. American capital propped up the economy of Weimar Germany, allowing it to deliver the reparations that permitted the Allies to pay their war debts to the United States and to buy American products. If something interrupted the flow of American export capital that fueled the whole arrangement, it would collapse with disastrous results. Germany would be unable to pay the reparations, the Allies would be forced to default on their war debts, and the floundering European nations would have to cut back on their purchases of American goods—with depressing effects on the American economy.

Just that sequence of events began to unfold when the Great Depression hit the United States in 1929 and investors withdrew funds from Europe. The crisis was compounded by an American blunder—the passage of the Smoot–Hawley tariff in 1931. It was the highest tariff in American history, and it led European nations to pass retaliatory protection measures. By 1932 American sales abroad had almost dried up altogether, adding to the glut on the domestic market. Hoover finally had the sense to proclaim a temporary moratorium on war debt repayments in 1931, in an attempt to shore up the world financial system. But when the Allies offered to cancel Germany's remaining reparations if the United States would relieve them of their debt permanently, he refused. The economic slide continued on both sides of the Atlantic. In Germany, the hardest-hit European nation, the depression undermined support for the democratic Weimar regime and paved the way for the coming to power of a militaristic demagogue, Adolph Hitler.

Japan versus China

By the time Hoover left office, there was serious trouble in the Far East as well. The core problem was in China, where Chiang Kai-shek's weak regime was exposed to the growing territorial ambitions of Japan. The Japanese economy was developing at a spectacular rate, and the government looked to nearby northern China for markets and raw materials. Japan's expansionist aims clashed with traditional American rhetoric about the Open Door—that is, equal commercial privileges for all powers in China. But American statesmen in the twenties were optimistic that differences with Japan could be settled peacefully. They won what seemed a great victory for peace and sanity at the Washington Naval Conference in 1921. During World War I, Japan, Britain, and the United States had all launched major shipbuilding programs, hoping to gain naval ascendancy in the Pacific. The Washington conference put an end to the arms race. The nations attending accepted quotas on the total number of battleships in their fleets and agreed to junk some existing ships. The Five Power Treaty fixed the relative naval strength of the United States, Britain, Japan, France, and Italy in the next decade at the ratio of 5:5:3:1.67:1.67. Japanese military leaders complained that it was the equivalent of Rolls Royce: Rolls Royce:Ford, but they were overruled by their government. The inequality had some justification, because the coastlines to be defended in the United States and the remaining colonies of the British Empire were so much greater than those of Japan.

The Washington conference also tried to resolve the delicate problem of the status of China, but with less success. It produced a Nine-Power Treaty that pledged the signatories to respect the sovereignty, independence, and territorial integrity of China. This victory for the Open Door policy was more apparent than real, however. The treaty provided no enforcement mechanism, and it was ambiguous as to whether or not it covered the portion of China on which Japan had particular designs—Manchuria. Subsequent diplomatic exchanges between the United States and Japan revealed a sharp difference of opinion on that point, but neither side pressed for a show-down on the matter. For the rest of the decade, the Japanese paid lip service to the Open Door, and attained the economic influence they sought in Manchuria without open military conquest.

The peace was shattered in 1931, when Japanese troops marched into Manchuria. In the three preceding years, Chiang Kai-shek had been resisting Japanese economic dominance in the region, rich in timber, coal, iron, and grain. He had built a new railroad to compete with the Japanese-owned South Manchurian Railroad, organized boycotts of Japanese products, and subjected Japanese nationals to harassment. These efforts to expel the Japanese from their sphere of influence inflamed Japanese public opinion and strengthened the hand of super-nationalistic elements. Continued cooperation with the western powers, they argued, meant subordination. Discrimination against Orientals in the United States and the British Empire and the inferior naval ratio accorded Japan at the Washington Naval Conference revealed the West's determination to deny Japan her rightful place in the sun. Such were the views of the army leaders who fabricated an incident in Manchuria to use as a pretext for a full-scale invasion. They acted without authorization of the civilian government, which apologized and promised to withdraw the troops. The civilian moderates lost out in the ensuing political struggle, however, and a new regime committed to expansion took power. The army remained in Manchuria, and Japan established the puppet state of Manchukuo there.

The United States condemned the seizure of Manchuria as a violation of the Kellogg–Briand Pact and the Nine-Power Treaty. Secretary of State Stimson announced his Non-Recognition Doctrine—the United States would not recognize the legitimacy of any political changes in China accomplished by force. But America would not go beyond moral condemnation. Stimson himself wanted to threaten to enlarge the U.S. Navy and to impose trade restrictions against Japan, whose economy depended heavily on the United States. President Hoover was unwilling to run the risk, remarking that it would do no more good than "sticking pins in a tiger." If the issue had been put to a popular referendum, the overwhelming majority of the public would undoubtedly have responded as Hoover did. Rhetoric about the Open Door in China was all very well, but few Americans favored a serious rebuff to the Japanese that might have led to a military clash. The moral gesture of non-recognition was much cheaper. But such gestures enrage others without restraining them. Extremists in Japan were not dissuaded by American chiding; instead they drew the lesson that future aggression would bring nothing more than angry words from Washington.

Fear of involvement was no American monopoly during the Manchurian crisis. Although the Japanese aggression clearly contravened the Kellogg–Briand Pact, the Nine-Power Treaty, and the charter of the League of Nations, none of the major powers were willing to undertake forceful action. There was much indignation in the capitals of Europe. Diplomats sent so many protest notes that American humorist Will Rogers remarked that "they have run out of stationery." Every morning, said Rogers, some country fired off a complaining memo to the Japanese, and every morning Japan sent another army to Manchuria. The League of Nations appointed a commission to study the problem, and in February, 1934 its assembly passed a resolution that denied recognition to Manchukuo and called for negotiations between Japan and China. But there were no sanctions to put teeth in it. For Britain and France, the real purpose of the League was to keep Germany in the subordinate place prescribed for it by the Versailles Treaty, not to play policeman in a remote area half-way around the world. When the Japanese refused to abide by the League's request and resigned from the world body instead, Western statesmen refused to consider trade sanctions or other tough measures.

FRANKLIN ROOSEVELT
AND THE QUEST FOR NEUTRALITY

In the early days of his political career, Franklin Roosevelt's views about America's role in the world closely resembled those of his much-admired cousin Theodore. While serving as Wilson's Assistant Secretary of the Navy, FDR called for strengthening the armed forces and denounced the "soft mush about everlasting peace which so many statesmen are handing out to a gullible public." If war was to come, he announced, he would "follow in the steps of T.R. and form a regiment of rough riders." World War I was no place for a troop of rough riders, however, and FDR remained at his desk in Washington. After attending the Paris Peace Conference as an observer, he was increasingly drawn to Wilson's idealistic vision of the American mission to create a new world order. How much his conversion was genuine and how much the result of a political calculation that the public had grown tired of martial rhetoric and become more receptive to appeals for disarmament and world peace is uncertain. In any event, he made the need for American entry into the League of Nations a major issue in his Vice-Presidential race in 1920. If it was a political calculation, it was a bad one—Cox and FDR lost by a landslide (though largely for domestic reasons).

Roosevelt didn't make the same mistake again. While jockeying for the Presidential nomination as Governor of New York, he ducked foreign affairs altogether. Asked by the press for his views on the Manchurian crisis and President Hoover's war debt moratorium, he offered only a "no comment." After his candidacy became official in 1932, complete evasion was no longer possible, and he bent with the prevailing winds. After the powerful isolationist publisher William Randolph Hearst attacked him as an internationalist on the basis of his earlier record, FDR repudiated his support of the League. "The League of Nations today," he claimed, "is not the League conceived by Woodrow Wilson." The reasons he offered to support that assertion were not persuasive, but it was an expedient stance. So too were his reversals on the war debt and tariff issues. In 1928 he had charged that America was "greedy" to insist on full repayment, particularly when it had a "discriminatory and exorbitant tariff policy" that made it "doubly hard" for the European nations to do so. In 1932 Roosevelt berated Europeans for their failure to meet their just obligations to the United States and backed away from his criticism of high tariffs. Once he concluded that an internationalist stance would lose more votes than it would win, Roosevelt was quick to disassociate himself from it.

He kept to that course, with rare exceptions, throughout his first and during much of his second term in office. Alleviating the domestic economic crisis was naturally his first priority. His first inaugural address devoted a bare sentence to foreign affairs, a vague pledge that the United States would follow "the policy of the good neighbor—the neighbor who resolutely respects himself and, because he does so, respects the rights of others." Europe was quickly given cause to wonder about the administration's respect for its rights when Roosevelt refused to support the efforts of the London World Economic Conference to stabilize international currencies. Roosevelt's policy made economic sense, because it freed the United States to manage its own currency in ways that would stimulate recovery and pressured European nations to abandon the gold standard and do the same. But his blunt message torpedoing the conference indicated that America would display little interest in anyone else's problems until its own economic difficulties were eased.

When the Roosevelt administration made at least a small gesture toward international cooperation, it was rebuffed by the isolationists who dominated the halls of Congress. In 1933, the World Disarmament Conference at Geneva was deadlocked because Germany demanded full military parity with other powers and France would not agree in the absence of political guarantees of her future security. Roosevelt sent a representative who tried to break the deadlock by proposing that the United States would meet with other nations when world peace was threatened, and that if one nation was judged the aggressor America would adjust its policies in order to avoid defeating measures of collective security adopted by the others. It was not a full commitment to join in economic sanctions, only a promise not to increase trade to such an extent that such sanctions would be undermined. However, even this limited involvement was too much for Congress. Senate amendments cut out the heart of the authorizing bill, and the measure died. In his first showdown with the isolationists, FDR was forced to beat a retreat.

The Depression decade was a disheartening time for anyone who believed in peace and democracy. In Germany the economic crisis sapped support for the Weimar government and strengthened extremist parties on both the left and the right—the Communists and Adolph Hitler's National Socialists (Nazis). The Nazis, who promised to avenge "the crime of Versailles," purge the country of its "subversive" Jews and Communists, and restore the German "master race" to power and glory, proved the stronger of the two factions. After an election in the summer of 1932, they became the largest single party in the parliament, and in January of 1933 the President of the Republic appointed Hitler as Chancellor. Hitler quickly seized absolute power. Legislative power was transferred to the executive branch of government; opposition parties and trade unions were banned; constitutional rights were suspended by decree; the courts were brought under the control of the Nazi Party; Jews were not only driven out of jobs in the government, the universities, and the professions, but were later subjected to violent terrorist attacks by storm troopers.

Hitler dreamed of becoming the master of Europe, but was cagey enough to proceed one step at a time, keeping his ultimate purpose veiled. For six years, without firing a shot, he won victory after victory at the bargaining table from opponents who believed that appeasement would put an end to his grievances and ensure the peace. But his appetite for power grew with each successive concession. At first Hitler proceeded cautiously, pressing Germany's claims for equal armaments at the World Disarmament Conference. The French refused after FDR's plan to support a collective security agreement was vetoed by the U.S. Senate, and in late 1933 Germany walked out of the conference and resigned from the League of Nations. In March of 1934, Hitler announced that Germany had secretly built an air force—in violation of the treaty of Versailles—and shortly thereafter declared that he would not be bound by any of the treaty's disarmament clauses. In 1935, compulsory military service was introduced; the next year German troops marched into the Rhineland, which had been a demilitarized zone under the treaty. The German army was still too small to prevail if France and Britain had resisted militarily, but they were unwilling to wage war, even one they were bound to win. They merely protested to the League of Nations, which deplored the invasion but voted no sanctions. Instead, the League invited Hitler to propose a new European security system. He obliged with ambiguous generalities and a pledge that he had no territorial ambitions.

Hitler's fellow dictator and ally, Benito Mussolini of Italy, was also on the move, and he too met with little resistance from the Western democracies. Italy had run a poor last in the European race for colonies in the underdeveloped world. The memory of her humiliating defeat by the natives in Ethiopia in 1896 still rankled, and Mussolini sought revenge and imperial glory by invading Ethiopia again in 1935 from the neighboring Italian colonies of Somaliland and Eritrea. The Council of the League of Nations condemned Italy and voted to impose a trade embargo. But conspicuously missing from the list of forbidden items was the one commodity that might have impeded the Italian military drive—oil. Out of fear of war with Italy, Britain and France had vetoed efforts to embargo oil. With planes, tanks, and poison gas, Italy crushed the Ethiopian tribesmen in eight months. The League's sanctions hit an unhappy middle ground; they were strong enough to antagonize Italy, but too weak to deter her.

Germany was Italy's only supporter in the conquest of Ethiopia. As soon as it was accomplished, the two fascist powers found an opportunity for joint action on behalf of another right-wing militarist with dictatorial ambitions—General Francisco Franco of Spain. In July of 1936, Franco led the Spanish army in a revolt to overturn the democratic Republican government; Germany and Italy provided equipment and "volunteers" to assist him. Their aid was decisive, because the Western democracies refused to sell the Republican government the planes and munitions it was entitled to buy under international law. Hoping to stop the Spanish Civil War, Britain and France formed an International Nonintervention Committee of nations pledged to support neither side. On paper, it was an even-handed policy; but in practice, only the democracies abided by it. Germany and Italy, although they were signatories to the nonintervention agreement, contributed $600 million and 65,000 troops to Franco's Fascist rebels. Hitler's Kondor Legion of 400 aircraft used the Spanish Civil War as a testing ground for new planes and tactics. The Republicans got far less help—scant funds and munitions from Russia and Mexico and only 40,000 untrained and ill-equipped civilian volunteers from Europe and the United States. As a result, the Spanish Civil War ended with the complete triumph of Franco's forces in March of 1939.

While Hitler and Mussolini were flexing their muscles in Europe, the Japanese were showing their strength in the Far East. The military leaders who had gained ascendancy during the Manchurian crisis of 1931 remained in power, and they sought to bring all of East Asia into a Japanese-dominated "co-prosperity sphere" once their control over Manchuria was consolidated. At the London Naval Conference of 1935, the Japanese denounced the 5:5:3 naval limitation formula and demanded full parity with America and Britain. When the parity was denied, Japan walked out and proceeded to carry out a major shipbuilding program. In the summer of 1937, the Japanese launched a full-scale military drive into China; by 1938, they controlled most of its eastern half. China appealed to the League of Nations as it had during the invasion of Manchuria, with the same discouraging results. The League found that Japan had violated the Kellogg–Briand pact and recommended that the signers of the Nine-Power Treaty meet to work out a course of action. The ensuing conference in Brussels was a fiasco. The Japanese didn't bother to attend, and the other eight countries could not agree on a single concrete action to aid China or restrain Japan.

The futility of appeasing the demands of expansive totalitarian powers finally became clear to even the most obtuse innocents in the aftermath of the Munich peace conference of 1938. After reoccupying the Rhineland, Hitler announced that his broader aim was to reunite all the German peoples of Central and Eastern Europe in a single state. This provided his rationale for invading Austria in 1938 and annexing it (the *Anschluss*). It was also the pretext for his move against Czechoslovakia, whose Sudetenland region had three and a half million Ger-

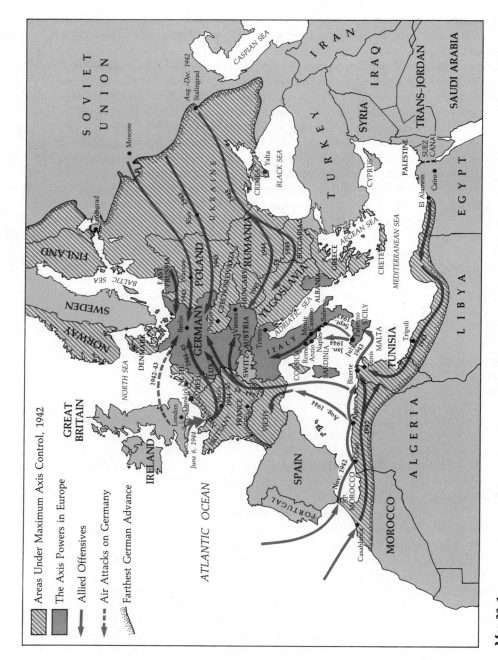

Map 28–1
World War II: Europe and North Africa

Areas Under Maximum Axis Control, 1942

The Axis Powers in Europe

Allied Offensives

Air Attacks on Germany

Farthest German Advance

man-speaking residents. Czechoslovakia was protected by a treaty with France, but France dared not honor its commitment to Czech independence. In a September, 1938 meeting with Hitler in Munich, the French and British prime ministers, Edouard Daladier and Neville Chamberlain, acquiesced to demands that the Sudentenland be given to Germany in exchange for Hitler's promise to seek no further territory. Skillful diplomacy, Chamberlain announced with satisfaction, had assured "peace for our time." Within six months, in March of 1939, Hitler broke his Munich promise and sent the German army in to seize the whole of Czechoslovakia. That was the end to appeasement. Britain and France promptly offered iron-clad guarantees to the next likely target of German aggression—Poland. Hitler, suspecting that they were bluffing and would back down once again, was confident in any event that Germany would win if a full-scale war did break out. In August, Hitler signed a non-aggression pact with Stalin—to ensure that the Soviet Union would not go to war with Germany unless attacked. In September, German tanks sliced through Polish defenses in a lightning attack, and Russian forces invaded from the east. The democracies could not mobilize in time to save Poland, which was swallowed up in less than a month. But Britain and France could no longer delude themselves with visions of "peace in our time." They immediately declared war on Germany, and began to prepare for an all-out struggle. World War II had begun.

American Responses

The Roosevelt administration was naturally dismayed by these repeated acts of aggression by hostile totalitarian powers. But its reactions were cautious and passive. They had to be, given the political climate. It is impossible to overestimate the strength of antiwar sentiment in the United States in the 1930s. The vast majority of Americans—certainly the vast majority of Congressmen—were determined that history would not repeat itself. Few Americans then doubted that U.S. participation in World War I had been a ghastly mistake. Leading historical studies, and the major investigation of World War I munitions-making conducted by the Senate's Nye Committee in 1934–36, conveyed the same disillusioning message as the antiwar fiction of writers such as Ernest Hemingway, John Dos Passos, and e.e. cummings: We had been maneuvered into the war by profit-hungry bankers and arms manufacturers.

Fears of involvement in European affairs were especially strong among certain groups with special ethnic or religious concerns. Several million Americans of German descent remembered the harsh treatment meted out to them during America's previous war against Germany, and believed that American participation then had deprived Germany of her legitimate rights as a great power. Few sympathized with the Nazis, but they had no liking for the authors of the Versailles Treaty either. Irish–Americans, a potent force in the Democratic Party, opposed aid to Britain because it had held Ireland in colonial subjection until 1922 and still controlled Ulster. Italian immigrants and their children saw Mussolini as a great man bringing glory to their mother country. American Catholics were not dismayed at General Franco's assault on the Spanish Republic, because they viewed the Republican government as an enemy of the Church. America's remarkable ethnic and religious diversity meant that taking sides in a European quarrel was bound to antagonize many millions of voters.

As Europe moved toward all-out war, therefore, the United States sought to insulate itself by means of the neutrality acts of 1935, 1936, and 1937. Loans to countries at war, like those given to the Allies during World War I, were banned. To prevent the accumulation of debts that might give Americans a stake in the final outcome, all trade had to be on a cash and carry basis. To ensure that no risk would come to American ships, belligerent vessels had to carry the goods from American ports. American citizens were forbidden to travel on the ships of warring nations so that there could be no more Lusitania incidents to whip up hostility in the United States. In effect, America was renouncing its traditional maritime neutral rights out of the fear that defending them could embroil us in another "unnecessary" war. The most important provision of the neutrality acts was the requirement that the President levy an impartial arms embargo whenever war broke out. This meant that all arms shipments to belligerents would be cut off, regardless of American sympathies and interests. It denied arms to Ethiopia as well as to Italy, to the Spanish Republic as well as to Franco's forces (which were getting all they needed illicitly from Germany and Italy). Although FDR pressed for amendments that would give him greater discretion in deciding when and how to impose trade restrictions, he approved the bills when the amendments were defeated. Out of an overriding fear of war, Congress made war more likely by serving notice that it would make no effort to distinguish between aggressors and the victims of aggression. Hitler, Mussolini, and the Japanese generals found the neutrality acts reassuring evidence that the United States would do nothing to block their designs.

After his reelection in 1936, Roosevelt hinted at the possibility of a more forceful foreign policy to deter aggression. His famous Quarantine speech, delivered in Chicago in October of 1937, warned that "the peace, the freedom, and the security of 90 percent of the population of the world is being jeopardized by the remaining 10 percent," and suggested that a quarantine of the aggressors might be necessary. Under questioning, however, he was unwilling to commit the United States to do anything specific. If Britain and France, whose security was most directly menaced by the spread of fascism, persisted in appeasement, the President of the United States was not in a position to pursue a drastically firmer course. In fact, it took a major lobbying effort by the administration to kill the most extreme isolationist bill ever to come before Congress. The Ludlow Amendment would have altered the Constititution to require a popular referendum before Congress could declare war. This audacious move to strip the President and the Congress of their traditional powers failed by only a few votes, even though FDR used every possible pressure to bring the Congress into line. It was striking evidence of widespread American determination to have peace at any price.

Nor were the people of the United States moved by humanitarian concern over the plight of the hordes of European refugees who sought to escape persecution by totalitarian governments. The restrictive and discriminatory immigration quotas of the 1920s remained in force, and efforts to loosen them attracted little support in

Congress. No one yet understood that Hitler would attempt to physically exterminate the Jewish people—the "final solution" was not ordered until 1941—but the savagery of Nazi anti-Semitism was perfectly plain. After a wave of synagogue burnings across Germany in November 1938, liberals proposed that 20,000 Jewish children under the age of 14 be admitted without regard for the quota. Opinion polls showed that two-thirds of the American public opposed even this small gesture, Roosevelt was unwilling to take a stand, and Congress refused to act. The wife of the U.S. Commissioner of Immigration remarked casually at a cocktail party that the trouble with the measure was that "20,000 children would all too soon grow up into 20,000 ugly adults."

EDGING TOWARD INTERVENTION—1939-41

With the Nazi invasion of Poland in September of 1939, American sentiments went overwhelmingly with the Allies. The insatiability of Hitler's ambition was clear. After Britain and France declared war, a U.S. public opinion poll found 83 percent pulling for the Allies, 16 percent neutral, and only 1 percent actually favoring the Nazis. Despite this sympathy, however, not one American in 20 polled favored a declaration of war against Germany. It took two more years for America to be drawn into the fighting, and then it was by an unexpected route.

When the war broke out in Europe, the neutrality laws required an impartial embargo on the sale of war materials to either side. Roosevelt found this an intolerable restriction in the light of the clearcut Nazi menace and asked Congress to lift it. The transparent purpose was to aid the Allies, but he shrewdly refused to make the case for repeal on that basis. Instead, he said that the arms embargo provision of 1935 had been a mistake, and that returning to "the ancient precepts of the law of nations" and resuming arms sales was the best means of keeping the United States out of war. The logic of the argument was strained, but a carefully orchestrated campaign allowed the measure to carry. It was ostensibly neutral— Germany as well as the Allies was allowed to make cash purchases of war materials and carry them across the ocean on her own ships—but in fact, the ascendancy of the British navy made the trade entirely one-sided. The American public—or at least the politicans who represented it—were willing to tilt that much toward the Allies, but still indulged in the fantasy that the neutrality act was really a step to protect the nation from involvement in the war. The rest of the 1939 neutrality act kept the other provisions of the earlier neutrality bills in force and gave the President power to ban American merchant vessels from specified war zones.

If the war with Germany had gone well for the Allies, America might have been able to preserve its neutrality. But it did not. After the quick German victory in Poland, there followed an interlude of several months in which nothing happened—the period of the "phony war." The three million man French army, generally believed to be the best in Europe, drilled confidently behind the impregnable fortifications of the Maginot Line that it had erected after World War I to prevent another German invasion. Britain rearmed feverishly. Optimists speculated that Germany was a bully who appeared strong only when fighting smaller countries like Poland. That illusion quickly vanished in the spring of 1940: The Germans conquered Denmark and Norway, and bypassed the Maginot Line by knifing through Holland and Belgium into France. The Allies had more fighting men, more tanks, and more artillery, but the Germans had a radically new and superior strategy—the *Blitzkrieg* (lightning war). They were the pioneers of modern tank warfare, using massive concentrations of armor to penetrate deeply behind enemy lines to destroy communications, and deploying airborne troops to seize key points ahead of the advancing Panzer tank divisions. The Allied generals, whose conception of warfare was 20 years out of date, were helpless before the onslaught. In six weeks, France was compelled to surrender. The British expeditionary forces, caught in a shrinking pocket of iron formed by encircling German forces at Dunkirk in Northern France, were nearly annihilated. 350,000 British troops were successfully evacuated only because Hitler impatiently sent his tank corps driving toward Paris, and a streak of bad weather kept Luftwaffe planes from wiping them out. Hitler was now master of Western Europe. Britain stood alone, and it seemed certain that she would either sue for peace or collapse under massive German air attacks. If by some miracle she survived, the British would hardly be in a position to launch a major counterattack. Only 21 miles of the English Channel separated England from a German invasion.

Taking Sides

The astonishing German conquest electrified the United States and transformed public opinion. A German victory over Britain seemed imminent, and that could put the British Navy in German hands and turn the Atlantic into a highway for German penetration of the Western Hemisphere. Congress spent the three months before the fall of France inconclusively debating Roosevelt's request for a slight increase in defense expenditures. As the power of Hitler's war machine became clear, Congress poured money into the defense budget. Total expenditures for 1940 were $12 billion, a fivefold increase. The first peacetime military conscription act in American history was passed, and shipments of war materials to Britain were stepped up as much as the neutrality legislation would permit. The crucial problem, however, was that Germany's wolf packs of U-boats were winning "the battle of the Atlantic," sending a large and growing proportion of merchant vessels bound for Britain to the bottom with torpedos. Winston Churchill—who had become British Prime Minister in May of 1940—had begun an intimate correspondence with FDR as soon as the war broke out and had developed a close personal relationship with him. He begged Roosevelt to provide him with retired U.S. destroyers for use in convoy duty to keep open the Atlantic lifeline. It was "a matter of life and death," Churchill said flatly. Roosevelt agonized over the issue during the summer. Such an action would violate the spirit if not the letter of the neutrality laws, and would amount to an open declaration of American support of England in its war with Germany. But in September, without consulting Congress,

FDR issued an executive order giving Britain 50 old but serviceable American warships in exchange for rights to establish American bases on British possessions in the Western Hemisphere and a British pledge never to surrender its fleet to Germany.

The destroyer deal outraged isolationists and sparked the formation of a new national antiwar organization, the America First Committee. The committee—whose leaders included Charles Lindbergh and General Robert E. Wood, chairman of Sears Roebuck—denied that Hitler imperiled American national interests, and maintained that the United States should keep out of the continuing struggle over the balance of power in Europe. With some justice, the Committee argued that the destroyer deal was an abuse of presidential power and that such a serious new commitment required Congressional approval. And the committee leaders effectively exposed an inconsistency in the administration's stance: If Germany was indeed strong enough to menace American security, they asked, how could American material aid alone be enough to guarantee Britain's survival? A policy of all-out aid short of war was not a viable long-run policy, America Firsters charged, but a step that could only end in full American participation on the side of the Allies.

The America Firsters underestimated the danger that a Nazi-dominated Europe would pose for the United States, but were quite accurate in their assessment that the line between all-out aid and actual participation could not be adhered to for long. However, they were unable to bring the issue before the electorate for a

AN INTERVENTIONIST VIEW, APRIL, 1941

We shall be in deadly danger the moment British sea power fails; the moment the eastern gates of the Atlantic are open to the aggressor; the moment we are compelled to divide our one-ocean Navy between two oceans simultaneously.

The combined Axis fleets outmatch our own: they are superior in numbers to our fleet in every category of vessel, from warships and aricraft-carriers to destroyers and submarines. The combined Axis air strength will be much greater than our own if Hitler strikes in time—and when has he failed to strike in time? The master of Europe will have at his command shipways that can outbuild us, the resources of twenty conquered nations to furnish his materials, the oil of the Middle East to stoke his engines, the slave labor of a continent—bound by no union rules, and not working on a forty-hour week—to turn out his production.

Grant Hitler the gigantic prestige of a victory over Britain, and who can doubt that the first result, on our side of the ocean, would be the prompt appearance of imitation Nazi regimes in a half-dozen Latin-American nations, forced to be on the winning side, begging favors, clamoring for admission to the Axis? What shall we do then? Make war upon these neighbors, send armies to fight in the jungles of Central or South America; run the risk of outraging native sentiment and turning the whole continent against us? Or shall we sit tight while the area of Nazi influence draws ever closer to the Panama Canal, and a spreading checkerboard of Nazi airfields provides ports of call for German planes that may choose to bomb our cities?

—Editorial, *New York Times,* April 24, 1941

clearcut verdict. Roosevelt, running for this third term, was too slippery to admit that his policies were moving the country down the road to war. And his Republican opponent, Wendell Wilkie, had foreign policy views almost indistinguishable from Roosevelt's. Two Midwestern Republican isolationist Senators, Robert Taft of Ohio and Arthur Vandenberg of Michigan, had been candidates for the GOP nomination. If either had been successful, the country might have benefited from a frank and searching debate over the real issue: Was Britain's survival important enough to pursue policies that were bound in time to bring America into the war? The nomination of Wilkie, spokesman of the eastern internationalist wing of the Republican party, kept the key question out of presidential politics. Wilkie favored the destroyer deal (FDR had taken the precaution of clearing it with him before going ahead), military conscription, and full support for Britain. His campaign stressed the economic failings of the New Deal and Roosevelt's breach of the two-term tradition. Only toward the end of the campaign did he take up foreign policy, charging that FDR was insincere in his pledges to avoid war and had made secret arrangements with Britain. With Wilkie surging in opinion polls, Roosevelt abandoned his earlier efforts to suggest that America faced real dangers that would require hard choices, and claimed that his reelection would guarantee peace. "I have said this before, but I shall say it again and again and again," he told a Boston audience the week before the election, "your boys are not going to be sent into any foreign wars." When Wilkie was informed of the statement he sputtered, "That hypocritical son of a bitch! This is going to beat me." Whether FDR's soothing and dishonest pledge really made the difference is debatable, but it undoubtedly helped him pile up his five million vote victory margin.

Lend-Lease and the Battle of the Atlantic

For another year, the United States edged closer to war while refraining from full commitment. Shortly after the election, Roosevelt received an urgent plea from Churchill, who reported Britain's dire need for more American supplies and declared that within months England would have exhausted its financial reserves and would be unable to pay cash for them. That led Roosevelt to take another giant step down the road to war—the lend-lease program. If your neighbor's house was on fire, FDR told Congress, you didn't sell him your hose to put it out. You lent the hose to him and took it back after the fire was out. The United States should do the same with the planes, tanks, and munitions Britain needed to keep afloat. After prolonged debate, Congress passed a $7 billion Lend-Lease Act in March of 1941, guaranteeing Britain access to America's full industrial potential. If the United States was not yet formally wedded to Britain, one observer remarked, lend-lease amounted to at least "a common alliance."

Getting the supplies safely to Britain through submarine-infested waters remained a grave problem. The 50 destroyers provided the previous year were not nearly enough to give adequate protection against a stepped-up U-boat campaign. Roosevelt dared not openly order the U.S. Navy to convoy supply vessels across the ocean and use force against German submarines. That would be an outright act of war. But he moved stealthily to make it possible. He extended America's position far out into the Atlantic by seizing Greenland from Nazi-occupied Denmark in April and occupying Iceland in July. The Navy was secretly instructed to cooperate with the British in the antisubmarine campaign. And when such cooperation provoked conflict with Germany, FDR distorted the facts to stir up anti-German feelings at home. When a German U-boat fired upon the U.S. destroyer *Greer* in September, Roosevelt called it an act of naked aggression that justified him in providing American naval protection for all friendly ships operating in "waters the protection of which is necessary for American defense." The public was not told that the *Greer* had been shadowing the sub for three hours before the attack and advising British planes in the area where to drop depth charges. The submarine commander had turned on his pursuer in self-defense. Roosevelt similarly distorted the circumstances surrounding the German attack on the *Kearney* and the sinking of the *Reuben James* the next month. He failed to report that both ships were engaged in antisubmarine activity; in November he used the incidents to persuade Congress to amend the neutrality legislation to allow the arming of American merchant vessels.

America and Germany were waging undeclared naval warfare in the Pacific by the late fall of 1941, but FDR was careful to leave the United States technically a non-belligerent. He knew that American participation was inevitable, barring a miraculous last-minute reprieve, but felt it essential to delay until he had solid backing from the American public and until the United States had done more to mobilize its forces. The American people were still profoundly ambivalent about what risks they would run to stop Hitler. Roosevelt's problem, as the British ambassador to the United States astutely wrote to Churchill in November of 1941, was to "steer a course between 1) the wish of 70 percent of Americans to keep out of war, and 2) the wish of 70 percent of Americans to do everything to break Hitler, even if it means war."

The Road to Pearl Harbor

The incident that ended American ambivalence and drew the United States fully into the struggle happened not in the Atlantic, but half-way across the globe, at Pearl Harbor, Hawaii on December 7, 1941. Japan's allies, Germany and Italy, promptly proclaimed war against the United States, bringing America into war in Europe and Asia simultaneously. The Japanese attacked in order to break the economic stranglehold the United States had imposed to prevent her from enlarging her Asian empire. Due to the Nazi *Blitzkrieg* in the spring of 1940, the defeated French and Dutch and the tottering British were in no position to defend their colonial possessions in Asia—French Indochina (Vietnam), the Dutch East Indies, British Hong Kong, Singapore, Burma, and India. Only the United States, if she was willing to run the risks that applying sanctions would entail, had the power to deter Japan from moving to add these to her Greater East Asian Co-Prosperity Sphere.

Although there was division within the Roosevelt administration, with Secretary of State Cordell Hull warning repeatedly against measures that might provoke Japan to war against the United States, American policy grew stiffer and stiffer over the 18 months preceding Pearl Harbor. In May of 1940, FDR transferred the permanent base of the Pacific fleet from California to Pearl Harbor. In July, after the installation of a new Japanese cabinet committed to forging stronger ties with Germany and Italy, the administration blocked the shipment of aviation gasoline to Japan; in September the ban was extended to scrap iron. A day later, Japan, Germany, and Italy signed the Tripartite Pact that made Japan a member of the Axis. In subsequent months, the list of commodities forbidden to Japan lengthened. The next summer, after Japanese incursions into Southern Indochina, the United States played its highest trump card. It forbade all exports of oil to Japan (which depended on the U.S. for 80 percent of its needs) and froze Japanese assets in the United States, cutting off all trade. The aim was to bring Japan to its senses and to

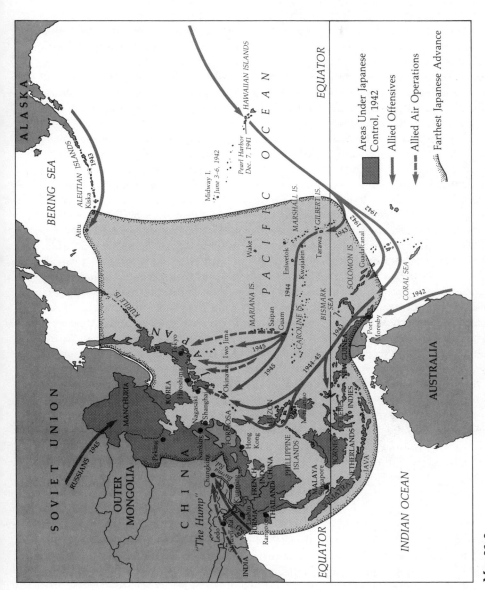

Map 28-2
World War II: The Pacific

Legend:
- Areas Under Japanese Control, 1942
- Allied Offensives
- Allied Air Operations
- Farthest Japanese Advance

accept America's demands—renunciation of further expansion in Asia and withdrawal from China.

With only a year's oil reserve on hand, Japan was faced with a choice of either completely renouncing the objectives that had been central to its foreign policy for a decade or going to war to conquer other lands with the resources it needed, such as the oil and rubber of the East Indies. Because expansion anywhere would meet with armed resistance from the United States, the Japanese military daringly decided upon a surprise attack upon American bases in Hawaii and the Philippines. Although their own intelligence estimates showed that the war potential of the United States was seven to eight times larger than Japan's, they gambled that a sudden knockout blow against the Pacific Fleet would stun the United States into making a peace that recognized Japanese hegemony in Asia.

American forces at Pearl Harbor were caught completely by surprise—battleships were anchored close together and planes were parked wing-to-wing, as though for the convenience of Japanese bombardiers. Why the attack was so unexpected has occasioned considerable historical debate. American intelligence officers had cracked the top secret Japanese diplomatic code, and deciphered messages which, in retrospect, seem to reveal precisely what would happen. The old theory that FDR knew of the Japanese plan and failed to order an alert to ensure that American losses would be great enough to win support for American entry into the war is now discredited. At least in part, America was unprepared for the attack due to the fact that a great many confusing and contradictory signals about Japanese plans were coming in the weeks before December 7; the United States lacked an agency capable of sifting the wheat from the chaff and communicating the important kernels with dispatch. American over-confidence and a degree of racist condescension toward Orientals also played a part. That little Japan would dare attack the mighty United States was hard to credit. One popular American belief was that the typical Japanese was too near-sighted to fly a plane. Such stereotypes may help to explain why American officials badly underestimated Japanese military capabilities. U.S. intelligence figures for Japanese plane production in late 1941 were 50 percent too low. Moreover, the range, speed, and maneuverability of the superb Zero fighter—the finest carrier-based plane of the day—and the training of Japanese pilots had been severely underestimated. Pearl Harbor was a painful educational experience.

The Course of Battle

America's entry into World War II was one of the two great turning points of the war, for it committed the world's strongest economy to defense of the Allies and defeat of the Axis powers. The other great turning point, we can see in retrospect, occurred six months earlier, in June of 1941, when Hitler invaded Russia and pulled the Soviet Union into the conflict on the Allied side. The attack on Russia, Hitler's greatest blunder, involved Germany in war on the Eastern Front before it had closed the door to war on the Western Front by delivering a knockout punch to Britain. It created a great vise that would close and crush the German army.

The non-aggression pact Hitler and Stalin had concluded in August of 1939 had removed the only remaining obstacle keeping Hitler from driving eastward—fear of war with the USSR. Stalin provided the necessary assurances; while German tanks had smashed into western Poland, the Russian army had seized the eastern third of the country. At the same time, the Soviet Union took control of the small Baltic states of Estonia, Latvia, Lithuania, and a slice of western Rumania, and demanded part of Finland to make her borders more defensible. The Finns put up startlingly stiff resistance in the Winter War of 1939–40, but in the end they had to give up the territory in question and sue for peace.

Had the German–Russian partnership been maintained, the outcome of World War II might have been different. Hitler had utter contempt for Slavic peoples and always intended to attack Russia one day. But his rash decision to go ahead in 1941 probably stemmed from his frustration over Germany's failure to wipe out the Royal Air Force in the Battle of Britain the previous summer, thereby making an invasion of the island impossible. He deluded himself into thinking that assaulting the Soviet Union would somehow help defeat Britain. The Nazis attacked with 150 divisions, the largest invading force in history, catching Russia completely by surprise. At first they sliced through the Russian lines like butter, advancing as much as fifty miles a day. By the end of November, they had penetrated 700 miles along a front 2,000 miles wide. They had Leningrad under siege and were fighting in the suburbs of Moscow. But in early December, at almost the same moment the Japanese attacked Pearl Harbor, the German forces were repelled from Moscow and forced to pull back for the winter. With the lend-lease equipment sent by Roosevelt when Hitler attacked, the Soviet Union offered enough resistance to avoid complete defeat and won the time to regroup while the brutal Russian winter made further fighting impossible. With the two previously uncommitted great powers—Russia and America—in the fray on the same side by the end of 1941, the global struggle took on an entirely new configuration.

Strategic Priorities

Had Americans been given a chance to vote on the matter, they would have given higher priority to the war with Japan than to the war with Germany. The treacherous nature of the Japanese "stab in the back" at Pearl Harbor and traditional hostilities toward Orientals both supported that inclination. But popular anti-Japanese feeling did not dictate American war strategy. Even before the United States entered the fighting, Roosevelt had promised Churchill to follow a "Europe first" policy. Germany was, after all, the greater military power, and the collapse of British and Russian resistance in Europe seemed far more dangerous than any gains the Japanese could make in the Pacific. Top military priority would be given to preparations for an American and British invasion of the continent to force the withdrawal of German troops from the Eastern Front and relieve pressure on the Soviet Union. In the opening years of the war, then, the American military effort in the Far East was essentially a holding action, designed to check or at least slow Japan's advance until the tide had turned in Europe. Meanwhile, the United

States sought to channel its productive might into producing the war materials needed by Britain and Russia, and to building up its armed forces to assist Europe first and then to deal with the Japanese.

Planes and guns, tanks and trucks soon poured from America's factories, much more rapidly and in much larger volume than the most optimistic planners had ever dreamed—almost 300,000 airplanes and over two and a half million machine guns, for example, by the war's end. Without this productive miracle, Russia and Britain could not have staved off defeat. The Soviet Union alone received more than $11 billion worth of supplies.

Until the Allied invasion of Normandy in June of 1944, America's main contribution to the European war took the form of material rather than manpower. British and American bombers flew through curtains of flak to pound targets in Nazi-occupied cities, but the much bloodier burden of the war on the ground was carried by the Russians. On the Eastern Front, the German and Red armies clashed in a series of enormous and savage battles. In the battle of Stalingrad, alone, in the spring of 1943, the Soviet victory was won at the price of casualties outnumbering all those suffered by U.S. forces in the whole of World War II! Hitler was able to throw the full weight of his forces into these duels because the United States and Britain failed to deliver on their pledge to launch a cross-channel invasion to reopen the Western Front. There were reasons for the delay—shortages of men and supplies, and British fears that losses would be intolerably high until Germany could be softened up by strategic bombing and ground attacks upon less well-defended peripheral areas like North Africa and Sicily. The failure to open up a second front across the English Channel, however, fed Stalin's suspicions that his allies preferred to stand aside while Russia and Germany bled each other to death, and increased his determination to win post-war settlement terms that would provide iron-clad guarantees of Soviet security.

The Red Army finally managed to beat back the last German offensive on the Eastern Front in the summer of 1943. It then rolled forward, driving the Nazis first out of Russia and then out of Eastern Europe altogether. The British and American invasion of Sicily in June, of Italy in September, and of France in June of 1944 helped make the Soviet advance possible because it forced Germany to transfer troops from the East to the West. The allied armies pressed the Germans back toward their own frontier. In December of 1944 a surprise German counter-offensive in Belgium nearly succeeded. But the Battle of the Bulge ended in German defeat—at a cost of the heaviest American casualties of the war (77,000)—and the allied drive for Berlin resumed. The vise around Germany tightened inexorably. In May of 1945, Berlin fell, Hitler committed suicide, and the Nazi regime toppled.

Japan and the A-Bomb

By then American military planners were worrying about how to force Japan to surrender without paying the enormous price in lives that an invasion of the islands would require. Despite the "Europe first" strategy, the United States quickly developed enough military power not only to blunt Japan's expansionist drive, but to launch counterattacks as well. Major naval victories at Midway and the Coral Sea in the summer of 1942 were followed by the successful invasion of Guadalcanal from Australia that fall. That marked the beginning of an "island-hopping" offensive designed to win positions close enough to serve as launching pads for a full-scale invasion of the Japanese mainland. The prospect was grim, because in battles like those at Guadalcanal, Iwo Jima, and Okinawa the Japanese had clearly been determined to fight to the last man. Another dismaying sign of their will to resist was their use of *kamikaze* tactics. Running short of experienced pilots, Japan gave men flying training of only a week and put them in the air. They didn't know how to land a plane safely, but that didn't matter, because they had the suicidal mission of crashing into American ships with a load of explosives. If the Japanese continued to show the same spirit, American intelligence estimated that an invasion would cost from half a million to a million American casualties and at least as many Japanese losses.

These frightful casualties were averted by America's discovery and use of a terrible new weapon, the atomic bomb. Scientists had advised FDR of the possibility of making nuclear weapons as early as October, 1939, but a crash program to build them was not begun until 1942. The Manhattan Project was a joint American and British effort, with $2 billion in funds and over half a million employees. The Russians, although officially allied, were not informed of the project, a clear indication of FDR's doubts as to the future course of U.S.–Soviet relations. The great fireball that arose over the desert at the Alamogordo, New Mexico testing grounds on July 16, 1945 represented a quantum jump in man's destructive powers. The decision as to how this superbomb should be used fell to Harry S. Truman, elevated to the presidency by FDR's death in April. Truman made the decision with little hesitation. At his orders, on August 6 some 80,000 people in the Japanese city of Hiroshima were incinerated; a second second attack on Nagasaki three days later killed at least 40,000 more. Upon hearing the news from Hiroshima, the elated Truman made the extraordinary remark that "this is the greatest day in history." A few days later, the Japanese government sued for peace.

Few historians today would agree that it was "the greatest day in history," and many question whether the atomic destruction at Hiroshima and Nagasaki was necessary. Some argue that Japan was closer to surrendering than American intelligence estimates allowed in 1945, and might have done so without the slaughter of so many innocent civilians. The chief obstacle to peace by then was America's insistence that the Japanese depose the Emperor, their most cherished symbol of national unity. If proof of the incredible destructive power of the atom bomb was needed, it has been suggested, a demonstration explosion in some unpopulated area would have been persuasive enough.

There is some force in these arguments. The raid on Nagasaki before the Japanese government could digest the lesson of Hiroshima was certainly trigger-happy and a crime against humanity. It was unwise to make removal of the emperor a condition for negotiation. Truman's statement after Hiroshima displayed striking insensitivity to what it would mean for mankind to live in the nuclear age. On the other hand, no one can say for certain how near to surrender Japan was in early August, and American planners did not have access to the

A SURVIVOR OF HIROSHIMA

The five of us, leaving our burning house behind us, hurried straight in the direction of Koi. We were already surrounded by a sea of fire. The streets were blocked with the fire and smoke of the ruined houses; and blazing telephone poles fallen across our path plunged us any number of times into the depths of despair. I don't know whether the people who lived there had already fled; at any rate there was no one in sight, and only once in a while we heard a moaning voice like that of a wild beast coming from out of nowhere. I had the feeling that all the human beings on the face of the earth had been killed off, and only the five of us were left behind in an uncanny world of the dead, and I had to shudder. As we passed the Nakajima School and came to Sumiyoshi Bridge, I saw several people plunging their heads into a half-broken water tank and drinking the water. I was very thirsty too, and I was so happy to see some people again that without thinking I left my parents' side and went toward them. When I was close enough to see inside the tank I said "Oh!" out loud and instinctively drew back. What I had seen in the tank were the faces of monsters reflected from the water dyed red with blood. They had clung to the side of the tank and plunged their heads in to drink and there in that position they had died. From their burned and tattered middy blouses I could tell that they were high school girls, but there was not a hair left on their heads; the broken skin of their burned faces was stained bright red with blood. I could hardly believe that these were human faces. As we came out to the main street and crossed Sumiyoshi Bridge, for the first time we met some living people of this world. No, rather than humans of this world it might be more correct to say we met humans of that other world, of Hell. They were all stark naked, their skin was rust-colored with burns and blood, their whole bodies were swollen like balloons....

—Arata Osada, *Children of the A-bomb,* 1959

documents later critical historians used to reach their verdict. Moreover, the military planners had a pertinent and painful recent experience with a similar prediction—their earlier optimistic intelligence estimates that Germany would collapse in the fall of 1944 had been off by several months. The idea of a demonstration explosion that risked no lives was debated, but ruled out as too risky. The United States only had two bombs on hand, and the mechanism for detonating them in the air had not been tested. A demonstration experiment with a bomb that turned out to be a dud would have been disastrous, a key scientist advised, adding, "and this was a very real possibility." If ending the war as quickly as possible with as little loss of American life was given absolute priority, the bombing of Hiroshima (but *not* the attack of Nagasaki) was defensible.

Critics of Truman's decision have emphasized the moral argument that the atom bomb destroyed innocent civilians rather than combatants. This is true, but the traditional distinction between soldier and civilians had been wiped out well before Hiroshima: The Nazis exterminated many millions of citizens in Europe, and the British and later the Americans disregarded the civilian–soldier distinction when they sent their heavy bombers over German and Japanese cities. The official policy of the American Air Force was to strike at precise military and industrial targets and to avoid direct attacks on population centers. But by the late stages of the war, American B-17s and B-29s were indiscriminately dropping loads of incendiary bombs over large enemy cities, hoping to undermine civilian morale and bring about societal collapse. The largest of these raids—the fire bombings of Hamburg, Dresden, and Tokyo—killed about as many people as died at Hiroshima. In 1945, crowded Japanese cities were being hit with the equivalent of one atomic bomb in TNT every two or three days. The average area destroyed in no less than 93 conventional attacks on Japanese cities was as large as that obliterated in Nagasaki; a March 1945 assault on Tokyo wiped out an area three times the size of Hiroshima. It is hard to see why it was any less moral to achieve similar effects instantly with a weapon that exposed fewer airmen to anti-aircraft fire.

Some historians have maintained that the decision to use the bomb was taken not so much to knock Japan out of the war as to intimidate the Soviet Union into following America's wishes. This view rests on the assumptions that Japan would have collapsed anyway at any moment *and* that the United States knew it with reasonable certainty—very doubtful propositions. It certainly is true, however, that the administration believed that in destroying Hiroshima and Nagasaki they were sending a message to the Russians. With the war in Europe over, the United States and the Soviet Union were increasingly at odds over political arrangements in Eastern Europe. Both sides were denouncing each other over the interpretation of vaguely worded wartime agreements between Roosevelt, Stalin, and Churchill. A monopoly on an inconceivably powerful new weapon, Truman and his advisers thought, would give the United States more leverage in the struggle with the Soviet Union over the shape of the postwar world. The bomb, said the Secretary of War Henry L. Stimson, was "a badly needed equalizer" in that contest, and it emboldened Truman to "get tough with the Russians." The results, as we shall see in the next chapter, were disappointing. Atomic diplomacy produced no concessions from Stalin; it merely strengthened his determination to put Eastern Europe under Soviet domination and to develop his own arsenal of nuclear weapons.

ON THE HOME FRONT

Some 400,000 Americans died in World War II, leaving behind grieving widows, parents, and friends. Most other Americans, however, had a surprisingly good time during the war years. The war accomplished what all the efforts of the New Deal planners did not; it brought sudden and complete economic recovery. In 1939, Secretary of Commerce Harry Hopkins, brooding over the appalling 17 percent unemployment rate, warned, "This country cannot continue as a democracy with ten million unemployed. It just can't be done." That grave and stubborn problem vanished as the defense industry sucked up the surplus labor pool left at the end of the Depression decade. Real war was the war on poverty that worked.

The economy surged forward at a phenomenal pace. The GNP per capita soared from $573 in 1940 to almost double that, $1,074, in 1945. Wartime inflation was partly responsible; but even allowing for that, real wages jumped 44 percent in four years. Of course there were some shortages. No new cars were available because Detroit's factories were producing planes, tanks, and jeeps. Gasoline, coffee, beef, sugar, and a few other commodities were rationed. But it was astonishing that America's factories and farms poured out enough goods to equip the 16 million men in our armed forces, and to supply much of the military needs of Britain and Russia as well, without deep cuts in production for domestic consumption. Instead, the standard of living at home improved considerably. No painful tradeoff between guns and butter was necessary. The economy generated an ample supply of both.

The principle cause of the wartime boom was the powerful stimulus to growth provided by massive deficit spending by the federal government. The deficits were the result of wartime necessity, not of the administration's conversion to Keynesian economics. During the war, defense needs required a tenfold increase in the federal budget, which reached $95 billion by 1945. Although the administration paid for as much of the war as was possible by increasing taxes sharply and by selling war bonds to the public, a gap that averaged $30 billion per year remained. It was just the shot in the arm the ailing economy needed. The continuing deficits later in the war, after full employment had been reached, overstimulated the economy and produced inflation. The price rise was not dramatic, however—only 28 percent between 1940 and 1945, a much lower inflation rate than in the closing years of the 1970s. The National War Labor Board, a joint union–business–government commission, held the line on wage increases, and the Office of Price Administration (OPA) was fairly successful in restraining wholesale and retail prices.

The virtual elimination of unemployment was a boon to the very poor, who had been hardest hit by the Depression. During the war, the distribution of income became modestly but significantly more equal, the only such shift in this century. In 1941, the least affluent 40 percent of Americans earned only 13.6 percent of all income before taxes; by 1946, the share had risen to 16.1 percent. The fraction of total income going to the most prosperous 20 percent fell from 48.8 to 46.1 percent. The drop was steeper still for the wealthiest 5 percent—from 26.5 percent to 20.7 percent. (These figures have remained essentially unchanged over the third of a century since the end of World War II.) Figures on income shares *after* taxes are regrettably unavailable, but they undoubtedly would show a somewhat greater shift toward equality. The graduated tax rate on high incomes was raised sharply during the war. Most of the burden of financing the war, however, fell on middle and lower income earners, because the minimum income taxed was lowered and rates were increased in all brackets. Roosevelt asked Congress for a tax that would have "soaked the rich," a 100 percent levy on all incomes over $25,000 per year, but Congressional conservatives rejected the proposal.

The acute labor shortage added to the bargaining power of labor, and the War Labor Board viewed the union cause sympathetically. The AFL and CIO consequently made great gains, with total union membership climbing from less than 9 million to over 15 million. Judged by the number of strikes and strikers, the war years were as turbulent as the late 1930s, but that measure obscures an important difference. The wartime strikes were spontaneous outbursts that were quickly settled and had no appreciable effect on production. The 1943 bituminous coal walkout, in which John L. Lewis and his men defied Roosevelt and public opinion to win a settlement making them the nation's highest paid industrial workers, was an exception. It was a costly exception for the labor movement in general, because it provoked Congress to limit the freedom to strike by passing the Smith–Connally War Labor Disputes Act. The measure required a 30-day cooling off period before a strike in a war industry, and set a precedent for other anti-union legislation that would come in the wake of the war.

Women and Blacks

The departure of 16 million men from the civilian labor force forced desperate employers to reexamine traditional sexual and racial stereotypes. It was necessary to employ "Rosie the Riveter" if that was the only way the ship could get built on schedule. The number of women workers climbed from 13 million to 19 million, many of them in what had always been "men's jobs." "Meet MRS. Casey Jones," declared a railroad job advertisement. "Casey's gone to war, so Mrs. Jones is out where 'man-size' jobs have to be done: in the round house, in the shops, in the yards." Even that ancient male bastion, the Army, gave in. Women were accepted for noncombatant service in 1942, and a quarter million enlisted before the war was over. The assumption that marriage and a career were utterly incompatible was undermined; three-quarters of the new female workers were married, and a third had children under the age of 14. The principle of equal pay for equal work won significant support from the War Labor Board, although enforcement was spotty. Many of these wartime employees chose to abandon their jobs after the war and others were laid off when war plants were shut down and reconverted. But the basic trend set in motion by the war was not reversed. Traditional ideas about "woman's place" regained their force in the popular culture of postwar America, but the much publicized "retreat into the home" didn't happen. The 1950 Census showed more women, and more married women, working than ever before, as has each decennial census since then.

The war wrought major changes in the lives of Blacks as well. The Great Migration from the South to the North had been interrupted during the stagnant thirties, but now it resumed on an even larger scale. Having suffered the most from unemployment during the Depression, Blacks now gained the most from the very tight labor market created by the defense boom. The acute labor shortage forced a lowering of discriminatory barriers imposed by employers and trade unions.

Traditional racist beliefs, already under attack by leading social scientists, were discredited by their association with Nazi theories of the supremacy of the Aryan race. The black press could now effectively denounce "race discrimination and segregation, mob brutality—the entire Nazi pattern of U.S. racial conditions." The black community displayed growing confidence and self-assertiveness. Membership in the NAACP soared from 50,000 to 500,000, and a newly founded interracial group, the Committee on Racial Equality (CORE) began to experiment with non-violent direct action tactics to overcome segregation. In 1941, A. Philip Randolph, leader of the Brotherhood of Sleeping Car Porters, won a major concession from the federal government by threatening a great black protest march on Washington to secure fair treatment of black workers in defense industries. To avert it, Roosevelt agreed to create a temporary federal Fair Employment Practices Commission, the first major step on behalf of black rights taken by an president since the end of Reconstruction.

The pattern of race relations in the armed services changed dramatically. The hundreds of Blacks who served were most often assigned to segregated units, and were frequently assigned to menial tasks away from the front line—the military equivalent of the "Negro jobs" to which they had been confined before the war. But they made important advances. Blacks were admitted to the Air Force and the Marine Corps for the first time, and the Army partially integrated its officer training schools and some of its combat units. The new mood of the black fighting man was displayed by a young first lieutenant named Jackie Robinson, who refused to take a seat at the rear of a segregated bus in a southern military camp. He was court-martialled and won his case, showing the cool courage he needed to endure the racial insults and the beanballs thrown at him when he became the first Black to play major league baseball in 1947. Such veterans returned to civilian life with new expectations and a new determination to fight for their rights.

The Plight of the Japanese-Americans

Although the war helped to break down some traditional racial and sexual barriers, it had profoundly negative consequences for one of America's racial minorities—the Japanese. The long tradition of anti-Oriental prejudice on the West Coast, where Oriental immigrants were concentrated, came to an ugly climax after Pearl Harbor. Rage at the sneaky nature of the Japanese attack blended with fear of Japanese disloyalty. Rumor (completely unfounded) had it that Japanese workers in Hawaii had cut great arrows in the sugar cane fields to guide the bombers to their targets. Could they be trusted in the event of an attack on the mainland? Neither the FBI nor the military intelligence agencies uncovered a whit of evidence of disloyal behavior in the Japanese-American community, but that did not allay the suspicion and hatred. California's Attorney General, Earl Warren, later a renowned champion of civil liberties as Chief Justice of the U.S. Supreme Court, described the Japanese menace with Alice-in-Wonderland logic. Many people, he said, were "of the opinion that because we have had no sabotage none has been planned for us. But I take the view that that is the most ominous sign in the whole situation." Newspapers, politicians, and patriotic associations clamored for action. A right-wing columnist declared that the "Japanese in California should be under guard to the last man and woman right now and to hell with *habeas corpus.*"

Shamefully, that is just what happened. In February, 1942 Roosevelt issued an extraordinary executive order that authorized the military to remove all "dangerous persons" from designated coastal areas and to confine them behind barbed wire in "relocation centers" for the duration of the war. As defined in the order, "dangerous" was not a matter of prior conduct or belief but of blood. It meant all persons of as little as one-sixteenth Japanese ancestry.[1] The result was that some 112,000 Americans of Japanese descent, two-thirds of them native-born American citizens, were driven from their homes and confined to barracks in the deserts of the Southwest. The Supreme Court cravenly upheld the internment policy on the grounds of military necessity, and denied that it abridged basic rights guaranteed in the Constitution. A later decision, when the war was winding down, forced a closing of the camps on a technicality, but left unchallenged the ominous precedent that the federal government may incarcerate an entire ethnic group without benefit of trial if it can claim some military justification.

World War II did not revive the intense nativist fears that provoked the "100 percent Americanism" drive of the First World War. Wagnerian operas continued to be performed, the German language was still taught, sauerkraut was not transformed into "liberty cabbage." Immigrants and their descendants from European homelands with which the United States was at war had a far easier time of it than had their brethren a generation earlier. Assimilation had proceeded to the point at which the loyalty of European ethnics could be taken for granted. But the increased tolerance did not extend to members of a small, politically powerless, unassimilated racial minority that had the misfortune to have ties with a belligerent power. The plight of interned Japanese was not comparable to that of the Jews in Nazi concentration camps. But it was a chilling demonstration of the arbitrary power of the modern state, even in a country with a written Constitution designed to guarantee basic liberties to all its citizens.

SUGGESTED READINGS

American foreign policy in the 1920s is examined in L. Ethan Ellis, *Republican Foreign Policy, 1921–1933* (1968), Joan Hoff Wilson, *American Business and Foreign Policy, 1920–1933* (1971), and Michael J. Hogan, *Informal Entente: The Private Structure of Cooperation in Anglo-American Economic Diplomacy, 1918–1928* (1977). Robert H. Ferrell, *American Diplomacy in the Great Depression: Hoover-Stimson Foreign Policy, 1929–1933* (1957) reviews the early Depression years. Elting Morison, *Turmoil and Tradition: A Study of the Life and Times of Henry L. Stimson* (1960) sheds much light on the entire period covered in this chapter.

---

[1] This definition of who was to be classified Japanese and hence dangerous was even more racist than the typical southern state's definition of a Negro as someone with at least one black great-grandparent. Having one Japanese great-great-grandparent was enough to call one's loyalty to the country into question.

John W. Wilz, *From Isolation to War, 1931–1941* (1968) and Arnold A. Offner, *The Origins of the Second World War: American Foreign Policy and World Politics, 1917–1941* (1975) are brief and lucid overviews. James MacGregor Burns, *Roosevelt: The Soldier of Freedom* (1970) and Robert E. Dallek, *Franklin D. Roosevelt and American Foreign Policy, 1932–1945* (1979) appraise Roosevelt's leadership. The strength of the isolationist impulse is clear from Manfred Jonas, *Isolationism in America, 1935–1941* (1969) and Arnold Offner, *American Appeasement: United States Foreign Policy and Germany, 1933–1938* (1969). On the crucial decisions of 1939–41, see William L. Langer and S. Everett Gleason, *The Challenge to Isolation, 1937–1940* (1952) and *The Undeclared War, 1940–1941* (1953), Bruce M. Russett, *No Clear and Present Danger: A Skeptical View of the U.S. Entry into World War II* (1972), Wayne Cole, *Charles A. Lindbergh and the Battle Against American Intervention in World War II* (1974), Charles Neu, *The Troubled Encounter: The United States and Japan* (1975), Joseph P. Lash, *Roosevelt and Churchill, 1939–1941* (1976), Robert A. Divine, *The Reluctant Belligerent: American Entry into World War II* (2nd ed., 1979), and Thomas A. Bailey and Paul B. Ryan, *Hitler vs. Roosevelt* (1979).

Roberta Wohlstetter, *Pearl Harbor: Warning and Decision* (1962) and Dorothy Borg and Shumpei Okomoto, eds., *Pearl Harbor as History* (1973) consider the controversy over Pearl Harbor. A. Russell Buchanan, *The United States and World War II* (2 vols., 1964) is a detailed account of the military struggle. America's wartime relations with other powers are treated in Gaddis Smith, *American Diplomacy during the Second World War, 1941–1945* (1965). Akira Iriye, *Power and Culture: The Japanese–American War, 1941–1945* (1981) makes illuminating comparisons between the two cultures. Plans for the shape of the postwar world are analyzed in Robert A. Divine, *Second Chance: The Triumph of Internationalism in America during World War II* (1967), and Michael Sherry, *Preparing for the Next War: American Plans for Postwar Defense, 1941–1945* (1977). For the debate over the decision to drop the A-bomb, see Herbert Feis, *The Atomic Bomb and the End of World War II* (1966) and Martin J. Sherwin, *A World Destroyed: The Atomic Bomb and the Grand Alliance* (1975).

Richard Polenberg, *War and Society: The United States 1941–1945* (1972), Geoffrey Perrett, *Days of Sadness, Years of Triumph: The American People, 1939–1945* (1973), and John Morton Blum, *V Was For Victory: Politics and American Culture during World War II* (1976) consider the impact of the war on American society and culture. On changes in the role of women, see Chester W. Gregory, *Women in Defense Work during World War II* (1974), Leila J. Rupp, *Mobilizing Women for War: German and American Propaganda, 1939–1945* (1978), and Karen Anderson, *Wartime Women: Sex Roles, Family Relations, and the Status of Women during World War II* (1980). For changes in race relations, see A. Russell Buchanan, *Black Americans in World War II* (1977). Roger Daniels, *Concentration Camps U.S.A.: Japanese Americans and World War II* (1971) and Michi Weglyn, *Years of Infamy: The Untold Story of America's Concentration Camps* (1976) describe the internment of Japanese–Americans.

Chapter Twenty-Nine

Affluence and Anxiety

World War II was an immense triumph for the United States at an astonishingly low cost. No country in history ever emerged from a major war in better shape. America lost little more than 400,000 men; the Soviet Union lost over 20 million, Germany almost 8 million, not counting the 6 million German and East European Jews slaughtered in death camps. When hostilities ceased, the United States was by far the strongest military power in the world—and the only one with nuclear weapons. It was by far the richest as well. In 1947, the United States held 6 percent of the world's population but produced 50 percent of its manufactures, 62 percent of its oil, 57 percent of its steel, and over 80 percent of its automobiles. The average American earned an income about fifteen times that of the average foreigner. Such economic and military superiority was a dangerously heady brew. It produced an intoxicating superconfident belief that nothing was beyond the power of the United States—that America had not only a mission to be the policeman of the world, but the ability to carry it out. In 1941, Henry Luce, the publisher of *Time, Life,* and *Fortune,* had proclaimed the beginning of the "American Century," in which "the most vital and powerful nation in the world" would act "for such purposes as we see fit and by such means as we see fit." By the war's end, that vision seemed much less fanciful than it had at its beginning. It was an unfortunate illusion, Americans would discover painfully.

Emblems of ecological awareness, the smokestacks of the Long Island Lighting Company stand out in sharp relief against the sky over Northpoint, Long Island.

COLD WAR AND CONTAINMENT

Russia—America's ally in what Franklin Roosevelt called a struggle between "the forces of justice and righteousness" and "the forces of savagery and barbarism"—had suffered a terrible pounding from Hitler's forces on the Eastern Front while Britain and the United States cautiously planned the invasion at Normandy. But the gunsmoke had hardly settled before the United States was in another global struggle, this time against its former partner. Again "justice and righteousness" were on one side, and "savagery and barbarism" on the other. But this time Russia was the barbarian, while both Germany and Japan were part of the forces of righteousness. It was "the free world" against "the slave world," democracy versus international Communism, in a contest that extended to every corner of the globe. The struggle came to be known as the Cold War, a somewhat euphemistic label for a rivalry that eventually led to tens of thousand of deaths in Korea and hundreds of thousands in Vietnam.

Why did the Cold War begin? Could it have been avoided? Was Russia or the United States primarily to blame? Most histories of the Soviet–American relations produced in the United States while the Cold War was at its height defended American policy, portraying it as a necessary response to Soviet aggression. More recently a number of younger "revisionist" historians have argued that Russia was more flexible and accommodating than the United States, and that what appeared to be aggressive moves on Russia's part were defensive measures in response to American efforts to create a worldwide empire.

Neither view does full justice to the complexities of the problem. No one can speak with any certainty on the matter, since western historians have never been given access to Kremlin records that would disclose Soviet motives. It is clear, however, that a good deal of tension and hostility between the United States and the Soviet Union was inevitable, given the differences between the interests and values of the two nations and the power vacuum in the world that followed the collapse of the Axis powers. Russia was indeed aggressive and expansionist. But it was moved by genuine security needs, and America reacted impatiently and insensitively to those needs. Fear of Communism, pride in the country's overwhelming economic and military power, and a righteous sense of the superiority of the American way of life led the United States to attempt to impose its will in every corner of the globe, to build what could indeed be fairly termed a world empire of sorts.

So long as they faced the common enemy of Nazi Germany, Russia and the United States were able to negotiate their differences successfully. They did it by agreeing to postpone the central issue—the character of the regimes that would rule Germany and Eastern Europe in the future. Serious conflict was bound to erupt once the fighting had stopped, however. The United States was committed to the restoration of independent nation states in East Europe. Its economic and political reasons for supporting the Wilsonian principle of self-determination were both idealistic and pragmatic. It hoped to establish profitable trade with those countries, and the American population included millions of immigrants who worried about the fate of their former homelands.

The Soviet Union sought security from external attack. Invading armies had swept through Eastern Europe and penetrated deeply into Russia three times in little more than a century—during the Napoleonic wars, World War I, and World War II. The Russians were determined to see that it never happened again. If Poland, Hungary, Bulgaria, Rumania, and the other small nations of the area were allowed true self-determination, there was every likelihood that their governments would be as hostile to the Soviet Union as they had been in the interwar years. If Germany too were left free to regain her commanding strength, these lesser powers might again fall into the German orbit and Russia would again be in peril. Soviet security and self-determination for Eastern Europe were tragically incompatible goals.

While the war against Germany continued, neither the American nor the Russian government chose to recognize the incompatibility. At the November, 1943, meeting of Roosevelt, Stalin, and Churchill in Teheran, Iran, the problem was glossed over. The second conference of the Big Three, at Yalta, Russia in February of 1945, did little more to resolve the issue. The Soviet government accepted a vague Declaration on Liberated Europe that promised free elections and governments "broadly representative of all democratic elements in the population" of East European nations, and the United States was content. The declaration did not define "free elections" or "democratic elements" or specify any enforcement mechanism. Because the Red Army was by then occupying almost all of East Europe, Stalin probably assumed that he would be free to conduct Soviet-style "free elections" that would return suitably pro-Russian regimes.

Roosevelt's critics soon charged that the Yalta agreement displayed his naiveté about Soviet intentions, that he had been duped into "selling out" Eastern Europe to the Communists. But Roosevelt surely grasped the essential point: The area was not America's to sell. The Red Army was there, and the capacity of the United States to influence future developments there was distinctly limited. FDR believed that the possibility of a peaceful, postwar world depended on American–Soviet cooperation, and that it was essential not to provoke the USSR unnecessarily. He hoped that he could induce Stalin to behave with some restraint in installing "friendly governments," but cannot have thought that they would be truly independent.

If Roosevelt indeed understood the power realities of the situation, he did nothing to inform the American public of their unpleasant implications. Fear of alienating a key element of the New Deal coalition—the masses of Polish, Czech, Hungarian, and other Eastern European ethnic voters—led the administration to insist that the Declaration on Liberated Europe would ensure genuine self-determination for those nations. The disappointment of those unrealistic expectations did much to feed Cold War hysteria in the United States.

Enter Harry S. Truman

Roosevelt died within a few weeks of Yalta, in May of 1945. His successor, Harry S. Truman, had little knowledge of foreign affairs, no experience in dealing with Stalin, and a distinctly combative temperament. He preferred the stick to the carrot, and told his advisors that if the Russians did not become more cooperative they could "go to hell." After a meeting with the Soviet foreign minister, he boasted, "I gave him a straight 'one-two' to the jaw." The mounting tension between the United States and the USSR that developed thereafter, however, was not primarily due to the change in American leadership. Even if Roosevelt had lived, the real differences in the objectives of the two nations would have surfaced when the need to unite against a common foe disappeared.

From the American point of view, the Russians were showing a callous disregard for their Yalta pledge to respect the right of self-determination for the peoples of Eastern Europe. Although the pattern varied somewhat from country to country, it was evident that to secure "friendly governments" the Russians were prepared to jail or shoot anti-Communist elements of the population and to establish puppet police states. They were doing the same thing in the portion of Germany occupied by the Red Army—what became East Germany. They were also insisting on such massive reparations payment from Germany as a whole that the United States feared economic chaos and an eventual Communist revolution would be the result. And when Russia dominated both Eastern Europe and Germany, there would be little to protect Western Europe from the same fate. France and Italy already had strong Communist parties that could provide entry points. After a costly struggle against a dictator with unlimited ambitions, who had violated agreement after agreement, American officials were quick to conclude that they now faced the same challenge from another quarter. As the distinguished journalist Walter Lippman remarked, a generation of American leaders "overlearned the lesson of Munich." In retrospect, it appears that the specter of a Soviet conquest of Western Europe was a delusion. The USSR did not have the economic and military strength to take over all of Europe, and Stalin displayed little interest in fomenting revolution there. But in the context of the time, with memories of Hitler still fresh, it was not a wildly unreasonable fear.

From the Soviet point of view, America appeared to be the aggressor. Russia had done the bulk of the fighting against Germany and had suffered appalling casualties. One American out of 450 died in the war; for the USSR, the figure was more than one in ten. Now the United States was denouncing and threatening Russia for actions designed to secure its borders from another invasion from the West. And America was doing more than talking. After the German surrender, the Truman administration promptly cut off all lend-lease aid and refused to grant the Soviet Union a major loan for postwar economic reconstruction without unacceptable political strings. In the absence of such a loan, the Russians felt they needed substantial reparations from Germany, but the United States resisted that too. Emboldened by her monopoly of nuclear weapons, America seemed determined to reshape the entire world in its own image and to impose a *Pax Americana* everywhere.

Convinced that it was under economic attack, the Soviet Union wiped out the last vestiges of independence in Eastern Europe, completing the process with the overthrow of the democratic government of Czechoslovakia in 1948. It imposed an "Iron Curtain" to seal off contact between East and West, to ensure that citizens ruled by puppet governments were exposed to no ideas but the party line. One annoying hole remained in the Iron Curtain: West Berlin was reserved for American occupying forces by wartime agreement, although it lay 200 miles within the Soviet zone of Germany. In 1948, the Russians attempted to close the hole by blocking ground transport through East Germany to Berlin. Only the airlift of massive amounts of supplies in American planes allowed the city to survive the year until the blockade was lifted.

Although both the United States and the Soviet Union were charter members of the United Nations, the new world peace-keeping organization, hope that the UN could be an instrument of accommodation was soon frustrated. The Russians viewed the UN, not without some justification, an as instrument of American domination. They rejected an American proposal for United Nations control of nuclear energy with the right to inspect all countries to prevent the secret building of atomic weapons. The Baruch Plan, as it was called, would have preserved America's nuclear monopoly until an international agency was established, and would have forced the Soviet Union to halt its atomic research. Besides, outside scrutiny of the USSR, with its concentration camps filled with political prisoners, was unacceptable to Stalin. Instead, Russia accelerated its efforts to build the bomb, and succeeded in 1949.

Containment

While the Russians consolidated their control over Eastern Europe and worked feverishly to break America's nuclear monopoly, the United States launched a crusade to counter Soviet expansion and to achieve a commanding position in the world. The announced aim of American foreign policy in these years was "containment" of Russia. The basic conception, however, was more dynamic and aggressive than that phrase suggests. To George F. Kennan, the State Department's leading Soviet expert, the first task was to contain the Russians by "the adroit and vigilant application of counterforce," but the larger aim was to exert enough pressure to roll back the Soviet sphere of influence and bring down the Communist regime.

One element of the containment strategy was economic assistance to European countries whose economies had been ravaged by the war. Without rapid recovery, it was feared, popular discontent might result in revolutionary upheavals that would produce even more Communist regimes. The Marshall Plan pumped $12 billion in aid to Western Europe from 1947 to 1950 and lifted its economy out of the doldrums, substantially benefiting American business at the same time. In 1950, the principle was extended to the less-developed countries of Asia, Africa, and Latin America through the Point Four technical assistance program. The sums involved were considerable smaller, however, and the effects correspondingly less impressive.

The corollary of containment was military force. The United States constructed a worldwide network of military alliances and a ring of naval and air bases around the Soviet Union. During the Cold War, an average of a million American soldiers were deployed on 4,000 bases in no fewer than 30 countries. The rationale for that awesome commitment was the Truman Doctrine of March 1947. The government of Greece, with aid from Great Britain, had been waging a civil war against an insurgent guerrilla movement. When the critical state of Britain's economy forced her to suspend aid, the Truman administration decided to intervene. In a dramatic speech to Congress, the President called for intervention on the grounds that it was America's duty to "support free people who are resisting attempted subjugation by armed minorities or by outside pressures." Totalitarian regimes "imposed on free peoples, by direct or indirect aggression," he warned, "undermine the foundations of international peace and hence the security of the United States."

The amount of military aid that Truman requested and Congress provided for Greece was modest, and it seemingly had the desired effect—the rebellion was suppressed. But, in fact, American aid made less of a difference than the decision of neighboring Yugoslavia to deny the rebels a sanctuary any longer. The coincidence fostered the unfortunate delusion that American money could easily buy desired political outcomes in other parts of the world. Furthermore, Truman's rationale for intervention was dangerously grandiose. Assistance to Greece could have been defended on such narrow pragmatic grounds as America's interest in assuring a friendly government in a country bordering the oil-rich Middle East. But Truman followed the urging of the key Republican foreign policy spokesman, Senator Arthur Vandenberg, who advised him that to win Congressional support he had to "scare hell out of the country." That he did, by defining the issue as nothing less than a great global struggle between freedom and slavery, and by charging the United States with the duty of being policeman for the world, responsible for intervening wherever "free peoples" were menaced by "aggression," even "indirect aggression," (whatever that meant).

Truman's message was a lurid and regrettably oversimplified interpretation of the issues at stake in the Greek civil war, an expression of a rigid "Cold War mentality" that later embroiled the United States in serious difficulties in other parts of the world. Supporting the repressive, right-wing oligarchy that ruled Greece was not a defense of "freedom" as most Americans understood the term. This U.S. intervention marked the beginning of the sanctimonious debasement of the language in which the United States called all pro-American regimes, however dictatorial, "free." Portraying the rebellion as an example of Soviet aggression was stretching the truth considerably. The guerrilla movement had deep indigenous roots in Greece, and the external aid it did receive came not from Stalin's Russia but from Marshal Tito's Yugoslavia, which had strained relations with the USSR and would break out of the Soviet bloc altogether within a year. Truman, however, glossed over these complexities and simplistically attributed all revolutionary ferment to a monolithic conspiracy directed from Moscow. This equation remained the cornerstone of American foreign policy for a long time to come.

However, in 1947, few American doubted the assumptions embodied in the Truman Doctrine. Although it was formulated by a Democratic chief executive, it was endorsed by a Republican-controlled Congress, and subsequently adhered to by Republican and Democratic administrations alike. The two parties naturally quarreled over the details of foreign policy, particularly in election years, but from 1947 there was an unchallenged bipartisan consensus on basics. Congress ceased to play the role of critic that it had performed in the debate over the Versailles Treaty and the neutrality legislation of the 1930s, and followed the lead of the President and military leaders. As Truman's Secretary of State, Dean Acheson, candidly remarked later:

> Bipartisan foreign policy is the ideal for the executive, because you cannot run this damn country under the Constitution any other way except by fixing the whole organization so it doesn't work the way it is supposed to work. Now the way to do that is to say that politics stops at the seaboard—anyone who denies that postulate is a son of a bitch and a crook and not a true patriot. Now if people will swallow that then you're off to the races.

The public and the Congress did swallow it for twenty years.

SOCIAL AND ECONOMIC TRENDS

The joy that Americans felt on V-J day, August 14, 1945, was not unmixed with anxiety. The wartime economy had soaked up the millions of unemployed people like a giant sponge, and had miraculously provided both guns and butter. Per capita incomes, in constant dollars, had grown by a third between 1939 and 1945. But anyone old enough to recall the cruel Depression decade had reason to wonder if yet another great crash might be on the horizon. It had been the war rather than the New Deal that had cured the last depression. A *Fortune* magazine poll revealed that 58 percent of the nation's businessmen expected another major depression.

Those fears proved unfounded. Instead of slumping, the economy continued to surge forward, with only minor interruptions, over the next fifteen years. The United States was becoming what economist John Kenneth Galbraith called *The Affluent Society* (1958), one in which virtually everyone was assured of at least a subsistence income, and in which the majority had a degree of choice over spending that had been previously confined to a small minority in the upper income brackets. Economists estimate that "discretionary incomes"—that is, money that can be used to satisfy *wants* rather than *needs*—begins at about the $7,000 mark (in 1972 dollars) for a family of average size. By that standard, less than a quarter of all the households in the nation had any discretionary income at all at the close of the Great Depression; but in 1960, some 59 percent did. It is revealing that the Metropolitan Life Insurance Company estimated that 48 million Americans, one in four, were overweight. One striking symptom of the new affluence was the phenomenal spread of television. There were only ten thousand sets in the United States in 1947; a decade later there were forty million!

Prosperity fed renewed confidence in the future, as the completely unanticipated postwar Baby Boom indicated. In 1936, the birth rate—which had been declining for more than a century—fell for the first time below the replacement level, the level at which 1,000 women would replace themselves with another 1,000 women of child-bearing age in the next generation.[1] Experts predicted that the population of the United States would soon level off at about 140 million. They were far off the mark. The 1960 census counted almost 180 million. Part of the cause was a modest rise in immigration from abroad, but the chief reason was that American mothers were raising larger broods of children. In 1936, the fertility rate was 2.1; in 1957, the peak year of the Baby Boom, it reached 3.7, and then fell gradually until it sank below the 1936 low point in 1972. Couples in the Depression generation were apprehensive about bringing children into a world in which they might not find jobs. Parents of the postwar generation did not have the same scarcity mentality.

The combination of fatter paychecks and larger families fueled an enormous postwar construction boom in areas close to but not within the boundaries of large cities—that is, in suburbs. The proportion of Americans living in metropolitan areas increased from 51 to 63 percent between 1940 and 1960, but almost none of that growth was in the central cities. It was in the peripheral suburban areas, where Levittowns and similar tract developments sprang up. Only 25 million people, one in five, lived in a suburb in 1940. By 1960, the figure was almost 60 million, one in three. Suburbia had become the new frontier.

In recent years, the shift of population from central cities to suburbs (which still continues) has been described as "white flight," attributed to white fears of rising crime rates and court-enforced racial integration of the schools. Such factors may induce some to move, but the suburban drift long preceded these developments

---

[1]The replacement figure is about 2.2 children, since a bit less than half of all newborns are female and since some of them will be sterile.

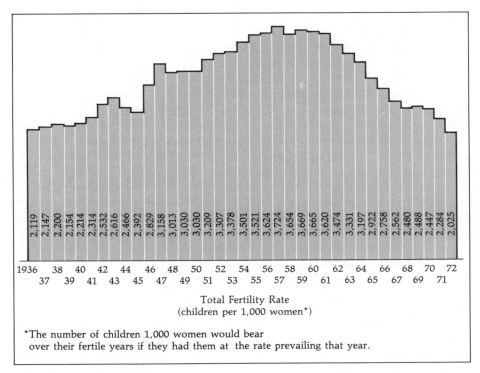

The bars are labeled with the following values from left to right:

2,119 | 2,147 | 2,200 | 2,154 | 2,214 | 2,314 | 2,532 | 2,616 | 2,466 | 2,392 | 2,829 | 3,158 | 3,013 | 3,030 | 3,030 | 3,209 | 3,307 | 3,378 | 3,501 | 3,521 | 3,624 | 3,724 | 3,654 | 3,669 | 3,665 | 3,620 | 3,474 | 3,331 | 3,197 | 2,922 | 2,758 | 2,562 | 2,480 | 2,488 | 2,447 | 2,284 | 2,025

1936 37 38 39 40 41 42 43 44 45 46 47 48 49 50 51 52 53 54 55 56 57 58 59 60 61 62 63 64 65 66 67 68 69 70 71 72

Total Fertility Rate
(children per 1,000 women*)

*The number of children 1,000 women would bear
over their fertile years if they had them at the rate prevailing that year.

FIGURE 29–1   The Baby Boom

and had deeper roots. It was largely the simple result of rising incomes, which allowed growing numbers of families to satisfy their desire for a home of their own in a quieter, cleaner, less cramped environment than most central cities could provide. The suburbs offered these advantages at a reasonable price, both because land values were so much lower and because government policy subsidized suburbanites in a variety of ways. Government funds built the high-speed highways that made it possible to commute long distances to work; the $26-billion federal highway program launched in 1956 was the biggest public works expenditure in American history. Guaranteeing home mortgages at low rates through the Federal Housing Authority and the Veteran's Administration—and allowing income tax deductions for mortgage interest payments—were other boons to suburban dwellers. With such encouragement, the proportion of Americans who owned their own homes soared from only 9 in 20 to almost 13 in 20 between 1940 and 1960, the highest since the Census Bureau had begun to ask the question in 1890.

Many of the new suburbanites found jobs in the rapidly growing white-collar occupations, as professional and technical workers, managers and administrators, or clerical workers. Shifts in the occupational structure increased the number of positions within large bureaucratic organizations—private corporations, governments, universities, hospitals—which required technical knowledge and specialized skills. The utilization of scientific and technical knowledge, more than anything else, brought the affluent society into being. Thus the fantastic growth of the electronics industry, which moved from forty-ninth to fifth place among the nation's industries between 1937 and 1958.

The growing importance of knowledge required a vast expansion of the society's primary institutions for advancing and transmitting knowledge. School expenditures rose from little more than $3 billion in 1940 to almost $25 billion in 1960. Only 42 percent of the 1930 fifth graders completed the twelfth grade, and 15 percent went on to college. More than six in ten (62 percent) of the 1952 fifth graders obtained high school diplomas, and a third of them attended college. Many of them who could never have financed their higher education were able to do so because of the G.I. Bill (1944), a measure almost as creative as the Homestead Act. It gave the 16 million men and women who had done military service the right to $500 a year in tuition and $75 a month for personal expenses at a college or trade school. Almost half of those eligible—7.8 million—seized the opportunity.

Although millions of people left the central cities for suburbia in the postwar years, the cities did not lose population. The places of new suburbanites were taken by newcomers, most of them from rural America. The farm population of the United States remained surprisingly constant in numbers in the 1920s and 1930s, at about 30 million (although it was a shrinking fraction of the total because the total was growing). After 1940, flight from the farm occurred on a massive scale. By 1960, over 16 million people had left the countryside, the largest such exodus in American history. The root causes were mechanization of production and depressed farm prices for much of the period, which together squeezed out marginal farms. Moreover, better-paying jobs were opening up in industry.

Many of those displaced from the land were southern blacks, who moved to northern cities. At the close of the Great Depression, a majority (51 percent) of the nation's blacks still lived in rural areas, almost all of them in the South. By 1960, the figure had fallen to little more than a fourth (27 percent). The number of Afro-Americans living outside the South jumped from 3 million to 7 million, a Second Great Migration three times as large as the one that occurred during World War I and the 1920s. As a result, the black presence was felt in the nation at large as never before, and the issue of civil rights took on a new urgency.

Important shifts in the role of women were taking place as well. Legend has it that the period of the Baby Boom and the growth of suburbia was the heyday of "the happy housewife," scathingly portrayed in Betty Friedan's best-selling *The Feminine Mystique* (1963). There was much merit in Friedan's assault on the constricting sexual stereotypes of the day, but she failed to see that a growing number of American women of her generation had been breaking out of the traditional mold. The best indicator was the increased involvement of married women in the labor market. A 1936 Gallup poll found that 82 percent of Americans believed that it was wrong for a woman to work if her husband was employed. In 1940 only 15 percent of married females held a job. That figure rose to 22 percent in 1944, and then fell slightly; "Rosie the Riveter" went back home when the men returned home. But only briefly. The proportion of working wives climbed steadily throughout the late forties and the fifties. By 1960 it stood at 31 percent, double the

THE PRESIDENT'S COMMISSION ON CIVIL RIGHTS CONDEMNS SEGREGATION, 1947

The separate but equal doctrine has failed in three important respects. First, it is inconsistent with the fundamental equalitarianism of the American way of life in that it marks groups with the brand of inferior status. Secondly, where it has been followed, the results have been separate and unequal facilities for minority peoples. Finally, it has kept people apart despite incontrovertible evidence that an environment favorable to civil rights is fostered whenever groups are permitted to live and work together. There is no adequate defense of segregation.... We believe that federal funds, supplied by taxpayers all over the nation, must not be used to support or perpetuate the pattern of segregation in education, public housing, public health services, or other public services and facilities.... A federal Fair Employment Practice Act prohibiting discrimination in private employment should provide both educational machinery and legal sanctions for enforcement purposes.

—President's Commission on Civil Rights;
To Secure These Rights, 1947

prewar rate. The proportion of employed women with children of preschool age tripled in those years. Well before there was an organized women's movement to attack it, the traditional notion that woman's proper place was in the home was slowly but surely losing its hold.

THE TRUMAN ADMINISTRATION

At the close of the war, President Truman asked Congress to adopt a series of liberal domestic measures, including an increased minimum wage, more generous unemployment and social security payments, national health insurance, and federal aid to education. He devoted very little effort to the job of seeing his "Fair Deal" enacted, however. Perhaps it was a hopeless task, because Congress had been controlled by a coalition of Republicans and conservative southern Democrats since 1938. The 1946 elections made the prospects of further reform even dimmer, as the Republicans carried both houses of Congress for the first time since 1928. They capitalized on an antiunion mood that was sweeping the country as a result of major strikes in the steel, coal, automobile, electrical equipment, and railroad industries. The 1947 Taft–Hartley Act, passed over Truman's veto, imposed new controls over unions and authorized the President to postpone strikes for an 80-day "cooling off" period. It was hardly a "slave labor act," as union leaders called it. It remains on the books today, and few workers feel enslaved. But it did represent a retreat from the 1935 Wagner Act, and marked an end to positive federal encouragement of union organizing.

Federal protection of the civil rights of black people became a major issue during the Truman administration. The movement of hundreds of thousands of blacks to northern cities where they were free to vote, made the Democratic party more responsive to their demands for equal treatment. Although far from radical, Truman condemned lynching and the denial of the franchise in the South, asked that the temporary wartime Fair Employment Commission be made permanent, and appointed the first federal Civil Rights Commission to investigate racial abuses and recommend remedies. In 1948, he issued an order that eliminated segregation in the armed services.

A number of circumstances converged to give momentum to the civil rights drive. The ideological struggle against Nazi racism weakened American racism. Cold War rivalries played a part; to continue to treat blacks as second-class citizens, it was argued, undermined the nation's claim to leadership in a world with many dark skinned peoples and gave ammunition to America's Communist rivals. The confidence, assertiveness, and political know-how of blacks themselves had increased as a result of the war. Many had better jobs and rising expectations. Those who did military duty in World War II had many bitter experiences, but they had been treated better than their brethren in earlier wars. Blacks were admitted into the Air Force and the Marines for the first time. The Army integrated its officer training schools, and at least a few of its combat units. Jim Crow practices were still prevalent, but they were coming under increasing attack.

At the outset of the 1948 campaign, the polls showing Truman running far behind the Republican nominee, Governor Thomas E. Dewey of New York. Truman won an amazing upset victory, however, thanks to Dewey's lackluster stumping performance and his own success at persuading the electorate that his opponent planned to "turn the clock back" and "do a hatchet job on the New Deal." Although the voters returned a Democratic Congress, power still lay with the old Republican–southern Democrat coalition, and Truman had no more luck in winning support for Fair Deal measures. Before his term was out, he found himself hopelessly on the defensive before charges that his administration was corrupt and "soft on Communism."

The Second Red Scare

The roots of the Second Red Scare lay in Truman's plan to win aid for Greece by "scaring the hell out of the American people." His crusading declarations on the menace of world communism helped to create the climate of fear that made it possible. In 1947, stung by right-wing charges that his administration was riddled with Communists and "fellow travelers," Truman set up loyalty boards to investigate all 2.5 million federal employees. He authorized them to discharge not only current Communist party members but any whose *past* political affiliations or sympathies made them seem "bad security risks." More than 2,000 people were fired or forced to resign, some for no greater crime than having expressed views some bureaucrat thought unconventional.

Rigorous through Truman's loyalty program was, it did not put the issue to rest. Disquieting developments both abroad and at home over the next few years raised fears of Communism to a fever pitch. In 1948, the Communist coup in Czechoslovakia revealed that a conspiratorial minority could overturn a stable democracy. In 1949, Russia exploded its first nuclear weapon, much sooner than American intelligence had predicted that it could. The same year, Mao Tse-tung's Red Army conquered China and forced Premier Chiang Kai-shek to flee to the island of Formosa (Taiwan). The next year, Communist North Korea invaded South Korea, starting a war that engaged almost six million American troops in a United Nations "police action."

While these events were transpiring, Congressional investigators were uncovering evidence—or seeming evidence—that Communists in high places were plotting to subvert the American government. In 1948, a former editor of *Time* with a history of mental instability, Whittaker Chambers, appeared before the House Committee on Un-American Activities to claim that during the 1930s he had been an underground Communist who had passed along classified documents to Soviet spies. He had obtained the material, he testified, from Alger Hiss, a fellow Communist who worked for the State Department. Hiss, then the President of the prestigious Carnegie Endowment of International Peace, denied all of Chambers' story, and was prosecuted for perjury (the statute of limitation for espionage charges had long run out). Historians are still debating over whether it was Hiss or Chambers who was lying; the most recent and thorough study concludes that it was probably Hiss. The jury, in any event, believed Chambers, and convicted Hiss in 1950. The jailing of a prominent New Dealer, a former clerk to Supreme Court Justice Oliver Wendell Holmes, whose distinguished character witnesses included Secretary of State Dean Acheson and Illinois Governor Adlai Stevenson, made many Americans wonder how many more Hisses there were to uncover. The Hiss case also showed the political capital there was to be reaped by exploiting the issue of Communism. One obscure member of the House Un-American Activities Committee, freshman Congressman Richard M. Nixon of California, used it as a springboard to leap into a Senate seat in 1950 and into the vice-presidency two years later.

Hiss's alleged crime had occurred more than a decade before, and the information involved was of a fairly trivial character. The atom-spy case that broke a month after his conviction was another matter altogether. In February 1950 the British government arrested the physicist Klaus Fuchs, who while working on the American atom bomb project at Los Alamos, New Mexico during the war, had transmitted secrets to Russian agents. Shortly after, the FBI accused David Greenglass, a technician also employed at Los Alamos, and his sister and brother-in-law, Ethel and Julius Rosenberg, of being Fuchs's accomplices.

At their trial, Greenglass confessed to espionage and was given a prison sentence. The Rosenbergs insisted that they were innocent, were sentenced to death, and were executed in 1953. Although there were many weaknesses in the case for the prosecution, there was much damaging evidence, which the Rosenbergs refused to answer by pleading protection from self-incrimination under the Fifth Amendment. It is probable that they had attempted to pass along information to the Soviets, at a time when the United States and Russia were allied in a common struggle against Hitler. But if they were spies, they were quite ineffective; the prosecutors were unable to establish that they had gleaned any secrets of real scientific value. The judge who sent them to the electric chair, however, claimed that they had surrendered "the competitive advantage held by the United States in super-weapons," and "undoubtedly" had "altered the course of history to the disadvantage of our country."

So menacing did the subversive threat seem to some that right-wing columnist Walter Winchell actually suggested that all American Communists be shot. Congress did not go that far, but it did pass the Internal Security Act of 1950, which rode roughshod over the freedom of speech and association. (It required Communists and Communist-dominated organizations to register with the government.) Truman's Attorney General, J.H. McGrath, spoke as if the country were honeycombed with traitors. Communists, he warned, "are everywhere—in factories, offices, butcher stores, on street corners, in private businesses. And each carries in himself the germ of death for society."

In this setting, the most spectacular demagogue of the era—Senator Joseph McCarthy of Wisconsin—rose to notoriety. McCarthy first won headlines in February of 1950 by claiming that he had in his hand a list of 205 Communists employed in the U.S. Department of State. In later speeches, he was cavalier about both the precise numbers and their precise crimes—referring variously to 205 "bad risks," 57 "card-carrying Communists," and 81 "subversives." He was a ruthless opportunist who never exposed a genuine party member, but used his chairmanship of a Senate committee and his capacity to grab headlines to smear the reputation of hundreds of innocent people. A Senate committee investigating his charges eventually concluded that they were "a fraud and a hoax," but McCarthy continued to make allegations of disloyalty in high places, and many Americans believed him. When the chairman of that committee ran for re-election to the Senate, McCarthy helped to engineer his defeat by circulating a faked photograph showing the man in friendly conversation with a Communist party leader. Even such militantly anti-Communist cold warriors as Secretary of State Dean Acheson and Secretary of Defense George Marshall, McCarthy claimed, were part of a "great conspiracy," aimed at weakening the United States and strengthening the Soviet Union. He had the doubtful distinction of adding a new word to the language. "McCarthyism" is "the political practice of publicizing accusations of disloyalty or subversion with insufficient regard for evidence."

Bogged Down in Korea

After North Korea invaded South Korea in June 1950, Truman sent American troops to conduct a "police action" under the cover of UN authorization. Korea was of no strategic importance, and had earlier in the year been declared outside America's "defensive perimeter" by the Secretary of State, the Joint Chiefs of Staff,

REPORT OF A SENATE COMMITTEE
INVESTIGATING SENATOR MCCARTHY'S CHARGES, 1950

At a time when American blood is again being shed to preserve our dream of freedom, we are constrained fearlessly and frankly to call the charges, and the methods employed to give them ostensible validity, what they truly are: A fraud and a hoax perpetrated on the Senate of the United States and the American people. They represent perhaps the most nefarious campaign of half-truths and untruth in the history of this Republic. For the first time in our history, we have seen the totalitarian technique of the "big lie" employed on a sustained basis. The result has been to confuse and divide the American people, at a time when they should be strong in their unity, to a degree far beyond the hopes of the Communists themselves whose stock in trade is confusion and division. In such a disillusioning setting, we appreciate as never before our Bill of Rights, a free press, and the heritage of freedom that has made this Nation great.

—Tydings Committee Report

and Far Eastern commander General Douglas MacArthur. But Truman viewed the attack as another step toward fulfillment of the Communist master plan for world domination. Whatever the difficulties of fighting an Asian land war half way around the world, the lesson of Munich was that the appetite of aggressors only grows with eating. At first American forces were on the defensive, but a brilliant surprise assault behind enemy lines in September sent the invading forces staggering back north of the 38th parallel boundary. Although Mao Tse-tung warned that China would not permit the conquest of its neighbor and ally, the prospect of "liberating" North Korea by force was too tempting to resist. General MacArthur persuaded Truman that the Chinese would never dare fight the United States. He was wrong. The American army fought its way almost to the Chinese border, the Yalu River. But then hordes of Chinese troops swept it back into South Korea. After that, battles see-sawed back and forth, with neither side able to make a breakthrough.

McArthur wanted to break the stalemate by bombing China, blockading its seacoast, and supporting Chiang Kai-shek in an invasion from Formosa. The President and the Joint Chiefs were unwilling to take the risk, and decided instead to fight a "limited war" carefully confined to Korea itself, even though a decisive victory might not be attainable on that basis. Invading the North and provoking Chinese intervention had been a disastrous miscalculation. Increasing the pressure on China might have proven even more disastrous by prompting retaliation from the Soviet Union. The Soviet air force could have struck at American bases in Japan and Okinawa, for example, and submarines and planes could have attacked U.S.

PRESIDENT TRUMAN'S PERCEPTION OF THE ISSUE AT STAKE IN THE KOREAN WAR

In my generation, this was not the first occasion when the strong had attacked the weak. I recalled some earlier instances: Manchuria, Ethiopia, Austria. I remembered how each time that the democracies failed to act it had encouraged the aggressors to keep going ahead. Communism was acting in Korea just as Hitler, Mussolini, and the Japanese had acted ten, fifteen, and twenty years earlier. I felt certain that if South Korea was allowed to fall Communist leaders would be emboldened to override nations closer to our own shores. If the Communists were permitted to force their way into the Republic of Korea without opposition from the free world, no small nation would have the courage to resist threats and aggression by stronger Communist neighbors. If this was allowed to go unchallenged it would mean a third world war, just as similar incidents had brought on the second world war.

—Harry S. Truman, *Memoirs*, 1955

warships operating in Korean waters. The resulting damage would have forced consideration of even more provocative countermeasures, such as bombing targets within Russia. Once this deadly cycle of challenge and response was set in motion, there would be no certainty that it could be stopped at a point short of a nuclear war that would devastate both countries.

Fighting a limited war under these circumstances was prudent, but difficult to justify to the American public. Having recently waged a total war and won a total victory over the Axis powers, and having been told by their leaders that Communism was an equally aggressive and dangerous foe, Americans found it difficult to see why the United States should be fighting in Korea with one hand tied behind its back. Lengthening casualty lists without advances on the battlefield, fears that the administration was "soft on Communism," and scandals involving some of Truman's close friends gave the Republicans powerful arguments in the 1952 campaign. In addition, they had an almost unbeatable candidate in war hero Dwight D. Eisenhower, who had been Supreme Allied Commander during World War II. Eisenhower was undoubtedly the most popular man in America at the time, possibly the most popular American of the century. "Ike" was not a polished, elegant orator like Adlai Stevenson, his Democratic opponent. Reporters covering him on the campaign trail groaned, "He's crossing the 39th platitude again." But his engaging grin and folksy manner were far more appealing to the ordinary voter. His hometown—Abeline, Kansas—lay at almost the exact geographical center of the United States, and he seemed the very embodiment of "the middle way." He was an extremely shrewd politician who managed to appear a statesman and not a politician at all.

Eisenhower hammered away at the corruption issue, and promised to "clean up the mess in Washington." He pledged that he would bring the Korean War to "an early and honorable end," and would go to Korea himself to see that peace was achieved if elected. He left it to his running mate, Richard Nixon, and other Republicans to work the issue of Communism for all it was worth. Nixon repeatedly attacked Stevenson as "Adlai the appeaser," a "Ph.D. graduate of Dean Acheson's cowardly college of Communist containment." Joseph McCarthy was fond of referring to Stevenson as "Alger" rather than "Adlai" and then "correcting" himself. Eisenhower took the high road in the campaign, without sacrificing the political benefits to be gained by denouncing the New Deal and Fair Deal years as "twenty years of treason" by the "Commicrat Party of Betrayal." It was a successful strategy. In November, he swept to victory by a 55–45 margin. Stevenson carried only nine states, seven of them in the "solid South."

THE EISENHOWER YEARS

Eisenhower did travel to Korea the month after his election, and the peace negotiations were brought to a successful conclusion in July 1953. It is not clear why the North Koreans and Chinese finally agreed to come to terms. Perhaps they responded to Eisenhower's veiled threats to escalate the war. But the change may have had more to do with the death of Joseph Stalin and his replacement by younger Russian leaders more receptive to "peaceful coexistence." Peace in any event was won.

It was preserved during Eisenhower's two terms in office, although the air was filled with the rhetoric of "rollback" and the threat of dangerous confrontations with the Soviet Union over the "captive nations" of Eastern Europe. The United States waged a fierce propaganda war with instruments like Radio Free Europe, urging revolt by the peoples behind the Iron Curtain. When actual revolts occurred, however—in East Germany in 1953, and in Hungary and Poland in 1956—America stood by helplessly while the Soviet army moved in to crush the rebels. To have provided support for the "freedom fighters" would have risked nuclear war, and the administration shied at that possibility. Although the United States refused to verbally acknowledge that Eastern Europe had for the foreseeable future been drawn into the Soviet "sphere of influence," its actions admitted the reality.

In this respect and others, Eisenhower's foreign policy resembled that of the Truman administration more than it differed. Eisenhower rushed ahead to complete the worldwide chain of military bases ringing the USSR and China that Truman had begun. Through a series of military pacts like the Southeast Asia Treaty Organization (SEATO), the administration sustained the commitment of the Truman Doctrine to support "free peoples threatened by direct or indirect aggression." Eisenhower sent the marines into Lebanon for a few months in 1958 when its government was threatened by insurrection. In addition to providing military and economic assistance to anti-Communist, pro-American regimes around the world, Eisenhower authorized the Central Intelligence Agency to wage covert war against governments it considered too radical. CIA influence helped topple leftist regimes in Iran in 1953 and Guatemala in 1954.

Despite these basic continuities, there were some significant differences between the foreign policies of the Truman and Eisenhower administrations. Eisenhower cut Truman's defense budget from $50 billion to $40 billion and held it there during his eight years in office, partly because he believed in balanced budgets and thought there was a serious danger that the United States would "spend itself into bankruptcy." It was also because his long military experience had exposed him to both the horrors of war and the military-industrial complex's insatiable hunger for more money. In 1956 he wrote a friend:

> Some day there is going to be a man sitting in my present chair who has not been raised in the military services and who will have little understanding of where slashes in their estimates can be made with little or no damage. If that should happen while we still have the state of tension that now exists in the world, I shudder to think what could happen in this country.

In perhaps the most important foreign policy decision of his administration—the decision not to intervene in Vietnam in 1954—Eisenhower showed greater restraint than either his predecessor or his successor likely would have. The French had been fighting to maintain their colony in Indochina against Ho Chi Minh's national liberation movement since the end of World War II. After the 1949 Communist revolution in China, Truman—deciding that maintaining the French empire in Southeast Asia was crucial to the containment of world Communism—had extended military aid. By 1954, the United States was footing 80 percent of the bill for the war in Vietnam, but that was still not enough to bail out the French, who most Vietnamese regarded as alien oppressors. After the Vietminh won a decisive victory at the 1954 Battle of Dien Bien Phu, the French asked for an American air support.

Many people in the administration, including Secretary of State Dulles and Vice President Nixon, favored action, including the dispatch of American troops. The Joint Chiefs of Staff even suggested the use of nuclear weapons. The British and Congressional Democrats Eisenhower consulted urged caution, however, and he followed their advice. He said that he would neither use that "terrible thing" nor send American fighting men. As he wrote prophetically in 1963—before massive American involvement in the Vietnam War—"The jungles of Indochina would have swallowed up division after division of American troops. Furthermore, the presence of ever more white men in uniform probably would have aggravated rather than assuaged Asiatic resentments." In addition, he said, the United States had "a tradition of anti-colonialism," and its "moral position" was "more to be guarded than the Tonkin Delta, indeed than all of Indochina."

Eisenhower's restraint kept America out of war in Southeast Asia in 1954. Another decision he made shortly after, however, created conditions that helped to bring about her later military involvement in Vietnam. The French and Vietminh reached an agreement that ended the war at the 1954 Geneva Conference. Ho Chi Minh withdrew his forces from the southern half of Vietnam with the understanding that free elections would be held within two years to determine who would rule a unified Vietnam. The promised elections were never held. Skeptical that the elections in the North would be truly free, and fearful that Ho was so popular that he would win even if they were, the Eisenhower administration instead decided to back the temporary ruler of the South, Ngo Dinh Diem, and to establish an independent South Vietnam as an anti-Communist bastion similar to South Korea. Economic assistance, arms, and military advisors for Diem seemed a very small investment compared with the cost of the Korean War (or the probable cost of having joined the French in the fighting in 1954). Eisenhower kept the peace, it appeared, without sacrificing honor. As for the long-run costs of subverting the Geneva accords, creating the state of South Vietnam, and attempting to preserve it with American power, they would become clear later. For the moment, Eisenhower's policy seemed a success.

The ending of the Korean War, the death of Stalin, and the absence of other dramatic threats to the status quo created opportunities for diplomatic contacts between the United States and Russia that were unimaginable in the tensest early years of the Cold War. Eisenhower met with the leaders of the Soviet Union, Britain, and France at Geneva in 1955 and offered his "open skies" proposal for halting the nuclear arms race, which would have given each side complete freedom to fly over and photograph the other's territory in search of violations. Russia rejected the plan, but the summit conference itself was a recognition that the two sides had a strong common interest in settling their differences without nuclear war. The shooting down of a high-altitude American U-2 spy plane over the Soviet Union in early 1960 inflamed relations between the superpowers again, but they were certainly more amicable than they were when Eisenhower first took office.

Domestic Policy

Eisenhower appointed a cabinet made up of wealthy businessmen; critics referred to them as "eight millionaires and a plumber" (the Secretary of Labor). His choice for Secretary of Defense was Charles E. Wilson, President of General Motors, the nation's largest defense contractor. Wilson saw no conflict in owning $2.5 million in GM stock while making decisions of vital importance to his company because "what was good for the country was good for General Motors and vice versa." When confronted with evidence of rising unemployment during the brief recession of 1954, Wilson insisted that anyone who truly wanted to work could get a job. He preferred "bird dogs" to "kennel-fed dogs," he said, "one who'd get out and hunt for his food rather than sit on his fanny and yell."

The President, however, was not a doctrinaire, conservative ideologue but a pragmatist who had no interest in repealing the New Deal. He was more eager to balance the budget that he was to keep the economy at full employment, and refused to run deficits to counter business downturns in 1954, 1957–58, and

1960–61. But he resisted right-wing demands to turn the clock back. "Should any political party attempt to abolish Social Security and eliminate labor laws and farm programs," he wrote in 1954, "you would not hear of that party again in our political history." A "tiny splinter group" favored that, he said, but "their number is negligible and they are stupid." Instead, Eisenhower backed a broadening of Social Security coverage, federal aid to schools, and the creation of a Department of Health, Education, and Welfare. Although his Secretary of Agriculture, Ezra Taft Benson, denounced the Truman administration's profligate subsidies to farmers, expenditures for them actually rose sixfold during his tenure.

Eisenhower was an ardent anti-Communist. He agreed with Senator McCarthy's professed aims, and purged the civil service with new "loyalty" investigations that resulted in the firing of 2,600 "security risks" and the resignation of 4,300 others. The criteria for determining what a "security risk" was were broader and vaguer than ever before, and the safeguards for the accused were fewer and weaker. Although McCarthy's wild accusations soon became an embarrassment, Eisenhower refused to speak out against him. He told his brother he would not "get in a pissing contest with that skunk." When McCarthy attacked the State Department for carrying in its overseas libraries books by supposed radicals—such as Sherwood Anderson, Theodore Dreiser, John Dewey, and Arthur Schlesinger, Jr.—their books were taken off the shelf. When McCarthy denounced a career diplomat Eisenhower appointed to an ambassadorship as a "security risk" because the man had been FDR's interpreter at the Yalta conference, he was promised that no more "controversial" figures like that would be given office. McCarthy at last overreached himself in 1954, when he conducted nationally televised hearings designed to show that the U.S. Army was "shielding Communist conspirators." That was too much for moderate Republicans who had previously found him a useful weapon against the Democrats. When they abandoned him, the Senate voted to censure McCarthy for "conduct unbecoming of a member," and his career was over.

Progress in Civil Rights

The most important domestic policy decision of the decade was made not by Congress or the President but by Chief Justice Earl Warren's Supreme Court. In 1954, in *Brown vs. Board of Education*, the nine justices unanimously held that racially segregated public schools denied black students the "equal protection of the laws" guaranteed in the Fourteenth Amendment of the Constitution. Since the late 1930s, the Court had been striking down Jim Crow practices in a variety of areas, including higher education, voting rights, transportation, and real estate. The *Brown* decision was the real revolution, however. The Court now endorsed Justice John Marshall Harlan's courageous dissent in the *Plessy* case more than half a century before. Harlan had said that the "thin disguise of 'equal' accommodations will not mislead anyone, or atone for the wrong done this day." "Separate educational facilities," declared Chief Justice Warren's opinion, "are inherently unequal."

MARTIN LUTHER KING'S STRATEGY, 1958

The nonviolent resisters can summarize their message in the following simple terms: We will take direct action against injustice without waiting for other agencies to act. We will not obey unjust laws or submit to unjust practices. We will do this peacefully, openly, cheerfully because our aim is to persuade. We adopt the means of nonviolence because our end is a community at peace with itself. We will try to persuade with our words, but if our words fail, we will try to persuade with our acts. We will always be willing to talk and seek fair compromise, but we are ready to suffer when necessary and even to risk our lives to become witnesses to the truth as we see it.

The way of nonviolence means a willingness to suffer and sacrifice. It may mean going to jail. If such is the case the resister must be willing to fill the jail houses of the South. It may even mean physical death. But if physical death is the price that a man must pay to free his children and his white brethren from a permanent death of the spirit, then nothing could be more redemptive.

—Martin Luther King, *Stride Toward Freedom*, 1958

In subsequent cases, the Court allowed school boards "a reasonable time" in which to implement the decision, and interpreted the phrase in a manner that allowed considerable foot-dragging. Six years later, 89 percent of the South's school districts still had dual systems. But it was clear that the Court would keep up the pressure for desegregation, and that any chief executive would use whatever force was necessary to uphold the law. Eisenhower refused to endorse the *Brown* decision publicly, not because he opposed it (he didn't), but because he believed it was the Court's duty to interpret the law and his to enforce it. He did just that in 1957 when he sent federal troops to Little Rock, Arkansas, to protect black children entering the high school from angry white mobs.

While the NAACP's Legal Defense Fund worked tirelessly to prepare cases for the federal courts, other black Americans were experimenting with other forms of activism. A year after the *Brown* ruling, the young minister Martin Luther King, Jr., led the blacks of Montgomery, Alabama, in a boycott of the city's segregated bus system. The city gave way before the force of this demonstration of King's principle of nonviolent direct action, and eliminated segregated transportation. In a similar demonstration early in 1960, black college students in Greensboro, North Carolina, sat down at lunch counters reserved for whites and refused to leave unless they were served. The sit-ins spread rapidly, and soon Woolworth's and other national chain stores operating in the South opened their facilities to black and white customers alike.

The gains blacks won from court decisions and direct action were impressive. In other ways, however, the Eisenhower years were less satisfactory. During the war and immediate postwar years, Afro-Americans made notable economic progress. At the close of the Great Depression, the average black American family earned only 39 percent as much as the average white family. The ratio of black-to-white family income edged steadily upward thereafter, reaching the 57 percent mark in 1948. The advance was due to the fact that earnings in northern factories, even for unskilled work, were well above what sharecroppers received in the South. Throughout the 1950s, however, the ratio hovered around or below 57 percent year after year, even though continuing black migration out of southern agriculture should have pushed it up further. The explanation is not clear, but it may have been because blacks were the hardest hit in each of the Eisenhower recessions. As the last to have been hired, they were the first to be fired.

There was some truth to the Republican claim that the Eisenhower years were years of "peace and prosperity." But the prosperity was uneven, and the commitment to an independent South Vietnam would shatter the peace before long. The seeds of the turbulent sixties were sewn in the tranquil fifties.

SUGGESTED READINGS

Godfrey Hodgson, *America in Our Time* (1976) is a provocative synthesis covering the period from the close of World War II to the 1970s. On the origins of the Cold War, see John L. Gaddis, *The United States and the Origins of the Cold War, 1941–1947* (1972), Daniel Yergin, *Shattered Peace: The Origins of the Cold War and the National Security State* (1977), Charles S. Maier, ed., *The Origins of the Cold War and Contemporary Europe* (1978), Thomas G. Paterson, *On Every Front: The Making of the Cold War* (1979), Walter LaFeber, *Russia and the Cold War, 1945–1980* (rev. ed., 1980), William Taubman, *Stalin's American Policy* (1980), and Gregg Herken, *The Winning Weapon: The Atomic Bomb and the Cold War, 1945–1950* (1981).

Social and economic trends in the 1940s and 1950s are reviewed in Geoffrey Perrett, *A Dream of Greatness: The American People, 1945–1963* (1979), Robert Sobel, *The Age of Giant Corporations: A Microeconomic History of American Business, 1914–1970* (1972), John L. Shover, *First Majority–Last Minority: The Transforming of Rural Life in America* (1976), Robert C. Wood, *Suburbia: Its People and Their Politics* (1959), Herbert J. Gans, *The Levittowners: Ways of Life and Politics in a New Suburban Community* (1967), and Richard Easterlin, *Birth and Fortune: The Impact of Numbers on Personal Welfare* (1980). John P. Diggins, *Up From Communism: Conservative Odysseys in American Intellectual History* (1975), George H. Nash, *The Conservative Intellectual Movement in America since 1945* (1976), and Job L. Dittberner, *The End of Ideology and American Social Thought: 1930–1960* (1979) explore the rightward drift of intellectual opinion. Conflicting views on the second Red Scare are presented in Earl Latham, *The Communist Controversy in Washington* (1966), Walter and Miriam Schneir, *Invitation to an Inquest* (1973), Allen Weinstein, *Perjury: The Hiss–Chambers Case* (1978), David Caute, *The Great Fear: The Anti-Communist Purge under Truman and Eisenhower*

(1978), Victor S. Navasky, *Naming Names* (1980), and William L. O'Neill, *A Better World: The Great Schism: Stalinism and the Intellectuals* (1982). Ernest R. May, *"Lessons" of the Past: The Use and Misuse of History in American Foreign Policy* (1973) presents a particularly fascinating account of the Korean intervention. See also Bruce Cummings, *The Origins of the Korean War* (1980).

Samuel Lubell, *The Future of American Politics* (1951) perceptively analyzes the ethnic basis of the New Deal coalition and the impact of postwar developments on the electorate. Lubell's *The Revolt of the Moderates* (1956) carries the story into the Eisenhower years. On the Truman administration, see Barton J. Bernstein, ed., *Politics and Policies of the Truman Administration* (1970), Alonzo B. Hamby, *Beyond the New Deal: Harry S. Truman and American Liberalism* (1973), Burt Cochran, *Harry Truman and the Crisis Presidency* (1973), and Robert J. Donovan, *Conflict and Crisis: The Presidency of Harry S. Truman, 1945–1948* (1977), and *Tumultuous Years: The Presidency of Harry S. Truman, 1949–1953* (1982). Eisenhower's performance is analyzed in Herbert S. Parmet, *Eisenhower and the American Crusades* (1972), Townsend Hoopes, *The Devil and John Foster Dulles* (1973), Charles C. Alexander, *Holding the Line: The Eisenhower Era, 1952–1961* (1975), and Robert A. Divine, *Eisenhower and the Cold War* (1981). For a discussion of the Supreme Court's most important civil rights decision in the era, see Richard Kluger, *Simple Justice: The History of Brown v. Board of Education and Black America's Struggle for Equality* (1975).

Chapter Thirty

From Camelot to Watergate

By the late 1950s, it had become fashionable for social critics to complain that American life was bland and complacent. "We live in a heavy, sanctimonious, stultifying atmosphere," wrote one in 1960. The past decade, he declared, had been "the dullest and dreariest in all our history." The period that followed—the stormy sixties and early seventies—can be described in many ways, but "dull" is certainly not one of them. The era offered an abundance of drama—and not a little tragedy.

JOHN F. KENNEDY AND THE NEW FRONTIER

Dwight Eisenhower was 70 when he retired from office in 1961, the oldest man ever to occupy the White House until Ronald Reagan. His successor, John F. Kennedy, was 43, the youngest ever elected and the first chief executive born in the twentieth century. Kennedy promised adventure along a "New Frontier." He would "get the country moving again," after eight years of alleged drift and stagnation. The White House would be a new Camelot, the mythical court of King Arthur. By the time Kennedy was assassinated, in November 1963, the country was indeed "moving again." It was moving straight into a quagmire—the longest, most unpopular, and least successful war in American history.

In his televised campaign debates with Vice President Richard Nixon, Kennedy echoed the apocalyptic charges made by Republicans like Nixon and Dulles in 1952. The election of 1860, he said melodramatically, had centered on the question

Despite the emotional appeal of its "flower power" slogans, the Peace Movement of the 1960s could not transform bullets to blossoms.

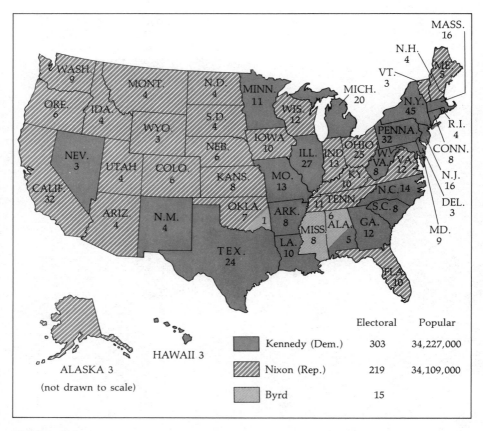

MAP 30–1
The 1960 Election

of whether the nation could exist half-slave and half-free. The question for 1960 was "whether the world will exist half-slave and half-free, whether it moved in the direction of freedom or in the direction of slavery." The balance had been tipping toward slavery in recent years, he declared, because of the laxity and softness of the Eisenhower administration. Just as the Republicans in 1952 had accused Truman of "losing" China to Communism, Kennedy blamed Eisenhower for "losing Cuba to Communism" by failing to prevent Fidel Castro's 1959 revolution. It was essential that the United States be "first—not first if, and not first but, and not first when—but first." The Republicans had gravely underestimated the Communist menace, and had skimped on military spending. The Russians had stronger conventional forces, and there was a growing "missile gap" as well. Although some differences with the Soviet Union might be settled through peaceful negotiation, Kennedy declared, the United States should only negotiate from a position of strength, not when "the power balance" was moving away from us."

Although these were the central themes of Kennedy's campaign, his victory at the polls was not a ringing popular endorsement for a more militant foreign policy. Kennedy defeated Nixon by fewer than 120,000 votes, 0.17 percent of the total; it was the most even division of the popular vote in American history. And issues of foreign affairs had less effect on the outcome than questions of personality, economics, and religion.

Each of these worked to Kennedy's advantage. He was a more skillful and photogenic television performer than Nixon, who looked as if he had a bad case of "5 o'clock shadow." The economy was in the doldrums again, always a handicap for the party in power; in the month before the election, the unemployment rolls increased by nearly half a million. Kennedy's Catholicism lost him votes in white Protestant areas, especially in the South, but won him even more from Catholic voters elsewhere.

Taking the Offensive

Had any one of these circumstances been different, Kennedy would probably have lost the race to Nixon. Certainly his election was not a mandate for sweeping changes in public policy. But Kennedy proceeded to act as if he had such a mandate in the realm of military and foreign affairs, his central preoccupation during his three years in office. He was a confident, arrogant, macho prophet of a new nationalism, a latter-day Teddy Roosevelt. "The trumpet summons us again," he declared in an inaugural address rich in martial rhetoric. Freedom was "in its hour of maximum danger," and the United States its sole defender. In the great struggle against Communism, America would "pay any price, bear any burden, meet any hardship." "The complacent, the self-indulgent, the soft societies," he said a few weeks later, were "about to be swept away with the debris of history. Only the strong can possibly survive."

Kennedy was not always so bellicose. His Peace Corps was an imaginative and idealistic venture that enlisted the talents of young Americans in projects for economic and social betterment in the underdeveloped world. One motive, of course, was to prevent social unrest that might bring to power radicals who were antagonistic to the United States. But if the Peace Corps was in that sense an instrument in the Cold War, it involved constructive rather than destructive competition.

Kennedy's space program, a crash effort to put an American on the moon within a decade, might be considered another example of constructive competition. It is dismaying, however, that the program could have been justified on solid scientific grounds, but was instead sold to the American public by appealing to their wounded pride. The Russians were ahead in the race to the moon, said Kennedy, and they had to be bested if we were "to win the battle that is now going on around the world between freedom and tyranny."

Upon taking office Kennedy quickly discovered that the United States was in fact much stronger militarily than he had claimed during the campaign. Intelligence reports revealed that his allegations about the decline of American power relative to that of the Soviet Union were false. There was no "missile gap" and there never had been; the United States had a much superior nuclear striking force. Kennedy nevertheless demanded a sharp increase in appropriations for both nuclear and conventional arms, and Congress supported it. America had to offer further proof of its toughness, even though it was well ahead in the arms race. The possibility that this would only frighten the Russians into more hardline positions and provoke them to increase their arsenal did not disturb him.

The new chief executive's eagerness to strike a blow for freedom accounted for his impetuous approval of an invasion of Castro's Cuba in April 1961. Most of the 1,400 men who landed at the Bay of Pigs were native Cubans who had gone into exile after the 1959 revolution, but they were trained, equipped, and transported to Cuba by the CIA. Plans for the operation had been laid in the closing days of the preceding administration, but it is uncertain whether Eisenhower would have given final approval to it. It was a flagrant violation of international law, an imperialist adventure, and its chances of success rested entirely on the validity of the wishful assumption that Castro had so little popular support that an invasion would trigger a mass upheaval against his regime. But Kennedy was impatient to seize the initiative in the Cold War, and this seemed a bold way of doing so.

The invasion did not spark the hoped-for anti-Castro uprising, and the exiles were quickly overwhelmed by the Cuban army. Kennedy appeared before the world as a clumsy Goliath and Castro as a David. The Soviet Union, already dismayed by the American military build-up and by Kennedy's bellicose utterances, affirmed its support for Castro and stepped up the volume of aid to Cuba. It was a calamity from every point of view.

Writers sympathetic to Kennedy claim that he learned much from this on-the-job training, and displayed greater caution and maturity in his subsequent conduct of foreign affairs. He did learn some minor lessons—not to be so credulous about the CIA's intelligence estimates, for example—but nothing that made him doubt his anti-Communist zeal or his faith in military solutions.

When he met Khrushchev in Vienna in June, only six weeks after this rankling defeat, Kennedy refused even to discuss possible changes in the status of Berlin, which the United States was still occupying under a temporary wartime agreement then 16 years old. He had reason for suspicion about Soviet intentions. But his own position was extremely rigid, and after he returned to the United States his statements on the matter were inflammatory. The sole aim of the Russians, he suggested, was to test America's will to resist aggression, and they had to be stopped—even at the risk of nuclear war. In an outburst more appropriate to the hero of a Hollywood western than to the President of the United States, he declared that "if Khrushchev wants to rub my nose in the dirt, it's all over."

To demonstrate his determination, Kennedy called up reserve units, demanded more funds for the military, and proposed a national defense program to equip the nation with fallout shelters to allow it to survive a nuclear exchange. The civil defense appropriation he asked for was pathetically inadequate for the task, and the best-informed scientists pointed out that no shelter program could protect more than a small fraction of the population from extinction in an all-out nuclear war. But it was an alarming demonstration of the crisis mentality that gripped the administration, an indication that it was willing not only to think about the unthinkable but to plan for it.

The unthinkable came very close to happening during the Cuban missile crisis of the next year. Despite the failure of the Bay of Pigs invasion, the administration was still determined to topple the Castro regime. It blocked all trade and travel between the two countries, ended American aid to any nation that assisted Cuba, and used its political and economic leverage to secure Cuba's expulsion from the Organization of American States. Although it almost defies belief, later investigations of the CIA disclosed that its agents had received White House approval to work on plans to assassinate Castro, and had even enlisted the aid of the Mafia in the task.

The Soviet Union therefore had every reason to fear that its one political satellite in the Western Hemisphere was in mortal danger, and to step up its arms shipments to Castro. In the late summer of 1962, Russia decided to send nuclear as well as conventional arms, and began to construct missile silos for atomic rockets with enough range to reach most of the eastern United States. American U-2 spy planes overflying Cuba spotted these sites in October.

Putting nuclear warheads in Cuba was a provocative gesture. But it was not a violation of international law, unlike the Bay of Pigs invasion, nor was it a genuine threat to the military security of the United States. Russia had already placed Cuba under its nuclear umbrella, in effect, by announcing that it would do whatever was necessary to defend the island from another American invasion. Placing the missiles on Cuban soil simply made that commitment more unmistakable. Stationing nuclear weapons in other friendly countries was not a tactic invented by Russia but by the United States, which had long before installed missiles aimed at Soviet targets in such countries as Turkey and Italy. The Soviet action did not shift the military balance of power. Russia already had an ample stock of nuclear-tipped rockets that could cross the ocean in minutes to devastate the United States. As Secretary of Defense Robert McNamara admitted, "It makes no great difference whether you are killed by a missile fired from the Soviet Union or from Cuba."

Kennedy, however, took the installation of missiles in Cuba as yet another test of American will, a "deliberately provocative and unjustified change in the status quo" which could not be accepted "if our courage and our commitments are ever to be trusted again by either friend or foe." While he conceded later that the rockets would not have altered the balance of military power, he claimed they would have "appeared" to have changed the balance of power, and "appearances contribute to reality." Unlike the western democracies facing Hitler in the 1930s, the United States would show an iron determination that would give its world commitments "credibility." Instead of negotiating with the Russians, Kennedy handed them an ultimatum. The missiles had to go immediately or the United States would take them out by force. Soviet ships on the way to Cuba with more must turn back or face the guns of the U.S. Navy warships in the Caribbean.

The two weeks that followed were the most dangerous in world history. For days, Russian ships continued to steam toward Cuba, on a collision course with the American fleet. At last they were halted on Khrushchev's orders. "We're eyeball to eyeball," said the Secretary of State, gleefully, "and I think the other fellow just blinked." The Soviets backed down and agreed to take the missiles out, in exchange for an American promise to respect Cuban independence in the future. Kennedy's policy was in that sense a success. Whether this political victory over the Soviet Union was worth the risk of a total war between two nations capable of reducing each other to radioactive rubble may be questioned, however. Part of the blame rests on Khrushchev for having deployed the missiles 90 miles from American shores in the first place. But it was the Kennedy administration that recklessly embraced "eyeballing" tactics in response to that challenge, and Khrushchev who displayed the restraint and flexibility that prevented ultimate catastrophe.

Whether it was because the missile crisis forced some new awareness of what a nuclear war would mean, or because Kennedy felt that he had demonstrated his toughness so unmistakably that it could never again be doubted, his administration made some modest efforts to ease Soviet–American tensions not long after. In his June, 1963, address at American University, Kennedy declared that the two countries had "a mutually deep interest in a just and generous peace and in halting the arms race," to break out of the "vicious and dangerous cycle in which suspicion on one side breeds suspicion on the other, and new weapons beget counterweapons."

As a concrete step toward reduced tension, the United States and the Soviet Union set up a "hot line," linking the Kremlin with the White House to permit instant communications in an emergency. They also concluded a limited nuclear test ban treaty. It barred nuclear testing in the atmosphere, under water, and in outer space, but not underground. The ban eliminated an important source of atmospheric pollution, but it was far from being the great "breakthrough for peace" that some enthusiasts thought it was. Instead of fighting for a more meaningful and inclusive ban, Kennedy won the political support of military leaders by excluding underground tests from the agreement and by pledging an accelerated test program beneath the earth. In the seven years following the treaty, the United States exploded twice as many nuclear devices as it had in the entire 18 years preceding it!

The test ban treaty did not slow the arms race in the least—it accelerated it. But it was an important symbolic gesture that might have led in time to more substantial efforts toward peaceful accommodation between America and Russia. Kennedy's assassination in November of 1963 left that a matter for his successor. But the key decision that prevented further accommodation and inflamed relations once again was Kennedy's—the decision to go to war to preserve a non-Communist regime in South Vietnam.

Into the Quagmire

American efforts to contain Communism in Southeast Asia date from the Truman administration. Eisenhower had wisely refrained from military intervention to prevent the defeat of the French in 1954, but not so wisely supported the installation of the anti-Communist Diem regime in the southern half of Vietnam. The Diem government was a corrupt dictatorship, resolutely opposed to land reform to benefit the peasant masses. Despite an enormous program of American economic and military assistance—almost $4 billion had been spent by the time Eisenhower left office, and some 600 American officers were serving as advisers to Diem's army—a civil war was raging in the south. Diem's forces were unable to suppress the revolutionary National Liberation Front (the Vietcong).

When Kennedy entered the White House, he faced the question of what—if anything—to do about the increasingly shaky Saigon regime. One option was to conclude that the United States had already done all that it could do to help. If Diem had been unable to win the allegiance of the Vietnamese people with the massive aid he had already been given, his government did not deserve to survive. Kennedy rejected that course, and decided to employ American military power to do the job that Diem's army was incapable of doing. It seemed at first only a small step, a matter of just a few more American advisers, but by the time of Kennedy's death the number of "advisers" had grown to almost 20,000, and the struggle had been defined in a manner that soon led to the subsequent dispatch of hundreds of thousands of ground troops, the expenditure of hundreds of billions of dollars, and the deaths of 58,000 Americans and at least half a million Asians. Kennedy, of course, could not foresee these ultimate consequences of his actions. Historians, not historical actors, have the benefit of hindsight. But Kennedy had been advised of the potential dangers of his course, most forcefully by French Premier Charles de Gaulle at a meeting in early 1961. The United States, de Gaulle warned, should learn from the experience of the French in Indochina. "The more you commit yourself there against communism, the more communists will appear to be champions of national independence." Although you "will find officials who, by interest, obey you, the people will not consent. I predict to you that you will, step by step, be drawn into a bottomless military and political quagmire."

Why did Kennedy fail to heed this sound prediction? One reason, undoubtedly, was his fear of the domestic political consequences of the collapse of a regime closely aligned with the United States. Truman had been hurt by the charge that he lost China. Having used the same tactic himself against the Republicans, substituting Cuba for China, Kennedy would have found it acutely embarrassing to be accused of losing Vietnam.

Furthermore, Kennedy and virtually all of his advisers were utterly convinced that all revolutionary movements in the world were orchestrated from Moscow. The Joint Chiefs of Staff called the Vietcong uprisings "a planned phase in the communist timetable for world domination." Guerrillas fighting to overturn the Diem government could not be natives with legitimate grievances; they must be invaders from North Vietnam, acting on orders from China and Russia. (Although China and Russia were quarreling bitterly by this time, American leaders held obsessively to their view of monolithic Communism and ignored the fact.) The war was another case of external aggression like Korea. In fact, the Korean analogy was false. The National Liberation Front was not an invading army but an indigenous southern movement, and the weapons it fought with were largely American munitions captured from the South Vietnamese army. North Vietnamese military aid to the Vietcong, and the eventual entry of units of North Vietnamese troops into the fighting, came after and as a result of America's military intervention, not the other way around. The conception of the Communist "timetable," however, obscured these vital distinctions.

The need to keep the Communists from carrying out their "master plan" in South Vietnam seemed all the more urgent because of another closely related conviction of the Kennedy administration—the "Domino Theory." According to this notion, all of the countries of Southeast Asia were like dominoes lined up in a row; if one—South Vietnam—toppled, it would bring down another, which would in turn bring down another... "If we don't stop the Reds in South Vietnam," it was said in all seriousness, "tomorrow they will be in Hawaii, and next week they will be in San Francisco." It was a poor theory, one that took no account of the particular historical circumstances that fostered revolutionary upheavals in some parts of the world and inhibited them in others, but it was believed by many otherwise intelligent Americans at the time.

These assumptions, of course, were not peculiar to John Kennedy and his team;

they were shared by most Americans in public life in the early 1960s. Kennedy, however, was more likely to fall into the Vietnam trap than a man like Eisenhower. JFK was intensely combative, sure of his country's power and convinced that he could employ that power efficiently and rationally. The threat of an American nuclear response to some small and ambiguous instance of Communist aggression was simply not credible, he believed. As a result, the enemy had been left free to nibble away at vulnerable areas like Southeast Asia. The solution was to increase the nation's ability to fight "counterinsurgency" wars with elite troops who understood guerrilla tactics. The army's Special Forces (the Green Berets) were Kennedy's creation, his answer to the Vietcong; he kept a green beret on his White House desk. With the aid of the computers his Defense Secretary, efficiency expert Robert McNamara, installed in the Pentagon, the United States could measure out precisely the amount of punishment needed to put down any insurrection against a friendly government. The rising "body count" would be a precise gauge of success. Vietnam was just the laboratory Kennedy needed in which to test this rationalistic faith, and he was perhaps fortunate not to have lived long enough to see the havoc that it wrought.

Domestic Policy

Kennedy was preoccupied with global matters during most of his 1,000 days in office. The fact that he had no popular mandate for major changes in domestic policy, and the strength of the Republican–southern Democrat bloc in Congress, limited his freedom of action. He also had very little taste for the log-rolling, back-scratching patronage games chief executives must play to get Congress to do their bidding. He was happiest operating in a realm in which the tradition of bipartisan foreign policy gave him an exhilarating freedom of action.

Kennedy's most significant domestic initiative was in the realm of economic policy. His major spending on the military and space programs pumped badly needed funds into an economy that had been languishing when he took over. Kennedy didn't know much about economics—he had gotten a "C" in the introductory course at Harvard—but his advisers were outstanding proponents of "the new economics," who accepted Keynesian principles. Running a deficit in the federal budget, they persuaded him, would stimulate growth without inflation so long as there were large numbers of people out of work. The economy could be "fine-tuned," so it would grow at a healthy pace without either unemployment above a minimal "frictional" 4 percent or rising prices. In accord with this theory, when the economy began to slump in 1962, Kennedy recommended a major tax cut without a corresponding reduction in expenditures. Congressional conservatives refused to go along until after his death, but in 1964 they approved the tax reduction as a tribute to the murdered President. The theory of "fine-tuning" was attractive, but in reality political pressures would work to keep expenditures normally above revenues, exerting inflationary pressure. Between fiscal year 1965 and fiscal year 1980 the federal budget was in deficit all but one year, the price level more than doubled, and unemployment remained a recurrent problem. The total federal deficit was $15 billion in the 1950s and $63 billion in the 1960s; in the 1970s it was a staggering $420 billion. Economists of different persuasions now disagree about what to do about "stagflation," but "the new economics" offers no magic formula to guarantee full employment and stable prices at the same time.

During the Kennedy years, major advances were made in the area of civil rights, but few resulted from the President's leadership. During the 1960 campaign, Kennedy had his brother Robert make the gesture of securing Martin Luther King's release from a Georgia prison, and he pledged that he would ban discrimination in federally assisted housing with "a stroke of the pen." It took him two years, until after the 1962 elections, to issue that executive order. Robert Kennedy's Justice Department was more responsive to black complaints than Eisenhower's, but it also bowed to political expediency in allowing the appointment of several southern white racists to federal judgeships. The President was afraid of alienating J. Edgar Hoover, head of the FBI, who was convinced that civil rights activists were dangerous subversives. The FBI not only failed to protect civil rights workers from violent attack; it bugged Martin Luther King's hotel rooms and leaked information to smear him.

The momentum of the black revolution sweeping the South had become so great by 1963, however, that Kennedy felt compelled to act. King's Southern Christian Leadership Conference, the Congress of Racial Equality (CORE), and the Student Non-Violent Coordinating Committee (SNCC) organized a great wave of demonstrations to bring down the Jim Crow system. The nightly television news pictured the violence southern whites directed against peaceful black protesters. In Birmingham, Alabama, in the spring of 1963, Sheriff "Bull" Connors' troops attacked demonstrators with dogs, fire hoses, and electric cattle prods, and a bomb in a black church killed four children. In August, 200,000 people attended King's March on Washington for Jobs and Freedom, the largest public demonstration ever held in the nation's capital. Early that year, only 4 percent of Americans rated civil rights the most important national issue; by the fall, 52 percent did. Until then Kennedy had been worried, according to one adviser, that the drive for black rights would "divide the American people at a time when the international scene required maximum unity." By 1963, it was clear that the movement would not go away, and the President climbed on the bandwagon. The administration sent a major civil rights bill to Congress, with a ban on discrimination in public accommodations, and increased federal authority to protect black voters and speed school desegregation.

The civil rights bill and the tax cut, both bogged down in Congress at the time of Kennedy's assassination, typified the fate of domestic reform on the New Frontier. A number of other significant domestic innovations were proposed by the administration—federal aid to education, a national medical care program for the aged, creation of a new department of urban affairs, and federal funds for urban mass transit, for example—and there were other progressive proposals well along in the planning stage, most notably a package of measures to alleviate poverty in the United States. But none had been passed, or even seemed to have much chance of passing, in November of 1963. There were many reasons for that failure, including the political complexion of Congress. But a major reason was the President's own

I HAVE A DREAM

Even though we face the difficulties of today and tomorrow, I still have a dream. It is a dream chiefly rooted in the American dream. I have a dream that one day this nation will rise up and live out the true meaning of its creed: "We hold these truths to be self-evident, that all men are created equal."

I have a dream that one day on the red hills of Georgia, the sons of former slaves and the sons of former slave-owners will be able to sit together at the table of brotherhood.

I have a dream that one day even the state of Mississippi, a state sweltering with the heat of injustice, sweltering with the heat of oppression, will be transformed into an oasis of freedom and justice.

I have a dream that my four little children will one day live in a nation where they will not be judged by the color of their skin but by the content of their character.

I have a dream that one day every valley shall be exalted, every hill and mountain shall be made low, the rough places will be made plain, and the crooked places will be made straight, and the glory of the Lord shall be revealed and all flesh shall see it together.

Free at last, free at last, thank God Almighty.

—Martin Luther King, 1963

sense of priorities. If he had not been so fearful that the United States was a "complacent," "self-indulgent," "soft" society "about to be swept away with the debris of history," and so certain that America had a vital stake in preventing revolutionary change in every corner of the globe, he would have been free to employ his considerable energies and talents to the task of building a better America. Instead, his chief legacy was U.S. involvement in Vietnam.

THE GREAT SOCIETY AND THE GREAT UPHEAVAL

The astonishing assassination of John F. Kennedy in Dallas on November 22, 1963, under circumstances that some still find mysterious, made Lyndon B. Johnson President. In his ability to press Congress into action, Johnson was more successful than any leader since Franklin Roosevelt. The years of "the Great Society," however, were also years of convulsive social unrest on the part of blacks, antiwar activists, and students from the "counterculture." The "liberal consensus" Johnson represented cracked apart under the pressure of racial tensions and an unpopular war, destroying his Presidency and altering the shape of national politics for a generation.

Johnson was a peerless manipulator who understood Congress the way few American Presidents have, a genius at wheedling, cajoling, and twisting arms to get what he wanted. After the 1964 election, in which the Republicans put forward the right-wing extremist Barry Goldwater as their candidate, he had greater leverage than any chief executive since FDR after his landslide victory in 1936. 1964 was an even bigger Democratic sweep than 1936. Johnson won 61.1 percent of the popular vote, the biggest margin in history, and Democrats controlled more than two-thirds of both the House and the Senate.

Johnson had two domestic aims. He wanted to use the power of the federal government to secure equal rights for blacks, and to enlarge the welfare state. He was strikingly successful at both. Under his urging, Congress passed the sweeping Civil Rights Act of 1964, a considerably stronger measure than the version that had been proposed by Kennedy. It guaranteed blacks access to all public accommodations, including hotels and motels, and authorized the Justice Department to sue to enforce desegregation. It created an Equal Employment Opportunities Commission to prevent any firm with more than 25 employees from discriminating against anyone on the base of race, religion, sex, or national origin. The next year, the Voting Rights Act outlawed literacy tests and other subterfuges that had been used to keep southern blacks from the polls, and prevented southern communities from changing their electoral systems and procedures without clearance from the Justice Department. It was a Second Reconstruction, more thorough and far-reaching than the first.

The welfare state was expanded in several ways. There was Medicare for the aged, federal aid to education for the young, a new Department of Housing and Urban Development for city dwellers, and Medicaid, food stamps, the Job Corps, and a host of other programs for the poor. In 1960, the sum of all federal "transfer payments" to individuals was $25 billion. In Johnson's last year, the figure was almost two and a half times that. Because many of the programs were permanent, and had levels of benefits indexed to rise with inflation, they would reach an immense $271 billion by 1980.

The Great Society program was not without flaws. Some complex measures were devised with such haste that they sometimes worked at cross purposes. Although critics charged that the administration was blindly throwing money at problems without a clear sense of just how it would solve them, the amounts involved were large only by comparison with what had gone before, not by comparison with the need. Over 30 million Americans had incomes below the poverty line in the late 1960s; spending on programs for their benefit worked out to be $250 a year per person. The War on Poverty was misnamed and oversold. It was not an "unconditional war" for "total victory," as Johnson claimed, but a modest skirmish, described in overblown rhetoric that created expectations that could not be satisfied without action of a much more dramatic character than Johnson ever contemplated—a federal guarantee of a decent minimum income to every American along the lines pioneered by advanced welfare states like Sweden. Instead, the poverty program remained squarely within the American liberal tradition, attempting to provide new opportunities for individuals to compete rather than attacking the extreme inequalities that resulted from competition. Its seemingly most radical component—Community Action Programs to spur neighborhood organization with "maximum feasible participation" by the poor themselves—deflected attention from larger national issues to local grievances, and provoked destructive and futile conflict with the big-city political machines. The slogan "community control" was a panacea that ignored the need to challenge the distribution of wealth and power at the national level, and antagonized groups whose aid might have been enlisted in such a challenge.

Escalation of the War in Vietnam

Some of the imperfections of the Great Society might have been ironed out if the Johnson administration had continued to devote most of its attention to domestic affairs. But it did not. Kennedy had left it with the legacy of an open-ended commitment to preserve a non-Communist South Vietnam, and Johnson honored it at a fearful price. One reason that Johnson trounced Goldwater so handily in the 1964 race was that he seemed less likely to involve the United States in a war in Asia. Goldwater sounded trigger-happy; he opposed the nuclear test ban treaty, called for the bombing of North Vietnam, and argued that the President should allow military commanders in the battlefield the freedom to use "nukes" whenever they saw fit. Johnson, by contrast, pledged that "we are not about to send American boys nine or ten thousand miles away from home to do what Asian boys ought to be doing for themselves," and "not going north and drop bombs."

It is hard to view these promises as anything less than a deliberate (and successful) effort to deceive the American people, the most flagrant of many in the painful history of U.S. involvement in Southeast Asia. Within 48 hours of assuming the Presidency, Johnson had assured the U.S. ambassador in Saigon that he "would not be the President who saw Vietnam go the way of China." In the year before the 1964 elections, the Joint Chiefs of Staff had told him again and again that a far more intensive American effort would be required to prevent such a loss, and had pleaded for a widening of the war. Johnson gradually gave in to these pressures, and authorized an acceleraton of covert warfare against North Vietnam—the dispatch of commando teams across the border on sabotage raids, and the use of American naval vessels to attack coastal installations in the North. The public was kept in ignorance.

There were limits to what could be done covertly. Open escalation of the American effort ran the risk of challenge from Congress, which alone had the Constitutional authority to declare war. In August of 1964, the administration found a pretext for asking Congress for a free hand. Two American destroyers cruising off the coast of North Vietnam, in the Gulf of Tonkin, claimed they had been fired on by North Vietnamese torpedo boats. If the attack actually took place—there is reason to suspect that the entire incident was a fiction—it was surely justified by the clandestine American raids on the North that had been going on for months. But the President insisted that the Navy had been an innocent victim of

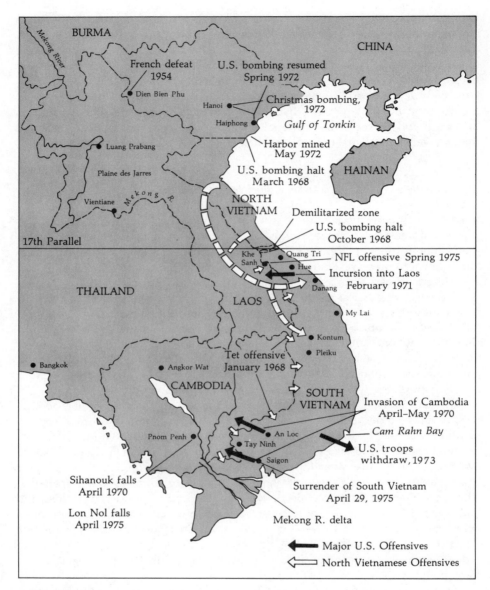

MAP 30–2
The Indochina War

"open aggression on the high seas." Congress consequently voted the Tonkin Gulf Resolution, giving the administration the authority to "take all necessary measures" in Southeast Asia, by margins of 416 to 0 in the House and 88 to 2 in the Senate. Johnson now had a blank check, and needed only to wait until after the election to fill it in and cash it.

Early the next year, with the election safely behind, the United States began large-scale bombing in Vietnam. Johnson resisted the military's request for an all-out assault to bomb the enemy "back to the Stone Age." It was to be a delicately calibrated, gradually increasing effort to inflict just enough pain to "break the will" of the North Vietnamese and compel them to cease their aggression. Johnson personally supervised the selection of targets in many instances, vetoed proposed raids close enough to the North Vietnam-China border to provoke Chinese intervention, and called intermittent bombing halts to see if Ho Chi Minh had at last seen the error of his ways. For all of this apparent restraint, however, during Johnson's years in office the United States dropped one and a half times as many bombs on the tiny country of Vietnam as it had in the European and Asian theaters together during World War II.

The bombing of the North was designed both to "strike at the source of the aggression" and to lift the morale of the government in Saigon. Saigon needed more than a morale booster, however. After a military coup toppled Diem in late 1963, no competent successor emerged, and a series of inept generals came and went in dizzying succession while disaffection spread and Vietcong strength grew in the countryside. The United States sought to arrest the deteriorating situation with airpower, but to no avail. Areas in which the control of the central government was weak were declared "free fire zones" and pounded mercilessly with high explosives, napalm, and chemicals to destroy the crops on which the guerrillas fed and strip the leaves from the jungle trees under which they hid. Such devastation of their countryside, not surprisingly, won few peasants to the cause of the "free world."

Control of the countryside could not be won by raining death and destruction from the skies alone. It required ground troops—and troops with a greater will to fight than those of the well-equipped but inert South Vietnamese army. At the same time that Johnson authorized the bombing of North Vietnam, he began to dispatch American soldiers to "do what Asian boys should be doing for themselves." By the end of 1965, there were almost 180,000; before another year was out, almost half a million. Each new shipment was justified as the final one. The generals could always see "the light at the end of the tunnel," and could promise prompt and decisive victory with just a little more manpower.

The military thought the task would be simple. "The French didn't kill enough," remarked one general. "If you kill enough you win the war." American soliders on "search and destroy" missions produced a "body count" of enemy dead that indicated steady progress toward that end, and B-52 bombers wiped out untold thousands more.

It is true the "if you kill enough you will win the war." But the military underestimated how many Vietnamese would be "enough," and overestimated the willingness of the American public to tolerate the killing and to pay the price in American casualties. The enemy proved capable of absorbing much more punishment than Washington had thought possible, largely because of the political meaning the war had for them. As Charles de Gaulle had warned President Kennedy long before, the more the United States assumed the responsibility for shaping the future of the country, the more the Vietcong and the North Vietnamese came to seem the legitimate defenders of the Vietnamese nation against another white colonial power. Despite the staggering casualties they received, the rebels continued to mount powerful resistance. At the beginning of 1968, they summoned up the resources for the surprise Tet Offensive, captured several provincial capitals, and attacked the American embassy in Saigon. The American military asserted that the Tet Offensive was "a complete failure," the last gasp of a beaten foe, but nevertheless advised that 200,000 more American troops would be needed to carry out the mopping-up.

By then, the political consensus to support a further escalation had vanished. The American public normally trusts its President in a time of war, and they had for a long time. Six months after the major enlargement of the war in 1965, almost two-thirds of those polled approved the move. But the casualty lists grew ever longer: 5,000 dead and 16,000 wounded in 1966, 9,000 dead and 32,000 wounded in 1967, 14,000 dead and 46,000 wounded in 1968. After the Tet Offensive, the military's repeated assurances that they needed just a little more time and a few more men lost credibility, and a majority of the public came to believe that the contest was unwinnable.

The Campus and the Ghetto

While battle raged in Southeast Asia, protest seethed on the campus and in the ghetto. The Baby Boom generation had reached college; by the late 1960s, campus youths outnumbered farmers by 3 to 1, railroad workers by 9 to 1, coal miners by 50 to 1. Many of them were ready for revolt at the prospect of being drafted after they left school to fight in a war that Congress had not declared. At "teach-ins," open meetings to discuss Vietnam, they learned information that made them doubt the rationale for American intervention. The number who took the radical view that capitalist "Amerika" was waging an imperialist war to prevent the "liberation" of South Vietnam was not large. Only 12 percent of the students polled in 1970, the height of the movement, identified themselves as "New Left," and by no means all of them had such extreme beliefs. Those who shouted down speakers defending government politics, bombed buildings, and marched under Vietcong flags got the headlines, though. The war fed feelings of resentment at all authority that had first surfaced in the "free speech" riot at the University of California at Berkeley in 1964. In the late sixties, militant activists protesting such symbolic links between the university and the government as ROTC and campus recruiters from Dow Chemical (the maker of napalm) occupied campus buildings and battled police—the "pigs"—sent to remove them. Between January and June of 1968 alone, 221 major demonstrations were held.

Similar unrest with much more serious consequences was occurring in black neighborhoods in northern cities—a wave of race riots. The first major riot—in the Watts district of Los Angeles in the summer of 1965—destroyed $40 million in property and left 34 dead. Newark, Detroit, and dozens of other cities erupted in 1967, the longest and hottest of the "long hot summers," with 83 deaths and over $100 million worth of damage. In city after city, black mobs looted stores, burned buildings, and fought with the police, firemen, and national guardsmen working to restore order. No one has yet adequately explained what caused these upheavals, nor why it is that they occurred in a spasm of about four years and then vanished. However, they were clearly expressions of black rage against discrimination and poverty, spontaneous symbolic assertions of a claim to receive more than the small share of society's resources that normally trickled into the ghetto. Certainly they made plain that the civil rights bills that guaranteed blacks full legal and political equality had not overnight eliminated racial tensions in American society.

Later investigations revealed that the riots were not organized by leaders; very little direction of the crowds took place. Whites responded to them with special fear and dismay, however, because they coincided with the emergence of a new style of black leader—militant spokesmen for "black power." Martin Luther King had preached a gospel of love and nonviolence, and had been willing to work with white sympathizers. In the mid-1960s, frustrated by white resistance, Stokely Carmichael and other SNCC leaders turned their backs on all white "honkeys" and on nonviolence and called for "black power." "Black is beautiful," they said, and black control over "the economics and politics of our community" was essential. Black power, declared Carmichael, would "smash everything Western Civilization has created." Rap Brown, his successor as head of SNCC, remarked that "John Brown is the only white man I could respect, and he's dead." Huey Newton, a leader of the Black Panthers, called on blacks to arm themselves: "We make the statement, quoting from Chairman Mao, that political power comes through the barrel of a gun."

Few of the rioters in Detroit or Newark can have thought in such terms. However one interprets the riots, they were not attempts at a revolutionary insurrection. These wild utterances by militant extremists, however, were unfortunate at a time when the central cities were exploding in flames. They fed "white backlash," the feeling that government support of the drive for black equality had gone too far. In 1964, only 34 percent of American whites believed that blacks were demanding "too much"; by late 1966, it was up to 85 percent. Richard Nixon, with his appeals to "law and order," would effectively play on such fears in the 1968 election.

The 1968 Election

In late 1967, a little known Democratic Senator from Minnesota, Eugene McCarthy, decided to challenge Johnson for the Democratic nomination as a peace candidate. Observers who failed to grasp the extent of popular unease over Vietnam found it laughable that he could make the effort to topple an incumbent President who had been elected by the most lopsided margin in history. Johnson was unbeatable. But after the March, 1968, New Hampshire primary—after the Tet Offensive—they stopped laughing. McCarthy won an amazing moral victory by placing within a few hundred votes of Johnson. Three days later, the rival the President feared most—Senator Robert F. Kennedy—announced that he too was in the race, and shortly afterward, a secret Wisconsin poll disclosed that the President was headed for a crushing defeat by McCarthy in that state's upcoming primary.

Johnson could not comprehend it. A few years before, he had been as popular as any chief executive in the nation's history. Now he was a prisoner in the White House, afraid to appear in public for fear of encountering antiwar demonstrators calling out, "Hey hey, LBJ, how many kids did you kill today?" Only 36 percent of the voters approved his overall leadership, and barely a quarter (26 percent) approved his Vietnam policies. The Tet Offensive had given the lie to the administration claim that the war was nearly won, and all that the military could recommend was to send still more men. That was politically impossible, and yet it was just as impossible politically for Johnson to win over the voters who were gravitating toward McCarthy and Robert Kennedy by admitting that his Vietnam policy for the past three years had been misguided. The only escape was to leave the fray altogether by refusing to run for reelection.

Although Johnson hated him and would have pulled every string he could to keep him from the nomination, Robert Kennedy appeared the favorite for the Democratic nod. But on the night of his victory in the California primary, he fell to an assassin's bullet. Gone was the only Democratic candidate with the enthusiastic backing of blacks and antiwar activists who had also appealed to trade unionists, the white ethnics, and the urban Catholics who had been crucial components of the New Deal coalition. Kennedy could call for an end to the war without sounding unpatriotic, and defend the civil rights revolution without seeming to endorse the breakdown of all law and order.

With Kennedy dead, the Democrats waged fratricidal warfare at their nominating convention at Chicago. Inside the hall, the battle was between Senator McCarthy and Johnson's chosen successor, Vice President Hubert Humphrey. In the streets outside, a related struggle raged between militant student demonstrators and Mayor Richard Daley's police, who clubbed and teargassed the students into submission with undisguised relish. The Humphrey forces easily controlled the nomination, but it was a victory of questionable value. The antiwar wing of the party threatened to sit out the contest in November, while right-wing Democrats began to rally behind the banner of a third-party candidate, Governor George Wallace of Alabama. Wallace denounced blacks, student radicals, and "permissive, pointy-headed intellectuals," and declared the war could be won if the military were given a free hand. His impressive showing in primaries in northern as well as southern states—34 percent in Wisconsin and 30 percent in Indiana— showed that "backlash" sentiments were widespread.

Republican Richard Nixon was the victor in November. His campaign stance on Vietnam was one of studied evasiveness. Like Eisenhower in 1952, Nixon pledged to end the war "with honor," but he refused to specify how, alluding only to a "secret plan" that would be unveiled in due time. Like Wallace, he hammered away at Democratic "permissiveness" as the cause of crime, riots, and campus disorders, and promised to restore "law and order." "Our schools," he said, "are for education, not integration." The contest between Nixon and Humphrey was close; only half a million votes, 0.7 percent of the total, separated the two. But Wallace won almost 14 percent, so the two law-and-order candidates together were preferred by more than 57 percent of the electorate.

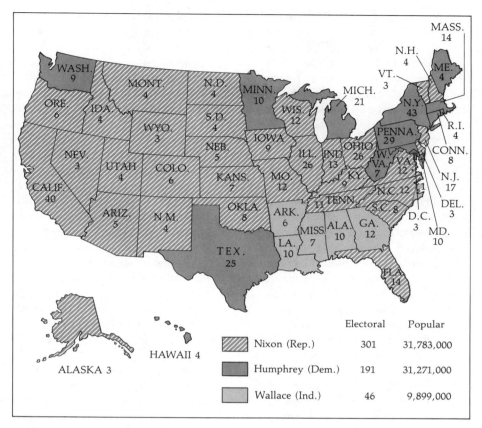

	Electoral	Popular
Nixon (Rep.)	301	31,783,000
Humphrey (Dem.)	191	31,271,000
Wallace (Ind.)	46	9,899,000

MAP 30-3
The 1968 Election

Most impressive were the inroads the Republicans made among groups that had been strongly Democratic since the New Deal—low income, blue-collar whites. Although Humphrey was strongly endorsed by organized labor, only 47 percent of skilled workers and 38 percent of unskilled or semiskilled laborers cast their ballots for him. The war and the race issue overrode the social-class political allegiances that had been normal since the Great Depression.

THE NIXON YEARS

During the campaign, Nixon had pledged to "bring us together," to restore unity in a society that seemed to be tearing apart. His leadership did create a new consensus of sorts. By 1974, it had convinced a large majority of Americans that Nixon should be impeached for "high crimes and misdemeanors" and thrown out of office.

Nixon entered the White House pledged to end the war in Vietnam. It took him four years to honor the pledge. His secret plan for peace was "Vietnamization." The United States would build up South Vietnam's military forces, but would withdraw its own troops. The number of American fighting men in Vietnam fell from over half a million when he took office to 39,000 by September 1972, and the number killed or wounded in battle dropped sharply as well. It was a popular step, and so too was the administration's announcement that the draft was to be phased out.

The people of Vietnam continued to die, however. Vietnamization did not work. The South Vietnam army had every advanced American weapon it wanted, but lacked the discipline and will to fight shown by the Vietcong and North Vietnamese forces. The United States tried to turn the situation around by even more aggressive use of American air power. During Nixon's first four years in office, American planes dropped twice as many bombs on Southeast Asia as *all the allies* together had used against Germany and Japan in World War II, killing tens of thousands of villagers and turning much of the countryside into a wasteland. Although the administration denied it publicly, for 14 months the air assaults were directed against neighboring Cambodia as well, in an effort to cut off the flow of supplies to the rebels. When that failed, Nixon ordered an invasion of Cambodia by South Vietnamese and American troops in the spring of 1971. Despite it, the rebels still managed to find the food and arms they needed and fought on. The major effect on Cambodia was to trigger a civil war that ended in the installation of a Communist regime some years later.

The invasion of Cambodia had two very important consequences for the administration, one immediately apparent and another that would not become clear for some years. The immediate effect was a storm of protest on American campuses. Demonstrations were held at more than 400 colleges and universities, and 250 institutions were forced to close temporarily. At Kent State, in Ohio, panicked National Guardsmen fired into a crowd and killed four youths; at Jackson State, in Mississippi, local police shot two black students to death.

How much the general public was moved by the demonstrations is unknown. But Richard Nixon was certainly moved by them—moved into taking a series of actions that led to his eventual political downfall. Nixon was always a hypersensitive and suspicious man, and the wave of antiwar protest on the campuses seems to have unhinged him. Convinced that student radicals were engaged in a conspiracy to subvert the republic, he began to lay secret plans for the gathering of political intelligence about their activities through such illegal tactics as burglaries, wiretaps, and the opening of mail. Nixon had already authorized wiretaps on thirteen government officials and four journalists he thought had been involved in leaking the news about the bombing of Cambodia. In July of 1970, he approved the "Huston plan" to coordinate such activities by the FBI, CIA, and the Defense Intelligence Agency. When Hoover refused to risk the FBI's reputation, the administration decided to create a special secret White House strike force, the "plumbers." Their targets were not only student radicals but anyone critical of the administration, including journalists and officials of the Democratic Party, whose offices in the Watergate Hotel were the site of the later Watergate burglary. Thus, when Dr. Daniel Ellsberg, a former Pentagon employee, leaked the sensational secret history of U.S. involvement in Vietnam, the Pentagon Papers, to the *New York Times*, G. Gordon Liddy and E. Howard Hunt broke into his psychiatrist's office in search of information to discredit him.

Previous Presidents—including FDR, John F. Kennedy, and Lyndon Johnson—we now know, had sometimes abused their powers in search of intelligence about opponents. Nixon did it more; he did it more zealously, and he did it as part of a plan to concentrate power more tightly within the White House than it had ever been before. He conceived of himself as a counterinsurgency President, at war against a hostile establishment. Under his direction, his staff compiled an "enemies list," and pressured the Internal Revenue Service to give rough treatment to the tax returns of the people on it. This was part of a broad effort, Presidential counselor John Dean later testified, to "use the available Federal machinery to screw our political enemies." "Anyone who opposes us, we'll destroy," said a top White House aide who eventually did time in prison for his role in the machinations. "As a matter of fact, anyone who doesn't support us, we'll destroy."

Victory in 1972

Such "hardball" tactics were hardly necessary to ensure Nixon's reelection in 1972; the Democratic Party seemed to be self-destructing. The deep divisions between urban bosses and union leaders and advocates of "the new politics" that had crippled it in 1968 were still there. But this time, the leaders of the new politics controlled the convention because of new delegate quotas intended to "democratize" the party. Senator George McGovern of South Dakota, who called for immediate withdrawal from Vietnam, easily won the nomination. His campaign was a disaster from the first, after it was revealed that his proposed running mate had undergone electric shock treatment for a mental disorder. His ill-considered welfare and tax-reform proposals, and his image of permissiveness on such issues as crime, student protest, draft resistance, and the drug laws severely hurt his campaign. Although McGovern tried to seize the initiative by claiming that the administration had been implicated in the break-in at the Democratic National Headquarters in June, the press and the public paid no attention. Apparently they believed Nixon's assurance that John Dean had conducted a "complete investigation" of the affair, and had found that "no one in this administration was involved in this very bizarre incident." A week before election day, Nixon's National Security Advisor Henry Kissinger put a final nail in McGovern's coffin by announcing that negotiations in Paris for an end to the war were almost completed, and that "peace is at hand."

The election was a landslide, second only to Johnson's 1964 triumph. Nixon won everywhere but in Massachusetts and the District of Columbia, taking 60.8 percent of the popular vote. The peace Kissinger promised did not come, and the negotiations broke down. To step up the pressure, Nixon then ordered the largest bombing raids on North Vietnam in the entire history of the war, the savage

"Christmas bombing" of Hanoi and Haiphong. Whether it was because of that or because of signals from a war-weary Russia and China, a deal was finally struck in January of 1973. Nixon claimed that it was truly a "peace with honor." Critics objected that the terms were little different from those that could have been negotiated when Nixon first took office, and that four years of carnage and destruction could have been avoided. The agreement did not in fact bring peace, only American withdrawal from a war that soon flared up again and ended in a victory for the insurgents. In May of 1975, Vietcong and North Vietnamese troops stormed into Saigon while the last American officials raced to the helicopters that would take them to safety. The longest war in American history, one which cost that nation 58,000 lives and $350 billion, thus ended in complete failure. It did not result in the "liberation" of South Vietnam, as some radicals claimed; the massive flight of the "boat people" and North Vietnam's subsequent invasion of Cambodia exposed the tyrannical character of the regime to all but the most innocent. But it is hard to doubt that the effects of American intervention were anything but disastrous for all concerned.

In their prolongation of the Vietnam War, Nixon and Kissinger wore the same Cold War ideological blinkers that had unfortunately drawn the United States into the conflict in the first place during the Kennedy and Johnson administrations. In other respects, however, they pursued a more flexible foreign policy than anyone had anticipated. Despite Nixon's long record of militant anti-Communism and his old habit of branding opponents as "pinkoes" and "fellow travelers," he took major initiatives to promote friendlier relations with the two great Communist world powers, China and Russia. His visit to China in early 1972 meant that the U.S. government had abandoned at last the fiction that Chiang Kai-shek's government on the island of Formosa was the true representative of the 800 million people of China, and its consequent insistence that "Red China" be denied membership in the United Nations.

There were new overtures to the Soviet Union as well, to allay Russian fears that the United States was becoming too closely aligned with their rival. The policy of "detente" with the USSR did not produce any spectacular changes in Soviet-American relations, but new trade agreements facilitating the sale of American wheat in Russia and the beginnings of negotiations for strategic arms limitation (SALT) were small steps in the right direction.

These foreign policy achievements won Nixon gratifying recognition as a statesman in the capitals of the world, and fed his ambition to be an imperial president. The trend toward the concentration of power in the hands of the chief executive had been going on for much of this century, notably so in the Roosevelt, Kennedy, and Johnson administrations. But under the Nixon administration it proceeded more rapidly than ever before. Disdainful of the Congress, which remained under Democratic control throughout his years in office, he vetoed bill after bill, and refused to spend duly appropriated funds that he believed excessive, illegally "impounding" them instead. He controlled a vastly enlarged White House staff (more than triple the size of John Kennedy's) responsible to no one but himself, and attempted to operate the government with minimal interference from

Congress. Buoyed by his smashing triumph over McGovern, he reorganized his administration to ensure that only ardent Nixon loyalists would have power, and announced plans to bring the federal bureaucracy under tighter White House control.

Nixon's Downfall

It was too late, because in the next year and a half a wave of scandals that drove Nixon from office came to light. In October of 1973 Vice President Spiro Agnew resigned to avoid prosecution for having taken bribes from contractors and cheating on his income tax. The press discovered that Nixon himself owed the Internal Revenue Service more than $400,000 in back taxes and penalties, and had spent $10 million of the taxpayers' money on improvements and security arrangements for his mansions at Key Biscayne, Florida, and San Clemente, California.

Most damaging of all was the unraveling of the conspiracy of silence over Watergate. The members of the "burglary team" who were caught bugging the Democratic National Headquarters had kept their silence until after the election, in return for promises of plenty of cash and eventual pardon conveyed to them by White House counsel John Dean. When federal judge John Sirica threatened them with stiffer sentences than they had expected, one broke and confessed that the deed had been ordered by officials of the Committee to Re-Elect the President. Hearings by Senator Sam Ervin's investigating committee produced a lengthening chain of evidence that the break-in had been authorized by high officials in the White House, and a growing number of related "White House horrors." "What did the President know and when did he know it?" Republican Senator Howard Baker asked repeatedly. In July of 1973 came the astonishing news that a quite precise answer could be given to that question, because Nixon had secretly taped all of his conversations in the Oval Office. When the special Watergate prosecutor, Archibald Cox of the Harvard Law School immediately subpoenaed the tapes, Nixon refused, claiming an absolute right of "executive privilege." When Cox insisted, Nixon fired him, prompting the protest resignation of Attorney General Elliot Richardson and his chief aide, among the most respected members of the administration. Cox's replacement, Leon Jaworski, kept up legal pressure for the tapes, and forced the release of some, one of them with a mysterious buzz obliterating eighteen-and-a-half minutes at what appeared to be a crucial part of the conversation. White House aide General Alexander Haig's explanation that the buzz was caused by "some sinister force" was not reassuring.

The details of this fascinating and astonishing story are too complex to enter into here. Suffice it to say that Nixon was driven ever deeper into a corner. The Supreme Court insisted that he give up more and more tapes, and each disclosure was more incriminating. In March of 1974, a federal grand jury indicted seven top Nixon aides for their involvement in the cover-up; it also secretly named the President as an "unindicted co-conspirator," because the prosecutor advised that

PRESIDENT NIXON'S TAPE SECRET, APRIL 26, 1973

NIXON: With regard to the tapes... I don't think it should ever get out that we taped this office, Bob. Have we got people that are trustworthy on that? I guess we have.

HALDEMAN: I think so.

NIXON: If it does, the answer is yes. We only, but we only taped the national security, uh, information. All other, all other, all other information is scrapped, never transcribed. Get the point? That's what I want you to remember on those, if you will.... I think that's very important, very important. You never want to be in a position to say the President taped it, you know. I mean taped somebody.

HALDEMAN: Well, the whole purpose of this was for national security....

NIXON: I know, but I just don't want this to be—I just don't want that tape, for example, I don't want you to, I don't want to disclose that to Ehrlichman or anybody else, I mean that's just something—I know what you can tell Ehrlichman. Just say you went over it and it's about the same as...

HALDEMAN: I've already, what I said to him is that the tape—he knows I went over it, of course. Uh, I said, "It basically says what the President recalled."

the law prevented the indictment of a chief executive. Nixon took the fight to the public in the spring by releasing his own "edited" version of transcripts he was still struggling to keep secret, but even these sanitized versions contained ugly material and made people wonder how much worse the originals were. In July, three days after the Supreme Court ordered the release of still more tapes, the House Judiciary Committee recommended that Nixon be impeached for obstruction of justice, abuse of presidential power, and failure to enforce the law by turning over subpoenaed tapes. Before the matter could be brought to the floor of the House, a crucial revelation was made. The newest tapes scheduled for release included a conversation between the President and his Chief of Staff, Robert Haldeman, which provided unmistakable evidence that from the beginning the conspiracy to cover up Watergate had been orchestrated by Richard M. Nixon, who had told lie after lie to the American people. With his impeachment and conviction now a sure thing, Nixon had no alternative but to resign in disgrace. That the President of the United States felt compelled to tell the public "I am not a crook," as Nixon did in November 1973, was amazing enough. The revelation that he was not telling the truth when he said it boggled the imagination. No chief executive could survive that damning stain on his reputation.

SUGGESTED READINGS

Godfrey Hodgson, *America in Our Time* (1976) is the best overview. For other general accounts, see William O'Neill, *Coming Apart: An Informal History of America in the 1960's* (1971), and Ronald Berman, *America in the Sixties* (1968). Arthur M. Schlesinger, Jr., *A Thousand Days: John F. Kennedy in the White House* (1965) and Theodore Sorenson, *Kennedy* (1965) are admiring accounts by insiders. David Halberstam, *The Best and the Brightest* (1972), Henry Fairlie, *The Kennedy Promise: The Politics of Expectation* (1973), and Garry Wills, *The Kennedy Imprisonment: A Meditation on Power* (1982) are sharply critical.

James L. Sundquist, *Politics and Policy: The Eisenhower, Kennedy, and Johnson Years* (1968), Otis L. Graham, Jr., *Toward a Planned Society: From Roosevelt to Nixon* (1976), James T. Patterson, *America's Struggle Against Poverty, 1900–1980* (1981), and David Calleo, *The Imperious Economy* (1982) treat the major domestic policies of the period. Herbert Dinerstein, *The Making of a Missile Crisis* (1976), David Detzer, *The Brink* (1979), Glenn T. Seaborg and Benjamin S. Loer, *Kennedy, Krushchev, and the Test Ban* (1982), and Richard J. Barnet, *Intervention and Revolution: The U.S. and the Third World* (1969) consider foreign affairs. On Vietnam, see R.W. Tucker, *The Radical Left and American Foreign Policy* (1971), Frances Fitzgerald, *Fire in the Lake* (1972), Herbert Y. Schandler, *The Unmaking of a President: Lyndon Johnson and Vietnam* (1977), Guenter Lewy, *America in Vietnam* (1978), Michael Charlton and Anthony Moncrieff, *Many Reasons Why: The American Involvement in Vietnam* (1978), George C. Herring, *America's Longest War* (1979), and Leslie H. Gelb, *The Irony of Vietnam: The System Worked* (1979). Radical politics and cultural styles are analyzed in Peter Clecak, *Radical Paradoxes: Dilemmas of the American Left, 1945–1970* (1973), Irwin Unger, *The Movement: A History of the New Left, 1959–1972* (1974), and Morris Dickstein, *Gates of Eden: American Culture in the Sixties* (1977). On the ghetto upheavals and civil rights struggles, see Robert M. Fogelson, *Violence as Protest* (1971), August Meier and Elliot Rudwick, *CORE: A Study in the Civil Rights Movement, 1942–1968* (1972), Carl M. Brauer, *John F. Kennedy and the Second Reconstruction* (1977), Dorothy K. Newman, et al., *Protest, Politics, and Prosperity: Black Americans and White Institutions, 1940–1974* (1979), David J. Garrow, *Protest at Selma: Martin Luther King, Jr., and the Voting Rights Act of 1965* (1978), J. Harvie Wilkinson III, *From Brown to Bakke: The Supreme Court and School Integration, 1954–1978* (1979), William H. Chafe, *Civilities and Civil Rights: Greensboro, North Carolina and the Black Struggle for Freedom* (1980), Harris Wofford, *Of Kennedy and Kings: Making Sense of the Sixties* (1980), and Clayborne Carson, *In Struggle: SNCC and the Black Awakening of the 1960's* (1981).

Garry Wills, *Nixon Agonistes: The Crisis of the Self-Made Man* (1971) is a penetrating study. Leonard Silk, *Nixoneconomics* (1972) and Jonathan Schell, *The Time of Illusion: An Historical and Reflective Account of the Nixon Era* (1975) assess Nixon's domestic achievements. On foreign affairs, see Henry Brandon, *The Retreat of American Power* (1973), Roger Morris, *Uncertain Greatness: Henry Kissinger and American Foreign Policy* (1977), and Stanley Hoffman, *Primacy or World Order* (1978). J. Anthony Lukas, *Nightmare: The Underside of the Nixon Years* (1976) is the most satisfactory account of Watergate.

Chapter Thirty-One

In Our Times

Historians, a thoughtful writer on current affairs has observed, "are scholars who tell us later what it all means, after time has burned off passing detail, and left the ridges of change bare." History is the art of hindsight—of piecing together the puzzles of the past after one knows how the story has turned out. We are still too close to the history of the United States in the past decade to be able to see it from the historian's perspective. Time has not yet bared the "ridges of change" that shape the flow of current history. The historian's own subjective preferences and prejudices consequently will be more evident than when he deals with more remote events. Nevertheless, it is essential to attempt to make some sense of recent developments, even though the provisional account that can be written today will undoubtedly seem superficial and biased before very long.

THE POLITICS OF STAGFLATION

Gerald R. Ford, a long-time Congressman from Michigan who Nixon had named Vice-President after Spiro T. Agnew was forced to resign, replaced Nixon in the White House in August of 1974. It was a difficult time for anyone, but particularly for a Republican, to occupy the Presidency. Popular disillusionment over Vietnam and Watergate was reflected in public opinion polls that revealed public confidence in government officials had slumped sharply since the mid-1960s. In two

Amid headlines involving the arms race, inflation, and Central American revolutions, many Americans felt the most pressing problem of the early 1980s was unemployment.

hundred years, a magazine commented, the United States had gone "from George Washington, who could not tell a lie, to Richard Nixon, who could not tell the truth." Ford's immediate decision to issue Nixon a "full, free, and absolute" pardon for any crimes he committed as President was an understandable attempt to sweep the memory of Watergate under the rug and spare the country the trauma of seeing a former chief executive put behind bars. But it invited suspicion that Nixon had made his abdication conditional upon an agreement that he could remain above the law, much as Vice-President Agnew had avoided jail for accepting bribes by pleading no contest and resigning his office. The Republican Party's inability to disassociate itself from Watergate resulted in a Democratic landslide in the November, 1974 elections. The Democrats won an additional 43 seats in the House and 4 in the Senate, giving them edges of 291 to 144 and 61 to 37 respectively. The new President's prospects of winning approval for legislative innovations were severely circumscribed as a result.

Gerald Ford kept Henry Kissinger on as Secretary of State, and his foreign policy followed the main lines laid down by Richard Nixon. Strategic Arms Limitations Talks with the Soviet Union resulted in a 1974 treaty, SALT I. It did nothing to reduce the mammoth nuclear arsenal both sides had by then accumulated, but pledged that neither would build destabilizing anti-ballistic missiles that might tempt one to launch a nuclear first strike. After the October, 1973 Yom Kippur war between Israel and various Arab states, Kissinger's "shuttle diplomacy" helped to bring about a cease-fire and a promise of the Israeli Knesset (Parliament) to end military occupation of the Sinai Peninsula in exchange for Egyptian recognition of Israel's right to exist. An incident in the aftermath of final collapse of South Vietnam in 1975, however, showed that the Ford administration could be trigger-happy. After the Communist Khmer Rouge came to power in Cambodia, its forces seized an American merchant vessel, the *Mayaguez*, for violating Cambodia's territorial waters. While negotiations to secure the release of the *Mayaguez* were proceeding, Ford sent in the Marines to rescue the crew by force. The 38 crew members were freed, but at the cost of 15 American deaths, 3 missing in action, and 50 wounded. The figures suggested that Ford's decision to fight was impetuous, but the action was popular. Frustrated by their prolonged inability to use America's crushing margin of military superiority to pacify Vietnam, Americans rallied around the flag at this flexing of the nation's military muscle.

President Ford's management of the economy was considerably less popular. At the outset of his presidency he defined inflation, then running at the rate of 11 percent a year, as America's number one domestic problem. To conquer it, he pursued tight money policies that plunged the country into the worst recession since the 1930s. Unemployment soared to over 12 percent in the peak month of 1975, and averaged 8.5 percent for the year. Thereafter, the Ford administration, prodded by Congressional Democrats, shifted to expansionary monetary and fiscal policies. Federal spending was increased at the same time that taxes were cut, producing federal deficits of $71 billion for fiscal year 1975 and $66 billion for 1976. Under that stimulus, unemployment began to fall, but the inflation rate also started to climb once again. Both unemployment and inflation remained well above what they had been in the prosperous sixties; "stagflation," it was becoming clear, was

TABLE 31-1
Inflation, Unemployment, and "Discomfort Index"
for Selected Years

	Percent Increase, Consumer Price Index	Percent of Civilian Work Force Unemployed	Discomfort Index (Inflation plus Unemployment)
1961	1.0	6.7	7.7
1965	1.7	4.5	6.2
1970	5.9	4.9	10.8
1971	3.4	5.9	9.3
1972	3.4	5.6	9.0
1973	8.8	4.9	13.7
1974	12.2	5.6	17.8
1975	7.0	8.5	15.5
1976	4.8	7.7	12.5
1977	6.8	7.0	13.8
1978	9.0	6.0	15.0
1979	13.3	5.8	19.1
1980	12.4	7.1	19.5
1981	8.9	8.7	17.6
1982	3.9	10.6	14.5
1983*	4.9	10.8	15.7

*Estimated

not a problem to which there were easy answers. Since the early seventies, the "discomfort index" (inflation plus unemployment) has remained two to three times as high as in the Kennedy and Johnson years (see Table 31-1).

Neither the President nor the Congress grasped the full significance of the most important economic challenge of the Ford years—the successful attempt of the Organization of Petroleum Exporting Countries (OPEC) to use its monopoly power to send world oil prices skyrocketing. For a dozen years after its founding in 1960, OPEC was ineffectual. The United States was producing enough petroleum to meet most of its own needs and part of those of other Western countries, and OPEC members lacked the discipline to agree on a price for exported oil and stick to it. In the sunny Eisenhower years, the age of massive, overpowered gas guzzlers with tail fins, the world price of oil was *ten cents* a barrel (as compared to about $30 in the early 1980s). The working and living patterns of Americans were premised on an unending supply of extremely cheap energy. The first indication of an end to that world that could waste energy was the OPEC oil embargo of October, 1973, and the decision of the oil-producing nations to jack up petroleum prices four-fold over the next six months, the first of a series of shock waves the effects of which were still being felt in the United States a decade later. The pretext for the embargo was Western support for Israel in her latest war with the Arabs, but what gave OPEC the clout to make it hurt was that the United States, Europe, and Japan had by then grown heavily dependent on Middle Eastern oil for transportation, heating, and industrial power. A third of all the petroleum used in America, for example, came from abroad, and by the end of the decade the proportion had risen to half.

The Ford administration made a modest attempt to force Americans to adjust to new realities by proposing an increase in the federal tax on gasoline to reduce consumption, and decontrol of oil prices to stimulate domestic production. But Congress, shrinking from actions that would likely enrage many voters, defeated the plan. U.S. oil prices continued to be pegged at levels far below those in other industrial nations; the retail price for gasoline was 39 cents a gallon, as compared to 72 cents in Britain, 87 cents in West Germany, and 95 cents in France. The perverse effect of standing pat was that it encouraged high consumption and discouraged domestic production (because prices were kept artificially low by controls). As a result, the United States became progressively more dependent on oil imports from one of the most volatile and unstable areas of the world. Long lines at gas stations in the winter of 1973–74 should have made plain the need for a new energy policy, but most Americans attributed the shortage to hoarding by greedy oil companies.

Although he had the advantage of being the sitting President, Gerald Ford was too moderate in his views for the increasingly powerful and restless right wing of the Republican Party, and he barely wrested the nomination from its favored candidate, Governor Ronald Reagan of California. In the November elections, however, Ford came very close to defeating the Democratic dark horse, an obscure one-term governor of Georgia, Jimmy Carter. Carter had taken advantage of reforms in the system of presidential primaries to secure the nomination by tireless grassroots campaigning, ignoring the Democratic Party hierarchy. He frittered away the enormous lead over Ford he had enjoyed in the polls at the time of the conventions, but held on to edge out the incumbent by two percent of the popular vote. Carter downplayed issues and ran "against Washington," stressing that he was an outsider uncontaminated by any association with the Washington power structure. He won by recreating the old New Deal coalition, carrying every southern state and enough northern industrial states to put him over the top.

The Man from Plains, Georgia

Jimmy Carter was a fervent "born-again" Christian, who pledged to "see us once again have a nation that's as good and honest and decent and truthful and competent and compassionate and as filled with love as the American people." "I will never lie to you," he promised. His sincerity could not be doubted, but the job of presiding over a divided nation proved to be more difficult than he had anticipated. At first, Carter showed a certain flair for populist public relations gestures many found appealing. He was the first President ever photographed in blue jeans, he chose to walk down Pennsylvania Avenue to the White House after his inauguration rather than ride in a limousine, and he dramatized the need for energy conservation by wearing a thick sweater rather than a business suit in his television message on the subject. But appealing directly to the people was no substitute for working effectively with Congress. Although both houses were controlled by members of his own party, many Congressmen were alienated by Carter's evident disdain for the Washington scene. Neither the President nor his chief advisors, almost all of them drawn from his close circle of Georgian backers, understood the need to curry favor with key figures in the Congressional establishment. Carter "simply did not *like* politicians," one of his top aides admitted later; he had no taste for wheeling and dealing to get his way. When urged to get to know some Congressional leaders by playing tennis with them, he dutifully made a list, checked off the names after he had played once with each, and that was the end of the matter.

The Carter administration was no more effective at dealing with stagflation than its predecessor had been. In his first years in office, the new President followed expansionary policies to restore full employment. Unemployment declined moderately as a result, but the inflation rate increased two-and-a-half times between 1976 and 1979. By early 1980, the Consumer Price Index was soaring at an annual rate of 18.2 percent, the highest in American history. At that appalling pace, the value of a pension or other fixed source of income would be cut in half in a mere five years. A loaf of bread cost $.24 in 1970, $.89 in 1980; a one-pound can of coffee had risen from $.91 to $3.69. Although the newly-appointed head of the Federal Reserve Board, Paul Volcker, put the brakes on by tightening control over the money supply in late 1979, it did more to increase joblessness than to check inflation, which was even higher in 1980 than the year before. Per capita income in constant dollars, up 37 percent in the 1950s and 34 percent in the 1960s, began to decline shortly after Carter took office, and fell 5.5 percent in the year 1980 alone. The discomfort index in 1979 was the highest on record since the 1930s, and it was higher still in 1980 (see Table 31-1). Money wages were climbing, but prices were rising even faster. For the first time since the 1930s, the standard of living of the average American dropped, and the United States slipped to number eleven in the world in per capita income, behind most of Western Europe.

The causes of the inflationary spiral were debatable, but a major one was another surge in the price of imported oil. By the late 1970s the people of the United States were burning up 16 million barrels of petroleum a day, half of which came from abroad. After quadrupling in 1973-74, the price of OPEC oil rose by only 25 percent over the next four years; in that period, demand did not grow much more rapidly than supply. The revolution that overthrew the Shah of Iran in the fall of 1978 and eventually brought to power the Ayatollah Khomeini shut down Iran's rich fields and created shortages that allowed OPEC to raise prices again, from $15 to more than $30 a barrel. Even more annoying to American consumers than more expensive gas were infuriatingly long lines at the pump and the threat that they would not be able to fill their tanks whenever they wished.

The Carter administration perceived the urgency of the energy crisis. What it failed to grasp was how to prod Congress into resolute action to deal with it. Shortly after he took office, Carter declared that the battle to conserve energy was nothing less than "the moral equivalent of war," and proposed a sweeping program to cut imports and spur domestic production by raising oil prices. He called for a stiff tax on gasoline and on oversized automobiles, decontrol of domestic petroleum prices, and subsidies for conservation measures and the development of coal, solar, and nuclear sources of energy. The plan was hastily conceived, and Carter and his team of outsiders were unable to persuade either the public or the Congress that drastic measures were required. After eighteen months of lobbying by powerful interest groups, only a few of Carter's most innocuous proposals were adopted. After three years, a more comprehensive but still greatly watered-down energy package scraped through. American consumption of imported oil fell off steeply in the early 1980s; however, the main cause was not the new legislation but a severe recession that shut down many industrial establishments. It seemed a safe bet that economic recovery in the future would bring further energy shortages and upward pressure on prices.

The President had a somewhat freer hand in the conduct of American foreign policy, and Carter employed it with mixed success. He denounced what he regarded as the Machiavellian practice of making alliances with repressive regimes around the world, and declared that supporting individual human rights would be "the soul of our foreign policy." The policy influenced the easing of political suppression in some dictatorships aligned with the United States, particularly in Latin America. But it was not put into practice in such cases as the Shah's Iran, South Korea, or the Philippines, and it did nothing to mellow the rulers in the Kremlin. The administration removed a major irritant in our Latin American relations by negotiating a treaty ceding the Panama Canal to the government of Panama—over the cries of right-wingers who insisted that "the canal is ours, we stole it fair and square." Carter's canal treaty won the necessary two-thirds approval in the Senate by a margin of a single vote. Tensions with Communist China also eased after Carter extended full diplomatic recognition to the People's Republic in December of 1978, bringing to fruition Richard Nixon's "opening to China." In a brilliant feat of personal diplomacy, Carter also attempted to defuse the Middle Eastern powder keg by persuading President Anwar Sadat of Egypt and Prime Minister Menachem Begin of Israel to meet with him at Camp David in September of 1978, a major step down the road that led to a peace treaty between Israel and the nation that had long been the most powerful exponent of Arab nationalism.

The most important relationship in world politics is that between the two superpowers with the ability to reduce most of the planet to radioactive rubble— the United States and the U.S.S.R. Carter took office as a supporter of detente as practised by Henry Kissinger during the Nixon and Ford administrations. Despite his dismay at the Soviet Union's disregard for human rights, he struggled patiently to hammer out a Strategic Arms Limitation Treaty that would effect an equilibrium of nuclear forces by limiting the number of warheads and delivery vehicles on both sides and barring the development of new thermonuclear weapons. The SALT II treaty, drafted in early 1979, aroused the ire of the same right-wing Senators who opposed the Panama Canal "giveaway"; they maintained, with more emotion than reason, that the terms of the treaty were slanted in favor of the Russians. What promised to be a furious political struggle came to an abrupt end at the end of the year, when the Soviet Union sent troops into Afghanistan to support a pro-Soviet puppet regime that was having difficulty suppressing an uprising by Moslem rebels. In response, the disillusioned President put SALT II on the back burner, declared an embargo on shipments of American grain and high-tech products to the U.S.S.R., and organized support for an international boycott of the 1980 Moscow Olympic Games. Abandoning the quest to put a lid on the arms race, Carter announced that the United States would build a new arsenal of MX missiles, and make them invulnerable to Soviet attack by shuttling them around on 4,000 miles of underground tracks in the western United States.

The foreign policy issue that most damaged Carter politically was one over which he had virtually no control. In November of 1979, an angry crowd of Iranians stormed the U.S. embassy in Teheran and took 53 Americans hostage. The condition for releasing them, they announced, was that the United States deliver the Shah (then in the U.S. for medical treatment) to the Ayatollah Khomeini's revolutionary regime for trial. Carter was desperately eager to avoid a replay of the *Mayaguez* incident, politically popular though that show of force had been, and insisted that the United States do nothing that might imperil the lives of the hostages. The issue had to be resolved by peaceful negotiation. Months of inconclusive talks with a succession of alleged spokesmen for the Iranian government followed, while every night the television news reported that the twentieth, the fortieth, the ninetieth, the one hundred twentieth day of captivity had ended.

After almost half a year had elapsed, the President felt compelled at last to attempt a military solution—a helicopter raid to free the captives. When the details of the operation are made public some day, it may seem less wildly misguided than it appeared at the time. All that the American people knew then—and all that they know today—is that the April, 1980 rescue attempt was botched and that it left eight American soldiers dead in the desert. In the eyes of the world, and of the American people themselves, the United States appeared an impotent giant. Negotiations then resumed again, to bear fruit only after the 1980 elections were over. It is not easy to point to an alternative policy that would have been clearly preferable to that pursued by the Carter administration; certainly none of the President's political rivals articulated one. But the whole affair was profoundly humiliating. It gave Carter an image of weakness that he could not shake, and increased public receptivity to the Cold War platitudes that were the stock-in-trade of his Republican opponent in the November election, Ronald Reagan.

The Reagan "Revolution"

In the 1980 presidential contest, Carter was trounced by Reagan, a photogenic former actor who proved to be a superb campaigner. Reagan carried 44 of the 50 states, and the GOP gained twelve Senate seats, taking control of a house of Congress for the first time since 1954. The Republicans offered reassuringly simple solutions to the problems that beset the nation. Echoing John Kennedy's 1960 charge that the Eisenhower administration had allowed the Russians to open up a "missile gap," Reagan claimed that Carter's laxness had produced a "window of vulnerability" that might tempt the Soviets to launch a nuclear strike and that a

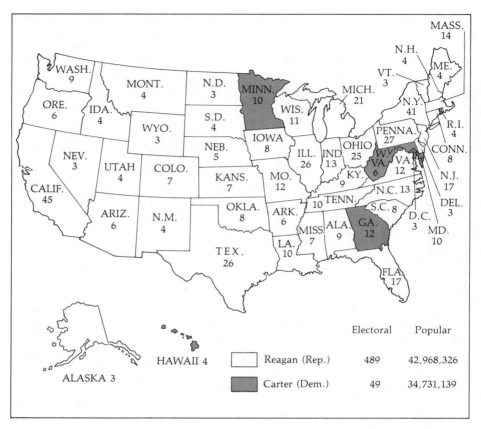

MAP 31–1
The 1980 Election

crash buildup of both nuclear and conventional forces was needed to restore the United States to a commanding position in the world and insure the peace. Chronic inflation had a simple source and remedy. Its "main cause," according to Reagan, was "the massive continuing deficit of the federal government." Cutting "big government" down to size and balancing the federal budget, he claimed, would solve the problem. Eliminating the deficit and balancing the budget would not require higher taxes; it could actually be done, Reagan contended, with lower taxes. Paring down wasteful social programs that diminished incentives to work, reducing taxes, and eliminating restrictions on entrepreneurial freedom would get "government off the backs of the American people" and produce a tremendous surge of economic growth. A healthy dose of "Reaganomics," "supply-side economics," would restore the patient to glowing health.

Some observers took the election results as a popular mandate to roll back the Great Society, the beginnings of a "Reagan revolution" that would produce an electoral realignment as decisive as those of the 1890s and 1930s. Close inspection of the electoral returns, however, made it seem questionable that a new, long-term "Republican majority" had taken shape. Some groups that traditionally leaned toward the Democrats did indeed defect to Reagan. "Born-again" white Protestants, for example, strong backers of Carter in 1976, opted for Reagan by two to one in 1980. He won 51 percent of the Catholic vote, and almost 40 percent of normally liberal Jewish votes. But whether the election was a positive mandate for Reagan or a repudiation of Jimmy Carter was debatable. Some 38 percent of the voters told pollsters they had pulled the lever for Reagan because they disliked Carter so much, a group twice as large as those giving any other reason for their choice.

Whether or not Reagan had a strong popular mandate for a dramatic change of course, in his first days in office he proceeded to act as if he had been given one and the Congress appeared to agree. At his recommendation, the Congress slashed $35 billion from food stamp, school lunch, and a variety of other health, education, and welfare expenditures. At the same time it approved virtually every item on the Pentagon's wish list and launched the largest peacetime military buildup in American history. It endorsed the supply-side recipe for economic growth by enacting a gigantic tax cut, estimated to amount to $750 billion over the next five years.

The vaunted economic boom, however, failed to materialize. The inflation rate fell off sharply during the first two years of the Reagan presidency, but it did so because the economy was falling into an ever-deeper slump. The rise in unemployment and the decline in industrial output were steeper than in any year since the difficult transition from a war to a peacetime economy was made in 1946. 1982 was the fourth year in a row in which the real earnings of the average American slipped. This dismal showing, and the widespread belief that Reagan's tax breaks and cuts in social programs were skewed in favor of the well-to-do scotched Republican hopes that the 1982 Congressional elections would be comparable to those of 1934, when Franklin Roosevelt's party strengthened its grip on the legislative branch. Instead, the Democrats gained 26 seats in the House of Representatives and won 27 of 36 gubernatorial races.

At the time of this writing—the spring of 1983—the Reagan administration's economic program seemed in considerable disarray. The President was determined to press for further whopping increases in the military budget. The new Congress seemed equally adamant it its refusal to approve further major cuts in social welfare expenditures. Even if those are forthcoming, the combination of the tax cuts mandated in 1981, the depressed level of tax revenues resulting from the continued recession, and the demands of the Pentagon will result in a staggering deficit. Over the entire decade of the 1970s, the federal government ran up $420 billion in red ink, a sum Reagan denounced as profligate. In the single fiscal year that begins on July 1, 1983, his own administration anticipates a deficit of well over $200 billion, and the picture for the "out" years in the future looks little better. Having taken office pledging a fully balanced budget by 1984, the best that the President can now pledge is that the budget will be "trending towards balance" by the end of the 1980s—with an imbalance of $126 billion, far larger than any under Nixon, Ford, or Carter, in the year 1988. Fear that these immense projected deficits would trigger another round of inflation was the major reason that long-term interest rates remained extremely high despite the abrupt slowing of inflation.

The most painless and effective damper on the soaring federal deficit would be to put a lid on the nuclear arms race by negotiating a settlement with the USSR Although the Reagan administration denounced supporters of the growing popular movement for a negotiated nuclear freeze as dupes of the Russians, it professed willingness to explore arms control agreements between the two superpowers. The sincerity of its commitment was doubted by many. Key administration officials spoke blithely of "prevailing" in a "protracted" nuclear exchange; one declared enthusiastically that all it would take to survive a thermonuclear holocaust was "a shovel and three feet of dirt." Optimists could take some comfort in the fact that Reagan's long record as an ardent cold warrior gave him the political freedom to arrive at an arms control settlement that more "dovish" politicians would find politically suicidal, much as Richard Nixon's past record made it easier for him to withdraw from Vietnam and to establish relations with Communist China than it would have been for a Democratic President. Whether Reagan would in fact take advantage of that freedom to reduce the risks of the thermonuclear conflagration that might mean the end of civilization, however, was far from clear.

THE DECLINING—BUT CONTINUING—SIGNIFICANCE OF RACE

Although the 1980s will surely hold many surprises, we can predict with considerable confidence that the issue of relations between white and nonwhite Americans will remain central. Extraordinary advances have been made within the past generation, changes that are little short of revolutionary. And yet the United States is still far from a color-blind society, and the question of the role of black people within it will remain an urgent one for the foreseeable future.

Some sense of the amazing progress in race relations that has been made since the Great Depression may be gained by comparing the best-selling novel and popular film of the Depression decade, *Gone with the Wind,* with the 1977 television film *Roots,* which reached an audience rivaling that of the Superbowl. The black people in *Gone with the Wind* were portrayed in a manner familiar to southern apologists for slavery a century earlier—as happy, docile, lazy, childlike Sambos, suitable for nothing more challenging than menial service under close supervision by benevolent whites. The highly popular weekly radio program "Amos and Andy" conveyed much the same image. The scientific reference works of the day were if anything even more demeaning. Negroes, according to the supposedly authoritative *Encyclopedia Britannica,* had a distinctive unpleasant odor and a "less voluminous brain" than whites. They were "on a lower evolutionary plane," "inferior," "more closely related to the highest anthropoids" than to other human beings.

In *Roots*, by contrast, blacks appeared as unfailingly intelligent, enterprising, and heroic victims of cruel and greedy whites. Whether many white viewers were actually persuaded by this inversion of older racial stereotypes is impossible to say.

TABLE 31-2
Black Occupational Progress, 1940–80

	Percent Employed as Professional, Technical, Managerial, or Administrative Workers				
	1940	*1950*	*1960*	*1970*	*1980*
Black males	3	4	5	8	20
White males	17	19	23	25	32
Black as percent of white	18	21	22	32	63
Black females	5	7	8	11	20
White females	19	18	17	19	25
Black as percent of white	26	39	47	58	80

The point is that an ardently pro-black film like *Roots* could never have been shown to a national audience until fairly recently. That it was in 1977, and was a huge success, is a symbol of much else that has happened.

One major area of change has been the occupational sphere. At the close of the Great Depression, less than half a century ago, a majority of American blacks still lived in the South. More than a quarter of them were sharecroppers, farm laborers, or farmers, and over half were nonagricultural laborers or domestic servants. Only a handful—3 percent of the males and 5 percent of the females—worked as professionals, technicians, managers, or administrators. Now less than 3 percent of the nation's blacks work in agriculture, and most of this small remnant are no longer tenants or laborers but farm owners; in 1969, only a fifth of the 100,000 black-operated farms in the United States were occupied by tenants. The proportion of black males in upper-level white-collar jobs has soared from 3 to 20 percent, and of females from 5 to 20 percent (see Table 31-2). The proportion in menial laboring or service jobs has fallen from over half to one-third. Half of all employed blacks today are either skilled craftsmen or white- or pink-collar workers. The rapid emergence of this new black middle class has been one of the major social changes of our era.

This dramatic upgrading of the black labor force could not have taken place without a great rise in the educational level of the black population. Before World War II, blacks in the early stages of their careers (ages 25–34) had an average of only seven years of schooling, three and a half years less than their white counterparts, and that seven years was obtained in inferior segregated schools in most cases. Today the racial gap in years of school completed has almost vanished. Other measures of educational achievement—the proportion graduating from high school and the rate of college attendance—show similar progress. As recently as 1950, only 83,000 blacks were enrolled in college; today the figure is over a million.

These educational and occupational advances, in an economically expanding society, have multiplied the earning power of the average black person and raised larger numbers of people from abject poverty. In the late 1930s, the median income of black families was only a third that of native whites. Even after the great gains made by blacks during World War II, four in ten earned less than $3,000 a year (in 1974 dollars), well below the poverty line, and only one in six made more than $7,000. By 1974, only 14 percent of black families eked out their existence on less than $3,000 and well over half had $7,000 or more. One of the key effects of this new affluence has been a sharp rise in the proportion of blacks who own their own homes, up strikingly from 23 percent in 1940 to 44 percent in 1980.

The political advances made by the black community have been equally impressive. At the end of the Great Depression, they were denied elementary political rights throughout the South, where more than three-quarters of them lived. Less than 5 percent of the blacks residing in the eleven ex-Confederate states were registered to vote. Legal barriers to political participation were absent in the North, but the poverty and limited education of most northern blacks kept them from turning out at the polls, and their numbers were too small to count for much anyway. There were only a handful of black elected officials in the entire country. Mass migration to the North, the civil rights movement, and the Voting Rights Act of 1965 have together put an end to black political isolation and powerlessness. By 1971, 62 percent of southern blacks were registered to vote, only a shade below the white rate. White candidates have been forced to take black interests into account wherever Afro-Americans form a strong voting bloc, and growing numbers of blacks are pursuing political careers. In 1977, there were 17 blacks in Congress, 299 in state legislatures, and 162 serving as mayors. Today there almost 6,000 black elected officials and another 20,000 employed as government administrators or policy technicians. Blacks are still underrepresented in politics, but their political leverage has increased notably.

The Other Side of the Coin

To say that black people have come a long way—a very long way—in the past generation is not to say that all is well, and that the United States has successfully resolved the race issue. The division between the races is still the most important and dangerous cleavage in American society. For all of the gains made by the rapidly expanding black middle class, there is also a large and growing black "underclass," much of it locked into the vast ghettoes of New York, Chicago, and other metropolitan centers. In large central cities, the percentage of whites with incomes below the official poverty line fell 5 percent in the course of the 1970s, but the proportion of impoverished blacks increased 21 percent. In 1981, 34 percent of blacks, 9 million people, lived in poverty, as compared with 11 percent of whites. Black unemployment rates are double those for whites in every age group, and for black teenagers they exceed 50 percent in many cities. The high level of joblessness is one source of the soaring ghetto crime rate, most of whose victims are black.

The best measure of the continuing economic disadvantage of blacks is the

TABLE 31–3
Black Educational Gains, 1940–75

	Median Number of Years of School Completed (ages 25–34)	Percent High School Graduates (ages 25–34)	Percent in College (ages 18–24)
1940			
Blacks	6.9	11	2
Whites	10.4	39	9
Black as percent of white	66	28	22
1975			
Blacks	12.4	69	21
Whites	12.8	82	27
Black as percent of white	97	84	78

ratio of their mean earnings to those of whites. Although black incomes have risen spectacularly within the past generation, part of the reason is that the incomes of all Americans have been going up. The following figures reveal how much blacks have caught up with whites: In 1939, the average black family earned only a bit more than one-third of its white counterpart. Much of that huge differential had been wiped out by 1970, when the ratio stood at .61, before slipping slightly in the 1970s. To advance from about a third to three-fifths of the white average is certainly progress. On the other hand, three-fifths is well below equality. By an odd and depressing coincidence, it is just the weight the Founding Fathers assigned slaves for purposes of political representation and taxation.

The failure of blacks to attain full economic equality with whites is not a simple measure of the extent of continuing racial discrimination in the American economy. Differences in the earnings of ethnic groups today are largely due to a

TABLE 31–4
Black Family Incomes, 1947–74
(in 1974 dollars)

Percentage Earning	1947	1974
Less than $3,000	42	14
$3,000 to $6,999	41	31
$7,000 to $9,999	9	16
$10,000 or more	8	38

TABLE 31-5
The Ratio of Median Black
to White Family Income, 1939-80

Year	Ratio
1939	.37
1950	.54
1960	.55
1970	.61
1980	.58

complex of demographic factors. Blacks, for example, are still more concentrated in the South than whites, and southern wage levels are below the national average. Blacks are less well educated, on the average, than whites, although younger blacks are rapidly catching up on this score. Part of the racial gap in earnings stems from that differential. Whites today are seven years older than blacks on the average, and that increases their incomes because employment earnings rise with experience. When we control some of these distorting influences by comparing black and white families in the North and West in which the head of the household was under 35 and both parents were working in 1976, the blacks actually earned a shade more—$16,715 to $16,691.

There are grounds for optimism that the movement toward equality will continue. The average black educational level will rise as the older generation educated under Jim Crow retires from the labor force and college-educated Afro-Americans are launched into careers. On the other hand, there are many alarming signs, including the tremendous rise in the proportion of black families headed by females without a husband present, which has almost doubled within the past two decades. In 1978, less than half (49 percent) of all black children under 18 were living with both parents as compared to six of seven white children. Some argue that it is ethnocentric to think that such families are "deviant" and "pathological,"

TABLE 31-6
Proportion of Families Headed
by a Woman with No Husband Present

	Black	White
1940	18	10
1960	22	8
1978	39	12

and argue that this household form is a functional adaptation to ghetto circumstances. Whatever the merits of that argument, the association between residing in a household without a male head and poverty is extremely strong. In 1977, 51 percent of such black families had incomes below the poverty line, but only 14 percent of two-parent households lived at that level. And it is clear that children who grow up in miserable poverty are scarred by the experience in a variety of ways that limit their opportunities to live a happy and productive life.

Another cause for concern is that the administration that swept into power in the 1980 elections appears to be insensitive to blacks and the poor in general. Reagan's deep cuts in social welfare programs and his faith in "trickle-down economics" may prove disastrous for the black community. Even relatively affluent black professionals have reason to worry, because fully half of them—as opposed to only a quarter of white professionals—are employed by a federal, state, or local governmental agency. The major contraction in the governmental sector that the administration hopes to achieve, if it comes, may cost many of them their jobs.

The Ethnic Revival, Immigration, and the American Future

One of the most important and least widely understood facts about the United States today is that it has once again become a major recipient of immigrants. The Immigration Act of 1965 repealed the highly restrictive system that had been in operation since the 1920s. It put a much higher ceiling on total immigration, provided many avenues of entry above the quotas, and removed the former preference shown for applicants from northern and western Europe. In the 1970s, five million newcomers entered the United States legally; in 1980 alone, the figure was over 800,000, plus an unknown but clearly large number of illegal aliens. America presently takes in more than twice as many immigrants as the rest of the world combined!

Hardly any of today's arrivals come from the major sending societies of any earlier era—Britain, Ireland, Germany, Poland, Russia, or Italy. Most are Asians— principally Chinese, Japanese, Koreans, Philippinos, or Vietnamese—or Hispanics. Whether they will assimilate into the society as fully as their predecessors remains to be seen, and may in time become a major political issue. In culture, language, religion, and race, these "new" immigrants are more distinct from white Americans than the "old" and "new" immigrants of the past. Many of the Asian newcomers have been strikingly successful educationally and economically. But they are arriving at a time in which pressures to Americanize have relaxed; the concept of the "melting pot" is under attack and "cultural pluralism" has become fashionable. Indeed, some federal and state programs seem designed to retard assimilation. Hundreds of millions of dollars a year, for example, now support bilingual education in more than 70 different languages. Some advocates of these efforts claim that their aim is to facilitate the transition to English, not to perpetuate ethnic separatism. But clear evidence that they have that effect is lacking. Likewise, amendments to the 1965 Voting Rights Act guarantee the right to ballots in languages other than English to those who wish them, even though a knowledge of English remains a prerequisite for naturalization. The tradition that English is the national language is even under attack from some quarters, particularly in the Southwest. Perhaps a common national language is not a necessary precondition for a cohesive and harmonious society, as they argue. The examples of strife-ridden Canada and Belgium, however, are not encouraging. American society has long balanced unity and diversity, and it would be well not to forget the need for unity in a world in which people are killed every day in conflicts triggered by ethnic animosities.

The recent expansion of various "affirmative action" programs to cover immigrants who happen to be nonwhite is likely to prove a particularly divisive issue. Government-mandated affirmative action requirements began in the late 1960s in response to a widespread perception that American blacks had been kept too long at the back of the bus by white prejudice, and that special efforts were needed to ensure their full equality. Whether legally imposed "goals," "timetables," or "quotas" were effective means to that end was debatable, but the argument that blacks had faced unique handicaps was compelling. The subsequent lengthening of the list of "racial minorities" to include Orientals and Hispanics, however, was far more questionable. It was difficult to see why an engineer from Spain, an architect from Argentina, a nurse from the Philippines, or a chemist from Korea who came to the United States to improve his or her lot should have any privileges not available to American whites. In earlier times, Chinese and Japanese Americans certainly suffered from grave disabilities because of their race, but by the 1970s both communities ranked well above presumably "advantaged" American whites by every measure of social status, be it median family income, proportion in high-ranked jobs, or rates of college graduation. The cases of the two largest Hispanic groups, the Mexicans and Puerto Ricans, are more complex, but they were never as strongly segregated and stigmatized as American blacks, and one can doubt the wisdom of granting them special protection as "minority races." If nonwhites continue to have a privileged legal status, it may well fuel a new drive to restrict the immigration of those who benefit from it.

FAMILY PATTERNS AND SEX ROLES

No period of American history has seen such sudden and sweeping changes in sex roles and family patterns as our own. Although the women's movement suffered a major defeat in the early 1980s when the Equal Rights Amendment failed to win approval from the necessary three-fourths of the states, the sexual revolution had already won the day.

The idea that a woman's proper place—at least a married woman's place—is in the home was still very widely held in the 1950s, even though a sizable minority of wives were in fact employed. "Our readers are housewives, full time," said the editor of a leading women's magazine. "They're not interested in the broad public issues of the day. They are only interested in the family and the home." Today a majority (51 percent) of married women hold jobs, and no less than 80 percent of those under 35. Hard though it is to believe, in the Eisenhower era, a wife's earnings could not legally be counted in determining how large a mortgage a family could get from the bank. Men alone, it was assumed, were the only true breadwinners; that a woman too could pursue a career that generated a steady income was simply not recognized. Now only the most affluent families can contemplate purchasing a home without two paychecks.

The massive movement of women into the labor force—an increase of 27 million in the past two decades—did not suddenly catapult females into a position of economic equality with men. Far from it. Most of the new workers were employed as low-level information processors, as secretaries, clerks, and receptionists. Or they were low-level people processors—nurses, sales clerks, teachers, dental assistants, or social workers. These are predominantly female occupations, with many part-time "in-and-out" workers, dead-end vocations that are poorly paid. Employed women earn only about three-fifths as much as male workers. The gap has been narrowing a bit of late, partly because of antidiscrimination legislation and partly because increasing numbers of younger women are now obtaining the credentials to enter well-paid occupations that previously had few females. A third of the 1981 graduating class at Harvard Medical School were women, as were 30 percent of all the graduates of American law schools, and 10 percent of those taking engineering degrees. The gap will not disappear, however, until a generation of females with the same career aspirations and drives as males appears on the scene, and until the problem of how to raise children without impeding the career advancement of their mothers is resolved.

The clash between career aspirations and child-rearing responsibilities has become less acute than it used to be, however. One reason is that norms governing family size have changed dramatically in recent years. At the beginning of the postwar Baby Boom, 49 percent of Americans believed that the "ideal" family had four or more children; in 1980, only 16 percent thought that. Since the cresting of the Baby Boom in 1957, the birth rate has fallen steadily, and it now stands at 1.7 children per woman of childbearing age, well below replacement levels. Taking out the time to see one or two children through infancy is obviously less of a career interruption than doing it for four or five. Various forms of institutionalized day care and greater and greater sharing of domestic tasks in two-career families are also easing the burdens on working wives. In 1980, 42 percent of the public believed that both sexes should share responsibility for cleaning the home, for example, still a minority but up substantially from the 24 percent who took the egalitarian view only a decade before.

Only a quarter of a century ago, the great majority of Americans thought that a woman could only find her true identity by "finding a man." In 1957, some 80 percent believed that a female who failed to marry must be "sick," "neurotic," or "immoral"; only a quarter thought so in 1980. (Some readers may find the 1980 figures still astonishingly high rather than strikingly low, but the magnitude of the change is certainly remarkable.) Most young women today do not feel the pressure to rush into marriage that their mothers had, and they are not doing so. The proportion of females aged 20 to 24 who were unmarried rose from 28 percent in

1960 to 43 percent in the late 1970s. Whether this will result in a lower marriage rate overall, or is only an indication that marriage is being delayed a few years is unclear from recent evidence. But for people in their thirties, the marriage rate has been rising recently.

The choices open to women—and men—to lead their lives in ways an earlier generation would have considered unconventional have multiplied greatly. The transformation of sexual mores recently has been amazingly rapid and thorough. As late as 1967, a whopping 85 percent of the public believed that "premarital sex is morally wrong," a view taken by just 37 percent a dozen years later. In 1968, a dispute between the administration of Barnard College and a student who wanted to share an apartment with her boy friend rated a national news story. By 1980 the Census counted more than a million unmarried couples living under the same roof, and no one paid much heed.

One of the choices an increasing number of Americans have been making—the decision to end a marriage they find unsatisfying—distresses defenders of the traditional family. The divorce rate has indeed been skyrocketing. In 1910 there were ten marriages for every divorce in the United States. By 1940, the ratio was down to six to one; in 1980, it was only two to one. At the current rate, half of the couples marrying this year will end up in divorce court. The trend is clear, but its causes and implications are hard to assess. Conservatives who attribute it to more permissive sexual attitudes and "Women's Lib" are obviously mistaken, because it had been going on long before either of those developments. It is not evidence of growing dissatisfaction with marriage *as an institution*, as many claim, because the rate of remarriage has increased just about as rapidly as the divorce rate. We cannot even be sure that it shows that more Americans than ever before are contracting marriages that turn out to be desperately unhappy. Legal, religious, and social constraints upon divorce are much weaker than they were in the past, and escape from an intolerable partner is far easier.

It is possible, therefore, that the high rate of broken marriages means the opposite of what most people assume. It could be that more Americans than ever are finding satisfying marriages, even though many of them don't until the second time around. Considering the sweeping cultural changes we have been living through of late, it is very striking that the proportion of Americans who claimed to be dedicated to "the ideal of two people sharing a life together" did not decline at all during the 1970s; it was 96 percent in 1970 and still 96 percent in 1980. Whatever else may have changed, that continuity is impressive.

THE USES OF THE PAST: A CONCLUDING OBSERVATION

This chapter opened with the caveat that it is impossible to view our own time with the full perspective that historians will later be able to bring to it, after time has "left the ridges of change bare." To admit that, however, is not to concede that the past is irrelevant to our present or future condition. History is not a "policy science"; knowing about it will not dictate how we vote on any current issue. But

Hegel was too pessimistic in saying that all we learn from history is that we do not learn from history. As Franklin Roosevelt said wisely long ago, a sense of the past can help us "to gain in judgment for the creation of the future."

How? Certainly not by providing any simple laws of the "X always leads to Y" variety, which is what Hegel and many others sought in vain. The historical record, alas, includes no easy recipes to guarantee future peace or prosperity. The utility, the relevance, of history lies in the fact that the troublesome problems of today are rarely altogether new; nor are those of tomorrow likely to be. The vast majority are variations, sometimes only slight variations, on themes that preoccupied our predecessors as well. To know how they grappled with and resolved (or failed to resolve) them permits us to place the events in tonight's news in a deeper and more meaningful context.

Of course the present is not the past, and speculating about "what Lincoln would have done" about racial conflict in the 1980s, say, is the height of folly. But it is surely impossible to hold an informed opinion about our current racial difficulties without having a grasp of where they came from, which necessarily entails a command of history that goes back to Lincoln's time and even earlier. It is essential to know, for example, that blacks are not recent voluntary migrants but the descendants of people who were brought here as slaves two to three centuries ago; that until very recently they were an overwhelmingly rural people who had been deprived of the opportunity to have any voice in public affairs and had received a second-rate education at best; that they entered urban America at a time when the economy offered fewer prospects for unskilled people than was the case when the Irish, Italians, Poles, and others first came to the United States. The roots of the race problem reach back to the very beginning of American history, and any intelligent response to it must be sensitive to its special historical configurations. Likewise, to judge whether the current crisis in Central America is likely to become "another Vietnam" or "another Munich" demands a knowledge not only of current conditions south of the border, but of the long history of American involvement in Latin American affairs and of those alleged historical parallels. A sense of the past will not put an end to political debate. Different observers may draw different policy conclusions even if they agree on the shape of the historical record. But they will have a more accurate and sophisticated grasp of the issues at stake and the possibilities for action than those who lack such knowledge. For that reason, history is an indispensable tool if we are to "gain in judgment for the creation of the future."

SUGGESTED READINGS

Peter N. Carroll, *It Seemed Like Nothing Happened: The Tragedy and Promise of America in the 1970's* (1982) is the most recent general survey. Theodore H. White, *America in Search of Itself: The Making of the President, 1956–1980* (1982) is a fascinating account of political changes from Eisenhower to Reagan. The decline of party loyalty is analyzed in Everett C. Ladd and Charles D. Hadley, *Transformations of the American*

Party System (rev. ed., 1978). Biographies of recent key political figures include Richard Reeves, *A Ford, Not A Lincoln* (1975), Betty Glad, *Jimmy Carter: From Plains to the White House* (1980), Hendrik Smith, et. al., *Reagan the Man, the President* (1981), and Lou Cannon, *Reagan* (1982).

On the most difficult and most important issue facing mankind, see Michael Mandelbaum, *The Nuclear Question* (1979), Jonathan Schell, *The Fate of the Earth* (1982), Robert Scheer, *With Enough Shovels: Reagan, Bush and Nuclear War* (1982), Lawrence Freedman, *The Evolution of Nuclear Strategy* (1982), George F. Kennan, *The Nuclear Delusion: Soviet–American Relations in the Atomic Age* (1982), and Harvard Nuclear Study Group, *Living with Nuclear Weapons* (1983). James Fallows, *National Defense* (1981) is incisive. For an assessment of the aims of America's chief rival, see Adam B. Ulam, *Dangerous Relations: The Soviet Union in World Politics, 1970–1982* (1983). Robert Stobaugh and Daniel Yergin, *Energy Future: Report of the Energy Project at the Harvard Business School* (1979), Lester C. Thurow, *The Zero-Sum Society: Distribution and the Possibilities for Economic Change* (1980), Richard J. Barnet, *The Lean Years: Politics in the Age of Scarcity* (1980), and David Calleo, *The Imperious Economy* (1982) clarify the economic alternatives.

William J. Wilson, *The Declining Significance of Race: Blacks and Changing American Institutions* (1978) assesses recent changes in race relations. On the continuing debate over racial policy, see Nathan Glazer, *Affirmative Discrimination: Ethnic Inequality and Public Policy* (1975), Allan P. Sindler, *Bakke, DeFunis, and Minority Admissions: The Quest for Equal Opportunity* (1978), and Thomas Sowell, *Race and Economics* (1975) and *Ethnic America: A History* (1982). For contrasting views of the white ethnic revival of the 1970s, see Michael Novak, *The Rise of the Unmeltable Ethnics: Politics and Culture in the Seventies* (1972) and Orlando Patterson, *Ethnic Chauvinism* (1977). Marvin Harris offers some provocative observations about the changing position of blacks and of women in *America Now: The Anthropology of a Changing Culture* (1981). For other valuable discussions of sex roles and family patterns, see Mary Jo Bane, *Here To Stay: American Families in the Twentieth Century* (1976), William H. Chafe, *Women and Equality: Changing Patterns in American Culture* (1977), Sara Evans, *Personal Politics: The Roots of Women's Liberation in the Civil Rights Movement and the New Left* (1978), Christopher Lasch, *Haven in a Heartless World: The Family Besieged* (1977) and *The Culture of Narcissism: American Life in an Age of Diminished Expectations* (1978), and Daniel Yankelovich, *New Rules* (1981). Andrew Hacker, *USA: A Statistical Portrait* (1983) summarizes what the 1980 Census reveals about the state of the nation. See also Victor R. Fuchs, *How We Live: An Economic Perspective on Americans From Birth to Death* (1983).

For a superb discussion of how our often inaccurate images of the past have shaped foreign policy decisions, see Ernest R. May, *The "Lessons" of the Past: The Use and Misuse of History in American Foreign Policy* (1973).

Index

Daley, Richard, 736
Danton, George Jacques, 193
Danvers, MA, 91
Darrow, Clarence, 598, 602
Dartmouth College vs. Woodward, 281
Daughters of the American Revolution, 655
Davis, Jefferson, 338, 358, 486
Davis, John W., 584, 646
Davis Bend, MS, 362
Dawes Severalty Act, 437–38
Daytona, FL, 589
Dean, John, 738, 740
Dearborn, MI, 558
Death Rates, in colonies, 10–12, 20–22,
    28–30, 53, 63, 75, 89–91; in 19th century,
    334–35, 411–12
De Bow's Review, 244, 283
Declaration of Independence, 143, 150, 159,
    161, 165, 191, 284, 402
Declaration on Liberated Europe, 697
Declaratory Act, 135
Debs, Eugene V., 472–73, 536, 551, 581
Defense Intelligence Agency, 738
De Gaulle, Charles, 726, 733
De Lancey, James, 118
De Lancey, Stephen, 94, 118
Delaware, 80, 83, 113, 161, 167, 174, 312,
    325–26, 336
Delaware River, 82, 83
Democratic Party, in Civil War era, 337,
    351–53, 361–63, 373; formation of, 286–87,
    291, 294; in 1850s, 304, 308, 310–23; in late
    19th century, 486–87, 491–99, 505–506;
    and the New Deal, 642–43, 654–60,
    668–69; since the New Deal, 701, 706,
    710–11, 718–20, 730, 735–37, 739, 744–50;
    in Progressive era, 534–38
Democratic Review, 304
Dempsey, Jack, 588
Denmark, 90, 676
Depression of 1873, 399
Depression of 1893, 399, 491–97
Depression of 1929, 634–60
Detroit, MI, before the Civil War, 128, 200,
    214, 267, 269, 312; in late 19th century,
    410, 414, 418; in 20th century, 564, 579,
    599–600, 602, 604, 647, 652, 734
Dewey, George, 505
Dewey, John, 714
Dewey, Thomas E., 706
Dias, Bartholomew, 7–8
Dickinson, John, 136
Diem, Ngo Dinh, 713, 725, 733
Dien Bien Phu, Battle of, 712
Dillingham, William, 557
Discourse on Government, 311
*Discourse on the Constitution and Government of
    the United States*, 311
District of Columbia, 308, 343, 604
Dix, Dorothea, 294, 612

Dominican Republic, 501, 530
Dominion of New England, 115–16, 124
Donovan, William J., 677
Dorchester, MA, 48, 425
Dos Passos, John, 568, 587, 673
Douglas, Stephen, 276, 314, 319–23
Douglass, Frederick, 297, 299, 364–65, 595,
    622
Dow Chemical Co., 734
Drake, Francis, 18
Dreiser, Theodore, 406, 412, 587, 714
Dresden, Germany, 687
Drew, Daniel, 400–401
DuBois, W.E.B., 598, 600, 606–607
Dudley, Thomas, 56
Duke, James B., 402
Dulles, John Foster, 712
Dunkirk, 676
DuPont, Pierre, 570
Dutch, 80, 82, 86, 108, 110, 113, 114, 138, 276,
    547
Dutch Reformed Church, 100–101
Dutch West India Company, 82, 100, 113

East Anglia, 45
East India Co., 18, 20, 138
East St. Louis, IL, 604
Eastland Co., 18
Education, in Antebellum South, 249–50;
    of Blacks; 243, 392–93, 755–57; Common
    School movement, 226–27, 294; G.I. Bill,
    704; in late 19th century, 392–93; of
    women, 614, 761
Economic Interpretation of the Constitution, An,
    176
Edison, Thomas, 566
Edwards, Jonathan, 73, 101–102
Egypt, 746, 750
Ehrlichman, John, 742
Eighteenth Amendment, 560–61, 583
Eisenhower, Dwight D., 710; domestic pol-
    icies of, 713–16; foreign policies of,
    711–13
Electoral College, 172, 180, 189, 192–93, 280,
    286, 323, 365
Elementary Arithmetic, 334
Eliot, John, 50
Elizabeth, Queen of England, 18–19, 40–41
Elkhorn Creek, WI, 263
Elkins Act, 528
Ellington, Duke, 607
Ellis Island, 71
Ellsburg, Daniel, 739
Elmira Female College, 614
Emancipation Proclamation, 295, 343–44,
    346, 360
Emergency Bank Act, 644
Emerson, Ralph Waldo, 221, 292, 322
Encomienda System, 14

Gadsden Purchase, 306, 439
Gag Rule, 298
Gage, Thomas, 135, 138, 142, 145
Galbraith, John K., 702
Galena, IL, 332
Gall, 434
Galloway, Joseph, 141
Gama, Vasco da, 7–8
Garfield, James A., 584
Garrison, William Lloyd, 296–300, 320
Garvey, Marcus, 607–608
Gaspee, 138
Gates, John W. "Bet-a-Million," 400
General Accounting Office, 582
General Electric Co., 654
General Federation of Women's Clubs, 624
General Managers Association, 472
General Motors Co., 566, 569–71, 653–54, 713
Genet, Citizen, 187
Geneva, Switzerland, 38, 39, 41, 554, 664, 669
Geneva Conference, 713
George III, King of England, 129, 143, 144, 156, 157, 160, 175, 338
Georgia, 498, 594; in Antebellum period, 234–35, 237, 253, 259, 281, 326; during Civil War and Reconstruction, 334, 338, 347–48, 358, 362, 371–72; as a colony, 69, 86, 113, 116; in Revolutionary era, 132, 167
German Reformed Church, 98–99
Germans, 150, 192; in colonies, 80, 84–87, 100, 119, 122; in 19th century, 216, 276, 313, 445, 475–76, 485–86; in 20th century, 543, 547, 550–51, 557, 561–62, 604, 673, 691
Germany, relations with before World War I, 414, 473, 500, 502–503, 505, 531–33; and World War I, 542–48, 551–52; in 1920s and 1930s, 638, 664, 666, 669, 671; and World War II, 675–76, 680, 682–84, 698–99
Gershwin, George, 607
Gettysburg Address, 355
Gettysburg, Battle of, 334, 348
Ghent, Treaty of, 199
G.I. Bill, 704
Giants in the Earth, 444
Gibbons vs. Ogden, 281
Gilbert, Humphrey, 19
Gilman, Charlotte Perkins, 622
Gladden, Washington, 514
Glorious Revolution, 115, 116, 146
Goldwater, Barry, 651, 730–31
Gompers, Samuel, 467–70, 473, 475, 491–92, 532, 652
Gone With the Wind, 754
Good Hope, Cape of, 7, 8
Good Neighbor Policy, 665
Goodyear, Charles, 209
Goshen, CT, 95
Gosset, Thomas F., 594

Grand Army of the Republic, 484
Grand Canyon, 528
Granger Movement, 440, 447
Grant, Ulysses S., 332, 335, 342–43, 348–50, 355, 362, 366, 374–75, 458, 478
Granville, Earl of, 92
Great American Desert, 432–33
Great Awakening, 101–104, 145–46
Great Barrington, MA, 408
Great Britain, colonies in North America, 16–57, 66–71, 80–84; friction with U.S., 1793–1814, 186–88, 197–200; and Greece, 700; imperial system, 106–24; imperial system breaks down, 126–46; Industrial Revolution, 109, 111, 209, 234; Revolutionary War, 150–57; technological borrowing from, 208–209; and World War I, 542–48, 551–54, 558; and World War II, 673–84
Great East Asian Co-Prosperity Sphere, 671, 680
Great Gatsby, The, 587
Great Lakes, 128, 156, 201, 212
Great Migration (Puritans), 36, 45–53, 86–87
Great Migration (Southern Blacks), 598–608
Great Northern Railroad, 525
Great Plains, 313, 408, 432–49
Great Society, 729–31
Greece, 700–701
Greeks, 599
Greeley, Horace, 204, 319
Green Berets, 727
Greenback Party, 440, 495
Greenglass, David, 707
Greenland, 679
Greensboro, NC, 715
Greenville, Treaty of, 200–201
Greenwich, OH, 263
Greer, 679
Griffith, D.W., 605
Grimke, Angelina, 295, 297
Grimke, Sarah, 295, 297
Gross National Product (GNP), in Antebellum period, 218–19; in late 19th century, 352–53, 384, 392, 450, 502; in 20th century, 566–67, 575, 634–65, 657–58, 688
Guadalcanal, 685
Guadalupe Hidalgo, Treaty of, 306, 439
Guam, 505
Guardian, The, 598
Guatemala, 712
Guinea Company, 18
Gulf of Tonkin Resolution, 731–32

Haig, Alexander, 741
Haiti, 501, 530, 540
Haldeman, Robert, 742
Haley, Alex, 64
Half-Way Covenant, 56, 101
Halifax, Earl of, 116

Halleck, Henry, 342–43
Hamburg, Germany, 687
Hamilton, Alexander, 171, 173, 177, 182, 183, 184, 185, 186, 188, 189, 190, 191, 193, 194
Hamilton, Andrew, 119–20
Hammond, Senator James, 234, 242
Hampton Court, 41
Hampton Institute, 595
Hancock, John, 94, 137, 142, 143
Hannibal, MO, 212–13
Harding, Warren G., 580–82, 664
Harlan, John Marshall, 498, 714
Harlem, New York, 600, 602–603, 607–608
Harlem Renaissance, 607
Harpers Ferry, VA, 322
Harper's Weekly, 228, 359, 437, 501–502
Harrison, Benjamin, 488–89, 503
Harrison, William Henry, 200–202, 288
Hartford Convention, 199, 278
Hartford, Treaty of, 114
Harvard College, 44, 47, 100, 401, 418, 598, 727
Harvey, W.H., 493
Hat Act, 109
Havana, Cuba, 504
Havemeyer, Henry, 400
Hawaii, 501, 503–505, 690
Hawkins, John, 18
Hay, John, 472, 533
Hayes, Roland, 607
Hayes, Rutherford B., 375
Haymarket Riot, 472
Hearst, William Randolph, 668
Hegel, G.W.F, 763
Helper, Hinton Rowan, 248
Hemingway, Ernest, 587, 673
Henry VIII, King of England, 16, 38
Henry the Navigator, Prince, 7
Henry, Patrick, 87, 91
Henry St. Settlement House, 513
Hepburn Act, 528
Hermitage, The, 286
Hester St., 407
Hetch-Hetchy Valley, 529
Hillsborough, Lord, 137
Hindus, 608
Hiroshima, Japan, 685–87
Hiss, Alger, 707, 711
Hitler, Adolph, 666, 670–73, 675–76, 680, 682–84
Holland, 45, 68, 80, 82, 138, 154, 186, 499, 676
Hollywood, 579
Holmes, Oliver Wendell, 342
Holmes, Oliver Wendell, Jr., 483, 551, 707
Holy Alliance, 500
Home Owners Loan Corporation (HOLC), 644
Homer, Winslow, 205
Homestead Act, 353, 441–44, 484
Homestead Strike, 470, 472, 491

Hoover, Herbert, 549, 582, 584; domestic policies of, 632, 639–43; foreign policies of, 664–68
Hoover, J. Edgar, 544–55, 728, 738
Hopi Indians, 9
Hopkins, Harry, 650, 655, 687
House, Edward, 543, 546
House of Burgesses, 21, 26–28, 114, 140, 143
House Un-American Activities Committee, 707
Houston, TX, 585
How the Other Half Lives, 423, 512
Howard, O.O., 361, 364
Howe, Julia Ward, 336
Howe, Louis, 642
Howe, William, 145, 153
Howells, William Dean, 612
Hudson, Henry, 80
Hudson River, 45, 82, 83, 281
Hughes, Charles Evans, 537–38, 659
Hughes, Langston, 607
Hull, Cordell, 680
Hull House, 514
Hull House Maps and Papers, 514
Humphrey, Hubert, 736–37
Hundred Years War, 5
Hungarians, 697
Hunt, E. Howard, 739
Hunter, Robert, 512
Huston Plan, 738
Hutchinson, Anne, 55–56, 98, 102
Hutchinson, Thomas, 138, 139
Hyatt, Henry, 273
Hyde, Edward, 116

Ickes, Harold, 655
Idaho, 304, 423, 441
If Christ Came to Chicago, 512
Illinois, before the Civil War, 200, 216, 229, 248, 256, 261–76, 284, 298, 314, 317, 319–20; in the late 19th century, 336, 360, 441, 457, 472, 489; in the 20th century, 626
Immigration Act of 1965, 759
Immigration Restriction League, 557, 562
Impending Crisis of the South, 249
Incas, 9, 10, 12, 13, 24
Indentured Servants, 23, 26–27, 29, 31, 33–34, 66–69, 85, 89
Independence, MO, 304
India, 8, 557
Indiana, 200–202, 215, 229, 252, 261–76, 336, 484, 583
Industrial Revolution, in Britain, 109, 111, 209, 217, 234; in U.S., 184, 204–30
Industrial Workers of the World, 467, 550, 617
Influence of Sea Power Upon History, The, 501
Ingersoll, Robert G., 483
Inns of Court, 41
Internal Revenue Service, 735, 741

A 3
B 4
C 5
D 6
E 7
F 8
G 9
H 0
I 1
J 2